HUMAN DEVELOPMENT: A SCIENCE OF GROWTH

HUMAN DEVELOPMENT: A SCIENCE OF GROWTH

JUSTIN PIKUNAS, Ph.D.
Professor of Psychology
University of Detroit
Certified Consulting Psychologist
Detroit, Michigan

With Chapters by
Eugene J. Albrecht, Ph.D.
Associate Professor and Chairman
Department of Psychology
Villanova University

Robert P. O'Neil, Ph.D.
Assistant Professor and Certified Psychologist
University of Detroit

McGraw-Hill Book Company
New York, St. Louis, San Francisco
London, Sydney, Toronto
Mexico, Panama

To the college student who is
interested in a most fascinating
subject: man as he develops

.

HUMAN DEVELOPMENT: A SCIENCE OF GROWTH

Formerly Published under the Title of *Psychology of Human Development*

Library of Congress Catalog Card Number 68–9048

1 2 3 4 5 6 7 8 9 0   MAMM   7 6 5 4 3 2 1 0 6 9

Preface

Eight years have passed since the appearance of the first edition of this work, entitled *Psychology of Human Development*. During these years research in most areas of human development has moved rapidly in terms of both theoretical systems and experimental findings. The converging contributions from psychology, biology, medicine, education, and sociology are establishing a science of growth. Many current theories, hypotheses, and facts from many branches of science have been incorporated in the present completely rewritten edition, to revitalize the text and bring it up to date. Indeed, an attempt has been made to show the whole of human development in the total environment. Developmental continuities and discontinuities, as well as patterns found at each level of life throughout senescence, have been spotlighted in order to facilitate understanding of the person at every phase of life.

In the present edition, as in the first, the emphasis remains on the psychological processes and their various aspects. The continuous interaction of the individual with his sociocultural environment is the basis for both personality development and adjustment. The evolving self-concept and its effects on behavior control as well as interpersonal relationships are brought to the fore. This interaction with persons of different ages is stressed, since not only is the infant or child affected by his parents and other adults but he in turn also affects them in myriad ways. Because each individual is highly influenced by his sociocultural environment, the role of various environmental, societal, and cultural factors is stressed throughout the text. By emphasizing the self-concept of the individual throughout life, we give continuity to the interpretation of behavior changes.

The often neglected levels of life—adulthood and senescence—are given extensive treatment. This revision meets the need to convey a better understanding and genuine appreciation of early adulthood, especially since most of the students for whom the book is intended are young adults.   A new chapter on late adulthood is added in order to achieve a complete presentation of the life cycle.

The revision will fulfill its raison d'être by providing a fuller understanding of the individual's changes throughout his life span.   Furthermore, its facts, principles, and illustrations, drawn from many sources, may prove useful as guidelines in the prediction of behavior at various levels of human life.   The text contains many facts but also many generalizations.   The latter are a necessary part of any comprehensive textbook on the present subject at the current level of scientific achievement in the study of human growth and its deterioration.

Acknowledgments.   Without the work of several contributors this revision would not have been possible.   Dr. Robert P. O'Neil gave added assistance by reading several sections of the manuscript and contributing to their development.   Because of illness Dr. Eugene J. Albrecht, who participated in the planning of the first edition and wrote four chapters of it, was unable to collaborate in the writing of the present edition. Appreciation is expressed to Drs. Nancy Bayley, Katherine M. B. Bridges, Charlotte Buhler, Luella Cole, Evelyn Duvall, Lawrence K. Frank, Robert J. Havighurst, Dorothea McCarthy, Bradley M. Patten, Sidney L. Pressey, Robert R. Sears, and the following publishers and organizations for permission to reprint their copyrighted material: McGraw-Hill and its Blakiston Division, John Wiley & Sons, Basic Books, Russell Sage Foundation, Joint Committee on Health Problems in Education of the National Education Association and the American Medical Association, Society for Research in Child Development, New York Academy of Science, the Psychological Corporation, and a number of professional journals.

Justin Pikunas

To the Student

Human development and its progress throughout life is a very difficult subject to master, even if some of its contents appear obvious or known to the reader. Such subjects as human anatomy and physiology often exhaust the medical student's time and patience. Yet how simple they seem when compared to the perplexing varieties of behavior, complexities of personality, and individual differences at various stages of life. There are good reasons for taking Alexander Pope's eighteenth-century advice seriously: "The proper study of mankind is Man." We feel it is desirable to begin right from the start—where man is conceived—and to follow his journey throughout life as he contends against and copes with the forces within himself and his total environment.

For appropriate orientation it is advisable to read a chapter prior to its class presentation. Facts, concepts, and theories emphasized by the instructor can then be underlined, possibly in different colors, to signify different degrees of importance. Additional concepts, theories, and illustrations introduced by the instructor ought to be transferred into a notebook as fully as possible.

Taking notes is an essential part of the learning process. Making class notations on the right-hand pages of the notebook and using the left-hand pages for notes from your textbook and related readings is helpful in tying up information on a subject. Questions at the end of each chapter give you an opportunity to check your comprehension of the major ideas presented in the text. Moreover, chapter summaries, based in part on your answers to the review questions, ought also to be kept in your notebook.

A mere knowledge of fundamentals is not sufficient at the college level; yet this comes first, because details without general organization do not produce meaningful knowledge. In the first reading of a chapter, try to get the major ideas. Then read the chapter a second time—that's where your study really begins—underlining the major ideas and picking out any points you missed the first time. Having your own system of marking facts will be a useful guide for note-taking and reviewing.   Keep in mind that the chapter headings and subheadings are designed as aids for organizing and learning.   The individual grows and acts as a whole; his psychological processes are not divided, though the rubrics may seem to point to this.

Additional reading of past and current research studies is equally important for progress in mastering the subject matter.   It is advisable to try to read from the selection of references following each chapter. The volumes of *Psychological Abstracts, Annual Review of Psychology, Child Development Abstracts and Bibliography, Research Relating to Children*, and *Developmental Psychology* are other comprehensive sources for selection of developmental research articles and reports.   At the college level, there is really no substitute for reading of original research reports.   In a final count, the student uses the lecture material, textbook, and readings as three sources of learning supplementing each other. Although he may consult with his instructor, integration of these materials is largely a task of his own.

Contents

Part 9.   Late Phases of Life

Part 1

Basic Approach to Developmental Study

Since the emergence of scientific psychology nearly a century ago, man has vastly extended his fund of knowledge about himself. More important than the specific facts acquired, however, were the invention and refinement of various methods and techniques for furthering explanatory knowledge. By the ingenious use of these methods, the psychologist can anticipate continuing success in attaining the threefold goal of growth science: understanding, predicting, and controlling the course of human development and behavior. He can look forward hopefully to new insights into the intricacy of the human organism and personality and the consistencies of growth and behavior, as well as the factors influencing them.

Intelligent comprehension of human development must be built upon clarification of the nature of growth science, cognizance of the methods for investigating developmental continuities and transitions, and understanding the hypothetical explanations for the patterns of growth and maturation. Section I, in its three chapters, presents a review of these subjects.

THE NATURE OF
GROWTH SCIENCE

In the modern world of today, with its expanding culture and technology, racial and ideological conflicts, population explosion, and increasingly complex social differentiation, man faces many difficulties in his quest for adjustment, maturity, and happiness. New tasks and decisions, challenges and hazards overtake him; change rather than stability is the order of the day. These outside problems complicate the frustration each man faces as he grows and matures from the earliest stages of life to the period of old age. Yet this complexity of the physical world is barely comparable to the marvelous intricacy of the human organism and personality.

As a person reviews his own life, it becomes clear that he is not the same today as he was two or ten years ago. He is still the same individual, since the ultimate nature of his being has not been transformed, but many of his motivational and behavioral characteristics are far different. Such common expressions as "Don't be a baby" or "Act your age" indicate that what is normal behavior at one age is unacceptable at another. The needs, drives, desires, and aspirations of the individual undergo not only frequent modification but also major revision. Beliefs and attitudes, emotional responses and intellectual abilities—indeed, all the dimensions of personality—change

3

throughout man's life span. The kinds of changes which take place are determined by both hereditary and environmental factors, particularly the kinds of stimulation the person receives during his formative years of life. Since the person faces constant changes, problems, and decisions as he goes through life, it is crucial that he know and understand himself. The arm-chair speculations, the old wives' tales, and the advice of earlier times— many of which have endured until the present day—have been found sadly wanting. True, literature verifies the fact that some deeply penetrating analyses of human nature and behavior have been achieved in the past, but it also reveals many accepted absurdities. It has, therefore, become the task of science to evaluate critically what has been believed previously, thereby deepening man's current knowledge of himself.

As a major branch of science, psychology deals chiefly with man's under-standing of himself. Using scientific methods, it studies mental processes, motivation, and behavior in order to predict and to control them. *Develop-mental psychology* is dedicated to just one aspect of this search for knowl-edge; it seeks understanding and control of the basic processes and dynamics underlying human behavior at the various stages of life. Its investigation encompasses the growth and maturation of the individual organism, its cogni-tive and emotional powers, as well as its personality structure. Any factors which promote or retard any aspects of development must also be considered. Within this broad range of interests, the types of interaction between the human organism and the environment also require careful study. As a core for the science of growth, developmental psychology deals with all the pro-cesses contributing to becoming an infant, a child, an adolescent, and a mature adult. A dynamic yet precise representation of human needs and goals can be sketched within the developmental framework of the various levels and phases of life. By now the field of developmental psychology in-cludes "practically all topics in general psychology and uses nearly every method available for the study of behavior" [23, p. 102].

Developmental psychology is an *ontogenetic* study of the human organism from conception to death. Not the species, but the individual, with his direc-tion of growth in his environment and culture, forms its major concern. So that man may better know and understand himself and those around him, developmental psychology seeks to discover the sequential changes in human personality. With scientific methods and the aid of specialized techniques, it seeks to find order in what appears to be chance and hazard, or even chaos. With this knowledge of order and sequence, the individual should be able to help his fellow man in times of stress instead of merely remaining a perplexed spectator. He should also be better able to understand his own motivation. He should be more capably equipped for the future. This expectation should not be interpreted to mean that the mere knowledge of facts and principles automatically establishes an individual as a well-adjusted person.   Nor should the reader assume that developmental psychology is the study of how to live successfully and happily.   It is rather an area of systematic, logical observation leading to scientific interpretation of growth and behavioral patterns throughout life.   The growth patterns at various levels of life form the subject matter of developmental psychology.   In keeping with the *orthogenetic* principle, we see the human organism as destined for a normal course of growth which ensures the realization of his genetic potential unless detrimental environmental factors distort, damage, or prevent this actualization.   A young person is especially in danger of deviation in growth and behavior since he is almost completely dependent upon his immediate environment.

The sequential changes that occur in human growth and behavior include the progressive unfolding of different dimensions and powers, as well as the decline, with eventual deterioration, of the organism's functional abilities. Thus, intellectual development encompasses both the emergence of its functions in the years of childhood, its perfection during adolescence, and its gradual impairment in the later years of adulthood and senescence.   Though behavioral scientists usually stress the beginning and early phases of life, the significance of later periods cannot be disregarded.   Developmental psychology forms a nucleus for a budding interdisciplinary science of growth embedded in the findings of recent biological and behavioral research [11]. Contributions to the science of human growth have come primarily from areas of psychology and biology, but sociology, education, pediatrics, psychiatry, even anthropology and public health have also participated.

Although the roots for a growth science can be traced back to Aristotle, the unfolding of the theory of evolution brought it to life.   It was G. Stanley Hall who expanded Darwin's theory of biological evolution into a system of behavioral *recapitulation*.   According to Hall's theory, as the child relives the phyletic stages of animal evolution and primitive phases of the human past, the postpubertal individual manifests "the higher and more completely human traits" [14, p. xiii].   Before attaining adult maturity, the adolescent experiences within himself the blows of the rising modern era of technology and culture.   Hall's influence was broadened by his many students of human development at Clark University.   His voluminous writings, especially "The contents of children's minds on entering school" (published in the first volume of *Pedagogical Seminary*, 1891), his original two-volume work *Adolescence* (1904), and a volume on the psychology of the second half of life, *Senescence* (1922), exerted a major forward thrust upon man's study of himself.

By inviting Sigmund Freud and Carl G. Jung to the United States in 1909, Hall indirectly established psychoanalysis as another major influence in

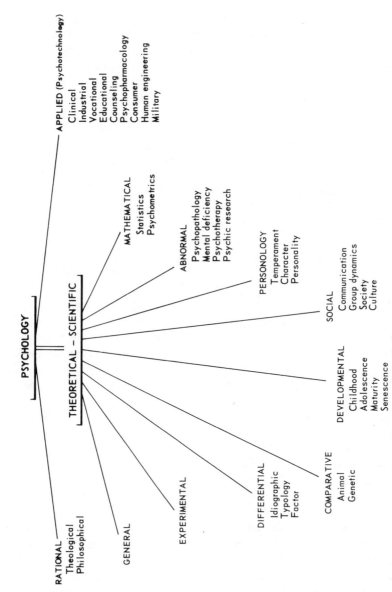

Figure 1-1 Divisions and branches of psychology.

developmental psychology in this country, now especially evident in Erik Erikson's concept of the eight stages of man. In the early 1960s a third major influence arose, that of Jean Piaget, spearheaded by his theories on cognition, communication, and morality. Today Hall's works are just a part of history, but Freudian psychoanalysis is still showing considerable vitality. Piaget, Erikson, Buhler, Frank, Gesell, Bayley, Sears, and other exponents of the budding growth science will be given more detailed analysis in Chapter 10 and other sections of the present book.

As can be seen in Figure 1–1, developmental psychology is closely allied to comparative and social psychology. In developmental psychology, comparisons are often made between infants and children, adolescents and adults, as well as among various classes of the population. In *comparative psychology*, the scientist explores various forms of animal behavior in order to understand similar simple patterns of behavior as they appear in man. In an early study, Wilhelm Preyer [18] compared infant reflexes, instincts, and emotional reactions to those of various animals by showing the similarities as well as the differences among them. Charles Darwin [8] studied emotional reactions at human and animal levels and found considerable similarity in their expressions. He postulated that most of man's expressive actions are inherited from and so shared with a number of animal species. *Social psychology* studies various relationships among individuals and the influence other persons or groups exercise upon the individual. Since most individuals live in family groups and many are members of schools, churches, and other organizations, they cannot be studied or understood outside of their social milieu.

APPROACHES TO THE STUDY OF HUMAN DEVELOPMENT

As shown in Chapter 2, there are several general approaches to a systematic analysis of the developmental pattern and its phenomena. Depending upon the various methods and techniques used, certain advantages and disadvantages are inherent in each approach.

One approach is to treat specific dimensions of growth and behavior one by one throughout the entire life-span—or at least throughout some continuous portion of it. When, for example, social behavior is discussed, a writer starts with the presocial behavior of the newborn infant, continues through the emergent social tendencies characteristic of childhood, adolescence, and adulthood, and concludes with the restriction of social interaction in old age. By following this procedure, an aspect of growth is examined throughout life. This *dimensional* approach has the decided advantage of maintaining continuity of subject and thought; the student reads the entire sequential pattern with the current discussion clearly related to what happened before.

Karl C. Garrison [2] and Sidney L. Pressey and Raymond G. Kuhlen [6] follow this dimensional approach almost to the letter.

Reliance on quantified studies and the application of developmental norms is a major feature of this approach. Knowledge of group averages and the rate at which abilities unfold is important for parents and teachers—in fact, for all persons concerned with human growth and welfare. Such normative data is essential for the clinician in diagnostic work. Any rigorous application of such group norms is, however, exceedingly dangerous. Just because an individual is slightly ahead of or behind "schedule" does not necessarily mean that he is precocious, retarded, or disturbed. Most of the current "norms" represent averages for comparatively small groups of individuals. Actually, it may be that no one in the normative group exactly represents the means reported. Therefore, it is essential to keep in mind that there is wide variation within the group when such norms are being applied to an individual case. Moreover, as will be seen in Chapter 3, neither the growth of different structures and organs nor the acquiring of abilities and traits proceeds at a uniform rate. A healthy child who is ahead of schedule in regard to some functions and achievements may be noticeably behind the norms in others. Much parental anxiety and worry would be alleviated if these basic facts of inter- and intraindividual variability were fully recognized.

The dimensional approach does have a major limitation. Man is not merely a social being, an emotional creature, an intellectual entity—he is all of these and more all at the same time. His social interaction with others cannot be isolated from his feelings or intellectual functions, or from the multitude of other components which make him what he is. These powers do not merely converge in his person, they fuse with each other to a significant extent. He acts as a unified whole. Hence, to consider only one aspect separately from the others is to ignore the totality of the human person. Even for the sake of achieving continuity of thought this cannot be completely justified.

The second general approach to the study of human development consists of a comprehensive examination of man's capacities and behavioral functions at each developmental level. The goal of the *developmental-level* approach is an understanding of the *whole* person with his various abilities and achievements, dynamics and motives, needs and problems as they appear in each phase of life. Rather than seek to answer a question such as "What is the general course of intellectual growth and decline?" this approach attempts to clarify questions such as "What are the typical behavior patterns and dynamics of the infant, the preschool child, or the pubertal adolescent?"

It should be noted that at one developmental level a particular growth or behavior variable is exceedingly important; at another level this same aspect is relatively unimportant or perhaps even nonexistent. Physiological changes are of crucial significance in prenatal, early postnatal, and pubertal periods of life but are of much less importance in later childhood and early adulthood. Being accepted by one's peers is a major goal of the older child and young adolescent, pressing the individual to alter his feelings and behavior toward conformity with his age group. The very young child, on the other hand, is not concerned with peer acceptance. The emotional, social, and intellectual aspects of man are a few of the dimensions of his total personality which are very important after the earliest levels of development have been passed.

The general weakness of the developmental-level approach is much the same as the strength of the dimensional approach: continuity with respect to some growth aspect of the individual. Conversely, the weakness of the dimensional approach, its theoretical but unrealistic isolation of a quality, is offset by the basic strength of the developmental-level approach: maintenance of a view of the total individual at any one period or stage. As some other authors have done [1, 4], we too have selected the developmental-level approach for the study of human development. In order to capitalize on the advantages of the dimensional approach, Chapters 3 to 5 present an overall discussion of major aspects of development and of factors affecting them. By including this approach we hope to show the total environment and its role in the development of the total human person. An examination of the distinguishable developmental levels constitutes the content for the remaining chapters of the book.

DEVELOPMENTAL LEVELS

By dividing the human life-span into various stages, the investigator encounters a number of problems. First, some stages are not sufficiently distinct from those which precede or follow them. Thus, the infant does not suddenly enter childhood or the adolescent early adulthood; some characteristics typifying a new stage are acquired and shown at earlier levels. Second, the criteria for judging what constitutes a level of development are difficult to discover. Should the length of infancy, for example, be defined in terms of chronological age, of bodily growth, or of speech ability. Moreover, what criteria should be used in considering bodily growth or the state of language development? Would an X-ray record of the calcification of the bones and success on a picture vocabulary test be sufficient indexes for these two aspects of growth? If not, how does one select the best measures for adequate appraisal of these factors? A study by Horace B. English [9] shows that most of the seventy-four developmental psychologists who answered the writer's questionnaire objected to the notion of distinct stages of development. One-third of them set the beginning of childhood at one year of age. The majority saw puberty as a physiological condition and not a division of the life span.   About half of them considered the onset of adolescence at twelve and that of old age at sixty-five.   Less than one-third set maturity at twenty-one.   Though some clarifying studies exist, the problem of continuities and discontinuities will probably exist for many years.   Nonetheless, many outstanding exponents of human development from G. Stanley Hall up to the present have embraced the concept of stages.   Moreover, Freud [12], and Piaget [17] aiso, conceptualize fairly clear-cut stages in their studies of sexuality, cognition, and other major aspects of growth and maturation. John E. Anderson [7, p. 40] also affirms the stage concept and summarizes his view in the following manner:

> The enlargement of the life space proceeds by stages, each of which may involve a varying period of time for acquisition followed by a period varying in length during which the growng person adapts to his new found functions and properties.   Thus there are sudden as well as gradual transformations of behavior with each change followed by a period of gradual adaptation.

A child who walks and talks, for example, has a different orientation to his environment than a child who merely creeps and babbles.   The sexually mature adolescent possesses a different pattern of motivation from an older child whose sex glands are not as yet functioning.   Erik Erikson [10] speaks of core conflicts during succeeding stages of development, and Robert J. Havighurst [15] enumerates the tasks to be mastered at each level of development.   The "critical periods" hypothesis is also consistent with the stage approach.   It points to the significant differences in the capacity to learn affective and social responses at various ages in the early phases of development.   A lack of sensitivity to stimuli seems to occur in an organism when the exposure comes too early or too late [19, 20, 22].   After surveying studies related to animals and humans, Philip H. Gray [13] placed the critical period for imprinting in human individuals in infancy, from the age of about six weeks to about six months; stimulus deprivation of the organism at this time can be seriously damaging.   He provides evidence which suggests that "wild children" and delinquent adolescents may have lacked imprinting, in addition to stressful experiences, during the period of infantile helplessness.   J. P. Scott [19] places the start of the critical period for maximum emotional disturbances at approximately seven months, when the critical period of primary socialization ends.

In the study of the life span to follow, a serious attempt has been made to define each developmental level in terms of behavior patterns and traits distinguishing it from earlier and consequent phases.   In other words, the basis for dividing the life span into developmental levels is demonstrated by the emergence of new qualities, as well as significant changes in trends and achievements within the basic pattern of behavior at each given stage. Although there are general age limits for each of these stages, one should always keep in mind that such limits are only approximations of the average course of development: one person passes into the next developmental stage months or even years before another person of the same chronological age. Also, the passage may be partial, that is, in terms of only certain developmental aspects. It should also be recognized that considerable differences exist among various cultures, as well as among different socioeconomic classes within the same culture: average longevity, social demands and pressures, developmental tasks and hazards all vary. The present investigation concerns primarily the individual in the American culture and society.

For the purpose of systematic presentation, the life span is arbitrarily divided into the following thirteen levels; Figure 1–2 shows their graphic representation.

1. *Prenatal period.* The time prior to birth, when major bodily structures, organs, and functions are established to form a biological basis for psychosocial development.

2. *Neonatal period.* The first weeks of life, during which the newborn infant, or neonate, makes radical adjustments to the demands of the extrauterine environment.

3. *Middle infancy.* The second postnatal phase, during which the baby grows at a very fast rate and actively explores his immediate environment. His search for new experiences, relationships, and meaning intensifies, but he is restricted by his limited mobility and power of communication.

4. *Late infancy.* The period during which the human individual enlarges his world greatly by the frequent use of movement, including walking, running, and climbing. Now he is a toddler. Mobility is effectively supplemented by a major means of communication, verbal language. New emotions and increasing awareness of self are other factors adding to complexity of behavior at this stage.

5. *Early childhood.* The preschool years, during which the child improves upon his previously acquired abilities and skills, gains in independence, develops a concept of himself, but remains largely restricted to the family environment.

6. *Middle childhood.* The first years of school life, during which numerous social and intellectual changes occur, partly as a result of the child's intense interaction with peers. He learns many new skills and is exposed to the fundamentals of culture through various means of mass communication.

7. *Late childhood.* The two to three years preceding the onset of puberty,

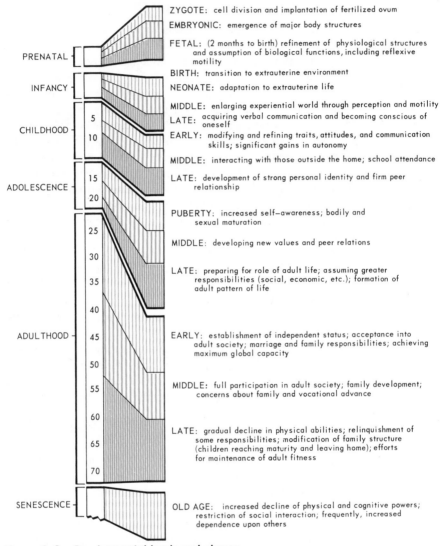

ZYGOTE: cell division and implantation of fertilized ovum

EMBRYONIC: emergence of major body structures

FETAL: (2 months to birth) refinement of physiological structures and assumption of biological functions, including reflexive motility

PRENATAL

BIRTH: transition to extrauterine environment

INFANCY

NEONATE: adaptation to extrauterine life

MIDDLE: enlarging experiential world through perception and motility

LATE: acquiring verbal communication and becoming conscious of oneself

CHILDHOOD

5

10

EARLY: modifying and refining traits, attitudes, and communication skills; significant gains in autonomy

MIDDLE: interacting with those outside the home; school attendance

15

ADOLESCENCE

LATE: development of strong personal identity and firm peer relationship

20

PUBERTY: increased self—awareness; bodily and sexual maturation

25

MIDDLE: developing new values and peer relations

30

35

LATE: preparing for role of adult life; assuming greater responsibilities (social, economic, etc.); formation of adult pattern of life

40

ADULTHOOD

45

EARLY: establishment of independent status; acceptance into adult society; marriage and family responsibilities; achieving maximum global capacity

50

55

MIDDLE: full participation in adult society; family development; concerns about family and vocational advance

60

65

LATE: gradual decline in physical abilities; relinquishment of some responsibilities; modification of family structure (children reaching maturity and leaving home); efforts for maintenance of adult fitness

70

SENESCENCE

OLD AGE: increased decline of physical and cognitive powers; restriction of social interaction; frequently, increased dependence upon others

Figure 1–2 Developmental levels and phases.

during which the child strongly identifies with his peers. He grows into peer society and becomes group-minded with persons of his own sex.

8. *Puberty.* The period during which rapid physiological, psychosexual, emotional, and social changes occur. This is also the stage often marked by increased self-awareness, ambivalence in motivation, and friction with parents and teachers, as well as peers.

9. *Adolescence.* Although puberty is a phase of early adolescence, the

adolescence proper continues approximately five years, during which there tends to be much vacillation, uncertainty, and change before the individual matures for the responsibilities of adult life. It may be a period of intensified conflict during which many life-determining decisions are made, even before a clear self-identity is acquired and an adult pattern of life is embraced.

10. *Early adulthood.* The period in which the individual enters into adult society and culture, chooses an occupation, and usually establishes a family. There is frequently a stabilization of his system of values and interests along with character formation.

11. *Middle adulthood.* The years of consolidation and evaluation of previous achievements and aspirations. This period is normally the peak of civic and economic development, the stage of highest status in adult society.

12. *Late adulthood.* The period of gradual physical and cognitive decline, characterized by increased stability and self-assertion. There is an increased reliance on the habitual and ideological. Adjustment difficulties arise here as children marry and leave the home.

13. *Senescence.* The years of deteriorating sensory acuity and motor skills. Decline of vocational interests, accompanied by partial withdrawal from social functions, produce difficulties even in relying on the past and the habitual. There is an increased preoccupation with the past and the self.

QUESTIONS FOR REVIEW*

1. Considering the numerous changes within and around the individual, what does he need most with respect to himself and others?
2. Explain the concept of developmental psychology and its place among the divisions of psychology.
3. In what ways are child psychology and the psychology of adolescence related to developmental psychology?
4. What practical values might developmental psychology offer the student, over and above those provided by a knowledge of general psychology?
5. What advantages and what limitations are found in the dimensional and the developmental-level approaches to developmental study?
6. What is the value of establishing developmental norms for various aspects or phases of growth? What is the danger in applying such norms to individual persons?

* The questions at the end of each chapter test the student's knowledge of the subject matter. If read at the beginning, they provide a preview of the topics, concepts, and problems upon which to focus. Answered after studying a chapter, either individually or in class discussion, they form a summary of its principal points.

7. What difficulties does the investigator encounter in dividing the life span into different segments?

REFERENCES

I. Selected Reading

1. Goodenough, Florence L., and Leona E. Tyler. *Developmental psychology.* (3rd ed.) New York: Appleton-Century-Crofts, 1959. A widely known text in which the developmental-level approach is used. Though it covers all phases of life, early periods are emphasized.

2. Garrison, Karl C. *Growth and development.* (2nd ed.) New York: Longmans, 1959. Various dimensions of growth, including personality, are successively presented.

3. Gordon, Ira J. *Human development: Readings in research.* Chicago: Scott, Foresman, 1965. A good selection of studies on several major concepts and early levels of development, including adolescence.

4. Hurlock, Elizabeth B. *Developmental psychology.* (3rd ed.) New York: McGraw-Hill, 1968. It examines the individual at successive periods throughout life with a stress on childhood and adolescence.

5. Kuhlen, Raymond G., and George G. Thompson. *Psychological studies of human development.* (2nd ed.) New York: Appleton-Century-Crofts, 1963. A selection of fifty-nine articles grouped according to major aspects of development.

6. Pressey, Sidney L., and Raymond G. Kuhlen. *Psychological development through the life span.* New York: Harper & Row, 1957. A fine presentation of the developmental approach in which various aspects of growth are traced through the life-span.

II. Specific References

7. Anderson, John E. Dynamics of development: System in progress. In D. B. Harris (Ed.), *The concept of development.* Minneapolis: University of Minnesota Press, 1957. Pp. 25–46.

8. Darwin, Charles. *The expression of the emotions in man and animals.* Chicago: University of Chicago Press, 1965 (originally published in London, 1872).

9. English, Horace B. Chronological divisions of the life span. *J. educ. Psychol.,** 1957, **48**, 437–439.

10. Erikson, Erik H. *Childhood and society.* (2nd ed.) New York: Norton, 1963.

11. Frank, Lawrence K. Human development: An emerging scientific

---

* Journal titles are abbreviated throughout the References, but in most cases their full titles are given in the Selective List of Journals.

discipline.   In A. J. Solnit and Sally A. Provence (Eds.), *Modern perspectives in child development.*   New York: International Universities Press, 1963. Pp. 10–36.

12. Freud, Sigmund.   *Three contributions to the sexual theory.*   New York: The Journal of Nervous and Mental Diseases Publishing Co., 1910.

13. Gray, P. H.   Theory and evidence of imprinting in human infants.   *J. Psychol.,* 1958, **46,** 155–166.

14. Hall, G. Stanley.   *Adolescence: Its psychology and its relation to physiology, anthropology, sex, crime, religion, and education.*   New York: Appleton-Century, 1904.   2 Vols.

15. Havighurst, Robert J.   *Developmental tasks and education.*   (2nd ed.) New York: Longmans, 1952.

16. Hess, E. H.   Imprinting.   *Science,* 1959, **130,** 133–141.

17. Osterieth, P., J. Piaget, et al.   *Le problème des stades en psychologie de l'enfant: Symposium.*   Paris: Presses Universitaires de France, 1956.

18. Preyer, Wilhelm.   *Die Seele des Kindes.*   Leipzig: T. Grieben, 1881 (*The mind of the child,* translated by H. W. Brown.   New York: Appleton, 1888).

19. Scott, J. P.   Critical periods in behavioral development.   *Science,* 1962, **138,** 949–958.

20. Scott, J. P.   The process of primary socialization in canine and human infants.   *Monogr. Soc. Res. Child Developm.,* 1963, **28,** No. 1.

21. Spitz, René A.   Hospitalism, an inquiry into the genesis of psychiatric conditions in early childhood.   *Psychoanal. Stud. Child,* 1945, **1,** 53–74.

22. Spitz, René A., with K. M. Wolf.   The smiling response: A contribution to the ontogenesis of social relations.   *Genet. Psychol. Monogr.,* 1946, **34,** 57–125.

23. Stevenson, Harold W.   Developmental psychology.   *Annu. Rev. Psychol.,* 1967, **18,** 102–128.

RESEARCH METHODS

Developmental psychology utilizes the research tools which help to answer questions about phenomena that appear to be related to age. It seeks answers to questions related to antecedent-consequent growth relationships, to the trends in cognitive, creative, and other capacities at various ages, and to considerations of the ways in which present performance or motivation influence future behavior. These questions are important in the developmental study of the individual or group. In many of these studies, the investigator must show how a reaction pattern has evolved from an earlier state and what conditions are responsible for the change. These kinds of problems and questions, have generated the need for appropriate methods for dealing with them. Accordingly, many distinct methods and techniques have been constructed and used in developmental research designs. When compared to the early approaches to studying development, the current research methods represent a great advance in design complexity, objectivity, and accuracy.

Until the relatively recent rise of psychological methodology, the methods for studying growth or maturation were for the most part limited to subjective observation of children and acquaintances or to philosophically based essays on the nature of the growing child. Although they were not subjected to the rigors of the scientific method and procedure, some of these early attempts led to the formulation of important questions. In the seventeenth century, Comenius [11] wrote about 150 essays on the nature of the child and his educational needs.   He was the first to emphasize the child's distinctness from the adult in both physical and mental makeup.   In 1762, Jean Jacques Rousseau's *Emile* [23] appeared.   It inspired naturalistic education and a laissez faire approach in child management.   In 1881, Wilhelm Preyer's famous book *Die Seele des Kindes* was published, and it was translated into English in 1888 as *The mind of the child* [22].   This work, based in part on controlled observation, and supplemented by a number of ad hoc experiments, served for nearly half a century as a model for developmental research.   Oral questioning gave rise to the construction of questionnaires in which carefully selected items pertaining to particular behavior or adjustment areas were compiled as means for obtaining data from groups of children, adolescents, and adults.   G. Stanley Hall, in 1891, was the first American psychologist to apply this technique to the study of children's knowledge [14].

Nancy Bayley [8] assumes that "All behavioral research, including studies of restricted and atypical populations and behaviors, should be oriented to the subjects' age or stage of development as well as their other characteristics."   This certainly would add to the meaningfulness of findings.   Diversity and originality in psychological research were recommended by outstanding participants in an educational research seminar [25].   Research studies in developmental psychology are periodically reviewed in *Annual Review of Psychology* [9, 16].   Humphry F. Osmond [19] wrote a very intriguing article surveying and illustrating basic technical, exploratory, and marginal kinds of research.   Galileo, Max Planck, Heinrich Kluver, and Fleming were among those shown as creators of great ideas and research projects.   Hints were given for recognizing men with great ideas among current researchers.   Interest and success in designing exact techniques and procedures for critical and systematic investigation of specific developmental problems are enterprises seen only in recent decades of the twentieth century. A brief examination of scientific method will aid in understanding the specific methods and techniques used in modern developmental research.

THE SCIENTIFIC METHOD

In the various fields of empirical science, the scientific method offers a structure and procedure for acquiring valid knowledge.   In its basic form this method may be summarized as follows:

1. *Problem.*   Some definite problem is chosen for investigation.   Broad generalizations and unobservable phenomena cannot be directly investigated.   For example, the researcher might be interested in discovering whether children raised in an institutional setting differ in their language development from children raised at home.   But what is meant by these terms?   "Raised at home" may sound simple and clear,

but is it? Is being raised at home with both parents the same as being raised with only one parent? Is it the same to have the mother at home during the day as to have her working? Any accurate statement of the problem must include an operational definition of "raised at home." Or again, what is "language development"? Has language developed when the child uses a simple word meaningfully, uses all the parts of speech, or uses sentences of various types? Obviously the solution to the original problem will depend upon the way in which its various elements are specified.

2. *Hypothesis.* Considering related studies and the facts the investigator already knows, he makes an inductive inference or a calculated guess as a tentative explanation of the problem. The formulation of a hypothesis is essential to carrying out the remaining steps of the scientific method because it aids the investigator in designing his total research project and in selecting methods for collection and analysis of data. The scientist may devise alternative hypotheses and design experiments to test each of them.

3. *Collection of data.* Testing of a particular hypothesis depends partly on the skillful selection of a method for systematic observation or measurement. In developmental psychology, for example, operant conditioning, cinemanalysis, and psychometric and projective tests are utilized. By applying the selected methods, the investigator collects data for analysis and interpretation. All methods are utilized for the same purpose: accumulation of precise, reliable, and verifiable data.

4. *Analysis and interpretation of data.* The data accumulated by the application of the selected measurement device is subsequently subjected to rigid analysis. Typically this involves application of certain statistical procedures. The hypothesis is evaluated in terms of the statistical findings. The investigator asks to what extent the set of data rejects or fails to refute the hypothesis as originally stated. A definite relationship is often established with a stated probable error. It should be noted that the analysis of data usually neither proves nor disproves the hypothesis: it is always conceivable that the observed results might have been the product of some unknown factor. This is why the repetition of various studies, including experimental ones, is useful. Not all of them verify the original findings; some of them yield contrary results.

5. *Conclusions.* The final step in the scientific method is the formulation of conclusions based upon the findings of the investigation and other sources of information. In view of propositions made by other studies, new hypotheses may be formulated. Actually, each time some new relationship or lack of relationship is discovered, new problems arise requiring further investigation.

In a scientific study the variable that the researcher introduces and controls is termed the *independent* variable. The resulting response being observed by the scientist is called the *dependent* variable. It is the aim of the investigator to determine whether or not the introduction and manipulation of the independent variable are accompanied by changes in the dependent variable. Naturally any other factors or conditions which might influence the dependent variable must be taken into consideration. Whenever possible, such factors are held constant, or at least carefully observed, so that their influence will not distort the relationship between the variables. A careful analysis of pertinent relationships between behavior and age as a basis for prediction of behavior is an application of this procedure [17].

Generally, the basic reasoning process involved in scientific inquiry is *inductive*—going from specific observations or measurements to broad conclusions and generalizations. Yet *deductive* reasoning also is an integral part of science. In this approach, the scientist infers specific relationships or explanations from a theory or a set of principles [21]. For example, if we know that all live newborns cry, it is then logical to deduce that this is what will happen when an expectant mother gives birth to her first offspring.

GENERAL APPROACHES TO DEVELOPMENTAL RESEARCH

In the investigation of age-related variables and relationships, two basic approaches are available. These are the cross-sectional and the longitudinal approaches. Each has advantages and disadvantages, the more important of which will be considered. As shown in Figure 2–1, a number of specific methods and tools can be used in either approach.

Cross-sectional approach. In this widely used approach, samples of individuals from different age levels are measured and compared on a specific factor or variable. Height or weight tables have been established by measuring groups of children at various ages. Changes in intellectual ability, for example, might be discovered by comparing the performance of representative samples of two-, three-, and four-year-olds. In other words, each sample represents a given age, with the differences between the samples, if statistically significant, being attributed to the difference between the ages.

Assuming that representative samples are employed, valid tests and measurements yield age norms for the general population. Subsequently, any individual from this population can be compared to the norm. Hypothetically any person within a city or state, even in the country or world, could be studied in a single day or week. By statistically evaluating such data, developmental changes throughout the entire life span could be charted. At the present time there are refined tests for the assessment of most structures and functions of growth. Intelligence, aptitude, vocational, and personality

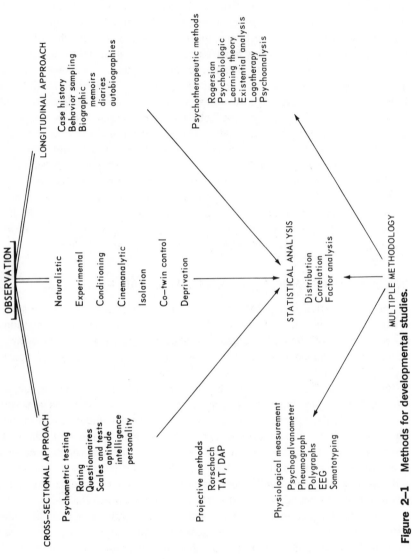

Figure 2–1 Methods for developmental studies.

tests are widely used for cross-sectional testing of individuals and groups. *The mental measurement yearbooks,* edited by Oscar K. Buros [10], provide periodic evaluative analyses of most psychological tests.

Despite the practical usefulness of the cross-sectional method, it has certain shortcomings. The individuality and totality of the person are usually lost. This criticism applies to any scientific study which isolates a single or a related group of characteristics from the total individual. Also inherent in this approach is the loss of developmental continuity. When diverse levels of development are compared, some important traits and features of intermediate phases are often missed. The one-year-old, for example, is typically quite accepting of those about him, the two-year-old is negativistic if not rebellious; and the four-year-old again tends to be quite accepting. Were only the one- and four-year-olds sampled, no significant developmental changes would be indicated in regard to this trait. By studying only fifteen-year-old boys, the variation in some developmental features is likely to be lost because these individuals will be at different levels of development, for example, some may be still prepubertal, others at the peak of pubertal changes, and still others full-fledged adolescents.

Longitudinal approach. In contrast to the cross-sectional assessment which views an individual or group at a specific age, the longitudinal approach studies the same persons over a long period of time. The investigator observes the increase in growth and other changes that occur during that period for each individual. He is also interested in what leads to what. As with the previous approach, the scope of the longitudinal study varies considerably, treating some things in a very limited way, such as gains in height or reading efficiency of a single person, or encompassing many dimensions of behavior and motivation within a large sample of individuals. In 1959, Alan A. Stone and Gloria C. Onqué [24] summarized 297 longitudinal studies in book form. Most of them treat of the emotional, social, and personality development of children. More recently J. Kagan [15] surveyed ten major longitudinal research projects in the United States in terms of samples, methods, and goals. For the future he suggests more rigorous application of methods and clearer delineation of problems. Comparison of the processes of growth and decline seems to be one of the least explored fields of longitudinal research [8].

One major advantage that the longitudinal method has over cross-sectional research is that of individualized analysis of the growth pattern. The person or group is not clocked by norms or standards. Another advantage lies in the absence of any likely source of sampling error. When in cross-sectional sampling different groups are used to represent selected age levels, it is assumed that the groups are really representative. When comparing one-year-olds with two-year-olds, for instance, it is assumed that in a year the first group will closely resemble the group that is now two years of age. It is always conceivable that such might not be the case.

In the case of long-term longitudinal studies, a definite problem arises. For many reasons a single investigator cannot study long periods of life. Unless a series of key investigators is arranged, the period of life under analysis has to be limited. The Berkeley growth study, the Stanford genetic studies of genius, and Gesell's developmental study—all were continued by later investigators with smaller samples than the originals. In most long-term investigations, the problem of maintaining contact with the participating subjects is a major one. Some of the participants lose interest in the project and others leave the community.

Case study. This is an exceedingly valuable longitudinal method for gaining comprehensive information about the various developmental areas of a single person. This type of study includes a wide variety of specialized investigations following a given outline such as that of Arthur E. Traxler and Robert D. North [26, pp. 271–274], for example. Basically, the case study consists of obtaining information about an individual's past history and relating this to his present personality structure and behavioral characteristics. Various procedures are used to gather necessary data concerning a person's history. Interviewing the person and one of his parents and obtaining medical, school, and employment records are common methods. In establishing the present level of development and adjustment, standardized tests and diagnostic interviewing are frequently employed. Which techniques will be employed for collecting significant data naturally depends upon the purpose of the case-history report.

In seeking to trace the relationship between the present and the past, the case study considers the person as he is and as he has been under relatively normal conditions of his life. It attempts to produce a picture of the whole personality. Such a procedure has definite advantages but also some limitations. On the positive side, it avoids the pitfalls that might be encountered by introducing artificial situations and variables. On the negative side, there is always the danger that among the myriad factors influencing human development some important variable may be overlooked or, conversely, overemphasized to the relative exclusion of some other. It might also be noted that, for the most part, case studies deal with persons who are disturbed or deviant in some way. Inasmuch as such samples are not representative of the general population, great care must be exercised in applying any conclusion to the normal individual. However, the person who has failed to adjust adequately often presents an exaggerated picture of a basically normal individual. For this reason, case studies of such individuals frequently advance the understanding of normal development or adjustment, and occasionally they point the way to further, more exact research. If, for example, in comparing the records of a sufficiently large sample of subjects certain consistent past events are found to be connected with a symptomatic mode of behavior, a relationship of causal significance may be suspected.

SCIENTIFIC TECHNIQUES

As was indicated in describing the third step of the scientific method, systematic observation is a leading characteristic of empirical science. The single technique of observing, however, is not applicable to the study of all scientific phenomena. Some procedures are especially suitable for testing one hypothesis but may be impractical or impossible for testing another. In considering the techniques which are widely applied in developmental studies, three points must be borne in mind. First, such methods and tools are not limited to developmental psychology or even to the science of psychology. Second, different methods are applicable to the same problem. Third, each represents a procedure suitable for a multitude of other purposes.

Experimentation. By far the most highly refined and most desirable tool is experimentation. Basically this consists of the systematic varying of some factor or group of factors and the observation of what then occurs to the subjects in this controlled situation. The experimenter seeks to determine whether a change in one variable is accompanied by a change in the subjects' responses. By way of illustration, let us consider an experiment in reaction time. An individual is instructed by the experimenter to press a certain button as quickly as he can after hearing a certain sound or seeing a light signal. Each time either stimulus is presented a timing device records exactly how long it takes the subject to respond. Other variables that might influence reaction time are held constant, or at least observed so that their influences may be evaluated. By repeated measurements the experimenter can determine whether there is a relationship between the independent variable and the dependent variable, between the type of stimulus and the speed of response.

In the foregoing experiment only one factor was altered and only one response observed. This, of course, represents the simplest type of experiment. Yet it may have value in a developmental study if this experiment is repeated from month to month or from year to year and the results are compared. More complex experiments involve the simultaneous manipulation of a number of factors so that the possible interacting effect of such variables can be ascertained. One should keep in mind the fact that the relationship between the experimentally manipulated variable and the observed result is not necessarily a cause-effect relationship. In the case of experimental studies, as with all other empirical investigations, such a relationship may merely signify that the variables are mutually related to some known or as yet unknown factors.

The control-group technique is one of a number of procedures employed to help regulate various extraneous conditions. In random control groups, two or more groups are tested and equated and one or two of them (excepting the control group) are exposed to the independent variable. In paired control groups, each subject in the group is paired with a subject in the other group or groups with respect to such variables as age, sex, socioeconomic status, IQ, and education. Measurements from several variables can be compared by statistical devices by holding one variable constant and finding correlations between the others. Many experimental procedures have been constructed that use Skinner's paradigm of operant conditioning, with verbal and nonverbal reinforcement and punishment [13, 20].

The chief value of experimentation is the speed with which data can be gathered, since the scientist does not have to wait for the natural occurrence of the phenomena. Also, the original investigator and others can repeat the experiment to verify results. Experimental techniques yield valuable information about individual differences among persons of the same age or of different age groups.

Despite the fact that experimentation is the most precise tool, it is not without some limitations. Artificial situations and stimuli make human responses less natural; suggestibility and distractions are difficult to control. Many problems cannot be attacked experimentally for ethical and humanitarian reasons [29]. The influence on human growth of some factor suspected to be seriously detrimental cannot be assessed, particularly if the experiment would have to be carried out for a prolonged period of time. Effects of radiation, for example, are of considerable interest, but moral considerations exclude the use of human subjects for any such experiments.

Isolation methods. A distinct application of experimental technique to longitudinal studies is illustrated by various isolation methods. In these, one group of subjects is offered the opportunity to experience some learning situation. A second group is not afforded the same opportunity. After a period of time, the two groups are compared in order to determine the influence of the experience upon achievement.

In many studies this procedure is carried one step further. The subjects not given the learning, the so-called "control" subjects, are offered it later in order to determine how quickly, if at all, they will match the first group of subjects. Thus, the first group, after its learning period, often demonstrates a marked advantage over the control group. But the control group usually requires far less training in order to reach the same degree of achievement. In such a case, it is reasonably inferred that some factor other than learning was involved in attaining proficiency. This factor, maturation, is an important developmental concept which will be considered in further detail in the next chapter.

Although isolation in its purest form is a strictly experimental approach wherein the amount of learning opportunity is controlled by the investigator, it may be extended to encompass large areas. In some cultures, for example, certain conditions are prevalent, whereas in other cultures they are largely or totally absent. The latter, therefore, is considered an isolated or control

group. All other things being equal, the differences in behavioral or personality characteristics may be attributed to the elements lacking in the cultural
environment. We really cannot imagine "all other things being equal," however, because of the tremendous complexity of any cultural group. Just the
same, in general terms, much useful information regarding human development can be obtained in this manner.

Despite the evident advantage of the isolation method for comparing the
haves and have-nots, it has distinct limitations. Long-term studies certainly
become impractical because of possible irreparable damage that might be
done to members of the isolated group. Moreover, the number of influences
that might be isolated diminishes rapidly as the person grows older: everyday
living provides many opportunities for individuals to develop the potentialities
studied. Consequently, use of this method has been restricted to basic learning processes occurring in the early years of life.

Co-twin control method. Often employed in conjunction with the isolation
technique, the co-twin method clearly illustrates the investigator's attempt to
control as many significant variables as possible in determining the relationship between hereditary endowment and psychological processes. This
method seeks to control the influence of heredity to the greatest possible
extent. Identical twins, persons who have developed from the same fertilized
germ cell and therefore possess virtually the same hereditary makeup, are
used as subjects. In an experimental isolation study, one twin (T) is exposed
to the experimental situation and the other twin (C) is not. Hence, both
environmental and hereditary factors are maximally controlled.

The leading studies of co-twin control were conducted by Arnold Gesell
and Helen Thompson [12] and Myrtle B. McGraw [18]. Both offer many
practical insights into the nature of development, especially the effects of
training on performance. Maximum rise in performance results from nurturing the desired response in a natural state of growth. McGraw observed
that the behavior patterns do not grow all at once but each has its own
period of rapid development. She made deliberate attempts to modify performance by giving one of a pair of possibly identical twins special training.
In some activities, such as walking, performance was about the same despite
early practice by one twin. In other activities, such as roller skating, the
trained twin became adept soon after he began walking. On the basis of her
varied experiments McGraw concluded that there are critical periods for human learning which vary for distinct ontogenetic activities; for each kind of
behavioral pattern there is an optimum period for rapid and efficient learning.

This method has proved very valuable in determining the relative importance of heredity and environment in the development of certain behavioral
traits and abilities, but its application is somewhat limited. Although it
represents the closest approximation to the ideal experimental procedure, it
has the drawback of sampling limitation; too few sets of identical twins of the

same age or developmental level are obtainable by the investigator. In addition, when older twins are used, another problem presents itself: the possible influence of different experiential backgrounds and personality factors. A recent survey of twin research [27] offered a partial solution for the criticisms raised, and discussed multivariate analysis of twin data. After several dramatic breakthroughs in genetics, this method for future research in human behavior genetics is becoming more valuable.

Still another use of the co-twin method is available to the researcher. Identical twins are still employed as subjects, but with no attempt to control their environment. The twins are reared in distinctive environmental settings, say in separate foster homes; or, as adults, they are exposed to decidedly different influences. They are then compared with respect to some specific trait, ability, or mental state. If the twins manifest significantly greater similarity than persons who have comparable environments but lack this hereditary resemblance, it must be concluded that the greater similarity of the twins is due to some hereditary factor. It can be noted in passing that research along this line has clearly demonstrated the important role of heredity in determining intellectual capacity and emotionality. Intensive research is currently being conducted to determine what, if any, hereditary basis exists for susceptibility to various illnesses, mental disorder, and types of personality.

Naturalistic observation. Observation in natural settings—hospital nurseries, schools, conventions, and recreational facilities—offers opportunity for repeated surveillance of infants, children, and adults. The undetected observer in the situation or behind a screen may study various activities and relationships among individuals, such as social contacts, feelings and emotions, or indexes of leadership, and record them. Natural and spontaneous behavior of individuals and groups is likely to make relationships among the variables observed more evident. The frequency of certain types of behavior can be more exactly assessed by time sampling. The time-sampling technique was first applied by W. C. Olson and Florence L. Goodenough.

The outcomes of naturalistic observation frequently suggest hypotheses for further research by the use of more accurate techniques. In the past, systematic observation of infants, children, and adolescents in hospitals, nursery schools, and other schools was utilized in the field studies of Charlotte Buhler, Jean Piaget, William E. Blatz, John B. Watson, and many others.

Biographical tools. Autobiographies and biographies, personal memoirs, diaries, and similar writings constitute records of human experience and behavior in various phases of life. By noting similarities and differences in recorded life histories, some useful information can be accumulated. Certain aspects of behavior and personality lend themselves very well to this type of study. Changes in the intensity of religious or ideological conviction, modifications of the self-concept; and the unfolding of creative ability are three examples of research problems which can be studied effectively by this technique.

Biographical sources are usually available only for the study of men of outstanding achievement [5, 6]. Diaries, however, have been used by G. Stanley Hall, Charlotte Buhler, and some others in their studies of adolescent behavior and motivation. From letters written within an 11½-year period, Gordon W. Allport [5] formulates a very intriguing analysis of an apparently neurotic lady.

Biographical material usually possesses a number of limitations. The accuracy of the author is one. When several biographies of the same person are compared great discrepancies are often found, particularly in the treatment of personal dynamics and motivation. Owing to the writers' attempted self-analysis of their own motivation, autobiographies also are subject to considerable error. But assuming that a set of such writings is quite accurate, there still is the practical problem of obtaining comparable material for analysis. What is considered important by one writer often is not even treated by another. Finally, the subjects of such literary works are, for the most part, not truly representative of any larger population. How many "average" men, for example, write diaries, publish autobiographies, or have their biographies written?

Interview. This is a technique that has many diverse applications. We are concerned only with the clinical employment of the interview. Clinical psychologists, psychiatrists, and psychoanalysts use this device for diagnostic and psychotherapeutic purposes. Etiological analysis of the past often discloses some definite relationships between certain frustrating or traumatic events in childhood and the resultant symptomatic patterns of the present. Many psychoanalytic sessions are devoted to the scrutiny of the individual's early experiences and relationships with significant persons. This discloses and often magnifies the drastic influence of antecedent events on the person's motivation and adjustment.

Clinical interviewing frequently provides a knowledge of the origins and development of maladaptive self-defenses, attitudes, and habits. As the number of similar cases increases the diagnostic conclusions gain in meaning. On the liability side one has to remember that the analyst may unconsciously prompt some answers or he may inaccurately interpret the bewildering complexity of data communicated by the client.

Statistical analysis. In developmental studies, most methods or techniques for investigating populations yield a large amount of quantitative data. The interpretation of such data is facilitated by the application of various statistical devices. The study of frequencies and distributions of scores, the computation of measures of central tendency (mean, median, and mode) and measures of variance, as well as correlations and factor analysis, add to the precision of the findings. Tests of significance determine the acceptance or rejection of the hypotheses formulated at the outset of research. What type of statistics will be employed depends on the type of research design which has been used.

Multiple methods. The application of two or more methods for more complex problems is a recent and welcome trend. When several methods are properly combined, each one offsets some limitations of the others. Some current research designs include interviews, questionnaires, and a number of psychometric and projective tests to see the joint effects of these methods applied to the study of the same problem in the same population. The safeguarding of extensive records and data for further studies also adds to the research and its training opportunities.

In all research designs it is imperative that the prescribed procedures are carefully executed, that experts are used to collect and treat the data, and that major findings are verified by repetition of original studies. In the designing of current developmental research projects, Freudian postulates and Piaget's hypotheses [28] are probably the two most frequently used sources. Such theorists as Kurt Lewin, B. F. Skinner, Robert R. Sears, Charlotte Buhler, Neal E. Miller, Erik H. Erikson, Robert J. Havighurst, and Talcott Parsons also offer many new concepts and constructs for further studies.

QUESTIONS FOR REVIEW

1. List and explain the basic steps in the application of the scientific method.
2. What are the characteristics distinguishing the inductive from the deductive approach in scientific study?
3. List the advantages and limitations of the cross-sectional approach in developmental studies.
4. What are the basic differences between the cross-sectional and the longitudinal approach?
5. In what way is the case-study technique related to the longitudinal method?
6. How does experimentation differ from environmental or natural observation?
7. Explain the two major uses of the co-twin control technique.
8. Identify the advantages and several typical limitations of the biographical techniques.
9. Explain the need for statistics in developmental studies.
10. Explain the use of clinical interviewing and the nature of the information gained.
11. Why should the investigator of human development employ several methods of research rather than just one?

REFERENCES

I. Selected Reading

1. Hoffman, Martin L., and Lois W. Hoffman (Eds.). *Review of child development research.* New York: Russell Sage Foundation, 1964 and 1966. 2 Vols. Volume 1 consists of twelve articles covering various research areas by thirteen authors, from genetics and effects of infant-care practices to the development of moral character and effects of the mass media. Volume 2 contains eleven articles by seventeen writers dealing with family structure, socialization, development of language, attitudes, motives and roles, and deviant patterns of early growth.

2. Mussen, Paul H. (Ed.). *Handbook of research methods in child development.* New York: Wiley, 1960. An extensive compilation of various methods and techniques of study by thirty experts, including research designs and particular applications of the techniques presented.

3. Scott, William A., and Michael Wertheimer. *Introduction to psychological research.* New York: Wiley, 1962. All the phases important to psychological research are clearly presented. The statement of concepts and questions in operational terms is emphasized.

4. Sidowski, Joseph E., et al. *Experimental methods and instrumentation in psychology.* New York: McGraw-Hill, 1966. The author and over thirty contributors deal with a large range of experimental techniques from conditioning to research on higher mental processes, offering suggestions for the use of a large number of instruments, polygraphs, and apparatuses.

II. Specific References

5. Allport, Gordon W. (Ed. and Interpreter). *Letters from Jenny.* New York: Harcourt, Brace & World, 1965.

6. Allport, Gordon W. The general and the unique in psychological science. *J. Personal.*, 1962, **30**, 405–422.

7. Anderson, John E. Child development research: The next 25 years. *Child Developm.*, 1960, **31**, 191–199.

8. Bayley, Nancy. The life span as a frame of reference in psychological research. *Vita humana*, 1963, **6**, 125–139.

9. Bell, Richard Q. Developmental psychology. *Annu. Rev. Psychol.*, 1965, **16**, 1–38.

10. Buros, Oscar K. (Ed.). *The sixth mental measurements yearbook.* Highland Park, N.J.: Gryphon, 1965 (reviews 1,219 tests).

11. Comenius, John Amos. *The school of infancy* (edited with an introduction by Ernest M. Eller). Chapel Hill: University of North Carolina Press, 1956 (originally published in German in 1633).

12. Gesell, Arnold, and Helen Thompson. Twins T and C from infancy to adolescence: A biogenetic study of individual differences by the method of co-twin control. *Genet. Psychol. Monogr.*, 1941, **24**, 3–121.

13. Greenspoon, J. The reinforcing effect of two spoken sounds in the frequency of two responses. *Amer. J. Psychol.*, 1955, **68**, 409–416.

14. Hall, G. Stanley. The contents of children's minds on entering school. *Ped. Sem.*, 1891, **1**, 139–173.

15. Kagan, Jerome. American longitudinal research on psychological development. *Child Developm.*, 1964, **35**, 1–32.

16. Kagan, Jerome, and Barbara Henker. Developmental psychology. *Annu. Rev. Psychol.*, 1966, **17**, 1–50.

17. Kessen, William. Research design in the study of developmental problems. In Paul H. Mussen (Ed.), *Handbook of research methods in child development.* New York: Wiley, 1960. Pp. 36–70.

18. McGraw, Myrtle B. *Growth: A study of Johnny and Jimmy.* New York: Appleton-Century-Crofts, 1935.

19. Osmond, Humphry F. The direction of research. In M. P. Lawton and Fay G. Lawton (Eds.), *Mental impairment in the aged.* Philadelphia Geriatric Center, 1965 (Proceedings of the Institute on Mentally Impaired Aged held at the Philadelphia Geriatric Center, April 6–8, 1964). See also Bush, Vannevar. *Science is not enough.* New York: Morrow, 1967.

20. Pikunas, Justin. Operant conditioning effects upon drawing content. *J. proj. Tech. & Person. Assessm.*, 1966, **30**, 172–176.

21. Popper, K. R. *The logic of scientific discovery.* New York: Basic Books, 1959.

22. Preyer, Wilhelm. *The mind of the child* (translated by H. W. Brown). New York: Appleton, 1888.

23. Rousseau, Jean Jacques. *Emile: Selections* (translated and edited by William Boyd). New York: Bureau of Publications, Teachers College, Columbia University, 1962.

24. Stone, Alan A., and Gloria C. Onqué. *Longitudinal studies of child personality.* Cambridge: Harvard (for the Commonwealth Fund), 1959.

25. Taylor, Donald W. (Chm.) et al. Educational research in psychology. *Amer. Psychologist*, 1959, **14**, 167–179.

26. Traxler, Arthur E., and Robert D. North. *Techniques of guidance* (3rd ed.). New York: Harper & Row, 1966.

27. Vandenberg, Steven G. Contributions of twin research to psychology. *Psychol. Bull.*, 1966, **66**, 327–352.

28. Wohlwill, J. F. Piaget's system as a source of empirical research. *Merril-Palmer Quart.*, 1963, **9**, 253–262.

29. Wolfensberger, Wolf. Ethical issues in research with human subjects. *Science*, 1967, **155**, 47–51. See also Bonner, Hubert. The role of the human sciences in the dehumanization of man. *Humanitas*, 1967, **2**, 227–246.

PRINCIPLES OF HUMAN DEVELOPMENT

This chapter consists of concise explanations of the basic elements and processes underlying human growth and maturation. Human development is an orderly and sequential phenomenon. This order and sequence become partially observable through discussion and illustration of the principal phases of development. It is hoped that each principle and sequence examined in this and the following two chapters will improve considerably the reader's perspective on the individual's growth and behavior in the total life span.

GROWTH PROCESSES

Human development is marked principally by three interrelated processes. These are differentiation, learning, and integration. Based on continuous additional growth by cell division, differentiation culminates in the formation of distinguishable tissues and organs. Starting about twenty-four hours after conception, cell reproduction is a lifelong process. Tissue formation starts in less than two weeks after fertilization of the ovum, as different cells are produced by the organizing cells which possess within them the DNA "blueprint" for genetic development. Periodically, the DNA molecules seem to give the body instruction on growth. Endodermic, mesodermic, and ectodermic layers of tissue appear. The outermost tissue, called the ectoderm, eventually produces the outer layer of the skin, hair, nails, skin glands, sensory cells, and the entire nervous system of the body. The middle layer, the mesoderm, produces the deeper skin layers, muscle cells, and the circulatory and excretory organs of the body. Finally, the endoderm produces the lining of the entire digestive system, the lungs, liver, pancreas, and many of the glands. Thus, various organs emerge within each layer of tissue and combine in a variety of systems, such as the central nervous system and the circulatory, reproductive, digestive, and excretory systems. These and related structural developments are presented in Chapter 6.

Physiological growth furnishes a basis for the formation of receptor, conductor, and effector systems, which make up the nervous system and help various motivational, behavioral, and personality variables to emerge and function. The receptors—our sense organs—are stimulated by various aspects of the environment. A "message" acknowledging the stimulation of receptors is transmitted to the brain by one group of conductors; another group conveys the brain's "orders" for action, again by way of the spinal column, to the various parts of the body. These (latter) conductors eventually lead to the effectors, which set muscles and glands into action. The human mind, using mechanisms of the central nervous system, unifies the specialized systems and organs into a functionally complete organization. Within the organism the various components form a whole which then integrates the activity of the parts. The process of integration is especially marked by the maintenance of the biochemical unity of the organism and by the emergence of a regulatory mechanism coordinating overt behavior with its goal. Hence the human individual uses the feedback that responds to selected sensory and probably symbolic stimuli in such a way that any deviation from the selected goal is continuously corrected and the right course of action is pursued.

Following birth, differentiation and integration are continually supported by external stimulation and learning experiences. *Learning* is the major way of acquiring a reserve of abilities and skills required for gratifying needs and adapting to the changing environment and culture. The growth processes establish the pattern for organism-environment interaction. Viewed from this perspective, behavior can be seen as a function of the developmental state of the organism in its environment.

For normative or comparative purposes, structural and functional growth is often expressed quantitatively in age units. The quantifications of intelligence testing into mental age (MA) and intelligence quotient (IQ) and of accomplishments in scholastic work into educational age (EA) are too well known to need any explanation. General vital capacity (VA), less well known, refers to the amount of air exhaled after a maximum inhalation; the vital index (VI) is set by dividing the cubic centimeters of air exhaled by the person's weight in kilograms. Carpal age (CA) is determined from the amount of calcium deposit in the wrist bones as seen in X-rays. Carpal age is often used as an index of general ossification. Height age (HA) and weight age (WA) are set by group averages for different ages separately for boys and girls. Dentition or dental age (DA) is a measurement of dental growth usually based upon the number of permanent teeth which have erupted. As a summary measurement, organismic age (OA) refers to the average of all structural measurements of an individual. In formulating the organismic age concept, W. C. Olson and B. O. Hughes [21], however, include some functional and achievement measurements, such as mental and reading ages. Organismic age divided by chronological age yields organismic quotient (OQ). Currently, this concept serves no useful function in the study of human development.

Arnold Gesell [16] introduced the developmental quotient (DQ) based on the maturity age of motor, adaptive, language, and personal-social aspects of behavior matched to age norms:

$$DQ = \frac{\text{maturity age}}{\text{chronological age}} \times 100$$

DQ points to the rate of growth and is useful in estimating deviations of development in the early stages of life. It is conceivable that a personality age (PA) and its quotient (PQ) will be established when structural comprehensive personality tests are devised and validated.

FACTORS IN SELF-REALIZATION

Self-realization refers to a lifelong process of developing and utilizing one's human qualities and capacities within the stimulating and restricting matrix of environmental forces. The principle of self-realization was first described by Carl G. Jung [19, pp. 171, 182] as a process of individuation in which the potential qualities and the contents of the personal unconscious are developed into the peculiar and idiosyncratic behavior of the individual. In its totality, self-realization essentially depends on three principle sources of stimulation: (1) heredity, (2) environment and culture, and (3) self-direction.

Heredity, chiefly determined by the chromosome composition of DNA (deoxyribonucleic acid) and RNA (ribonucleic acid) molecules, is unique for each human individual and remains a very important factor throughout life. Structural growth can be explained only through the decoding of DNA and possibly RNA messenger action, since without DNA cell reproduction could not take place. Enzyme action also depends on DNA functions [13, 23]. Structural growth is the basis for the neuromuscular and cognitive functions, both of which are basic for personality development. Heredity determines the rate of maturation and possibly sets the upper limits for all major growth processes. Even if the full quota of neurons in the brain develop, later millions of them may be lost as a result of fever, toxins, and injuries. They are the most differentiated body cells, and when lost, they are not regenerated. As will be shown in Chapter 4, hereditary *anlagen* (translated in a general way as dispositions) continue decoding messages and stimulating development throughout life. The actual level of development at any stage of life depends to a great extent on the need-gratifying and stimulating power of the environment.

Environment consists primarily of the various external events and stimuli which affect the individual. A child's social environment, for example, should gratify his biological, emotional, and spiritual needs and provide a variety of stimuli for intellectual development and personality formation. Frequent examples of ethical behavior by parents and others facilitate acquisition of desirable traits and personal integrity. In reverse, a lack of exemplary behavior and of moral education predisposes the child to the acquisition of socially undesirable traits and attitudes. Since Freud and Montessori, the boomerang effect of a harshly punitive discipline has also been often hypothesized. The "battered" children become highly aggressive and antisocial.

As the child grows and matures, he learns to become more selective about what he accepts. Increasingly, he assimilates only what he wishes to. *Self-direction* is shown when the child expands his understanding to a level at which he is able to make inferences and form estimations. By thinking abstractly and symbolically, the child shows that he is becoming less dependent on external stimuli and parental guidance. The ability to see alternatives and to choose his own activities is another sign of freedom from external pressures. The child's increasing self-reliance becomes a constant factor in his relationships, considerations, and decisions. Already at the age of about five the child can organize himself well enough to carry out some of his own decisions or wishes. Although it depends on hereditary and environmental stimulation, the self gains in autonomy from both and becomes a major organizer of behavior by the middle years of childhood. The developmental roles of heredity, environment, culture, and self-direction will be analyzed in Chapters 4 and 5.

Following a survey of many original studies in psychology and related fields, Charlotte Buhler [9] was able to distinguish four very basic tendencies of life, viz., need satisfaction, expansive creativity, order upholding, and adaptive self-limitation. Generally these tendencies are active in varying degrees, and each of them becomes predominant at certain levels of human development. The ultimate goal is self-fulfillment based upon optimal need satisfaction and creative expansion, achieved in the presence of internal order and adaptation to limiting situations.

Consistent with Kurt Goldstein, Abraham Maslow, and Carl Rogers, Buhler [8] classified the ultimate goal of life in terms of accomplishments rather than in terms of mere homeostasis. While some personality theorists see man as merely a biological organism, others hold that there is also purpose and meaning in man's life. The maximum realization of the individual's potentials and the resultant long-term achievements lead to a gratifying self-fulfillment at later stages of life.

The developmental tasks for each level of life will show the behavior patterns necessary for the unfolding of the total human person. Enumeration of the hazards encountered during early phases of development will reveal which forces are the disturbing and inhibiting ones. Lack of proper stimulation, for example, handicaps the child in developing his language skills and emotions. The child will not exhibit affection toward his parents if they do not first show it to him.

BASIC CONCEPTS

In the present text, many concepts of developmental psychology are defined and explained wherever they first appear. Terms and concepts that are not clarified are either self-explanatory in terms of general psychology or can be found in the Glossary at the end of the book. The student is urged to use the Glossary in order to get a fuller understanding of the terms used. Further information on psychological and related terms may be found in A comprehensive dictionary of psychological and psychoanalytical terms, edited by Horace B. English and Ava C. English [14], Handbook of psychological terms, by Philip L. Harriman [17], and Encyclopedia of educational research, edited by Chester W. Harris [18].

A brief clarification of key terms will be given here. Development is a very broad term which, first of all, refers to the process by which an individual's potentialities unfold and appear as new abilities, qualities, and characteristics. It includes the relatively permanent changes resulting from growth, maturation, learning, and achievement. Growth chiefly refers to the increment of bodily tissues, organs, structures, and systems. Maturation, in turn, refers to the emergence and attainment of maturity of bodily structures and functional powers mainly as a result of periodic genetic stimulation. Maturation may be defined as the progressive differentiation of structure and function. A certain degree of maturation, for example, is a necessary condition for learning efficiency. For a proper assimilation of various subjects, different degrees of maturity are required. A child cannot do something he is not biologically or functionally ready to do. If not urged, however, he will apply himself in only a limited way, even when his level of maturation is adequate. To illustrate: A child may shy away from other children and from visitors. Most children will not learn music just because a piano is available to them. *Achievement* is therefore a function of maturity, social stimulation, and self-application.

In its overall aspects, development includes attainment of any higher degree of differentiation, complexity, and functional efficiency in the human organism, as well as deterioration of structures and functions of the organism at later stages of life. Generally, development points to an irreversible change in an individual's pattern of action and reaction throughout life. It is identified as the integration of structure and function. Deterioration implies an impairment of tissue, organ, or system and a decline of any function arising from age or pathology. Allied to development is the concept of *aging* that starts at conception and ends with death. Aging increases with chronological age, but some organs and structures age at a faster rate than others. The same applies to functional powers of individuals. Two persons, one at thirty-five and the other at forty-five, may have equivalent biological age. Because of aging differences, the life expectancy for mentally defective persons is much lower than for intellectually bright groups.

ANALYSIS OF SPECIFIC PRINCIPLES

The course and pattern of human development may be partially explained or at least clarified by the following principles underlying growth, maturation, and behavior.

Growth and behavior follow genetic sequences. The physiological development of the human individual shows an orderly process of structural change marked by two interrelated types of sequence: (1) the cephalocaudal and (2) the proximodistal.

The *cephalocaudal* sequence, as the etymology of the word indicates, is the direction of early structural growth from the head, through the trunk, to the extremities. This means that the infant's head and brain grow faster and reach each level of maturity earlier than the heart, lungs, or other visceral organs. These have a priority of growth as compared with the hands or feet. At birth the head makes up over 20 percent of total body length, as seen in Figure 5–1; at maturity the ratio decreases and the head area accounts for only 8 percent of body length. Modern laboratory techniques show that metabolic activity maintains its highest intensity in regions of brain and neural structures in general. In later stages of life, the morphological changes due to deterioration are marked by the same sequence. Thus, the brain loses its weight and deteriorates at a faster rate than visceral organs do.   The hands and feet seem to produce the least deterioration or pathology in later stages of life.   Deeply localized organs and structures ache more often and become more easily damaged as a result of advanced age, illness, toxins, and infections [11].

The *proximodistal* sequence of maturation merely parallels the cephalo-caudal direction in terms of movement control.   Movements close to the body axis mature faster than movements of bodily parts located on its periphery. Head and eye control appear very early in postnatal life.   Whole arm and leg movements are seen long before elbow- and knee-joint control is exercised. The coordinated use of the feet and toes for climbing or jumping follows knee-joint control.

In its functional aspects, behavior follows the sequence from *general* to *specific* responses.   This sequence is inherent in all aspects of early develop-ment.   In emotional development, general excitement precedes the appear-ance of specific emotional responses, such as fear, anger, or delight.   Fear, in turn, differentiates into fear of specific objects, animals, or situations.   In acquiring speech, the child first learns a number of general nouns before he assimilates any specific ones, for example, he uses "car" for all motor vehicles before he applies proper names to each kind and make.   He learns and uses verbs before he picks his first adverbs.   It may also be noted that in old age the person encounters difficulties in recalling nouns before he does verbs.   Genetic order applies thus to both learning and forgetting.

This behavior sequence from general to specific may be further exemplified by such generalizations as from simple to complex, from unselective to highly selective, from concrete to abstract, from tangible to intangible, and from known to unknown.   The infant, for example, responds indifferently to the kind of clothing he is dressed in; the child shows some selectivity and prefer-ence; the adolescent is very specific about clothing he thinks is suitable. Because of the genetic order of development, learning is closely related to what the individual already knows.   The child's mind, for example, integrates new information effectively only if there is a foundation of similar knowledge. For this reason, children need simple object demonstrations and comparisons related to their past experiences in order to understand new data.   Feeding isolated facts and unrelated bits of subject matter to students does little to enhance learning.

The individual first perceives what is tangible; much later he begins to understand the less tangible and abstract aspects of reality.   The child learns, for instance, that some objects are at times "hot" long before he can understand the concept of heat.   Simple scribbling turns into drawing of observed objects; this drawing advances to accurate reproducing of aspects of reality before abstract and symbolic drawing is attempted.   It is impossible to follow etiquette and show cultural sophistication in childhood, but it should be required in early adulthood. These examples indicate how differential responsiveness expands as individual experience accumulates and explain why responses proper to a situation are more frequent at later than at early stages of maturity.

While genetic sequence is the same for all human beings, some exceptions are reported from time to time. A few children walk and run before they creep and some apparently never creep. Others may sing before they talk. Of course, there is an explanation for this. If a child goes from crib to playpen and is kept there for most of his waking time, he does not have space for engaging in creeping. Instead, he learns to rise to a standing position earlier, begins to balance himself, and moves to walking rather than creeping. If a mother speaks little but sings often and repeats some simple tunes, it is no surprise if the baby first imitates songs before he imitates words.

Various structures and functions of the organism have individual developmental rates and phases. All organs and systems of the human organism have different times for and rates of structural development. The brain, for example, grows at a very rapid rate during the prenatal and early postnatal stages and reaches practically its full weight and structural differentiation almost three years before the onset of pubertal changes. In fact, at two years of age its weight, over 1,000 grams, approaches 80 percent of its adult weight. The relationship of total body weight to brain weight approximates 1:8 at birth, but 1:41 at physical maturity. The thymus gland— located in the lower neck and upper thorax—grows early, functions maximally during the years of infancy and childhood, and ceases functioning by later adolescence. On the other hand, during the years of childhood there is very limited growth of the genital organs and system. Prior to the onset of puberty, this system has about 10 percent of its mature weight. Because of the variations in structural growth in various bodily systems, there is an insufficiency of balance and coordination in biochemical controls during the phases of rapid physiological growth, for example, infancy and puberty. Various systems and organs also show different rates of deterioration. Within the glandular system, for instance, the thymus gland decreases its functions with the advancing years of childhood, while the sex glands function maximally in the late teens and early twenties, and deteriorate functionally in the late forties in women and about two decades later in men. The other endocrine glands, for example, parathyroids and adrenals, maintain almost even functional capacity throughout life.

In an analogous manner, intellectual and social functions show particular cycles of development too, marked by rises, plateaus, and declines. The rate of speech development reaches its peak at five or six years of age, whereas socialization develops most rapidly during the middle phase of adolescence.   When properly taught, two or three languages can be successfully learned during the first six years of life, but it is very difficult to learn them in late years of adulthood.   Intellectual functions, as measured by individual intelligence tests, attain their highest efficiency about the age of seventeen or eighteen years, while the power of abstraction continues improving through the years of early adulthood.   Growth of character traits continues through-out adulthood.   Figure 3–1 shows graphically the hypothetical rate of growth of various factors and functions and facilitates comparison among them.

Unfolding abilities are spontaneously expressed.   There resides in the infant, child, adolescent, and adult a powerful impulse to grow and mature, to unfold new abilities, and to improve them by practice and revision.   Most of the capacities and potentialities inherent in the individual's nature ma-terialize or become activated in the first two decades of life.   Endowments and abilities are to a considerable degree irrepressible, yet activation of some of them may leave no room for the realization of related or antagonistic potentialities.

The tendency toward optimum functioning is vividly exemplified during the early stages of postnatal life.   As soon as the infant develops a new motor skill or language ability, he experiences a powerful impulse to practice it. When babbling or creeping takes a new form, exercising it may absorb the infant for hours.   He continuously repeats his newly acquired skill and seems

Figure 3–1   Hypothetical curves of growth for various factors of personality.

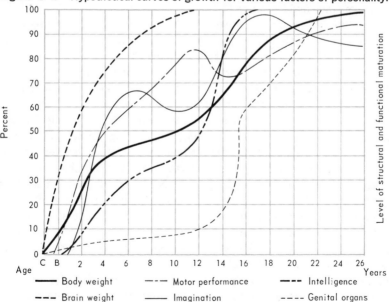

to derive great enjoyment from it.   Later, parental patience is often challenged by the child's frequent and repetitous questioning.   Probably the
child wants to get the idea straight in his mind before he feels ready to take
the next step along the same line of growth.   As soon as the child is managing well enough with one·type of experience, the foundation is laid for a
further differentiation, and before long he is ready to discard earlier practices
for the sake of the more advanced.   Thus, creeping is discarded as soon as
walking is well established, often at about the fifteen-month level, and "baby
talk" disappears in the latter part of the fourth year when the child advances
in speech efficiency.   Curiosity and desire for exploration, for new experiences, and for progress in the application of abilities and skills extend far
into the advanced stages of life and usually do not fully disappear even in old
age.   Restricted activity and lack of interest in old age are often due to the
general decrease of energy and ability, rather than to the lack of impetus to
apply what has been developed during the preceding stages of life.

Behavior is largely controlled by human needs.   Human needs spring
from the total man whose nature is actualized at various levels of life.
Throughout life physiological existence requires, for example, the need for
energy and a constant internal environment.   The energy is supplied by the
taking in of nutrients in foods and fluids, as well as by oxygen through breathing.   The internal environment is kept constant mainly by the functions of the
glandular and the central nervous systems.   This homeostasis, as it is called,
is marked by limited variations in metabolism, temperature, and blood pressure, in oxygenation and hydration [10, 11].

There are organic needs and drives for activity, and intellectual needs for
exploration and understanding.   Emotional needs for human contact and
affection have also been defined and substantiated [7, 12, 24].   Occasionally,
the child's very survival is threatened by a lack of frequent human contact
with the same person.   Needs for unconditional acceptance and status are
basic social needs.   Many behavior patterns instrumental in gratifying needs
are acquired and used throughout life.   In the course of development needs
for seeking stimulation and self-expression, for becoming normal and productive, for striving for independence and self-improvement become very important.   While all persons share to a considerable extent in all these and many
other needs, the degree of strength of each need and the avenues used to
gratify each differ greatly from person to person.   Deprivation through need,
when it continues, interferes with growth and adjustment, but as soon as such
a condition is alleviated by adequate supply, the organism tends to regain
its functional complexity.   Balance results when a continuous sequence of
arousal-action-reduction is established.

Behavior is a function of developmental status.   The idea that behavior
shows various qualities and features at different levels of development is
explained and illustrated in many sections throughout the book.   If one care-

fully observes the play activity of an infant and then that of a preschool child, he will be impressed by the differences in approach, complexity, duration, and other formal elements of play, despite the fact that the play material and situation may be practically the same.   If two individuals, one an infant and the other a child, used playthings in the same manner and engaged in the same activities, one would wonder about the child's level of development.   Is the child acting normally for his level of development?   Using as evidence of behavioral patterns and complexity the baby talk, and the clumsiness in psychomotor behavior of the child, the trained observer might infer that the child's level of maturity is approximately the same as the infant's.   Both would seem to be in the same phase of development, with this difference: the child is retarded, the infant is mature for his age.   In a case of severe retardation the individual will neither reach all the later developmental levels nor exhibit the complex behavior typical of the advanced stages of adulthood.

Thorough observation of each stage also seems to indicate that some characteristic traits or forms of adjustment, sometimes referred to as "problem behavior," are merely normal, necessary forms of experimentation leading to more integrative and adjustive behavior patterns in the advanced level of the same stage.   A careful study by Jean W. Macfarlane, Lucille Allen, and Marjorie P. Honzik [20] of behavior problems of normal children presents striking illustrations and table summaries of such undesirable behavior from babyhood to fourteen years of age.   Figure 3–2 illustrates changes in the frequency and severity of temper tantrums from five to fourteen years of age.

Human development is phasic.   The course of human growth and decline is marked by both continuities and discontinuities, slow modifications and rapid transformations.   A paradox results when the investigators who look for continuities find them and speak of human development as a continuous process, while more detailed investigation usually reveals rhythm in growth, shown by spurts and plateaus, as well as that which develops gradually into manifest phases.   In teething, for example, through X-ray, the underlying growth of all the first set and most of the permanent set of teeth is already visible at birth.   This is long before anything can be "seen" or otherwise detected.   Many teeth of the first set are already partly or wholly hardened.   Forerunners of later developments appear in other areas also.   Cooing and babbling exercises are recognized as underlying stages of forthcoming speech development.   Simple play activities are practiced long before complex patterns can be attempted.

Measurements of specific developments, such as height, vocabulary, or motor performance do not indicate uniformly increasing changes; rather, they show spurts, plateaus, or even regressions.   During the plateau periods, however, the incubation of previous learning takes place.   The earlier developments are integrated into a new pattern, and a readiness for new horizons

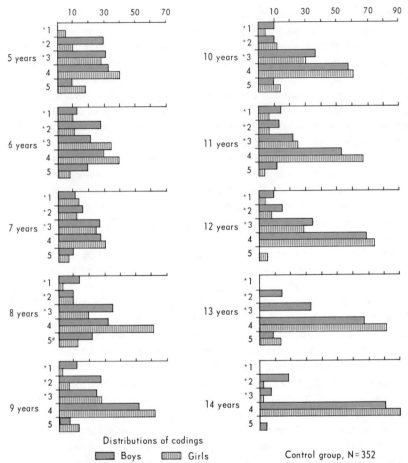

Figure 3–2 Temper tantrums. (Jean W. Macfarlane et al. *A developmental study of the behavior problems of normal children between twenty-one months and fourteen years.* Berkeley, Calif.: University of California Press, 1954, p. 55.) Coding (* = considered problems): *1 Severe explosions three or more times a week or daily screaming; *2 Occasional severe explosions or frequent screaming; *3 Infrequent severe explosions of frequent mild outbursts of temper; 4 Occasional mild temper tantrums; 5 Infrequent fretting; anger reaction practically nonexistent.

is acquired. Within the human organism and personality, there are many facets and traits to be developed. The growth of each affects the person's total configuration by modifying many aspects in some way. Development advances in a more or less integrated way, conditioned by the interaction of biochemical, psychological, and environmental factors.

Through preparational phases a person becomes well equipped to express himself in a more advanced manner. At this time a high degree of readiness for a particular form of learning is attained. If specific learning-eliciting stimuli are absent during a stage of development, the individual is deprived of the learning experience. As a result, the necessary foundation for later and more refined levels of development will not be established and any advanced learning of this kind will be hampered.

Forthcoming growth and behavior are predictable. Since development is an orderly sequence in growth, motivation, behavior, and possibly in personality organization, it seems logical that, if someone is an expert in developmental processes and behavior and is capable of diagnostic assessment, he can predict or at least estimate likely growth patterns of motivational structure, achievement, and probable tendencies of self-expression in a particular individual. Psychometric and projective testing and retesting over several years, wherever possible, enables the psychologist to estimate with considerable accuracy a person's abilities and to infer driving forces. Since every individual is fairly constant in rate of development, he can also predict the further course of growth and maturation. Such predicting, provided the test is valid, indicates that one child will be able to do college work because of his superior intelligence, while another child, being mentally retarded, will not catch up to the average level of performance.

One can foresee that a particular adolescent will not maintain an interest in music or engineering because he does not possess the aptitude, that is, the underlying capacity for the development and successful pursuit of this objective. Professional, individual interviewing and testing make many general predictions sufficiently substantial for some practical purposes. A word of caution is needed here: although prognosis, or prediction, is possible, such examination does not and cannot consider all possible factors influencing the behavior of a particular individual. For example, because of some particular person's unique experience, his efforts to compensate and overachieve may become so strong that further growth is possible. Such specific variables cannot always be estimated on the basis of objective test data. Prediction is usually more accurate in discovering limits rather than in identifying particular future acts or choices. If the individual's intelligence is low, the psychologist is justified in his conclusion that very intelligent performance will not be achieved, but how the individual will utilize his limited intellectual resources cannot, with accuracy, be predicted. The individuality and the personality of a human being are very complex and too deep to be fully subjected to psychological assessment. As a result, difficulties are bound to arise whenever one attempts to develop a total growth concept or to control behavior for either normal or deviant people. Much research is needed to improve the psychological tools and their application in order to increase the adequacy of prediction and efficiency of control for which science is striving.

The individual develops as a unified whole. Although there is no individual whose bodily functions, mental abilities, or personality organization cease to grow in complexity or maintain a biochemical and behavioral balance from phase to phase of development, the degree of biological and psychological growth and integration differs from person to person. Certain aspects of development appear uneven or to a degree dissociated in exceptional children and mentally disordered individuals. Aside from this lack of balance, a kind of intrinsic wholeness exists whenever an individual is capable of conducting his own life, even though this internal unification may not be adequately expressed in behavior.

Some writers associate puberty with physical and sexual maturation and seem to disregard the rises in imaginative, intellectual, and emotional development which take place at the same time. Changes in the self-concept and in personality at this stage are also frequently ignored. From stage to stage, there are many interrelationships among changes. With the exception of those who are greatly deprived or pathological, the principle of the unity of human development applies to all dimensions of growth.

All individuals are different. Though to an inexperienced eye some individuals, especially identical twins, appear much alike if not the same, careful observation reveals differences in most observable aspects, such as fingerprints and handwriting. Individual differences spring from many sources. Biological identity based on biochemical differences in heredity and metabolism is always a part of the individual and can never be lost [16, 22]. The rate of maturation, the child's position in the family, and the sequence of experiential events all vary in many ways from individual to individual. Each human being continuously changes, and individual differences become magnified as the person moves from one developmental level to the next. Nancy Bayley's study [6] of intraindividual differences illustrates this through various measurements.

The tendency to generalize about personality characteristics of races, nations, classes, and other groups is great indeed. Stereotypes are used to represent millions of individuals who may be similar in some features but substantially different in many others. Parents seem to forget this basic principle when they expect similar rates of development and achievement in their children.

QUESTIONS FOR REVIEW

1. Explain and illustrate the concepts of differentiation and integration.
2. Express as quantities two or three aspects of structural or functional growth in age units. Define the concept of organismic age.
3. Analyze the relationships among development, growth, and learning.
4. What are the principal factors on which self-realization depends? Clarify the principal role of one of them.

5. Identify Buhler's basic tendencies of life and indicate her "ultimate goal" in life.
6. Elaborate upon the concept of aging and its relationship to development and deterioration.
7. Explain how genetic sequence of growth applies to (a) the early and (b) the late periods of life.
8. Describe concisely the process of maturation of a bodily system and of a functional power.
9. Indicate the nature of several basic human needs and explain their role in behavior organization.
10. What measures can be used to predict developmental potentialities? Why is caution necessary in applying them?
11. What are the genetic sequences and regularities facilitating prediction?
12. What factors contribute to individual differences and how? Why do individual differences increase with age?

REFERENCES

I. Selected Reading

1. Bayer, Leona M., and Nancy Bayley. *Growth diagnosis.* Chicago: University of Chicago Press, 1959. Methods and techniques of assessment and prediction of normal and deviant development are presented and illustrated by 222 charts, figures, and tables.
2. Harris, Dale B. (Ed.). *The concept of development: An issue in the study of human behavior.* Minneapolis: University of Minnesota Press, 1957. Formulation of the concept of development by seventeen experts and its implications for behavioral and social sciences and for humanities are assessed.
3. Hurlock, Elizabeth B. *Child development.* (4th ed.) New York: McGraw-Hill, 1964. Chapter 1 presents changes, rates, and causes of development and methods of appraising them.
4. McNeil, Elton B. *The concept of human development.* Belmont, Calif.: Wadsworth, 1966. A paperback in the Basic Concepts in Psychology Series, presenting the characteristics of biological, psychological, and social development, including the sense of self.
5. Pikunas, Justin. *Fundamental child psychology.* (2nd ed.) Milwaukee: Bruce, 1965. Chapter 2 defines the basic concepts of child psychology and clarifies their relationships, while Chapter 3 presents the principles of development and their applications in interpreting child growth and maturation.

II. Specific References

6. Bayley, Nancy. Individual patterns of development. *Child Developm.,* 1956, **27**, 45–74.

7. Bowlby, John, M. Ainsworth, M. Boston, and D. Rosenbluth. The effects of mother-child separation: A follow-up study. *Brit. J. med. Psychol.*, 1956, **29**, 211–249.

8. Buhler, Charlotte. The human course of life in its goal aspects. *J. human Psychol.*, 1964, **4**, No. 1.

9. Buhler, Charlotte. Theoretical observations about life's basic tendencies. *Amer. J. Psychother.*, 1959, **13**, 561–581.

10. Cannon, Walter B. *The wisdom of the body.* (Rev. ed.) New York: Knopf, 1950.

11. Carlson, A. J., and E. J. Stieglitz. Physiological changes in aging. *Ann. Amer. Acad. Pol. Sci.*, 1952, **279**, 18–31.

12. Casler, L. Maternal deprivation: A critical review of the literature. *Monogr. Soc. Res. Child Developm.*, 1961, **26**, 1–64.

13. Crick, F. H. C. On the genetic code. *Science*, 1963, **139**, 461–471.

14. English, Horace B., and Ava C. English. *A comprehensive dictionary of psychological and psychoanalytical terms.* New York: Longmans, 1958.

15. Erikson, Erik. *Identity and the life cycle.* New York: International Universities Press, 1959.

16. Gesell, Arnold, and Catherine Amatruda. *Developmental diagnosis.* (2nd ed.) New York: Harper & Row, 1947.

17. Harriman, Philip L. *Handbook of psychological terms.* (2nd ed.) Totowa, N.J.: Littlefield, Adams, 1965.

18. Harris, Chester W. *Encyclopedia of educational research.* (2nd ed.) New York: Macmillan, 1960.

19. Jung, Carl G. *Two essays on analytical psychology* (translated by R. F. C. Hull). New York: Bollingen Foundation, 1953 (originally published in German in 1943 and 1945).

20. Macfarlane, Jean W., Lucille Allen, and Marjorie P. Honzik. *A developmental study of the behavior problems of normal children between twenty-one months and fourteen years.* Berkeley, Calif.: University of California Press, 1954.

21. Olson, W. C., and B. O. Hughes. The concept of organismic age. *J. educ. Res.*, 1942, **35**, 525–527.

22. Wald, George. Determinacy, individuality, and the problem of free will. In John R. Platt (Ed.), *New views of the nature of man.* Chicago: University of Chicago Press, 1965. Pp. 16–46.

23. Watson, J. D. Involvement of RNA in the synthesis of proteins. *Science*, 1963, **140**, 17–26.

24. Yarrow, L. J. Maternal deprivation: Toward an empirical and conceptual reevaluation. *Psychol. Bull.*, 1961, **58**, 459–490.

Part **2**

Fundamental Influences

Human development, behavior, and adjustment are often considered to be determined by heredity and environment. Closer examination, however, necessitates further division of the latter into such factors as family, peers, school, society, and culture. Moreover, man is a social and cultural individual who structures society and culture, creating highly complex organizations.

Developmental occurrences per se and the resulting configurations at each level of life set the stage not only for actual behavior but for later growth and adjustment possibilities. The self-concept and aspirations of the individual, although highly affected by his relationships with others, gain in motivational power as the years of childhood advance. This section will deal with the functions and stimulation value of all these factors and show their influence on the total growth pattern.

FACTORS INFLUENCING GROWTH AND BEHAVIOR

Human growth is manifested in several major areas. Physiological development of the organism is one of them. From an almost microscopic fertilized ovum unfolds the complex organism capable of functioning outside the uterus. During the gestation period behavior is very limited. Birth makes more individualized forms of expression possible. Among the behavior-organizing forces, emotional experience probably ranks the highest. The newborn has the ability to exhibit emotional excitement, and later various emotions emerge. Throughout life emotions vividly reflect various human relationships. As was shown in Chapter 3, needs rank high in eliciting rewarding types of behavior. Among the other behavior-organizing forces, cognitive functions perform an increasing role with age. Man is a rational animal—Homo sapiens.

Intellectual abilities are chiefly responsible for specifically human behavior, such as speaking, thinking, and creative self-expression. Most men symbolize and value: some write and others paint, and all are highly affected by what they read and view. Carl R. Rogers [24] suspects that there is an organismic base which determines the *valuing* process. This process synthesizes external impressions as well, and increases the development of personal motivation in the individual.

The importance of the social and moral aspects of development cannot be overemphasized. Most of the purely human powers depend on stimulation from people—the mother in particular. Advances in socialization and in emotional and moral sensitivity are determined mainly by others. Since the next chapter surveys major areas of growth, the present sections will analyze basic influences on which development depends, such as heredity, family, peers, school, and other environmental and cultural forces.

THE PERSON'S HERITAGE—A KEY TO HIS DEVELOPMENT

Generally, heredity includes the overall influences biologically transmitted from parents to offspring. What a person inherits and what he fails to inherit from his ancestors continue stimulating him throughout life. Sir Francis Galton estimated that a person inherits approximately 50 percent from his maternal line and 50 percent from his paternal line. He inherits in a decreasing geometric progression: about 50 percent from his two parents, 25 percent from his four grandparents, 12.5 percent from his eight great grandparents, and in the same decreasing ratio from still earlier ancestors. Galton's law of inheritance, however, is not actually accurate since some individuals inherit more from their paternal line, while others inherit more from their maternal line. Moreover, a person may inherit noticeably more from one of his grandparents than from others.

When speaking of the totality of biological inheritance, one uses the term *genotype,* since the organism is a derivative of genes. The changing characteristics of the organism as it develops throughout life constitute the successive *phenotype.* Development is an orderly succession of phenotypes but these, in turn, are dependent on the genetic code. A child as we see him is a phenotype.

Mendel's law of inheritance, based on dominant and recessive genes as carriers of phenotypical characteristics, does not explain genotypical traits. The Mendelian ratio of 3:1, obtained from the crossing of prebred lines, is also inaccurate for phenotypical factors of inheritance. The concept of genes, which is fundamental to Mendelian theory, has been outdated and replaced by three different structures (muton, recon, and cistron), each having specific (also heredity-transmitting) functions.

In 1944, Oswald T. Avery, Colin M. MacLeod, and Maclyn McCarty [6] isolated pure deoxyribonucleic acid molecules (DNA) and began assessing their great transforming activity. This activity depends on three substructures within the DNA (mutons, cistrons, recons) that contain genetic information in coded form. The smallest units of DNA molecule that can undergo changes are referred to as *mutons.* Any DNA unit capable of independent function is a *cistron.* Units effecting recombinations within the cell substances are called *recons*. These three are determiners of hereditary traits and, in a sense, are a refinement of the previously used gene concept. They probably contain the "blueprint" for genetic release according to which distinct cells, tissues, and organs are formed through the decoding of genetic structures from period to period.

Nearly a decade after the isolation of DNA, the Watson-Crick model of the DNA molecule was constructed [32]. It depicts DNA molecules as double helices of polynucleotide chains. When the double helix separates into two single threads, each of these forms a copy of the original double structure by the proper coupling of its bases (adenine-thymine, guanine-cytosine). Thus the genetic "alphabet" appears to consist of only these four "letters," and the number of permutations is 4^n.

Working on the assumption that the primary genetic information is apparently stored in the DNA molecules, J. G. Gall [13] unraveled a part of the genetic mechanism by eliciting certain enzyme actions at the insect level. Relying on his experiments with tissues of larvae *Drosophila* (the fruit fly), he found that segments of the chromosomal DNA unwind at specific intervals, transmitting bits of genetic decoding to RNA—a messenger strand which then carries them through the cell. The RNA molecule consists of a chain of half steps—media which are responsible for the formation of enzymes from amino acids. RNA responses, "right" or "wrong," accelerated, delayed, or otherwise, probably account for the biochemical individuality that each person has.

A decade of intense research ending in the early sixties brought the main details of protein synthesis to light. An orderly interaction of three classes of RNA—ribosomal, soluble, and messenger—controls the assembly of amino acids into proteins, the prime substances of life. J. D. Watson [31] has made it clear that not just details of this process but also many major points still require further explanation before selective protein synthesis and its consequences for heredity and embryology will be understood.

A major part of the genetic code came to light in 1963, when Francis H. C. Crick [11] published his deductions about the general nature of the code drawn from results of biochemical experimentation. In this revised genetic model, ". . . the base sequence of the DNA—probably of only one of its chains—is copied onto RNA, and this special RNA then acts as the genetic messenger and directs the actual process of joining up the amino acids into polypeptide chains. . . . One cistron one polypeptide chain" [11, p. 416]. Crick implies that it is reasonable to hope that the entire genetic code will be explained as additional research designs are completed. Apparently, the vocabulary of the genetic code is known but little of its grammar is as yet disclosed.

Hereditary differences probably result from (1) variations within chromosomes and their genetic structures of DNA, RNA, and other substances and (2) the almost unlimited combination possibilities in the process of fertilization.   The genetic code within the DNA provides the developmental direction and perhaps determines the upper limits for the quality and variety of responses that result from various types of external stimulation.

The individual's inheritance is determined during the process of fertilization.   This involves the pairing off of chromosomes and various subchromosome units such as DNA, RNA, and proteins.

The process of inheritance takes place within the cytoplasm and nucleus of the ovum when it is penetrated by and fuses with a spermatozoon.   When one considers the chance pairing of the subchromosome structures, the number of possible configurations is staggering, without even considering the interchange of DNA or protein molecules among chromosomes, which is also conceivable.   Inheritance is thus a base for the biochemical uniqueness of each individual, as he develops according to the pattern predetermined by his genetic code and the increasing interaction with his physical and social environments.   These, in turn, further, block, or distort the process of unfolding and the success in adaptation.

Ovulation and conception.   Ovulation usually occurs once during every menstrual cycle: one ripened ovum is released from one of the two ovaries into the Fallopian tube, where it slowly moves toward the womb.   If through sexual intercourse a large number of spermatozoa are deposited near the uterus at about this time, conception may result.   Ovulation regularly takes place about midway between two menstrual periods.   It most frequently occurs from ten to eighteen days after the beginning of a menstrual period.   However, there is not any time when ovulation cannot occur, since in rare cases even sexual excitement can produce it.   In other words, there are considerable differences between individuals as well as irregularities within each individual, for both ovaries usually take turns in ovulating.   The ovum, about 0.15 millimeter in diameter or about half the size of the printed period on this page, is one of the largest cells in the human organism.   This round, clear, shell-like capsule, weighing slightly less than one-millionth of a gram, contains a yolk which is used for self-nourishment during its germinal phase of development.   The yolk of the ovum makes this cell visible to the naked eye.

The spermatozoon, ejected by the testes into the penis, is one of the most minute cells of the body, measuring approximately 0.05 millimeter in diameter.   During intercourse the male usually releases millions of spermatozoa, about 500 million in each ejaculation.   The thin tail of the spermatozoon, which is about twelve times the length of the cell body, provides mobility by propulsion.   While only one spermatozoon is needed for conception, the mass of spermatozoa produce the enzymic action necessary for fertilization to take place. A low density of spermatozoa or relative weakness of the sperms produced make fertilization impossible. For about nine days after conception, the fertilized ovum, or zygote, drifts along, dividing itself into a cluster of many cells. It then becomes attached to the uterus wall, and, provided the uterus' membrane is receptive, the placenta is formed. The mother's blood, filtered thoroughly as its contents pass the placenta, provides nourishment, fluid, and oxygen for embryonic growth.

Sometimes two or more fertilizations occur at the same time because an ovary occasionally discharges two or more of its ripened ova. This leads to the multiple birth of fraternal twins, whose inheritances are probably as individual as those of any other siblings. Sometimes, as was mentioned earlier, a single fertilized cell divides into two completely separate halves, and two individuals, referred to as monozygotic or identical twins, develop.

The fertilized cell contains twenty-three pairs of small, threadlike particles called chromosomes with one-half of each pair coming from each parent. One pair of chromosomes, for example, determines whether a child will be male or female. Every ovum and about half of the spermatozoa have X chromosomes. The other half have a different chromosome, smaller in structure and lighter in weight. It is referred to as a Y chromosome. The female sex results if one X chromosome pair occurs in the fertilized cell. A male develops in the case of an X and a Y chromosome combination.

ENDOWMENT AND INDIVIDUAL GROWTH

Heredity is the leading factor responsible for many individual differences in growth and behavior. The rate of maturation, the growth in physical structure, blood type, susceptibility to some kinds of illness, skin pigmentation, and eye and hair coloring are all determined by inheritance. Sex-linked inheritance produces a number of conditions such as hemophilia, color blindness, baldness, speech-organ disorders, and probably several others. Temperamental and cognitive developments are stimulated by hereditary decoding. Whether intellectual development is directly controlled or merely determined by the instrumental complexity of the brain and other facilitating systems cannot be affirmed with any degree of certainty. DNA decoding of genetic information seems to set the direction for and determine the complexity of growth. The stimulating and facilitating influences of the total environment enable development to reach the upper limits of complexity. In most instances, where environment is below optimal stimulation, the growth potential is seldom fully realized, since various detrimental influences disturb, damage, or retard the course of physiological and behavioral unfolding. Insufficient language stimulation, for example, retards not only language development but cognitive differentiation as well.

Heredity includes susceptibilities to certain patterns of personality organization and disorganization. Mental disorders do not strike people at random but afflict those whose susceptibility is high and whose frustrations are intense during early levels of development. There is wide agreement that infants and children react to the same stimuli in innumerable ways and are differently affected by them. When children's deficiencies stem from genetic predispositions, these cannot be counteracted easily by any ordinary corrective measures [5, p. 718]. Some children are genetically disadvantaged, while others are genetically privileged. Still, the human individual is not completely "programed" by his genetic code but is capable of flexibility in growth and functioning. Though this flexibility is generally influenced by his environment, again he can escape complete determination and become capable of increasing self-direction.

The continuing influence of heredity is not as pronounced as some geneticists tend to believe. The influence of external factors becomes operative as soon as the placenta is established and the mother's condition is to a degree transmitted with many of her blood components to the developing embryo. As will be shown in Chapter 6, the mother's taking medicine, drinking alcohol, smoking, or becoming excited, all have some observable effect on the condition of the fetus.

Hereditary and genetic factors act as a matrix upon which various environmental occurrences exert a stimulating, suppressive, or distorting influence. Occasionally, the outside influences produce results which are far removed from the original hereditary endowments. The human individual is exposed to many losses, irreparable in some instances, as well as to partial or complete recoveries from many of them. The currently changing field of genetics offers a great deal of useful information to the student of human growth in recent journal volumes, especially those of *Science* and *Hereditas*. No one is completely the product of human heredity; there is continual interaction with the environmental forces, which we shall now consider.

LEADING ENVIRONMENTAL INFLUENCES

Environmental influences consist chiefly of six intimately interacting and partially overlapping factors: physical environment, family, peers, school, society, and culture. Each of these should be analyzed and its role in the development of a human individual studied.

Physical environment

The milieu in which a person lives is first of all physical in character. Various physical factors, such as climate, location in an open rural area or a congested city, as well as the size, place, and conveniences of a home, continually affect the person. If one takes a ride through any metropolitan area, he will be impressed by the variety and the changing atmosphere as he moves from the wealthy and attractively displayed homes of the suburbs to the congested and neglected slum areas of small, old, and disfigured houses and small businesses. In the slums there is perceivable pollution of the air and practically no place for children to play. In such areas, feelings of depression and dejection, if not aversion, contrast sharply with the delight one experiences in the pleasant suburban sections. The physical fitness and health of young people depend considerably on their surroundings. The ways in which personal needs, drives, and emotions are expressed are also related to the physical conditions of the home and the surrounding environment. The total value of stimulation increases as physical facilities are varied and improved.

Family

The nuclear family consists of the parents and their dependent children. This biologically based family is found in most societies. It is an enduring social unit based on marriage and recognized by an intimate sex or blood relationship. Sometimes a family is enlarged by including as a part of the household grandparents, adopted children, or some other relatives. But today the number of families living with grandparents is low and declining. As a primary group, the nuclear family has the greatest influences on its members, especially infants and children, since it regulates most of the other influences to which their children are exposed.

A family is comprised of individuals of differing experiential background, sex, and age. Such a primary group should be bound together not only by kinship but by intimate relationships marked by affection and mutual sharing in activities and concerns. Every family is distinguished by (1) the backgrounds of its members, each of which is in some ways different from the others, and (2) a number of dynamic relationships. These factors create the basis for close interactions and the atmosphere of the particular household. The larger the family becomes, the increasingly numerous are the relationships among its members. The husband and wife form two relationships with each other; when their first child comes, the number of interpersonal relationships triples. Figure 4–1 serves to illustrate this kind of extension of intrafamilial relations.

The size of the American family is oscillating. There was an ebb in the thirties, then a rise. Between 1940 and 1957, for example, birth rates for third and fourth children were climbing. Leveling off began in the late fifties and continued into the sixties [25]. As the number of children increases, the opportunities for interpersonal adjustment should expand. Research reports

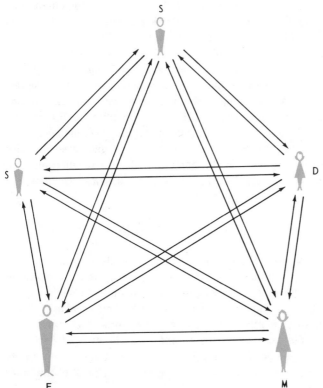

Figure 4–1 Intrafamilial relationships. Father (F) and Mother (M)—two persons, two relationships. When the first child (S) is born, there are three persons but six relationships among them; when the second child (D) comes, the number of relationships increases by six, etc.

on family life, however, give the impression of continued deterioration of integrity and cohesion. The rate of divorce, for example, is unabatingly climbing [28].

Ideally, the family's orientation grows out of commitments of husband to wife and vice versa, and of commitments of both to their children. Each member of the family attains a certain status which has certain effects on him, depending on family customs and size. To have status involves performing one or several roles. The impersonal society of today does not effectively support this situation. The decline in distinct status and responsibility, loss of function, and the decrease in "togetherness" of families and their members all contribute significantly to family disintegration [4]. Because of the dynamic character of family living, any combination of attitudes and relationships is possible within a modern family. Examples of high coherence, devotion, deep sentiment, and genuine commitment can be easily contrasted with instances of estrangement which include lack of caring, sharing, and providing.

The noted sociologist James H. S. Bossard [9, p. 57] identified the American family as a "transmitting" rather than a "generating" agency. The members of the family are "constantly contacting, bringing into the home, assessing, and evaluating the outside world. The home is a sort of crossroads, to which the outside world comes constantly." Most departures from home by children and adults alike provide a series of experiences instrumental in social weaning and learning, which, in turn, enrich their personalities. The family's socializing and humanizing functions are comprehensively analyzed in Evelyn N. Duvall's *Family development* [1]. This work stresses developmental tasks in various phases of family life and discusses at length basic patterns of interaction among members of various types of families.

In the culture of the United States the leading functions of the family encompass (1) bearing and raising children, (2) interpreting the environment, culture, and religion, and (3) developing personalities. All of these involve problems and conflicts, the efficient dealing with which preserves the family's integrity and coherence. In fact, the family is a workshop for the character fabric for life.

Parental roles. The far-reaching influences of the parents are made clearer by the principle of *primacy*, the assumption that the first acts or experiences in a given category or series tend to impress more and have more motivating force than later acts in determining future reactions of an individual. Since family life offers opportunities for most first experiences, its power to determine the future cannot be overlooked. Early family situations represent prototypes for the learned interpersonal relationships and attitudes toward other individuals and groups. Effects of such primal learning act as subconscious and conscious dynamic factors in later relationships and adjustments to various aspects of living. The earliest learning experience probably forms the pattern for the later information-processing capability of the individual. It is a major factor in setting the programing process of the human "brain-computer."

Relationships between the father and mother set the pattern for sibling associations, and these, in turn, determine the structural aspects for peer interaction. In each instance, modifications will occur, but they usually are incapable of producing substantial changes.

The role a father or mother plays may have extremely varying effects on a child and on the family as a whole. Children regard parents from their own deeply subjective points of view. Consciously or not, they expect gratification of their needs for stimulation, care, affection, and security.

The role the father of the family assumes has changed noticeably within recent decades. Fathers are taking on a larger share of parental activity and responsibility as the percentage of working mothers keeps rising. Because of automation and union influences, the father has more time at his disposal to spend with the family. This is especially true for those in the lower-income brackets. Apparently, the American industrial society is becoming less mother-centered in its child care and education. In addition to fulfilling the traditional functions of providing and arbitrating, the father is becoming more and more concerned with various aspects of child management and education. Studies of paternal deprivation suggest that there is a critical period, lasting from the time of weaning until entering school, when the father is very important to every child. Since the major factor in a boy's psychosexual development as a male is his identification with the father, paternal deprivation for boys "can be as serious as maternal deprivation" [21]. The adequacy of the father facilitates adjustment to the male population on the part of both sons and daughters. An absent or weak paternal figure is often revealed in the case histories of homosexuals and schizophrenics.

The influence of the father's personality traits takes effect as he comes in contact with the child and is instrumental in caring for his needs. If the father, for example, is tense and crude and disregards the child's attention-gaining devices, the child's ego becomes "deflated" and his anxiety is aroused. Consequently, his dependence on the mother is heightened because he needs consolation and tenderness. These compensative efforts are successful if the mother responds affectionately. The overall emotional climate of the home, resulting chiefly from father-mother interaction, is an important variable surrounding each individual of the family [15, 21].

Gratification of a child's needs and his tender care by the same person— the mother—is the basis of psychosocial development and security. Since the mother usually spends more time than any other person caring for her child, she easily becomes the "living personification" of what is good and desirable for the child. Affectionate mothering serves as a matrix for the development of sound interpersonal relationships. The amount of stimulation and of mothering granted to a child crucially affects his total growth and adjustment [8, 15]. Indeed, the mother holds the key to direction of the child's development and adjustment. Many mothers like stimulating their children and spend considerable time playing with them, talking, and encouraging them to activity. Others spend much time on their own affairs, barely caring for their children and protecting them from common dangers. At the same time many mothers are relatively free from tension and anxiety, while many others are anxiety-ridden and exhibit a considerable amount of symptomatic behavior. The effects of these and similar maternal conditions are largely unknown.

Talcott Parsons [22] observes that mothers "are continually about the house" and are doing relatively tangible work; therefore, it is "possible for the daughter to participate actively and usefully in many of these activities." From an early age she is being initiated into many important aspects of the feminine role. The father, however, spends much more time away from home than the mother, and many of the masculine functions at home are less tangible; therefore, their meaning remains to a large extent inaccessible to a boy. This leaves him with less "possibility of a gradual initiation into the activities of the adult male role." Possibly this helps to explain why girls generally conform much better to adult expectations than boys, who are often resistant to and defiant of adult notions of their behavior standard.

Attitudes and patterns in child rearing, supplied by 379 American mothers in Boston, are reflected in two tables from a detailed study by Robert R. Sears, Eleanor E. Maccoby, and H. Levin [25]. Table 4-1 shows women's attitudes toward having children. A woman who has been waiting and hoping for pregnancy is likely to accept and love her child. A woman who is displeased without reservation about her pregnancy is likely to show some indifference, if not rejection, toward her offspring. It is expected that a number of mothers will change their attitudes toward offspring significantly, following the birth of their children. Research is needed to follow up the ways in which attitudes toward pregnancy change and the ways in which they affect the offspring. The extent of use of tangible rewards by mothers in the same Bostonian sample is shown in Table 4-2. This study also notes the boomerang effect of corporal punishment when used for the behavior control of children. Paternal aggressiveness is countered by the growing aggressiveness of the child.

Various aspects of parental discipline reported in a number of studies were

Table 4–1. How mother felt when she discovered she was pregnant
(N = 379)

	Percent
1. Delighted; very happy; had been waiting and hoping for this	50
2. Pleased, but no evidence of enthusiasm (includes "This was a planned baby"—said matter of factly)	18
3. Pleased generally; some reservations	6
4. Mixed feelings; advantages and disadvantages weighed about equally	9
5. Generally displeased, although some bright spots seen	9
6. Displeased; no reservations	7
7. Not ascertained	1
	100

Source: R. R. Sears, E. E. Maccoby, and H. Levin. *Patterns of child rearing.* P. 32. New York: Harper & Row, 1957. By permission.

Table 4—2.   Extent of use of tangible rewards
(N = 379)

	Percent
1. Mother never uses rewards	12
2. Rarely uses rewards	18
3. Sometimes uses rewards	21
4. Fairly often uses rewards	22
5. Frequently uses rewards	19
6. Regularly gives rewards for "good behavior"; elaborate system for earning money or points; believes rewards are effective; evidence that this is a major technique for the mother	6
	100

Source: R. R. Sears, E. E. Maccoby, and H. Levin. *Patterns of child rearing.* P. 321. New York: Harper & Row, 1957. By permission.

recently summarized and reinterpreted through a series of factor analyses. Wesley C. Becker's [8] statistical results, represented in Figure 4—2, suggest three general classifications for categorizing parental behavior. They are restrictiveness versus permissiveness, warmth versus hostility, and calm detachment versus anxious emotional involvement. By combinations of these various traits, different types of parents can be classified. For example, the organized-effective parent is expected to rank high in warmth and restrictiveness; the indulgent parent is usually high on warmth and permissiveness. In addition to all the distinctions given in the figure, parental management of the child also differs as to the amount of stimulation the parent provides. Parents offering much and varied stimulation probably have fewer difficulties in child management as children grow older. Additional research is needed to assess the positive and negative effects of various amounts of parental stimulation, including overstimulation.

Child training. Methods of child care have been in flux throughout American history. In the changing American tradition of child rearing, Daniel R. Miller and Guy E. Swanson [20, pp. 5—23] distinguish four overlapping eras. Before the Civil War the focus was on methods designed to "break the child's will" because its will was thought to be intrinsically evil. The second period, from 1860 to 1941, was characterized by opposition to corporal punishment and emphasis on stimulating the natural development of the child as a unique individual. A regimented schedule of early training was prescribed in the twenties and thirties to build the child into an achieving and self-controlled individual. John B. Watson [30, p. 81] encouraged parents to treat children objectively and firmly, as though they were young adults: "Let your behavior always be objective and kindly firm. Never hug and kiss them, never let them sit in your lap." In the 1940s and 1950s progressive educators em-

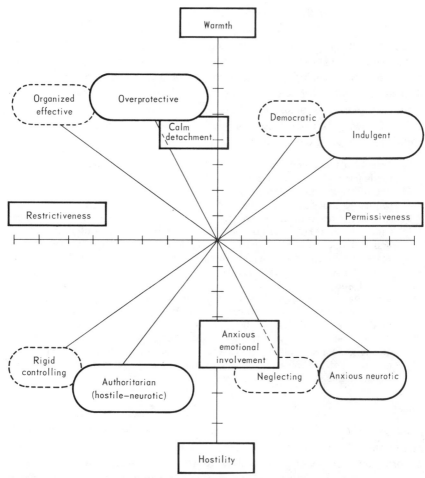

Figure 4–2 Becker's model for parental behavior. (Wesley C. Becker. Consequences of different kinds of parental discipline. In M. L. Hoffman and Lois W. Hoffman (Eds.), *Review of child development research.* Vol. 1. New York: Russell Sage Foundation, 1964, pp. 169–208. By permission.)

phasized meeting the social and adjustment needs of children in order to give them a good start in life. Preparation for flexibly meeting the changing social situation became very important. The child was allowed greater freedom to develop, even to the point of setting his own standards.

A child needs to feel safety within boundaries. The parental "yes" and "no" lay the foundation for order and morality. Just as many Swiss children learn three languages because they are spoken within the family environment, so the child generally learns many things from the members of the family.

While an adult usually handles specific situations in terms of general principles, the child handles general principles in terms of specific situations. Value and order must be often represented for the child. "The absence of a strong sense of value continuity in our society is a prime cause of the difficulty we face in helping the child to become personally ethical, socially democratic, and spiritually religious in which the ethical, the democratic, and the religious are consistent with each other" [16, p. 59].

The following is a case summary which illustrates the effects of several undesirable influences on an older child:

> *Fred* is a twelve-year-old boy, small for his age, with extreme aggressive tendencies and a lack of control. He is constantly starting fights in school and bullying other children. His record is one of extreme truancy, and consequently poor school achievement.
>
> Fred's parents have no control over him. His father is a heavy drinker, who gives Fred beer "so he won't have to steal it." His mother babies him and will not allow his teachers to reprimand him. In this environment, Fred is developing into a self-willed, antisocial, problem child. He is the leader of a gang of delinquents, and has led them into breaking into a school and almost destroying the interior. On his own he has set fire to a garage, and has even greater ambitions in this area.
>
> Despite repeated recommendations from school authorities, Fred is still in the custody of his parents, and his conduct is growing progressively worse. He lacks any concept of moral responsibility or social obligation and is generally impulse-dominated. Unless prompt care and a change of environment are initiated, Fred will probably become more delinquent and psychopathic.

Peers

Most persons enjoy associating with individuals who are similar in age, rank, and status. For most people opportunities for associating with peers exceed opportunities for relating themselves to younger or older persons. Senescents constitute a notable exception to this generalization because most of them prefer younger individuals, including children, rather than their own peers.

From about the age of four, there is a growing need for playing and conversing with another person of approximately the same age. An older child looks for a friend to whom he can confide his desires, problems, and aspirations. In peer groups he learns to give and take. Once the individual learns to identify with individuals of his own age, parental identifications lose some of their original strength. Important as they are, parental identifications become less pronounced as the child grows into peer society and its culture.

Self-identification with others frequently embraces screen stars, historical figures, and fiction characters also, but peers continue to be a major source of self-identification throughout adulthood. Peers, next to parents, are the most significant individuals in a person's life.   In them one finds many qualities for identification because, as Harry S. Sullivan puts it, "... the peculiarity exists that one can find in others only that which is in the self" [27, p. 22].

School

The home lays the foundation upon which teachers build.   Most major patterns of behavior are already functional by the time a child enters kindergarten or school, yet school experience is more than mere transfer or extension of early home and neighborhood learning.   The major growth of the child at ages five and six is cognitive and social.   Since kindergarten is a preparation for school, the teacher should give a great deal of attention to directing the child's emotions as he interacts with peers and provide opportunities for him to learn various forms of social activity.   It is beneficial for the child to discover early that in order to obtain approval he must act in a socialized manner.   Story reading, free drawing, handiwork, games, and songs are some of the typical means used by kindergarten teachers to arouse imagination, creativity, and self-expression in the five-year-old.   Culturally and economically disadvantaged children need social, emotional, and intellectual stimulation more than other children, because their background is usually meager in these respects.

The first major statistical survey of preschool education shows that about one-fourth of all children below the compulsory school attendance age were enrolled in various preschool programs in the 1964–1965 school year. The total number and percentage of all children in the population enrolled in nursery schools and kindergartens for each age were as follows: age three— 181,000 or 4.3 percent; age four—617,000 or 14.9 percent; and age five— 2,389,000 or 58.1 percent. An additional 11.1 percent of the five-year-olds were in regular schools.   Figure 4–3 shows the percentages enrolled in October 1964 according to family income with the lowest enrollment in the lowest income group.   Children of this group form the bulk of the disadvantaged-child population, who are most in need of regular preschool training to fill gaps in their experience and increase their abilities and skills to enable them to respond properly to the later demands of school.

The school's basic commitment to the psychosocial development of boys and girls is slowly giving way to a more concentrated focus on the cultivation of *intellectual* power.   Broad national policies and needs require heightened knowledge and skills in such subjects as mathematics, the basic sciences, English, and foreign languages.   Also, the continuation of education is stressed as an ever-increasing percentage of people seek college education. Teaching students how to cope with lifelong learning is another necessity

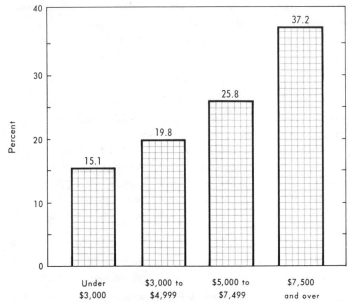

Figure 4–3 Percentage of three- to five-year-olds enrolled in nursery schools and kindergartens. (Statistic of the month. *Amer. Educ.*, 1965, **1**, No. 8.)

[18, pp. 20–23]. These two are the emergent functions uniquely suited to the school if school is going to face the great transformation of the space age.

Although at the present time practically all children are in school for ten to twelve years, regardless of motivation or ability, many children, especially those from the bottom of the socioeconomic pyramid, are neither capable in nor adjusted to the present-day school curriculum, which is geared to the education of middle-class children. Many lower-class children are culturally disadvantaged; others are physically, socially, or emotionally deprived. Frank Riessman [23] estimates that in 1950 fourteen large cities had one culturally disadvantaged child in ten, that in 1960 there was one in three, and he predicts that in 1970 there will be one in two. The schools of the 1970s will be facing problems of the highest complexity [22]. The influences of school are presented in more detail in Chapter 12.

Society

The matrix of human life is social in character. Establishing and changing interpersonal relationships are daily affairs. Modern society, with its large clusters of people in cities and suburban areas, provides almost unlimited opportunities for social intercourse. Automobiles, trains, ships, and airplanes permit a great extension of direct human interaction, while radio, television, and motion pictures serve as means of indirect contact.

The community is the first large social structure which serves as a framework for socioeconomic life. Small towns, suburbs, and other limited communities are not just geographic locations but are also a network of interpersonal relationships and economic structures which provide the most promising resources for meeting human needs at every level of development.

Careful observation of several large cities and rural areas will reveal great differences in neighborhoods and their inhabitants. Some American communities are well integrated and comparatively stable; the atmosphere is agreeable and consistent. The corrective influences of many such communities are sound and extensive. Yet many cities have districts in which the population is constantly on the move and community formation is weak and inefficient. Here the family receives little assistance in developing a child's civic obligations. Hence, the morale of the people is low and the disorganizing elements are strong; cultural values and expectations appear confused. In this type of community, the sociocultural ego—to use the concept of E. Durkheim—that is acquired through active participation in any system of society and culture cannot be sufficiently developed and integrated. Some stable communities are also rather unhealthy in their effects on their members since they foster an excessive "keep up with the Joneses" competition.

Socioeconomic subcultures and certain social groups have been distinguishable throughout the centuries. Originally class levels were based on economic assets, but personal endowment and education have since become significant in determining one's status. A social class is defined by Bossard as "an aggregate of persons having approximately the same social status in a given society." Social status implies "the arrangement of groups of people on a comparative scale, in terms of social distance and prestige as well as of reciprocal rights and duties" [10, p. 318]. Each social group usually displays an identifying mode of life and conduct. There is a similarity of occupational area and income, house type, geographical area, manner of speech, dress, interests, and leisure-time activities.

Several objective measures have been devised to establish the socioeconomic status of a particular individual or family [29]. The Index of Status Characteristics [29, pp. 22–25] assigns points for such factors as type of work, income resources, neighborhood, and type of home. For example, a laboratory technician who depends upon his salary as a source of income and lives in an apartment building situated in an average residential neighborhood would be placed in the lower middle class. Figure 4–4 illustrates some important differences in interests, education, etc., among youth (N=487) of the four social classes in a midwestern city of about forty-five thousand inhabitants.

In American society, there is more mobility in the class system and among classes than in most parts of the world. An individual born into a particular class usually dies in it, but there is possibility for considerable change, as illustrated in the popular opinion that any man's son has an opportunity to become President of the United States.

Traditionally three social-class levels are defined: upper, middle, and lower. In many studies each class is further divided into an upper, a middle, and a lower group, for instance, the middle upper and the lower upper classes. James H. S. Bossard [10] has appraised many studies of the American class system and concludes that general estimates place 3 to 5 percent of the

Figure 4–4 Social class and youth tendencies. The index scores have been computed from data in various tables to bring the five sets of data into one graph. (Robert J. Havighurst et al. *Growing up in River City.* New York: Wiley, 1962, p. 13. By permission.)

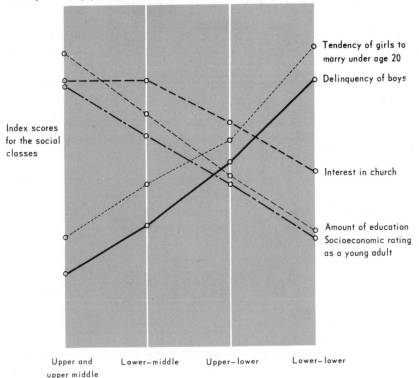

American population in the upper class, 38 percent in the middle class, and 57 percent in the lower class.

The living habits of each of these groups have been analyzed. Children in the lower class tend to be physically more aggressive and more independent, and to have earlier sex experiences. Middle-class individuals tend to be more controlling and demanding as parents. Many of them are ambitious people who frequently are striving to attain higher status and press their children to raise their status. Upper-class members enjoy more leisure activity, are educated in the leading colleges, and usually have an opportunity to develop their aesthetic appreciation to a higher level than the other groups.

The influences of social class on child-rearing practices have been studied by Davis and Havighurst in the Chicago area [12], by Sears, Maccoby, and Levin in Boston [25], and by Miller and Swanson in Detroit [20]. In these research studies it was found that middle-class families tend to have high educational goals for their offspring. They allow their children great freedom for activity during the day. Lower-class families tend to use more severe punishment in toilet training, while on the whole middle-class mothers utilize more subtle controls.

Other differences in child-rearing practices have also been noted among different classes of society. Miller and Swanson [20] studied 1,157 Detroit homes totaling 2,556 adults. The subjects were a representative cross section of urban and suburban households. In the group there were 582 mothers with children under nineteen years of age. Miller and Swanson distinguished within each social class groups designated as entrepreneurial and bureaucratic. The *entrepreneurial* group contained families in which the husband or wife was self-employed, employed in a small organization, or derived considerable income from fees; or in which either the husband or the wife was foreign-born or born on a farm. The *bureaucratic* husband worked for a relatively complex organization, depended on wages or salary as income, and was not faced with much risk-taking and competition. The study proposed that the two groups were influenced by different conditions and experiences. Hence, they would differ significantly as to particular child-rearing practices. "Children raised in individuated and entrepreneurial homes will be encouraged to be highly rational, to exercise great self-control, to be self-reliant, and to assume an active, manipulative stance toward their environment" [20, p. 57]. On the other hand, the bureaucratic family would stress accommodating and adjusting to the world, especially to the direction of the organizational structure of which it was a member. Also, children would be permitted a greater degree of spontaneity.

These expectations were tested in such practical matters as methods of weaning, toilet training, and reward and punishment. The findings confirmed some significant differences between the two groups, especially in the middle class. For example, entrepreneurial mothers in the middle class were prone to adhere to scheduled feeding, to use symbolic punishment, and to begin toilet training early. The researchers did not tend to find the significant differences between middle- and lower-class mothers which previous investigators had emphasized.

The clusters of people in metropolitan and large city areas contribute to the formation of mass society, which, in turn, develops a mass culture. This process is accelerated by mass education and exposure to the mass media of communication and mass entertainment. In mass culture, religious, political, and aesthetic values and related attitudes tend to become nearly homogeneous—people feel and think almost alike. Since the feelings and beliefs are not deeply anchored, an instability results, shown by high susceptibility to fashions and fads [32].

Television.   One of the most effective means of mass communication is television. It is significant as one of the many factors influencing home life. Since television operates with both pictures and sound, it offers a powerful stimulus to its viewers, children and adolescents in particular. The young child is highly susceptible to the values and attitudes advocated on television. One ought to keep in mind that TV is a means of conditioning (though highly reduced), reinforced by pleasant consequences and the comfort of watching.

Generally, programs have some educational value unless they are sensational or bizarre and deal extensively with crime and violence. Some commercial TV programs and most educational ones contribute much to the lifelong career of human learning. By word and illustration, they expand a person's reservoir of ideas and provide powerful incentives for new interests and activities.

Often TV stimulates the interests of a child by providing material which supplements the regular school curriculum. The child who watches a special science program or the reenactment of some historic event often becomes curious to read more on the topic. Some cloudy scholastic concepts can be made concrete and vivid by television. For example, a child is taught about a distant land in class, and after viewing a travelogue about that land, he achieves a vivid concept of the country.

Thrillers and mystery shows tend to spoil individual taste for better programs and to divert the viewer from reading and relaxation. A significant number of children and adolescents are permitted to watch late evening and even some midnight shows. These programs are often freighted with horror, sex, and violence, themes which naturally take their toll of the child's nervous system. The resulting tension not only affects the child's ability to sleep but also exerts a subtle influence by raising family friction because his patience threshold is cut down considerably. Spending as much as twenty hours a week before TV sets, as it is reported many elementary school children are doing [35], is certainly too much, even if the program selection is relatively good. Viewing long evening TV programs contributes to listlessness in school the next day. Continuous evening watching produces the "tired-child syndrome," also marked by loss of appetite, irritability, sleeplessness, or other more subtle detrimental effects. How can the child grow in sensitivity and kindness when the daily television makes cruelty and violence very exciting and attractive? Is not a large portion of the viewing time a school for delinquency and sadism? The togetherness of the family and the relaxed exchange of ideas among its members also suffer immensely. Alfred Bandura and Dorothea and Sheila Ross' study [7] of ninety-six preschool boys and girls shows that observation of models portraying aggression on film substantially increases the probability of aggressive reactions to subsequent frustrations. "Ss who viewed the aggressive human and cartoon models on film exhibited nearly twice as much aggression than did Ss in the control group. . . ." Harold L. Wilensky's survey of 1,354 men of the Detroit area [33] shows that men who have confidence in the major institutions of American society distrust TV and radio networks because of their poor programings and their detrimental effects on viewers and hearers.

Culture

Fundamentally, *culture* is the pattern of a people's life seen in terms of artifacts and creative achievements distinguishing large but similar societies. It encompasses all technology and civilization, law, morality, and religion, traditional and present trends, training and educational facilities, politics, arts, and recreation. With their unique personalities people create and affect culture, but in turn are also highly affected by its qualities and characteristics. Since culture is usually an end product of centuries of human endeavor, it cannot be easily or immediately changed; it maintains a certain stability from generation to generation. Cultural expectations and norms tend to be created and maintained. They influence everyday living and special occasions alike. Not only do they include education and marriage but also eating and feeding habits, as well as normal means of expressing affection and aggression.

The social classes pertain to the organizational structure of the population, while culture focuses on the customs, traditions, social graces, morals, beliefs, and roles which individuals play. Just as scientific insights further technology, artistic creativity enriches the culture.

Culture consists of learned behavior which results in standardized ways of believing and acting. Language and printed matter foster the transmission of culture from one generation to another. Parents transmit tradition to their children, and there is a partial carry-over to adults who immigrate from another society. Mass communication media provide the means for transmitting culture also.

American culture is a variation of Western Christian culture marked by pragmatism, high industrialization, superior technology, and a fast rate of change in styles, fashions, speech patterns, and fads. American culture promotes competition, specialization, and competence. Sex and power are often viewed as major positive valences.

The drive for monetary gain is strongly reinforced by emphasis on materialistic values and economic prosperity. A person feels he is failing unless his bank account is steadily growing or he is investing. To an Asian observer it seems as though most Americans are engaged in a marathon race in which those in the lead are phobic about those gaining at their heels, while those behind are envious, if not hostile, toward those ahead. Many feel they have been outdone by the Joneses and look for the avenues of least resistance to forge ahead. Is it any wonder that a large percentage of men and women in our present decade are tense, jittery, emotionally frustrated, and often unsure of their sex capacity and appeal? There is great room for improvement, and many are striving for this. American culture is perhaps comparable to Pandora's box, containing many destructive powers which are at present, however, divided among themselves and produce little harm for the total society.

In American culture the period of youth is, nevertheless, an ideal-filled stage of life. Vigorous commitment is demonstrated to individual dignity, personal and organizational liberty, and equal opportunities for all. Praise and reward are strong motivational forces. Savoir faire and optimism are common features. A saying attributed to the Seabees best describes this technical mastery: "The difficult we do at once, the impossible takes a little longer." Hospitality, helpfulness, and generosity are also marks of the American people despite the impersonal type of metropolitan society which tends to encourage disheartening detachment and exclusive interest in oneself or one's own family. To a large extent, American culture is a fusion of many cultural elements which give rise to many conflicting tendencies.

Sharing in the fundamental characteristics of the whole culture are various ethnic groups who display special culture preferences and features. Thus, there are religious groups which prescribe special food taboos, maintain various sacred rites of initiation, and insist on marriage within the subgroup. For example, there are the special dietary rules of the Orthodox Jewish people; their bar mitzvah exercises, celebrated to signify the thirteen-year-old male's coming of age and assuming of religious obligations; taboos against marriage outside the group; and the perpetuation of the Hebrew language through the training of the young.

Yet, despite race, national, and class differences, the industrial society presses people into a mold of unidimensionality and threatens expressions of individuality, creativity, and miniature esprit de corps [19, 33].

QUESTIONS FOR REVIEW

1. What factors make man distinct from other animals, and why is he identified as Homo sapiens?
2. What is heredity, and what makes heredity practically unique for each individual?
3. From where does an individual's inheritance come and when is it transmitted to him?
4. What is DNA, and what are its chief functions?
5. Describe the heredity of identical twins, and explain how it differs from the heredity of fraternal twins.
6. How does inheritance contribute to individual differences?
7. Since in the nucleus of the family each person is related closely to each other, how many relationships exist in a family of three persons? How many new relationships does a newcomer add to the network of associations?
8. What are the major parental influences on children? Analyze two of them.
9. Define the father's role and his major functions in a nuclear family.
10. Give some reasons why children need male and female models in the family.
11. Explain the principle of primacy and its role in motivation and adjustment.
12. Enumerate the persons and groups with whom the older child readily identifies himself.
13. What are some of the desirable and the detrimental effects of television viewing for children?
14. What are the major functions of the school and of the teacher?
15. In what significant ways do society and social class influence personal behavior?
16. Define culture and critically assess some traits of American culture.

REFERENCES

I. Selected Reading

1. Duvall, Evelyn M. *Family development.* (2nd ed.) Philadelphia: Lippincott, 1962. A comprehensive and well-written source on family life, stressing its tasks and patterns of interaction at different age levels.
2. Goodlad, John I. (Ed.). *The changing American school.* Chicago: National Society for the Study of Education, 1966. The second part of the sixty-fifth yearbook of the society, including works of twelve contributors. It exposes to the view of the reader the present school situation and the various forces molding its change.
3. Havighurst, Robert J., and Bernice L. Neugarten. *Society and educa-*

tion. (2nd ed.) Boston: Allyn and Bacon, 1962. A general reference book for American social structure, school and teacher, child's life space, and peer groups.

4. Sears, Robert R., Lucy Rau, and Richard Alpert. *Identification and child rearing.* Stanford, Calif.: Stanford, 1965. A major study of parental traits and their effects on children, including analysis of conscience.

5. Scheinfeld, Amram. *Your heredity and environment.* Philadelphia: Lippincott, 1965. An important source for heredity, including abnormalities, psychological traits, and human evolution.

II. Specific References

6. Avery, Oswald T., Colin M. MacLeod, and Maclyn McCarty. Studies on the chemical nature of the living substance including transformation of pneumococcal types. *J. exp. Med.,* 1944, **79**, 137–158.

7. Bandura, Alfred, Dorothea Ross, and Sheila A. Ross. Imitation of film-mediated aggressive models. *J. abnorm. soc. Psychol.,* 1963, **66**, 3–11.

8. Becker, Wesley C. Consequences of different kinds of parental discipline. In Martin L. Hoffman and Lois W. Hoffman (Eds.), *Review of child development research,* Vol. I. New York: Russell Sage Foundation, 1964. Pp. 169–208.

9. Bossard, James H. S. *Parent and child.* Philadelphia: University of Pennsylvania Press, 1953.

10. Bossard, James H. S. *The sociology of child development.* (2nd ed.) New York: Harper & Row, 1954.

11. Crick, F. H. C. On the genetic code. *Science,* 1963, **139**, 461–464. See also Garen, Alan. Sense and nonsense in the genetic code. *Science,* 1968, **160**, 149–159.

12. Davis, Allison, and Robert J. Havighurst. Social class and color differences in child rearing. *Amer. soc. Rev.,* 1946, **2**, 698–710.

13. Gall, J. G. Chromosomal differentiation. In W. D. McElroy and B. Glass (Eds.), *Chemical basis of development.* Baltimore: Johns Hopkins, 1958. Pp. 103–135.

14. Havighurst, Robert J. et al. *Growing up in River City.* New York: Wiley, 1962.

15. Hobart, Charles W. Commitment, value conflict, and the future of the American family. *Marriage Fam. Living,* 1963, **25**, 405–412.

16. Kagan, Henry E. Teaching values to our children. In Committee on studies for Golden Anniversary White House Conference on Children and Youth, *Children and youth in the 1960's.* 1960.

17. Kohn, M. L. Social class and parental values. *Amer. J. Sociol.,* 1959, **64**, 337–351.

18. Lee, Gordon C. The changing role of the teacher. In J. I. Goodlad

(Ed.), *The changing American school.* The sixty-fifth yearbook of the National Society for the Study of Education. Chicago: University of Chicago Press, 1966. Pp. 9–31.

19. Marcuse, Herbert. *One-dimensional man.* Beacon, N.Y.: Beacon House, 1964.

20. Miller, Daniel R., and Guy E. Swanson. *The changing American parent.* New York: Wiley, 1958.

21. Nash, John. The father in contemporary culture and current psychological literature. *Child Developm.,* 1965, **36**, 261–297.

22. Parsons, Talcott. Age and sex in the social structure of the United States. *Amer. soc. Rev.,* 1942, **7**, 604–616.

23. Riessman, Frank. *The culturally deprived child.* New York: Harper & Row, 1962.

24. Rogers, Carl R. Toward a modern approach to values: The valuing process in the mature personality. *J. abn. soc. Psychol.,* 1964, **68**, 160–167.

25. Sears, Robert R., Eleanor E. Maccoby, and H. Levin. *Patterns of child rearing.* New York: Harper & Row, 1957.

26. Stern, Curt. *Principles of human genetics.* (2nd ed.) San Francisco: Freeman, 1960. For tracing the expression of heredity in behavior, see Hirsch, Jerry (Ed.), *Behavior-genetic analysis.* New York: McGraw-Hill, 1967.

27. Sullivan, Harry S. *Conceptions of modern psychiatry.* New York: Norton, 1953 (original publication 1940).

28. *Vital Statistics of the United States: 1965.* Vol. 1. 1967.

29. Warner, W. L., M. Mecker, and K. Eells. *Social class in America.* New York: Harper & Row, 1960.

30. Watson, John B. *Psychological care of infant and child.* New York: Norton, 1928.

31. Watson, J. D. Involvement of RNA in the synthesis of proteins. *Science,* 1963, **140**, 17–26.

32. Watson, J. D., and F. H. C. Crick. The structure of DNA. *Cold Spring Harbor Symp. Quant. Biol.,* 1953, **18**, 123–131.

33. Wilensky, Harold L. Mass society and mass culture: Interdependence or independence? *Amer. soc. Rev.,* 1964, **29**, 173–197.

34. Wilkins, M. H. F. Molecular configuration of nucleic acids. *Science,* 1963, **140**, 17–26.

35. Witty, Paul. Some results of eight yearly studies of TV. *Sch. Soc.,* 1958, **86**, 287–289.

DEVELOPMENTAL ASPECTS
AND TRENDS

It has already been stressed that the individual develops as a whole, possessing an intrinsic unity throughout the entire life-span. It was also pointed out, however, that various systems and structures of the organism, as well as specific types of behavior, differ as to beginning point, developmental rate, and period of maximum functioning. The organismic and personality age trends and other significant growth aspects will be treated individually. Each of these aspects—physiological growth, emotional development, cognitive maturation, socialization, and the formation of the self-concept—will be followed through its own growth cycle, and their relationships to other factors will also be considered. Figure 5–1 is a schematic presentation of the general pattern of differentiation. In the prenatal stage, many structures and physiological functions begin to develop. After birth the structures become refined and the functions multiply continually throughout infancy, and to a lesser degree throughout childhood and puberty. Most growth is accomplished by early adolescence. Later adolescence and early adulthood are periods of functional culmination.

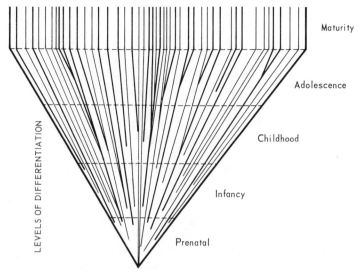

Figure 5–1 Differentiation of growth.   Each line indicates a new factor or function in the total structure of growth.

THE PHYSIOLOGICAL TREND

Physiological growth is anything but a smooth or continuous process.   Although the genetic curve is progressive for most systems and organs, there are plateaus, even deteriorations, for some structures as early as puberty. The plateau for growth of sexual organs during childhood and the shrinking of the thymus gland at puberty are examples of growth discontinuities.   The deterioration of most physiological structures and functions begins in middle adulthood and lasts throughout senescence.

The total pattern of physiological growth follows a cycle with spurts and plateaus which can be predicted.   Using the child's height, age, and roentgenograms (taken at eight or ten years of age) as an index of ossification in the wrist, adult height can be estimated with a fair degree of accuracy.   From the same wrist X-rays, the approximate time of sexual maturation can also be predicted [10].

The prenatal stage, the first year, and to a certain extent, early childhood are periods of tremendous physiological growth.   Development gradually tapers off during childhood until it reaches its low ebb at nine or ten years of age.   There is a renewel for about three years during puberty until finally it nearly ceases by the age of sixteen or eighteen.   The age at which pubertal changes take place and adult height is attained differs not only for boys and girls but also for individuals of the same sex.   There are many individual differences since every person has a distinct rate of physiological growth.   In the late 1960s the average age at which pubertal changes reach a peak is approximately twelve and a half years for girls and slightly over fourteen for boys. Increases in weight are comparable to those in height. Adult weight is usually reached in late adolescence. However, during later middle adult years there is usually a considerable gain in weight, often referred to as "middle-age spread." The waistline increases by several inches as amounts of surface fat accumulate in that region.

Even more striking than the changes in height and weight are those in proportions of various parts of the body from age to age. The proportion of the length of the child's head to his total height keeps decreasing, while the length of his legs continuously increases until adult proportions are acquired during puberty. Figure 5–2 graphically illustrates these changes as growth follows the cephalocaudal sequence.

Sidney L. Pressey and Raymond G. Kuhlen [21, p. 62] divide the life span into three major periods of physical development, with the first twenty years a continuous growth period. "The prime" is used to designate the years from twenty to approximately forty-five when the individual is at his peak. A slight decline follows, but it is mild until about the age of seventy, when a definite decline and weakness set in.

Physiological growth is highly affected by the amount of physical exercise, by emotional currents, and by dietary provisions. For internal chemical changes the number of needed nutrients is approximately sixty, many of which are essential for a child's or adolescent's welfare [17]. Individuals have different capacities to digest, absorb, store, and produce the necessary chemical substances from the foods making up their diets. Conversion of

Figure 5–2 Changes in proportions of the human body with age. (G. A. Baitsell. *Human biology.* New York: McGraw-Hill, 1940; after Stratz.)

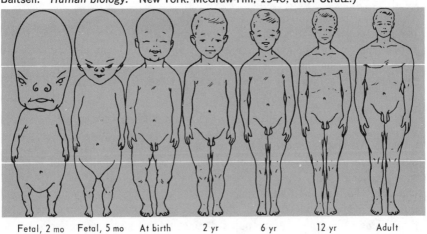

Fetal, 2 mo   Fetal, 5 mo   At birth   2 yr   6 yr   12 yr   Adult

nutrients into living matter involves the gastrointestinal organs and many other systems of the body.   For example, cells grow properly only if the composition of the blood and the amount of oxygen and fluids are within definite, rather narrow limits.   Strong emotional upsets inhibit the digestive system, and the individual loses his appetite.   Physical exercises speed up the nutritive exchange within the body.   The progress made in regulating human growth is remarkable but limited.   J. M. Tanner [28] has given a summary of acquired techniques in growth regulation in a 1963 publication.

Physical fitness is fostered by frequent exercise.   Although the kind and amount needed by one child or adult may be harmful for another, all children need some vigorous activities through which the muscles of the torso and limbs are used.   Muscles are meant to be used.   Physical exercises make children strong and vigorous.   For optimum physical development, children, it is said, "must have from four and a half to six hours daily of vigorous muscular exercise" [15, p. 56].   Winter and summer sports, basketball, and other athletic activities, if adjusted to the needs of the child, adolescent, or adult, further bodily growth and enhance endurance.   This, in turn, raises the individual's health and self-reliance—worthwhile gains for every person. Physical exercise is "the master conditioner for the healthy and the major therapy for the ill" [20].

SYNOPSIS OF EMOTIONAL DEVELOPMENT

The human individual is born with a capacity for emotional experience and behavior.   The events of his life, especially his relationships with parents and siblings and his exposure to emotionally challenging situations, conflicts, and frustrations will determine what emotions he will show as an adolescent and adult.

Our own experiences illustrate how emotions affect most behavior and influence a large segment of our reactions and activities.   Certain emotions are necessary for healthy living and adjustment.   Primarily an infant receives emotion.   He must feel sympathy, affection, and love from others before he can reciprocate.   Most emotions need stimulation for their development. Like every aspect of personality, distinct emotional expressions are acquired through observation and learning.

The aroused states of the young infant are only analogous to adolescent or adult emotional reactions.   However, early in the first year some responses are recognizable as emotional.   Based on Katherine M. B. Bridges' empirical assessment, Figure 5–3 shows the differentiation of various affective states during the first two years of life.   The diffuse excitement of the neonate, which is a function of general mass activity of the organism in need, pain, or discomfort, gradually assumes the quality of a pleasant or unpleasant reac-

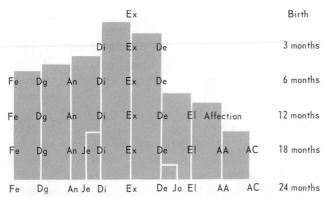

Figure 5–3 Bridges' chart of emotional differentiation. Key: AA—Affection for Adults; AC—Affection for Children; An—Anger; De—Delight; Dg—Disgust; Di—Distress; El— Elation; Ex—Excitement; Fe—Fear; Je—Jealousy; Jo—Joy. (Katharine M. B. Bridges. Emotional development in early infancy. *Child Develpm.*, 1932, **3**, 324–341.)

tion.   The resulting disgust and delight are in time further refined and develop into more subtle affective states.

Early childhood is normally the time when the individual greatly enlarges his repertoire of affective states and related behavior.   The various ways of expressing emotions are frequently altered.   The ability to communicate by speech replaces in part the use of motor activity as a necessary means of expressing emotions.   The young child becomes aware of the power of his emotions for influencing his parents, and learns how far he can go in expressing them.

At this period of development, attitudes and sentiments generally emerge. Attitude development begins after the child's emotions become fairly differentiated.   Positive or negative parental remarks about race, religion, authority, and other topics will be picked up by the child, along with corresponding attitudes.   Even with minimal instruction or training, preschool children acquire aesthetic, moral, and religious sentiments.   These are uncritically accepted in the child's fast-developing value system and act as powerful organizers as well as determents of behavior.   Envy and jealousy are vividly expressed at this level.   Children at this age are typically self-centered and rather demanding.   With proper training, however, fair play and a spirit of sharing can be inculcated in the child.

The emotional expression of children is very different from that of adults. Children's emotions are often explosive reactions to relatively trivial stimuli. On the other hand, because children are not yet subject to moods, these strong emotions appear and disappear quickly. Five minutes after a violent fight, the combatants may be playing together happily. The important point to bear in mind is that children can tolerate only a certain amount of excitement. Frequent emotional turmoil is more harmful to children than to adults. Children must learn a measure of self-control and frustration tolerance in order to avoid frequent arousal of emotions.

Middle and late childhood are periods of gradual emotional development. The child is learning more self-control through association with others. He is also refining the emotional states he is capable of experiencing.

Complete emotional differentiation is attained in adolescence. Before this period ends all the adult affective states can be experienced by an individual. Moods, virtually unknown in childhood, may plague the adolescent. One week he may be euphoric; the next week he may find life bereft of all joy. Adolescence is a period of oscillation between moods. Toward the end of adolescence, the reactions of the individual become more mature and adult-like, but emotions continue to play a leading role in motivation. One feature of emotional complexity peculiar to adolescence results from the intensification of the sex drive and experience of deep heterosexual love. In early adolescence there is usually an unrealistic idea of the love object. This makes a fusion of sexual object and love object difficult. It is not until late adolescence or early adulthood that the individual can attain the mature heterosexual love necessary for a lifelong marriage.

In adulthood, emotions do not develop any further but the maximum refinement of sentiments is attained. The next significant change in emotions comes in senescence, when emotional "disentanglement" occurs. There is generally a drastic reduction in social interaction and social emotions begin to play a much smaller role. Boredom and depression, irritability, faultfinding, and complaining rise noticeably with advancing age. The older person becomes increasingly disinterested, even apathetic. Emotional satisfaction is more and more often vicariously derived from memories of past events and achievements. Figure 5-4 attempts to depict schematically a genetic theory of emotions throughout life. Emotions will be further discussed in the treatment of various levels of life, including senescence.

COGNITIVE MATURATION

The process of cognition begins with perception—a function of external stimulation modified by internal coding. Perceiving is a process in which sensory input is unified and interpreted in accordance with a number of grouping tendencies and past experiences. From the developmental point of view, new and additional meanings are assigned to the previously undefined

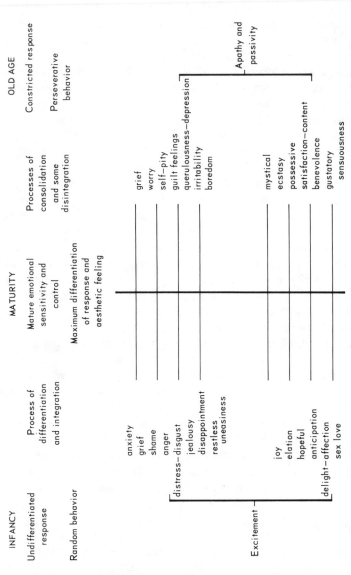

Figure 5-4 Schema of life-span emotional changes. (Katharine M. Banham. Senescence and the emotions: A genetic theory. *J. genet. Psychol.*, 1951, **78**, 175–183. By permission.)

sensory data. The rising awareness of persons, objects, situations, and relationships is a result of mental maturation, highly colored by the effects of original experiences, set, and attention.

It was Williams James who in 1890 in *Principles of psychology* wrote that "to the infant sounds, sights, touches and pains form probably one unanalyzed bloom of confusion." Does the infant's awareness of reality start that way? Recent studies suggest that the neonate has the capacity to respond distinctly to a considerable variety of stimuli. During the first five days of life, most neonates can be characterized as being consistently either slightly, moderately, or intensely responsive to stimuli, regardless of their modalities or natures [4].

The major spurt in perceptual development begins with birth and gradually levels off during the second year. The complexities of the perceptual process make it nearly impossible to delineate any definite phases of its growth, yet Jean Piaget's genetic analysis distinguishes various levels of perceiving specific factors and recognizing problems [19, pp. 414–434]. The world is structured but the growing person selects the structures to which he will attend and react; he even provides the missing parts on occasion. To perceive is "to know and comprehend the nature of a stimulus," to organize sets of stimuli never experienced before in terms of one of several alternative modes of perceptual organization. One cannot really know the single stimulus without understanding some properties of the sets within which it is contained [9].

Cognition refers primarily to conceiving, reasoning, deciding, judging, and theorizing, but as a generic term it encompasses all processes by which knowledge of an object is attained, including perception, memory, and imagination. The cognitive power makes men distinct from, and superior to, animals. Cognitive processes, although an integral part of man's nature, still must be developed. As is that of other functions, the developmental course of cognition is marked by periods of rapid development. For purposes of measurement and understanding, cognition must be translated into functional or operational terms. Hence, intelligence is commonly used to denote the achievements by which an individual forms concepts, makes decisions, and solves oral and performance problems. Performance resulting from the application of cognitive powers and functions is measured chiefly by individual intelligence tests, such as Stanford-Binet (Form L-M, 1960) and Wechsler Adult Intelligence Scale (WAIS, 1955).

The neonate shows virtually no distinctly cognitive behavior for some time after birth. Indeed, he lacks the proper means for it, since speech is the vehicle par excellence for cognitive functioning. However, the assessment of intelligence is occasionally made at three or six months of age. Seemingly, the more intelligent infant tends to develop faster in various aspects of growth; locomotion and perception are therefore often used in rating intelligence.

The actual demonstration of cognitive development is usually considered to be progress in verbal skill. The speed with which a child assimilates new words, his discrimination of differences and similarities, and the length of the sentences he uses are all fairly reliable indexes of intelligence. The child's curiosity is a great spur to his cognitive development. Although the frequent "What's that?" or "Why?" of a child at time annoys a busy parent, it is a major means children have for learning about the world around them. The type of questions asked is indicative of the level of intelligence. The young child wants to know "What?" or the name of a thing. "Why?" is the next question posed at about four and a half. The child realizes that most objects serve human needs and purposes and he is eager to know the function of any new object. Now he is aware not only of his needs and desires but also of some means of gratifying them. Then at eight or nine years of age the child is concerned about causes and effects. When he witnesses a new occurrence, he is interested in its cause.

During puberty, full cognitive capacity is attained. Following this peak at fourteen or sixteen years of age, refinement and polishing of many cognitive functions may continue. Special mental abilities and aptitudes are also shown at this time. As estimated by intelligence tests, cognitive functioning is at its best by the age of nineteen or twenty [29]. Adolescents are capable of propositional reasoning, theorizing, and questioning about ultimate reasons.

With adulthood comes a slackening in the exercise of cognitive functions for many individuals. Formal education is completed, and the problems of marriage and a vocation usually absorb the time earlier spent in developing the mind. If there is a considerable reduction in stimulation and application, a gradual reduction in cognitive alertness sets in early in adulthood.

In senescence, all aspects of cognition deteriorate at a moderate rate as do the other functions. There are many outstanding exceptions among clergymen, polticians, scientists, philosophers, and some professionals, but the generalization is correct for most individuals.

Piaget's theory of cognitive development

Jean Piaget postulates that the organism's interaction with the environment, chiefly through motor action, causes cognitive operations to emerge. Beginning with a basic state of organization and a basic process, adaptation, a spontaneous logical organization begins to occur. From the initial functions and structures of assimilation and accommodation come all other forms of knowledge. Cognition for Piaget is not a passive imprinting process, but action on reality. The driving forces of assimilation and accommodation produce self-structure. The action of the organism is thus central for the acquisition of cognitive operations and of distinct strategies for coping with the world [19, pp. 355–356, 386]. A core of unvarying attributes of organization and adaptation, governed by biological principles under the impact of experience, forms roots for cognitive activity. Physiological functioning presupposes a sort of organization which is extended into other functions, including the intellectual. Adaptation encompasses two interacting functions, assimilation and accommodation. This nucleus of processes produces structural units called schemas—a key concept in the genesis of intelligence. As a function of experience, the individual acquires an increasing number of operational schemas, that is, action sequences. Through corrective contacts with reality itself, the more efficient schemas supersede the cruder ones.

The process of *assimilation* may be illustrated by eating—incorporation of objects into oneself, while *accommodation* refers to the internal adjustments of the organism to the food. The early predominance of assimilation over accommodation changes in favor of the latter, and this is crucial for the establishment of advanced levels of cognition. Based on regularities, assimilation and accommodation become increasingly complementary. Cognition involves definite genetic steps. Certain components of each stage must be assimilated and accommodated before the next stage can occur. This rather simple operational framework becomes a very complex structure as the individual moves from one stage to another and the structural changes are explained by abstract logico-mathematical models. Prior to formulation of the analytic theory of cognitive differentiation in greater complexity, Piaget invented the concept of logical and intralogical grouping, which included group and lattice properties [1, pp. 172–187].

The first level of intellectual operation is called the period of *sensorimotor* intelligence. This level starts at birth and lasts until about two years of age; it involves differentiation between self and objects. It contains six stages, the first of which is marked by the predominance of reflexes during the first month of life. The establishment of primary and secondary circular responses covers the next two phases, marked by a rise of inner coordination and actions toward objects and events outside the self. Intentionality in activity appears, and subordination of means to ends is a hallmark of the fourth stage (four to eight months). The search for new behavioral means marks the last two stages of this period. This mental exploration of ways and means, as well as learning symbolic representations of desirable goals, paves the way for reasoning. The power to use symbolic function is a quality the child gradually acquires. Speech is a vehicle for progress in symbolization. Apparently, the amount of experience is crucial for setting the rate of intellectual growth [12, p. 357].

The second level of cognitive development, referred to as the period of preparation for and organization of *concrete operations*, begins at about two years of age and encompasses most of the years of childhood.   This period is divided into two subperiods: (1) preoperational representation (2–7), marked by beginnings of representational thought and intuition, and (2) concrete operations (7–11), when the child conceives of categories and the reversibility of a process.   Through frequent and often bewildering interchanges with siblings and peers, the child comes to grips with other viewpoints and gradually moves from a static egocentrism to the multiperspective reversibility—a hallmark of the grouping structure.   Arithmetic groups, logical and intralogical groupings, and various techniques of measurement emerge.   Even if viewed in varied forms, equivalence with regard to quantity, weight, volume, area, etc., can be recognized.   Once the grouping structures become concrete and operational, the world of representation (and that of measurement) gains in stability, coherence, and order.   The transition from concrete to formal operations becomes possible as thought processes continue abstracting from their sensorimotor basis.

The period of *formal operations* (11–15) is the crowning achievement of cognitive maturation.   It represents the final state of equilibrium toward which cognitive evolution has been moving since infancy.   Through active commerce with the world, the young adolescent moves toward logical and systematic reasoning and toward a search for general principles.   At this level he becomes impressed with and accepts the hypothetico-deductive "all-other-things-being-equal" method of investigation.   Bärbel Inhelder and Jean Piaget [13, pp. 344–353] show that the transition to formal operation signifies entrance into genuinely scientific methods of analysis.   Nontechnical experimental induction, based on the manipulating of a single factor with the others held constant, represents intellectual efficiency of the highest caliber. This principally deductive system, showing cognitive functions and underlying structures, was unearthed and empirically substantiated by Piaget and his associates (particularly Bärbel Inhelder, L. Apostel, P. Gréco, J. B. Grize, B. Matalon, and S. Popert) in their multivariate studies of the multiplicities of the child's verbal knowledge and performance.   The system is basically consistent with the cognitive development of mankind as reflected in anthropological studies.   In his epistemology, Piaget expresses belief that all physical, biological, and psychological laws can be integrated into a single, yet universal formula.

Intelligence testing and its applications

One of the controversial problems in the assessment of cognitive development is the measurement of intelligence and the practical application of IQs. There is considerable uncertainty as to just what intelligence tests do measure.   The theoretical foundations and specific rationales of the individual tests offer some insights into these measurements.   From a practical point of view, the psychologist assesses intelligence by requiring the subject to deal with various tasks and problems of increasing difficulty until he un-equivocally fails on each type of problem administered.   The efficiency level he reaches indicates functional development of cognitive powers.   A fairly accurate appraisal of intellectual performance is possible only by the appli-cation of individual tests, such as the Stanford-Binet or the Wechsler Adult Intelligence Scale.   Group intelligence tests, such as the Kuhlmann-Anderson or Lorge-Thorndike, are rough estimates of cognitive functions.

Widely used for several decades, in the 1950s the Stanford-Binet was in part restandardized for the third time in this country.   The Stanford-Binet L-M will probably retain its leading position as a test of child intelligence for some time to come.   In testing a ten-year-old child the examiner establishes his basal age (age at which he succeeds on all subtests) and tests him on higher levels until he fails all the subtests (ceiling age).   Giving credits for the lower ages and counting them up to the ceiling age gives the child his mental age (MA).   Instead of the IQ as a ratio between MA and CA (chrono-logical age), Form L-M utilizes the deviation IQ (that is, a standard score with a mean of 100 and standard deviation of 16 for each age).   The devia-tion IQ improves the IQ constancy from age to age.

General distribution of intelligence and other abilities is shown in Figure 5–5.   For comparative purposes, several sets of the more important scores are included.   At present, intelligence tests are frequently used for screening the mentally deficient, retarded, dull, average, superior, and gifted children in order to place them in the best available type of learning situations.   In a diagnosis of mental deficiency or mental retardation, the intelligence test, by classifying the individual according to degree of mental retardation, offers a prognostic evaluation also.   Figure 5–6 shows the general classification, frequency, and amount of dependency of each subgroup among those classi-fied as mentally deficient.

For purposes of prediction, intelligence tests are used sometimes as early as the third year and more reliably by school age.   By utilizing test results, exceptional children can be placed in situations which will prove intellectually stimulating and challenging, but not overpowering and frustrating.

LEARNING

The development of cognitive power is closely related to the increasing ability to learn.   With the exception of emotionally and mentally disordered persons, the level of intelligence as reflected by individual intelligence tests is usually consistent with the individual's power to learn.   As intelligence test scores

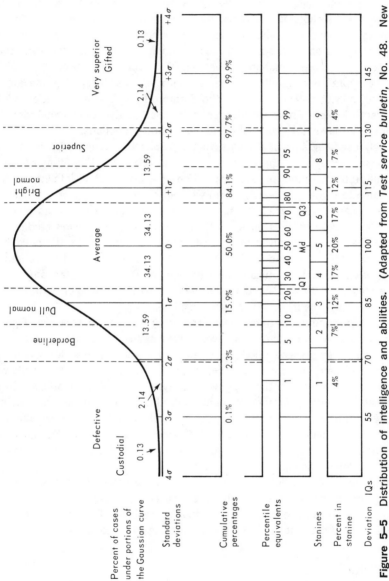

Figure 5–5 Distribution of intelligence and abilities. (Adapted from *Test service bulletin*, No. 48. New York: Psychological Corporation, 1955.)

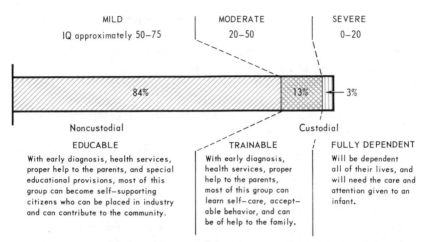

Figure 5–6 Classification of mentally deficient children. (Modified from Fact Finding Committee, Midcentury White House Conference on Children and Youth. *A graphic presentation of social and economic facts important in the lives of children and youth.* Washington: National Publishing Co., 1951.)

rise so does learning efficiency. A Minneapolis sample of 354 fourth- and sixth-graders showed that children's performance on different learning tasks is highly interrelated and that their rate of learning is significantly correlated with their intelligence level [26].

In the broad sense, learning includes all those motivational and performance changes that result from stimulation and experience. Learning is chiefly a function of increasing perceptual and cognitive efficiency as it is modified by the self. The capacity for learning new subject matter is also dependent upon maturity, adjustment, and the method of presentation. Teaching ballet to a five- or six-year-old often boomerangs, even if taught systematically. For this subject the feet are just not sufficiently calcified at that age for repetitious lifting and twisting of the body.

The individual utilizes many approaches and techniques in his attempt to adjust to the objective world and form the *eigene Welt*—a world of meanings and relationships of his own. Of utmost importance are sufficient opportunities for learning. Children and adolescents need a varied and constantly expanding environment which provides new experiences. In the case of the infant, a great deal of learning is the result of sensory stimulation. Looking at, touching, biting, hitting, pushing, and dropping are his methods of testing an object. If a baby is kept in the same room or playpen for long hours, he will suffer from this perceptual deprivation. A toddler who is confined to "keep him out of mischief" is missing many opportunities to learn. If parents consistently ignore the five-year-old's questions, they deny him a valuable learning experience. Providing exercises to fit the child's growing mind is a parental task of immense importance.

In adolescence, learning is of a much more complex nature. It takes in all aspects of life and includes a need for much nonacademic assimilation. Adolescents must learn necessary social graces, develop criteria for choosing friends and a marriage partner, and develop along cultural lines. In these areas opportunities for experience are essential. The adult must discover opportunities for these experiences to provide himself with a rich social, civic, and cultural life. Developing interests in subjects and activities besides one's occupation is beneficial to the adult. When retirement comes, hobbies and special interests are invaluable in rechanneling the energies no longer devoted to working. The growth of the mind is always assisted from the outside. Since our culture offers such unlimited opportunities for an individual's personal expansion, there are practically no limits for the individual's progress in learning and personal development [5].

The characteristic modes of learning include:

1. *Habituation*—exclusion of superfluous movement as a result of repetition.
2. *Imitation*—observable late in the first year of life and avidly practiced at about one and a half.
3. *Identification*—assumption of the status or role of a significant person (identification with parents is a dominant characteristic of early childhood, while peer identification begins in the later years of childhood).
4. *Conditioning*—operant conditioning in particular; the individual learns from his interaction with objects of his surroundings, and from the expressive and oral instruction of others he learns which actions are rewarded and which are not.
5. Sign and symbol *discrimination* is another important task for the acquisition of information.
6. Logical and systematic *thinking* facilitates dealing with less tangible aspects of reality, as does creative imagination.

After surveying research data on learning and conditioning, Gregory Razran [22] distinguished four levels and four sublevels of learning, coexistent at the higher evolutionary levels (but with higher levels normally dominant). As seen in Figure 5–7, at the highest level, *Symbolization* or *Sy* (*ABC . . . N*) learning configurations (percepts) become integrated and efferented to form word-symbols which, in turn, form sememes (meaning units). Through the synthetic operation of the mind, the person accumulates abstract and symbolic knowledge applicable in many social and cultural situations of life.

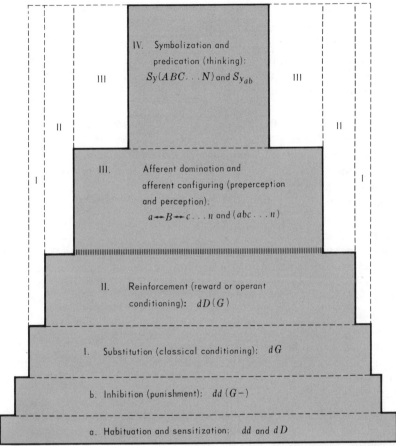

Figure 5–7 Razran's levels of learning. The universality of each level is represented by the width of its parallelogram; its functional efficiency, by the height of the parallelogram; and its total efficiency (functional efficiency × universality), by the area of the parallelogram. The phyletic antiquity of each level is indicated by its vertical position in the diagram. The dotted lines indicate the coexistence of lower and higher levels. (Gregory Razran. Evolutionary psychology: Levels of learning—and perception and thinking. In Benjamin B. Wolman (Ed.) and Ernest Nagel (Cons. Ed.), *Scientific psychology: Principles and approaches.* New York: Basic Books, 1965. Chap. 13, pp. 207–253. Fig. 13–1. By permission.)

THE PATTERN OF SOCIALIZATION

Socialization refers not only to the degrees to which an individual interacts harmoniously with others but also includes the factors which act upon the individual to change him from an autistic child to a socially mature individual.

As is true of other functions, the development from self-centeredness to sociability is neither continuous nor painless. Acquisition of communication and interaction skills is also included as a part of the socialization process. The progress in socialization is marked by learning to play roles and by acquiring social attitudes favoring fair play and cooperation.

Following the principle of primacy, it is safe to say that the nature of early social experiences will greatly influence later social success or failure. In this regard, parents are the earliest and most powerful socializing agents. Their relationship to each other and to the child is the one which the child will perceive as characteristic of many interpersonal relationships. Love of parents for each other and for the child will result in a warm, relaxed family relationship. The attitudes of parents toward their own associates will also be imitated by the child. Frequent arguing, gossiping, criticism, and expressions of disatisfaction with others will induce negative attitudes toward others in the child.

Just as serious as gratifying the child's needs is the responsibility of parents to act as representatives of society and its restrictions. Children must be taught impulse control, sharing, obedience, self-direction, and other related positive attributes which will equip them to deal effectively with others. Overpermissive parents damage a child's future when they permit him to have his own way too frequently. When their child faces the inevitable frustrations of life, he will be poorly prepared to cope with them.

As in other forms of learning, socialization requires suitable opportunities, and the earlier the better. The preschool child should have experiences with group activity. Learning the give-and-take necessary in the peer group is essential. Attitudes toward sharing and social manners learned in childhood tend to persist in modified forms throughout development.

Social interaction begins with the infant's differentiation between persons and things. He gradually learns to respond to parents, to discriminate between familiar and strange faces, and to imitate the actions and words of others. Social interaction is stimulated further by speech. The child learns to make his needs and feelings known not only by overt behavior but also by words. Parents can help their children by making it clear that speech is preferred to crying, tantrums, or other demonstrations.

The family is the primary socializing agent, and it remains the most influential in shaping the child's values and beliefs until approximately nine or ten years of age, when the peer group becomes the most influential factor. The gang age of preadolescence is characterized by intense loyalty to group standards. In early adolescence there is much dependence on peers, but self-direction and self-reliance gradually increase and by early adulthood many individuals have inner-direction and govern their own behavior.

The levels of socialization are fairly well defined and observable. The very young child is a self-centered creature and derives his satisfaction from self-initiated activity. This solitary play may be simultaneous as well, that is, although many children are playing in a room, there is very little interaction among them. The period of negativism which occurs from about two to three and a half years of age is an important step in the child's gaining of autonomy. It marks his first attempt at self-assertion as an individual. How this is handled by parents may mean the difference between a damaged child and a mentally healthy one.

Cooperative and competitive approaches are characteristic of middle childhood and are indicative of a rather advanced degree of socialization. The beginning of school life also comes at this time. This is a crucial step because the child must learn to accept an outside authority. Codes of behavior regarding taking turns, telling stories, informing on classmates, etc., are soon established by the group. The child's adherence to or deviation from these rules largely determines his degree of acceptance in a group. Readiness and ability to assume roles assigned by the group are fundamental for any satisfying group relationship. Group interaction and interdependence deepen until the onset of puberty, when the individual reverts for a while to a less social mode of living. This withdrawal is partial and temporary since most of adolescence is a group-dominated period, marked by a high degree of conformity and *esprit de corps*. The individual at this time is intensely concerned with establishing and furthering heterosexual friendships, but emotional sensitivity and heightened self-consciousness often hinder ease of communication between the sexes.

In late adolescence and early adulthood, the possible choices of a lifetime partner are reduced until the decision is made. The necessary adjustments to marriage are a significant developmental task and one indicative of a fairly high degree of socialization. Throughout adulthood, one's social horizon expands through friendships, business contacts, and acquaintances made in the community. With senescence, however, there is an increasingly sharp decline in new friendships, and a gradual loss, due to moving, retirement, or death of old associates. Senescent individuals tend to become withdrawn and apathetic, setting the process of socialization into reverse.

THE SELF-CONCEPT

The twin concepts of ego and self form the core of many controversial areas in current psychological theory. The self as the person views it and the self as the agent for activity are probably the leading ways of approaching this concept. In the first sense the ego is an object, in the second a subject. There is an evolving sense of self, and it tends to encompass both knowledge about self and the self as an organizer of behavior. What the brain is for the organism, the self is for personality. It is a central system for integrating and directing forces toward various forms of interaction with persons and objects. In agreement with George Mead, Harry S. Sullivan, and C. H. Cooley, John W. Kinch [14] says, "The individual's conception of himself emerges from social interaction, and in turn, guides or influences the behavior of that individual." Kinch feels that general agreement could be reached by using the following definition: "The self-concept is that organization of qualities that the individual attributes to himself." Since qualities include attributes and roles, this definition is superior to many others. Once the self is established, its behavior-directive power arises. A child of three, for example, feels that he has a mind of his own, and he applies it determinedly.

In the Freudian sense ego refers to the core of personality which expresses impulses and drives in conformity with reality demands. This idea of ego stresses the agent aspect of the self. Since ego includes nearly the same aspects of the person as the self and since most authors do not make clear distinctions between the two concepts, they may be treated as somewhat equivalent. While the ego embraces some unconscious processes, however, the self is anchored in the awareness and experience of identity. Most of the time an individual's actions are in accordance with his idea of himself. If a person perceives himself as intellectually inferior, whether or not this is objectively true, his actions will correspond to this subjectively perceived deficiency.

Consistency or continuity of behavior is a direct result of the self-concept. Although subject to maturation and to environmental influences, modification of the self-concept is usually gradual and slight. Experiences which would radically distort it, even favorably, tend to be denied reference to the self, as when people exclaim "It can't be true," "I wasn't myself," or "I lost my head." The degree of flexibility with regard to awareness differs, of course, from person to person, some persons tolerating a considerable range of modification and others showing much rigidity. As a rule, flexibility slowly declines with advancing age. Older persons show more rigidity than younger ones. With the advent of adulthood, there arises a natural desire for stability. For many individuals it is rewarding if in their social environment people continue reacting to them in the same or a similar manner as in the past.

Maintaining continuity of *identity* is another major function of the self. In spite of manifold changes in almost all aspects of personality as a result of growth and experience, the individual, nevertheless, recognizes that he is the same person he was ten, twenty, or many more years ago. Many qualities of a person change gradually. This allows self-identity to remain relatively constant throughout the life-span. Some mentally disturbed individuals, however, lose this sense of self-identity and misidentify themselves as extremely powerful or famous personalities.

The genesis of self. It is difficult to discover at what point in development the sense of self emerges. There is an increasing awareness of "me" and "not me," "I can" and "I can't," but when the individual becomes generally conscious of his own body, of his various abilities, of his "good me" and "bad me" is still matter for investigation. The fundamental difficulty with the self-concept is that we know about it only by inference. This is true for the person himself as well as for the observer [7, 27].

William Stern [25, pp. 444–446], the founder of the personalistic system in psychology, traces the development of the child's self-concept through the following phases:

1. The infant clings almost entirely to the present with its chance stimuli and to his sensations of pleasure and displeasure.
2. The child's attention becomes focused upon inner experiences, and processes of deliberation and choice become mingled with the sense impression and the response.
3. A dominant interest maintains a certain stability in spite of diversions tending to elicit other reactions.
4. The power of certain motivations which often have nothing in common with chance stimuli is felt. Such motives become permanent qualities of the child's personality.

Theodore R. Sarbin [23] has formulated an interesting theory concerning the genesis of the self-concept. It begins with a "somatic self" at birth, which remains the core of the self-concept. This somatic self consists of percepts pertaining to the neonate's body, such as sensations of hunger, dampness, or indigestion. This self is later supplemented by a "receptor-effector self," which consists of conceptions of the sense organs and musculature. The "primitive construed self," which follows from the previous two, is a rather vague awareness of self as an individual being. The "social self" emerges at approximately two years as a definite sense of self-identity and an awareness of different roles and of relationships with others. At this time, which marks the beginning of the period of negativism, "I" and "me" are used meaningfully. This rise in self-awareness, occurring at the beginning of the negativistic age, may be seen as the first manifestation of a genuine self-concept.

When an infant becomes aware of his own body and some of its processes, he learns to distinguish between himself and other people or surrounding objects. He has a growing awareness of his inner needs and drives, as well as the objects and conditions gratifying them. Individual selectivity appears, along with many likes and dislikes. The young child chooses to be led by his own desires and wishes. Resistance to parental control at the two- and three-year level can be understood in the light of the child's effort to assert himself. The way parents and others react to the child's behavior either encourages or inhibits him in the process of discovering his own selfhood. Acceptance by others leads to a self-accepting attitude and an ability to live comfortably with his emotions and to stand up for his own preferences and rights.   Self-acceptance is a necessary prerequisite for the development of a healthy personality.

Erik Erikson [8, p. 116] considers the emergence of personal identity as a very important element contributing to the ego structure.   This configuration results from the gradual integration of "constitutional givens, idiosyncratic libidal needs, favored capacities, significant identifications, effective defenses, successful sublimations, and consistent roles."   Through a synthetic process of the ego, personal identity becomes a part of ego identity sometime during the period of adolescence.   Erikson's well-known eight life crises, especially "the battle for autonomy," may be seen as milestones for the self-concept.

The self-concept, being a part of the personality, is influenced by the same factors which affect personality development.   Values are introjected by the self from parents, then from teachers and peers.   The young child, through identification with and training by parental figures, gradually evolves a self-concept consistent with these values.   Reinforcement is practically constant: behavior of the "good me" is rewarded; behavior of the "bad me" is punished.   The ease with which the self-concept can be influenced and its flexibility for change make moral and social training far easier then than later, when the structure of the self has become somewhat more deeply entrenched [24].   According to Harry S. Sullivan, "The self dynamism is built up out of this experience of approbation and disapproval, of reward and punishment." Later on the self dynamism "precludes the experience of anything corrective, anything that would be strikingly different" [27, pp. 20–23].

The theories cited thus far have presented some genetic aspects of the self. The origins of the self-concept are critically reviewed by Charlotte Buhler [6].   Table 5–1 shows her ideas concerning the main stages, relationships, and trends of this concept throughout life.   The research data, however, is fragmentary.   After reviewing the literature on the self, Ruth Wylie [31, p. 119] affirmed that there are "no longitudinal data on which to base a description of the development of the self-concept."   Because of the great differences in methods, subjects, and testing conditions, most cross-sectional studies have added little to the meager body of knowledge available.

The growing self-awareness within the child increases his behavior regulation.   His self-concept becomes a pivot for the integration of past and present experiences.   It establishes an order of priority in his response repertoire to various objects, persons, and situations.   Slowly the self-concept achieves the place of final arbiter in many conflict situations.   Tendencies to act in accordance with the self begin to dominate.   The self becomes an architect of the personality structure, as the individual tends to act more and more in terms of his own dispositions, abilities, and resources. This self-actualization begins early and continues throughout life, but many counteracting factors curb its attainment.

Throughout middle and late childhood, peers and reference groups begin to play a more dominant role, gradually displacing the parent as the primary modifier of the self-concept. The child more and more comes to identify himself with those of his own age and to adopt a code of behavior from the peer group. During middle childhood, the self-concept is fairly stable, owing to the relatively even rate of development of the different personality variables. However, with puberty there is a drastic change in the self-concept. The young adolescent perceives himself as an adult in some ways and in others as a child. Self-control and self-direction must be increased, even though independence from adults is in most cases still impossible for at least several years.

A peculiar problem in our society is the double standard which many parents use in judging their teen-age offspring. In some instances they expect them to act as young adults and judge them accordingly, while in other cases they treat them as children. Since a person's self-concept is in large part formed from others' evaluations of him, this inconsistency on the part of parents only compounds the adolescent's problems.

Because of the extensive changes affecting the adolescent in almost all the areas of his life, the self-concept is also in a state of flux during this period. The uncertainties of the future make the formulation of definite goals a difficult task. However, it is in the resolution of these adolescent problems and conflicts that the self-concept of the adult is born. The values and attitudes which are part of the self-concept at the end of adolescence are those which tend to remain as relatively permanent organizers of behavior.

In early adulthood with its new challenges and responsibilities, the self is tested and proved and by twenty-five or thirty years of age is completely formed. From this age on, the self-concept becomes increasingly resistant to change. In middle adulthood there is generally no change in the basic qualities of the self-concept, except the modification which comes with age and experience.

The increased longevity which man is enjoying today has concomitant drawbacks. With the policy of involuntary retirement so prevalent, the individuals at this time often experience drastic changes in their self-concept. After thirty, forty, or more years as breadwinners and contributing members of society, many of these individuals find themselves relegated to the position of second-class citizens. The ensuing self-devaluation often disturbs the total personality. This idea of growth and decline of the self-concept will be treated more fully in other sections of the text.

Table 5-1.   Buhler's basic tendencies and development of self

Ages	Need satisfaction	Self-limiting adaptation	Creative expansion	Establishing of inner order	Fulfillment
Birth to 1½ yrs	Trust and love, evolvement and discovery of self-sameness				
1½ to 4 yrs		Obedience and superego ideal vs. independence			
4 to 8 yrs			Autonomous, value-setting, ego-ideals aspect of task		
8 to 12 yrs				Attempts toward objective self-evaluation in social roles	
12 to 18 yrs	Sex needs and problem of sexual identity			Review and preview of self-development (autobiographical)	Fulfillment of and detachment from childhood

Table 5-1. Buhler's basic tendencies and development of self (continued)

Age				
18 to 25 (30) yrs	Tentative self-determination to role in society			
25 (30) to 45 (50) yrs		Self-realization in occupation, marriage, and own family		
45 (50) to 65 (70) yrs			Critical self-assessment	
65 (70) to 80 (85) yrs				Self-fulfillment
80 (85) to death	Regression to predominant need-satisfaction			

Source: Charlotte Buhler. Genetic aspects of the self. Ann. New York Acad. Sci., 1962, **115**, 730–764, p. 755. By permission.

QUESTIONS FOR REVIEW

1. Describe the pattern of physiological growth and explain the variations and changes from the prenatal to the adult level.
2. When do the basic emotions such as delight, disgust, anger, and fear appear? Describe Bridges' tree of emotional differentiation.
3. Identify three cognitive processes and explain their functions.
4. Describe Piaget's theory of cognitive development and explain his concept of accommodation.
5. Explain intelligence testing and identify two individual intelligence tests.
6. Explain the concept of learning and identify several means of learning.
7. How does socialization begin? When does the child become cooperative?
8. Define the self-concept and describe a theory of its formation.
9. Explain the effects of the increasing self-awareness of the child. What influence do parents have upon the development of a self-concept?
10. How is social development related to the self-concept?

REFERENCES

I. Selected Reading

1. Flavell, John H. *The developmental psychology of Jean Piaget.* Princeton, N. J.: Van Nostrand, 1963. Piaget's system of cognitive and related operations.
2. Murphy, Lois B. *The widening world of childhood: Paths toward mastery.* New York: Basic Books, 1962. Coping with the environment, inner crises, narcissism; includes the development of identity.
3. Royce, James E. *Man and his nature.* New York: McGraw-Hill, 1961. A philosophical exposition of human powers and motivation forming a neo-scholastic model.

II. Specific References

4. Birns, B. Individual differences in human neonates' responses to stimulation. *Child Developm.,* 1965, **36**, 249–256.
5. Bruner, Jerome S. The growth of mind. *Amer. Psychologist,* 1966, **21**, 1007–1017.
6. Buhler, Charlotte. Genetic aspects of the self. *Ann. New York Acad. Sci.,* 1962, **115**, 730–764.
7. Combs, A. W., and D. W. Sporer. The self, its derivate terms, and research. *J. indiv. Psychol.,* 1957, **13**, 134–145.
8. Erikson, Erik H. *Childhood and society.* New York: Norton, 1950.
9. Garner, W. R. To perceive is to know. *Amer. Psychologist,* 1966, **21**, 11–19.

10. Greulich, William W.   The rationale of assessing the developmental status of children from roentgenograms of the hand and wrist.   *Child Developm.*, 1950, **2**, 33–44.

11. Hunt, J. McVicker.   How children develop intellectually.   *Children,* 1964, **11**, No. 3.

12. Hunt, J. McVicker.   *Intelligence and experience.*   New York: Ronald, 1961.   See also J. P. Guilford.   Intelligence has three facets.   *Science,* 1968, **160**, 615–620.

13. Inhelder, Bärbel, and Jean Piaget.   *The growth of logical thinking from childhood to adolescence.*   New York: Basic Books, 1958.

14. Kinch, John W.   A formalized theory of the self-concept.   *Amer. J. Sociol.,* 1963, **68**, 481–486.

15. La Salle, Dorothy.   *Guidance of children through physical education.* (2nd ed.) New York: Ronald, 1957.

16. Loevinger, Jane.   The meaning and measurement of ego development. *Amer. Psychologist,* 1966, **21**, 195–206.

17. Macy, Icie G., and Harriet J. Kelly.   *Chemical anthropology: A new approach to growth in children.*   Chicago: University of Chicago Press, 1957.

18. Piaget, Jean.   *Les méchanismes perceptifs.*   Paris: Presses Universitaires de France, 1961.

19. Piaget, Jean.   *The construction of reality in the child* (translated by Margaret Cook).   New York: Basic Books, 1954.

20. President's Council on Physical Fitness.   *Adult physical fitness.*   1965.

21. Pressey, Sidney L., and Raymond G. Kuhlen.   *Psychological development through the life span.*   New York: Harper & Row, 1957.

22. Razran, Gregory.   Evolutionary psychology: Levels of learning—and perception and thinking.   In B. Wolman (Ed.) and E. Nagel (Cons. ed.), *Scientific psychology: Principles and approaches.*   New York: Basic Books, 1965.   Chap. 13.

23. Sarbin, T. R.   A preface to a psychological analysis of the self. *Psychol. Rev.,* 1952, **59**, 11–22.

24. Sears, Robert R.   Identification as a form of behavioral development. In Dale B. Harris (Ed.), *The concept of development.*   Minneapolis: University of Minnesota Press, 1957.

25. Stern, William.   *Psychology of early childhood.*   New York: Holt, 1930.

26. Stevenson, Harold W., and Richard D. Odom.   Interrelationships in children's learning.   *Child Developm.,* 1965, **36**, 7–19.

27. Sullivan, Harry S.   *Conceptions of modern psychiatry.*   New York: Norton, 1953 (originally published in 1940).

28. Tanner, J. M.   The regulation of human growth.   *Child Developm.,* 1963, **34**, 817–847.

29. Terman, Lewis M., and Maud A. Merrill. *Stanford-Binet Intelligence Scale: Manual for the third revision, form L-M.* Boston: Houghton Mifflin, 1960.

30. Tuddenham, Read D. Jean Piaget and the world of the child. *Amer. Psychologist,* 1966, **21**, 207–217.

31. Wylie, Ruth C. *The self concept: A critical survey of pertinent research literature.* Lincoln: University of Nebraska Press, 1961.

Part 3
Prenatal Growth and Birth

Parts 1 and 2 analyzed the principles and conditions under which human development takes place. This section will deal with the beginnings and earliest changes within the living organism. It will attempt to identify the factors in operation at conception and during prenatal life. Both beneficial and disturbing influences are treated, in order to present a more complete picture of this crucial phase of early growth.

Although the period within the uterus and the first days of postnatal life constitute a small portion of man's life-span, their significance is tremendous. The very survival of the individual is dependent upon the fine timing and coordination of a myriad of factors. The introduction of any hazardous elements or conditions can have far-reaching effects on the later well-being of the person. Inasmuch as the very bases of behavior, the neuromuscular, glandular, and sensory systems, are formed and integrated during this period, the individual's capacity to adapt himself to his environment is largely determined at this early stage. In addition to these formative processes, the necessary adjustments to extrauterine life, the individual differences evident at birth, and the care needed in the neonatal period are important factors in the future welfare of every human newborn.

PRENATAL DEVELOPMENT

The miracle of growth and development is never more perfectly illustrated than during the period prior to birth. During this time the organism changes from a comparatively simple, hardly visible, single-cell structure to a complex organism of billions of structurally and functionally different cells. The multiplication of cells is not, however, the most remarkable aspect of this period of growth. It is rather the differentiation of these cells into various functioning units which constitutes the most remarkable aspect and real essence of prenatal development. Thus, from the original single cell develop the cells and structures of the receptors, which are sensitive to specific stimuli; the muscle cells, which are capable of contracting and relaxing; glandular cells, which form and secrete a variety of chemicals; and the neurons of the nervous system, which perform a vast array of integrating and controlling functions.

The prenatal stage of development is usually divided into three phases. In each one, specific growth tasks must be accomplished. The fulfillment of these tasks, however, is not accomplished without encountering serious obstacles and dangers. Generally, under normal conditions these obstacles and dangers are overcome.

PERIOD OF THE ZYGOTE

The first phase of prenatal growth is termed the zygote period or period of the ovum. Beginning with the moment of conception, this period extends to about the end of the second week of gestation or pregnancy. As in the other stages of development, essential processes take place in this period. Moreover, definite dangers to the further development of the organism are present. Each stage of development, whether a prenatal stage or some period later in life, is dependent upon what has been accomplished during the preceding stages. In the case of the zygote, development is intrinsically bound to the hereditary disposition established at conception.

As indicated above, the period of the zygote begins with conception, when the nucleus of the male germ cell, the spermatozoon, merges with the nucleus of the female germ cell, the ovum. Ordinarily only one matured ovum is released from the ovaries and passes into one of the Fallopian tubes. In cases where several ova are released simultaneously, the occurrence of multiple births is possible. Through chemical action the male germ cells are attracted toward the ovum. Conception occurs when the ovum is penetrated and fertilized by a single spermatozoon. Although recent evidence indicates that the ovum may be penetrated simultaneously by more than one spermatozoon, conception in such cases fails to occur. But when the ovum is penetrated and fertilized by a single male germ cell, a wave of chemical changes takes place within the female cell, producing a "fertilization membrane." This prohibits penetration by additional spermatozoa [10, p. 12].

Following fertilization, the newly formed zygote normally passes down the Fallopian tube and into the uterus. During this time the uterine walls, through the action of hormones released by the ovaries, are being prepared for the reception of the zygote. Upon arriving in the uterus, the zygote becomes implanted in the wall, if it is sufficiently receptive, and for the first time, it begins to derive nourishment from the mother. (During the days preceding implantation the zygote has subsisted on nourishment provided by the yolk of the ovum.) Once the zygote is implanted, the organism starts its differentiation, and there is a rapid increase in size.

The period prior to implantation, however, has already witnessed notable developmental changes. During this period, the original zygote has continuously divided and redivided until a tiny globule of tissue exists. Moreover, its cells have begun differentiating into an outer layer, from which will develop the supporting structures of the growing organism, and an inner core, from which the new organism itself will develop.

The preceding description is a very brief account of the normal processes occurring during the initial stage of life. However, there are many other events which can take place. For example, the zygote may fail to pass into the uterus. In such a case, it may implant itself in some other area. Such "ectopic pregnancies," estimated to occur once in every 500 conceptions, almost invariably result in the eventual destruction of the organism [7, p.

176]. There is also the danger that, being nourished only by its own yolk, the zygote may perish before implantation can occur. In some cases too, the embryo is dislodged from the uterine wall and miscarriage occurs.

As already mentioned, usually only one ovum is released by the ovaries. In cases where two ova are released and fertilized (each by a different spermatozoon), the offspring are termed fraternal twins. From the discussion of heredity in Chapter 4 it is obvious that the hereditary similarity of such offspring is no greater than that of any other children born of the same parents. Consequently, the tendency of many parents to treat such children in the same manner and to expect the same degree of achievement from each is just as erroneous as to expect a younger child to live up to the norms established by an older sister or brother. This failure to recognize the basic individuality of the person is, as might be expected, even more common in the case of identical twins.

With the conception of identical twins (actually there may be more than two), a single ovum has been fertilized. In the process of cell division occurring early in the zygote period, the individual cells become separated and develop as individual organisms. The hereditary similarity of such offspring is usually complete; the only possible difference would be the result of imperfect cell division in the zygote. In physical appearance, such children often seem exactly alike. But each is a unique person, for neither the prenatal environment nor the sequence of events following birth is identical for such twins.

PERIOD OF THE EMBRYO

With the implantation of the zygote in the wall of the uterus, the second major prenatal period begins. This, the embryonic period, extends until approximately the end of the eighth week of gestation. During this period the rate of growth is tremendous. From a minute globule of tissue no larger than the head of a pin, the body enlarges rapidly in size, weight, and complexity. It is estimated that the fertilized ovum increases about ten thousand times in size by the end of the first month of pregnancy. The extensive changes are vividly illustrated in Figure 6–1, which represents the actual size of the developing embryo from one to seven weeks old.

During this stage the most important changes are not in size and weight, but in the differentiation of tissue into the various structures of the body. Whereas at the beginning of the embryonic stage the organism consisted largely of undifferentiated cells, by the end of the period all the major organs and systems have been developed. Thus, one finds in very rudimentary form

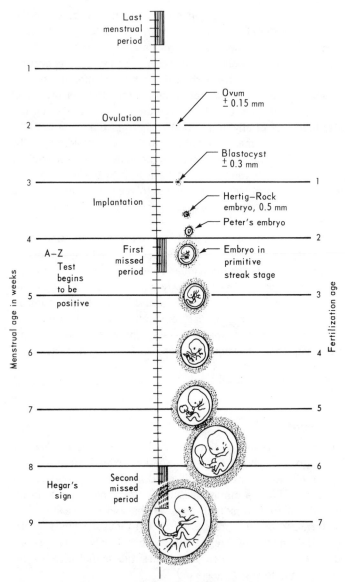

Figure 6–1 Early prenatal mitosis (diagrams showing actual size of embryos and their membranes, based on the mother's menstrual history). (Bradley M. Patten. *Human embryology.* (2nd ed.) New York: McGraw-Hill, 1953. By permission.)

the nervous system, including the brain and spinal cord; the specialized receptor mechanisms, such as the eyes; and the heart, lungs, digestive system, and other organs. Many of these structures and systems are still far from functional. Through the maturational processes of the weeks to follow they will be prepared for their work of sustaining the life of the individual. It should be noted, however, that by the end of the embryonic period the organism has acquired a definitely human form: it is no longer confusable with the embryo of an animal.

The sequence of development during the embryonic stage is quite systematic. Thus, each organ and organ system has a particular time for its emergence. Should a temporary disturbance take place at the time a particular system normally develops, that system will be temporarily or permanently impaired. If, for example, the delicate chemical balance of the mother is upset seriously, the effects on the growing embryo may be permanent, even if the normal balance is later restored. It is for this reason that certain maternal ailments are of particular significance during this period, although the same illnesses are relatively insignificant at a later stage of pregnancy.

The possibility that the embryo may be dislodged and a miscarriage result is also a danger at this period. With the passage of time, however, this threat becomes less. Thus, A. F. Guttmacher [5, pp. 195–206] has estimated that 72 percent of all miscarriages occur by the end of the third month of pregnancy. The causes for miscarriages vary: falls by or injuries to the mother, malnutrition, hormone imbalance, etc. An interesting relationship is found between the incidence of miscarriage and the sex of the embryo. It is estimated that for every 100 female embryos lost, 160 males perish.

PERIOD OF THE FETUS

Whereas the embryonic stage was largely characterized by the differentiation of tissue into the various bodily organs and systems, the fetal period is largely one of refinement and perfection of these systems. One by one, the systems and organs become functional. The fetal phase is also devoted to the preparation of the organism for the act of sustaining itself after birth. Thus, in the course of the fetal period all major organs and systems start functioning, and the organism shows distinctive characteristics of the human body. During the remaining months of prenatal development, the organs and activities necessary for the infant's survival after birth advance to the point of being functional, although they are not yet utilized, for breathing and swallowing. When this point is reached, the fetus is said to have achieved the age of *viability*. Typically this is at about the end of the seventh month of pregnancy, although cases of its beginning at the end of six months have been reported.

During the fetal period all bodily structures show great increase in size and complexity, and many are already in operation. The heart, for example, is beating, and the blood of the fetus is actively circulated. It should be noted, however, that even prior to this time there has been no direct connection between the circulatory system of the mother and that of the fetus. Rather, by means of the umbilical cord, the fetus has absorbed nutrition from the placenta, returning the waste through the same basic mechanism. The blood in the placenta is filtered, and only its particles, including nutritive materials and oxygen, pass to the fetus.

It is fairly certain that neurons (nerve cells) do not increase in number after birth, and their full quota is probably reached by the end of the fifth month of pregnancy. During the sixth month of pregnancy, the cells of the cortex arrange themselves in six layers and preserve this arrangement throughout the entire life-span. Additional neural synaptic connections facilitate perception and learning. Perhaps critical periods, acutely important for the development of some particular functions, are simultaneous with the rapid myelinization process, when a minimum of stimulation produces maximal synaptic patterning. While the rate of myelinization rises during infancy, the nerve fibers of the brain continue to develop throughout childhood and puberty.

Another sign of the gradual preparation of the fetus for extrauterine life is the development of a vast variety of reflexes and general movements. As the pregnancy progresses, such activity becomes increasingly frequent. There are wide individual differences in the amount of motility, some fetuses being active as much as 75 percent of the time, others as little as 5 percent. Although it is a rare occurrence, some hiccup. The basis for all these occurrences is naturally the functioning of the nervous system. In all likelihood the entire nervous system is developed by the end of the fifth month of pregnancy. Quite understandably, however, some parts of the nervous system are not functional until sometime after birth. Each form of activity shown by the fetal organism is "a step in normal development, hence a step in preparation for postnatal behavioral abilities. Furthermore, there is a tendency for voluntary acts, where and when they appear, to develop in a sequence based upon the earlier reflexogenic sequence of prenatal life" [6, p. 120]. ("Reflexogenic sequence" refers to the order of reflex emergence from simple to complex.) Usually, structures develop and are strengthened and exercised in the order in which they appear. This applies to their functioning as well. If it is born prematurely, the infant's chances for survival are reduced because the functions of some organs necessary for sustenance are not completely established. This problem and its psychological significance will be discussed in the next chapter.

INFLUENCES ON PRENATAL DEVELOPMENT

Although there has been much misunderstanding throughout history concerning the basic processes and mechanisms involved in prenatal life itself, possibly even more misunderstanding has surrounded the factors which influence growth and development during this period.   Much remains to be discovered in each of these fields, but considerable progress has been made.

Diet.   The eating habits of the expectant mother have been subject to much misunderstanding.   The old maxim that a mother must "eat enough for two" is one instance.   Despite the fact that the mother supplies all the nutrients for the growing fetus, it definitely is not true that she must eat for two.   Actually, overeating can be a major problem in childbearing since it places a burden of additional weight upon the mother [12].   Extreme malnutrition, of course, also presents a serious problem for the mother and the developing fetus.   This is clearly shown by the high incidence of deformed infants noted in war-ravaged European countries during and after World War II [13].   The proper nutrition of the expectant mother prior to pregnancy is a key factor in satisfactory nutrition during the period of gestation.   During the second and third trimesters of pregnancy the quantities of protein, calcium, iron, and iodine, as well as vitamins A, B-6 or B-12, C, and D, have to be moderately increased in order to meet the demands of fetal growth [2, 9].   Marked deficiency in certain vitamins, minerals, calcium, and proteins seriously affects the developing organism and may produce permanent defects within it [16].   Because the fetus is provided with needed nutrients on a priority basis, the mother suffers first from any deficiency.

Illness.   Depending on its duration, a serious physical problem or severe emotional strain during pregnancy affects the metabolism, oxygen level, and biochemical blood composition of the mother.   This, in turn, might interfere with the course of development of the new individual, for chemical substances unrelated to childbearing would be transmitted to the fetus' circulatory system despite filtration by the placenta.   Overindulgence in smoking and drinking also produces adverse effects on the fetus, as well as large amounts of toxins in the mother's system [15].   The most critical prenatal period is the second and third month of pregnancy, when the fetus' physiological organs and systems are formed.

Lester W. Sontag [14] was able to demonstrate that strong emotional reactions are usually irritating to the fetus.   The movements of fetuses, for example, increased several hundred percent while their mothers were under emotional stress.   Even when the disturbance was brief, heightened behavioral irritability of the fetus lasted as long as several hours.   An unusual amount of activity seems to correlate with a "hyperactive irritable, squirming, crying infant" after birth—a "neurotic" baby.

German measles, or rubella virus, when contracted during the first three months of pregnancy, often results in various malformations, including heart defects, congenital cataracts, and deafness. The first effective vaccine to offer lasting protection against rubella was the one produced by Meyer and Parkman in 1966. The preliminary results of inoculations of human subjects seem to be quite effective. The vaccine may end the dread of rubella, which swept the United States in 1964, affecting over twenty thousand children.

The bacilli of infectious diseases, especially venereal infections; viruses of measles and mumps; disturbed secretion of the pituitary, adrenal, or thyroid glands; toxins; excessive fatigue; and very young or very advanced biological age of the mother are among the causes of disturbed prenatal growth. The seriousness of the disturbance depends greatly on the severity and duration of the harmful influence, as well as the stage of development and strength of the neonate and the mother.

The mother's psychological adaptation to her pregnancy is influenced either favorably or unfavorably by her own adjustment to marriage and family life. Occasionally, fears and anxieties emerge, especially if the family increase was not intended. Joy and an overall feeling of gratification result when both parents have planned for the offspring. If the expectant mother is emotionally mature, and if her husband shows understanding of her situation and needs, there will be a favorable atmosphere. This safeguards her from excessive stress during this important phase of her life.

Generally an expectant mother should live her life as any healthy, active married woman would. She should avoid excesses of any sort but carry on most of her ordinary work and recreation. If her plan of living is well organized, it will provide a balance of work and relaxation [1, pp. 121–122]. If her health is precarious or external circumstances become stressful, consultations with an obstetrician or family physician should be of great assistance in avoiding serious complications. All medication must be reported to and controlled by one physician since the undesirable side effects of too much medicine are numerous.

QUESTIONS FOR REVIEW

1. Give some reasons why psychologists are interested in the prenatal phases of physiological development in the human individual.
2. After implantation of the zygote, what structural changes take place?
3. List several reasons for miscarriage and explain one of them.
4. Describe the functional capabilities of a fetus at about seven months of pregnancy.
5. Explain some of the basic functions of the brain and neural mechanisms.

6. What behavorial equipment is available to the individual after birth?
7. What are the main hazards during the prenatal period of growth?
8. Explain the concept of viability and that of blood incompatibility.
9. What do maternal diet and emotional well-being have to do with fetal development?
10. What relationships did Sontag discover in his study of expectant mothers?

REFERENCES

I. Selected Reading

1. Breckenridge, Marian E., ånd Margaret N. Murphy. *Growth and development of the young child.* (7th ed.) Philadelphia: Saunders, 1963. Chap. 3. Deals with physical and psychological adjustments arising during pregnancy.

2. National Research Council, Food and Nutrition Board. *Recommended dietary allowances.* National Academy of Sciences Publication No. 129, Washington, 1948. Discusses diet and its role for mother, baby, and child.

3. Patten, Bradley M. *Human embryology.* (2nd ed.) New York: McGraw-Hill, 1953. A comprehensive reference work on fertilization and the prenatal development of various somatic systems.

4. Stern, Curt. *Principles of human genetics.* (2nd ed.) San Francisco: Freeman, 1960. A general treatment of the laws and tendencies of early human development.

II. Specific References

5. Guttmacher, A. F. Miscarriages and abortions. In M. Fishbein and E. W. Burgess, *Successful marriage.* New York: Doubleday, 1955.

6. Hooker, Davenport. *The prenatal origin of behavior.* Lawrence, Kans.: University of Kansas Press, 1952.

7. Irving, F. C., and A. T. Hertig. A study of placenta accreta. *Surg. Gynec. Obstetr.,* 1937, **64**, 176–200.

8. Lieberman, M. W. Early developmental stress and later behavior. *Science,* 1963, **141**, 824–825.

9. Peckos, Penelope S. Nutrition during growth and development. *Child Developm.,* 1957, **28**, 273–285.

10. Raven, C. P. *An outline of developmental physiology.* New York: McGraw-Hill, 1954. See also Jerry Hirsch (Ed.), *Behavior-genetic analysis.* McGraw-Hill, 1967.

11. Rogers, Martha E., et al. *Prenatal and paranatal factors in the development of childhood behavior disorders.* Johns Hopkins University, School of Hygiene and Public Health. Baltimore: Johns Hopkins, n. d. (ca. 1955).

12. Shock, N. W.   Physiological factors in development.   *Rev. educ. Res.*, 1947, **17**, 362–370.

13. Smith, C. A.   Effects of maternal malnutrition upon the newborn infant in Holland.   *J. Pediat.*, 1947, **30**, 229–243.

14. Sontag, L. W.   The significance of fetal environmental differences. *Amer. J. Obstetr. Gynec.*, 1941, **42**, 996–1003.

15. Sontag, L. W., and T. W. Richards.   Studies in fetal behavior.   1. Fetal heart rate as a behavioral indicator.   *Monogr. Soc. Res. Child Developm.*, 1938, **3**, No. 4.

16. Warkany, J.   Congenital malformations induced by maternal nutritional deficiency.   *J. Pediat.*, 1944, **25**, 476–480.

THE HUMAN AT BIRTH

BIRTH

Birth is that process during which the developing infant is transferred from its uterine and liquid environment to that of the external world. Although it is impossible to set the exact date for the expected birth, it usually occurs at the end of the tenth lunar month, or about 266 days after conception. At birth, prenatal development is complete and is followed by infancy, a stage of lesser dependence and of many rapid changes.

About two weeks prior to birth, *lightening* takes place: the fetus descends into the lower abdominal cavity; the head of the fetus sinks into the pelvis, and its body falls a little forward. After lightening, the mother can breathe more easily because the upper abdomen and chest are relieved of pressure caused by the previous fetal position. The onset of labor is usually preceded by one or all of the following occurrences: (1) false labor pains caused by irregular, intermittent contractions of the uterus, (2) pink, blood-tinged discharge from the vagina, and (3) rupture of the membranes containing the fetus and amniotic fluid.

Birth is accomplished by rhythmic contractions of the uterine muscles at diminishing intervals, which exercise pressure, causing the expectant mother to feel pain and become more aware of the pending birth of her child. The successive and increasingly powerful contractions rupture the membranes containing the fetus and, after several hours of labor, send the infant into its new state of existence.

Three stages of labor may be distinguished. The first is characterized by uterine contractions. These continue to become more regular and harder and occur with greater frequency, lasting for longer periods of time. Also during the first stage of labor, the birth canal widens in preparation for the passage of the fetus. The second stage of labor brings about the actual birth of the child. The contractions are very hard, and the membranes containing the amniotic fluid often rupture early in this stage. In the third stage the placenta is expelled from the uterus. Since only the hospital will have all the equipment necessary to facilitate the process of birth and especially to meet any emergency that may arise during birth, including any special care the newborn may need, hospitalization is generally a necessity. When the first stage of labor—the longest—begins, it is time to inform the family physician or obstetrician and to prepare to leave for the hospital on his advice.

During the stages of labor, the mother should make repeated efforts to relax and rest between contractions and to bear down with her abdominal muscles while contractions are occurring. If she has little or no fear of this natural process, she is composed and therefore requires less analgesic (pain-relieving) medication. Although the average time of labor is approximately sixteen hours, it may last much longer or be considerably briefer. The length of the labor period is usually longest for the firstborn and shorter for later pregnancies. The contractions during the advanced stages of labor are severe and painful: they reach about 10 dols, normal sensitivity being approximately 11 dols. The psychological state of the patient makes pains more or less tolerable, but the frequently used spinal anesthetic affords much relief.

Many hospitals and obstetricians offer expectant mothers an opportunity to attend prenatal classes. One of the objectives of these classes is to teach the mother about natural childbirth in order to help her overcome fear of it. The mother is taught physical exercises and deep abdominal breathing which will help her to relax. At the time of delivery, the deep abdominal breathing will not only give the unborn baby better oxygenation but decrease the mother's pain. If the abdominal muscles are not tense, there will be less resistance to the actual progress of birth. It has been observed that this practice has reduced the time of labor by as much as two hours.

Hypnosis is also coming into use to facilitate the mother's relaxation and cooperation. In the hypnotic trance she is better disposed to assist at her own delivery. In some cases with complications such as heart weakness or a preceding spinal illness, that make the use of anesthetic or analgesic drugs inadvisable, hypnosis seems to be the only adequate substitute. To assure a successful hypnosis, one or two preparatory sessions are necessary for checking and raising the suggestibility of the expectant mother. No detrimental side effects are reported from hypnosis, and it is safe for the baby.

After childbirth, it is important that the mother rest for at least five to seven days. The trend today is for mothers to be out of bed within a day or two after the birth of the baby, depending upon the orders of the doctor. Getting up soon after delivery, referred to as *early ambulation,* seems to have definite advantages. The mother becomes stronger much sooner, there are fewer complications, such as thrombophlebitis (thrombus formation due to infection of the wall of the vein), and there is less discomfort since normal functions, such as bowel and urinary excretions, are resumed sooner if the mother is up and around. There seem to be very few, if any, disadvantages accompanying early ambulation for the normal, healthy mother, but other conditions, such as a heart disease or a very difficult delivery, may call for a modification of practice.

There should be very few visitors for the new mother both because she needs rest and because there is danger of infection being carried in to mother or baby. She should care for her baby at the assigned times. This helps her get acquainted with and feel concerned about the infant.

Many hospitals conduct classes for the mothers in their obstetrical divisions. In these classes the mothers are taught how to care for their babies' bathing, feeding, and dress, and to make a formula and diet. Films and other audiovisual aids are often used in these teaching programs. Acquiring a variety of skills in infant care, such as those related to dressing, bathing,

Figure 7–1   Infant and maternal mortality rates: U. S., 1930–1970. (*Health and vital statistics for the United States: Summary,* revised 1960; *The facts of life and death: Selected statistics on the nation's health and people.* National Center for Health Statistics, No. 600, revised 1965; and *Monthly vital statistics report, final mortality statistics, 1965.* 1966, **15**, No. 10.)

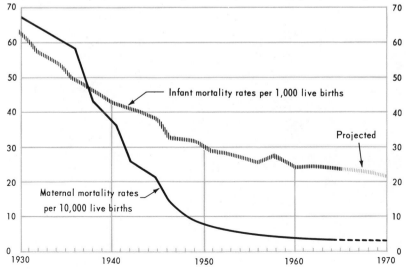

carrying, and feeding, gives the mother feelings of adequacy and security—feelings she really needs in infant rearing, especially for her first child. A number of mothers need assistance with housework for two to three weeks, in order to have frequent rest intervals, thus preventing contraction of infection due to a lowered state of resistance. Most mothers report the ability to assume normal duties within a week despite the postpartum bleeding.

Some U. S. population statistics will help to illustrate several important trends in the nation's vital data. From 1954 to 1964 the annual number of live births varied within the range of 4.0 and 4.3 million, but in 1965 it dropped to 3,760,358. In 1965, 97.4 percent of all births were in hospitals, 0.9 percent were attended by physicians outside hospitals, and 1.5 percent by midwives. The median weight at birth for live-born infants in 1960 was 3,310 grams, in 1963 3,290 grams, and in 1965 3,270 grams, or about 7 pounds 4 ounces for these years. Statistics also indicate the decreasing rate of fetal and infant deaths. A substantial decrease has occurred in the maternal death ratio per 10,000 childbirths: 1939, 39.7; 1950, 8.3; 1955, 4.7; 1960, 3.71. Figure 7–1 points out this continuing trend toward rapid decrease in deaths of mothers from 1930 to 1965, which is due particularly to the improvements in medical service.

As Figure 7–2 indicates, in 1947 nearly four million were born in the United States, the largest number in the history of the country until then. During that year, the birth rate soared to its highest point in decades. The predicted drop in the birth rate since 1947 has been smaller than expected,

Figure 7–2 Live births and fertility rates, 1910–1965. (*Monthly vital statistics report: Final nativity statistics, 1965, 1966,* **15**, *No. 8.*)

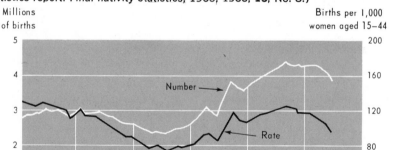

Table 7–1. Life data: United States

	Year				
	1940	1950	1955	1960	1965
Total births:					
Registered	2,360,399	3,554,149	4,047,295	4,257,850	3,760,358
Adjusted for underregistration	2,558,647	3,631,512	4,104,112		
Live birth rate per 1,000:					
Registered	17.9	23.61	24.61	23.7	19.4
Adjusted for underregistration	19.4	24.1	25.0		
Fetal deaths:					
Ratio per 1,000	31.3	22.9	22.7	22.2	
Total	73,802	801,300	91,907	94,452	93,200
Infants under one year, deaths:					
Ratio per 1,000	47.0	29.2	26.4	26.0	24.7
Total	110,894	103,825	106,903	110,873	93,200
Delivery:					
Physician in hospital	55.8%	88%	94.4%	96.6%	97.4%
Midwife			2.9%	2.0%	1.5%
Immature birth:					
2,500 grams or less			7.7%	7.7%	8.1%

Source: *Vital statistics of the United States: 1965*, Vol. 1, 1967; *Monthly vital statistics report*, Vol. 14, No. 12, 1966; and United Nations, *Demographic yearbook 1965*, 1966.

and the following decade even presented a slight rise. The 1960s witnessed a moderate decrease. As seen in Table 7–1 and Figure 7–2, the vitality of the nation continued unabated into the early 1960s. Since that time, the population of the United States has been growing at a decreasing rate.

THE NEONATE

The neonate is usually well equipped to respond and make a variety of adjust-ments to the demands of reality. The immense stimulation of the skin and deeper regions of the body produced by the contracting muscles of the uterus helps to activate the respiratory system, as well as the gastrointestinal and genitourinary tracts [13, p. 140]. These are the vital functions the newborn must be able to control (respiration, digestion, and elimination). The sudden exposure to a new environment necessitates this usually successful struggle for biological existence. The newborn infant's utter helplessness and vulner-ability engage assistance from people in the environment. "Defenseless as babies are, there are mothers at their command, families to protect the mothers, societies to support the structure of families and traditions to give a cultural continuity to systems of tending and training" [6, p. 151].

The early phase of infancy is marked by a rapid succession of developments in the physiological, motor, emotional, language, and perceptual aspects of growth. At this time, the newborn child attains a measure of integration and control over the various organs and functions of his body and gives increasing attention to the objects and persons of his surroundings. As a result, the infant expands his activities, decreasing his helplessness and enabling him to take his first steps toward an autonomous existence.

ADJUSTMENT AND DEVELOPMENTS

The beginning of life after birth is primarily a time for adjusting to the many situations encountered outside the mother's womb. The birth cry is a re-flexive inhalation and exhalation of air across the vocal cords, which are tightened by the shock or trauma associated with the change to the air pres-sure and temperature of the extrauterine environment. It marks the begin-ning of vocal communication of needs. During the first few weeks of post-natal life, sounds produced by the neonate are only vocal reactions of varying intensity to sensations, such as cold, hunger, dampness, pain, and digestive discomfort. Discomfort in the digestive system, for example, colic or indiges-tion, is one of the main reasons for neonatal crying.

The infant soon reaches a point at which he has developed new processes and activities, allowing him a less dependent existence. It is true that the various physiological developments prior to birth laid a satisfactory founda-tion for vital processes, yet for several days, if not weeks or months, their organization remains very precarious. This is especially true of the digestive system and of the neuromuscular system. Whether breast or formula feeding is introduced, physical growth in terms of weight shows a loss for several days. During the first four days of life, the neonate loses 6 to 9 percent of his weight or as much as 6 or 7 ounces before he begins to gain and recover it in seven to nine days. The early neonate phase is, in this sense, a plateau stage, but loss of weight is sufficiently balanced by other developments. Usually during the second week, there is a period of rapid growth which continues afterward, to a lesser degree, throughout the total span of infancy.

During the first phase of postnatal life the infant learns to cope with his particular environment by means of his senses and motor functions. He is very sensitive to tactual stimuli and to changes in his position. The baby quickly makes use of his somesthetic (skin and muscular) sensations. The temperature senses are sufficiently developed so that the neonate reacts vividly to cold or warm stimuli. The development of the taste and smell receptors is fairly advanced, and they contribute to the infant's process of nutrition. Opening and closing of the mouth occurs spontaneously as part of the infant's "search" movements and efforts to suckle. Salty, acid, or bitter solutions usually make the infant stop sucking, while sweet solutions elicit and maintain this reaction. Reaction to visual stimuli is marked by the closing of the eyes when a flash of light is applied to either one eye or both, and by expansion and contraction of the pupils in response to decreased or increased light intensity. Some auditory stimuli of ordinary intensity cause a momentary suspension of activity.

In addition to random motion, the neonate exhibits a considerable repertoire of behavior, such as fairly precise "search" movements, as well as sucking, swallowing, rejecting substances from the mouth, yawning, sneezing, holding his breath, and vocalizing. Hands and feet also produce several reflex patterns: the *Babinski* reflex, an upward and fanning movement of the toes as a response to stroking of the soles; the *Moro* reflex, a clutching movement of the arms and legs, resulting from a blow to the surface on which the neonate is lying and to intense sounds; knee jerk; palmar reflex; and rubbing the face. Nursing posture and startle response involve some coordination of parts of the body [5]. The newborn child also shows some fine sensory discriminations indicative of coded input [11]. Many of these responses are protective or need-satisfying and therefore continue to be exhibited in modified forms later.

Parents or observers also notice the neonate's capacity for emotional response. This is marked by pervasive excitement and is usually accompanied by crying and signs of displeasure. Relaxation and sleep signify lack of emotionally exciting stimuli. This restful state can be induced by picking the baby up and carrying him on the shoulder, by rocking him, and by feeding.

The quantity, quality, and complexity of sensory and motor responses increase at a considerable speed during the early months of postnatal life.

PROBLEMS OF SURVIVAL

Since the newborn child faces many new tasks, he is likely to have some difficulties early in life.   Growth and learning are determined largely by parental care, which either satisfies or frustrates the intrinsic biogenic and psychogenic needs.

One of the frequent problems related to the satisfying of biogenic needs is feeding.   In the hospital or at home, the scheduled feeding hours are often unsatisfactory since the baby is likely to get hungry early, cry himself to sleep, and show little initiative at the scheduled time.   Self-demand feeding usually does a better job, although it does not guarantee either sucking satisfaction or the intake of a sufficient amount of food.   The infant may show poor response to breast and formula feeding alike; diarrhea and vomiting are not infrequent.

Setting up a gratifying feeding situation is a task for mother and infant alike.   S. Escalona [7] and R. S. Illingworth [10] indicate the importance of the feeding method, noting that the emotional tone with which the baby accepts his food is often traceable to the mother's attitude and her level of relaxation while she is feeding him.   A baby can sense tension in the person who has intimate contact with him.   Quietly talking to the baby, handling him with slow and deliberate movements, and attempting to gain the infant's attention are all of considerable significance in avoiding feeding problems. Robert P. Odenwald [16, pp. 16–17] considers the periods of feeding the most important moments of the infant's life.   It helps to satisfy his sucking urge and offers psychological pleasure and emotional gratification for both the baby and his mother.   Whether nursed at the breast or bottle-fed, the mother's holding the baby in her arms while he is taking nourishment is of great importance.   There is no substitute for the affectionate care expressed at these moments, which every child urgently needs.

Although the average food intake per day during the first year of life is about two ounces to every pound of body weight, no definite amount can be stipulated; the quantity depends upon the neonate's level of maturity, which is difficult to estimate.   Prematurely born infants are capable of digesting only much smaller amounts of food than full-term babies.   Too often, however, parents believe that a certain amount of food must be taken in order to grow adequately.   As a result, they use various techniques to increase the amount and by doing this magnify discomforts within the digestive system. Both the amount of milk and the timing have to be flexible to adjust to the changing physiological and experiential states of the infant.

Many experiments have been conducted to study the genesis of the suckling response. A survey by S. Ross and others [18] of fifty-seven pertinent investigations points to the possibility of an instinctual drive, the functional activity of which increases when infants are exposed to sucking frustration. The experimental evidence does not point to any definite relationship between sucking variation and later patterns of behavior.

A condition known as *colic* can cause new parents much anxiety. Colic in infants is characterized by a sudden onset of loud and persistent crying with the knees drawn up to the abdomen. The abdomen is tense and distended. An attack may last 1½ or 2 hours, but in some cases it may continue many hours. The cause is frequently a digestive disturbance. One cause is air in the intestines which the baby swallowed during feeding and has not eliminated by burping. When the baby is able to expel the air through the rectum, he is usually relieved. Other causes of colic are overfeeding or an intake of formula that is too rich or otherwise disagreeable to the baby. Even the casein in milk can cause a digestive disturbance, and an allergy to a certain element in the diet can lead to much distress, in which case the type of feeding formula should be changed. Some babies who are allergic to cow's milk have to be fed goat's milk or milk made from soybeans. At times colic may be due to organic causes, such as appendicitis or intussusception, an entanglement of the intestines, which may require immediate surgical treatment. Whatever the reasons for a baby's high level of irritability, a pediatrician should be consulted and the baby treated according to the doctor's advice.

The expectant mother's adherence to medical regulations combined with the prenatal education in baby care offered by hospitals and other institutions have made major contributions to the prevention of early infancy diseases. This has also guarded the biological welfare of the infant against the "experimental" trial-and-error approach in the management of the first child during his first and most crucial year of life. Some dangers, however, still exist. Epidemic diarrhea in newborn infants is a serious condition which often results in death. For approximately 40 percent of infants, epidemic diarrhea is fatal [21, p. 790]. Pneumonia in neonates is serious, but with modern methods of treatment, barring other complications, chances of survival have increased. Syphilis also is now under better control since the discovery of penicillin.

The first day of life is the most critical for the neonate's survival. If the birth process is for some reason prolonged or if sedative drugs are used excessively or are used more than two hours prior to birth, the fetus may suffer a lack of oxygen, producing a state of anoxia; this anoxia, if prolonged, rapidly damages the sensitive tissues of the brain to the point of affecting the vital functions of the organism. Sedatives and analgesics, especially morphine, depress the infant's respiration so much that at birth there may be considerable difficulty in initiating the newborn infant's breathing. This is even more pronounced if a general anesthetic (instead of a spinal) is administered, in addition to sedatives. Great skill and caution must be exercised when these drugs are used, since individuals differ in their capacity to profit from them.

A direct source of danger to the survival of the neonate is birth injury resulting from delivery with surgical instruments or the excessive pressure caused by severe contractions or a too narrow passageway in the birth canal. Many newborn infants show a high tendency to hemorrhage, and some suffer from the interruptions of gas metabolism [19]. When delivery is complicated, a bone fracture, a neck injury, or damage to the spinal cord severe enough to cause paralysis and possibly death may result.

Brain injury due to pressure or anoxia may be so widespread as to deprive the newborn of his intelligence potential and lower his attainable IQ. Arnold Gesell [8], K. C. Pratt [17], and A. F. Tredgold [20] agree that various brain injuries accompanying birth account for about 5 to 10 percent of all mental deficiency cases. It might be added that the same causes often lead to complications and hinder the process of neonatal adjustment.

At times, certain physiological conditions and congenital malformations are present at birth which may threaten the infant's life. One normal physiological condition that presents some danger to the newborn infant is the mucus in his mouth which he may aspirate into his lungs as he breathes. To prevent this, immediately after birth, the obstetrician or nurse drains out the excess mucus from the baby's mouth and throat before he begins to breathe. In the nursery, babies are watched closely for any signs of difficult breathing or excess mucus.

There is an Rh hemolytic condition, known as *erythroblastosis fetalis*, which may afflict a fetus whose blood type is Rh+ and whose mother's type is Rh—. The Rh factor exists in about 85 percent of all humans. Rh incompatibility usually occurs when an Rh— mother is pregnant with an Rh+ fetus for the *second* time. During her *first* such pregnancy, Rh+ in the fetus' blood (inherited from an Rh+ father) sensitizes the mother, and she produces antibodies usually several weeks after delivery. These antibodies become activated about thirty weeks after the next conception of an Rh+ fetus. Some of them penetrate the placenta and cause a breakdown of the fetus' blood cells. If born alive, the baby becomes jaundiced and needs exchange transfusions in which some of his blood is drawn out and replaced with fresh blood. However, even massive blood transfusions save only about half the afflicted infants.

Eight years' research by three scientists (Vincent J. Freda, John G. Gorman, and William Pollack) has resulted in the discovery of a new vaccine, Rhogam, which after successful testing in 1968 was approved for marketing. Offering effective but temporary protection against Rh blood incompatibility, it must be administered once after every Rh+ childbirth.

Among the more frequent congenital defects which present danger to an infant's survival are hydrocephalus, spina bifida, and heart defects. The *hydrocephalic* condition (pressure of cerebrospinal fluid within the skull) eventually leads to death if untreated, and even with surgical intervention the life expectancy is short. *Spina bifida,* which is a defect of the spinal column, occurs in various forms. If it is a kind that involves the spinal cord directly, little can be done to prolong the infant's life, which usually ends as a result of secondary infection. Some kinds of spina bifida can be removed by a surgical procedure. Heart defects also may be various in kind. Some of them can be corrected providing the infant lives long enough to undergo surgery. Sometimes it is a full year before surgery can be performed, and during that time there may be many episodes of difficult breathing and upper respiratory infections, since this type of infant is especially susceptible to them. There are other congenital malformations equally dangerous but much less frequent, such as an abnormal opening in the trachea or a malformed digestive tract.

Attention has recently been given to babies born of narcotic-addicted mothers. It has been observed by obstetricians and pediatricians that babies born of addicted mothers manifest withdrawal symptoms after delivery, the severity of which depends upon the amount of drug taken and the time of the last dose prior to delivery, as well as the frequency with which the mother was accustomed to take the drug. Many babies of addicted mothers have died as a result of withdrawal reactions, especially if the baby's difficulty was unnoticed and therefore untreated. With treatment, the chances of survival are fairly good, and the baby can be cured of the addiction. Whether a baby cured of addiction will later in life be emotionally unbalanced and readily resort to narcotics is as yet unknown to science.

Premature births are often prolonged and cataclysmic, and subject the infant to greater than normal stress. The organism of the premature is somewhat fragile and generally not ready for birth [2; 3; 14, p. 73; 19]. His lungs may not be developed enough to allow for an adequate exchange of gases, or his digestive system may not be sufficiently developed to utilize milk and break it into the proper compounds for use in cellular life. Susceptibility to infections of various kinds is considerable in the premature infant since his immunity level is low. Secondary infections, such as pneumonia or diarrhea, may seriously threaten his life, even when he is several months old.

If a neonate weighs less than 2,500 grams (5 pounds 8 ounces) or has a gestation period of less than thirty-seven weeks, he is usually considered premature. Since 1950 the recorded percentage of premature births in this country has been about $7\frac{1}{2}$ percent and has varied only slightly from year to year.   Many hospitals do not discharge such infants until they reach their proper weight, unless they are one of triplets or twins.

Chances of mortality are inversely proportional to the infant's birth weight. About one-third of infant deaths under one year of age are due to prematurity, and almost one-half of the infants who die in the first month of life are premature babies [21, p. 698].   Figure 7–3 presents the causes of infant mortality under one year and reveals the changes in it for the decade from 1951 to 1961.   The decrease in the mortality rate is continuing, and the 1971 statistics may decline at a rate comparable to that which was witnessed from 1951 to 1961.

The psychological effects of prematurity are also numerous.   This fact per se arouses the concern and anxiety of parents, which in turn stirs up feelings and attitudes of overprotectiveness.   The difficulties in feeding the premature and the small amounts of fluid taken by the infant reinforce parental

Figure 7–3   Infant mortality: main causes by international lists (sixth and seventh revisions): United States, 1951 and 1961.   (*Trends in infant and childhood mortality*, 1961.   U. S. Department of Health, Education, and Welfare, Children's Bureau Statistical Series No. 76, 1964, p. 19.)

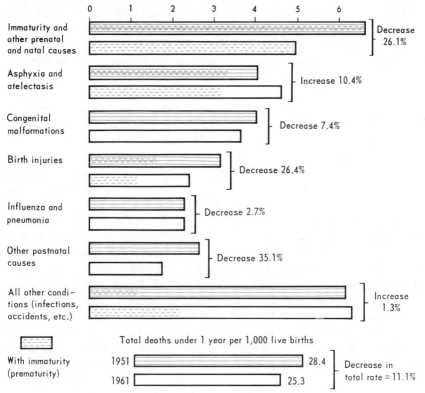

anxieties. Yet studies on prematurity suggest that, if the *corrected* chronological age (CCA) is used as a means to estimate growth and behavior, the premature baby develops satisfactorily [4]. The CCA of a premature infant is counted from the time of conception rather than birth. Thus, a premature infant born at thirty-five weeks of gestation has an age allowance of five weeks whenever his behavior or maturity is appraised in terms of age norms. If the overprotective attitude assumed toward the child persists, it tends to interfere with the normal course of his self-development. The need for assistance from others becomes deeply ingrained in the attitudinal system of the individual. Thus, the psychological impact on those who are born prematurely often continues throughout childhood and later.

INDIVIDUAL DIFFERENCES

After birth, individuals differ in all observable aspects. Much significance is attributed to differences in weight. The neonate normally is close to 20 inches in length and weighs approximately 7 pounds 3 to 4 ounces, but individual variation is great. Nearly two-fifths of those born in the 1960s weighed between 3,001 and 3,500 grams. On the average, female babies weighed 120 grams less than male babies [22]. In multiple births, the average weight is about 5 pounds. In some cases individuals of single birth have been as much as double the normal weight. (The weight of premature babies has already been taken up.)

Amounts of sleep and vocalization, characteristic positions the infant assumes, amounts and patterns of activity, eating patterns, and thresholds of sensitivity and acuity to various sensory stimuli, all differ in a variety of ways from one infant to another. One newborn infant requires feeding every 2½ to 3 hours, while another infant easily waits for about 4 hours. Differences in irritability and in response to external stimuli are often very marked. Some infants are highly reactive and irritable and awake at the slightest touch or beam of light. These reactions are a forecast of temperamental and cognitive differences which will influence these individuals' adjustments all through life. At birth one can even get a preview of the individual's body build. The infant may have small hands and feet, a short neck, and a rounded body. He may be small-boned and tend toward a slim structure, or he may be a sturdy muscular type. Infants in the same family, even fraternal twins, differ considerably. One twin, for example, may awaken frequently at night and have episodes of colic while the other sleeps peacefully.

As infants grow older, more and more differences can be seen. The ages at which teeth appear, the child first stands, takes his first steps, and speaks his first words vary as much as six or eight months from one child to another. One infant may be advanced in one aspect of development, such as creeping, standing, and walking, but slower in another area of development, such as speech. At the neonatal stage and later, baby girls are usually a little further advanced than boys in various aspects of development. Their ossification proceeds faster; locomotion, teething, and progress in vocalization also occur earlier. The rate of mortality is also lower for both premature and full-term girls. Female babies show more resistance to infection, colds, and other noxious influences.

QUESTIONS FOR REVIEW

1. What are the main signs indicating that the time for birth is approaching?
2. What is the chief means for pain control in childbirth and why must it be used cautiously?
3. Why is a hospital the most advantageous place for childbirth to occur?
4. Why should expectant mothers be trained? Does this apply to all mothers?
5. What do U. S. statistics show about the decline in maternal and infant deaths?
6. What are the most frequent difficulties in an infant's early postnatal adjustment? Elaborate upon two of them.
7. Explain the significance of crying and give several reasons for it.
8. Describe physical development during the first month of life.
9. List kinds of behavior of which the neonate is capable. Analyze their nature and effects on his adjustment.
10. How do various patterns of feeding affect the baby? Consider the mother's attitude.
11. Explain premature births and their effects on postnatal adjustment.
12. Discuss individual differences among newborn infants, including differences between boys and girls.

REFERENCES

I. Selected Reading

1. American Academy of Pediatrics. *Standards and recommendations on the hospital care of new born infants.* Evanston, Ill., 1964. An authoritative presentation of sound and desirable hospital practices.

2. Collaborative Perinatal Research Project. *Five years of progress.* National Institute of Neurological Diseases and Blindness, National Institute of Health, Bethesda, Md., 1963. A major investigation by fourteen medical institutions of the long-term effects of pregnancy and delivery following up forty thousand cases until 1972 when the offspring will be age seven.

3. Drillien, C. M., and R. W. B. Ellis. *The growth and development of the prematurely born infant.* Baltimore: Williams & Wilkins, 1964. A summary of a longitudinal study, involving over one thousand infants in Edinburgh, two-thirds of whom were premature.

4. Gesell, Arnold. *Infant development: The embryology of early behavior.* New York: Harper & Row, 1952. A careful physiological and medical study of early development and factors contributing to behavior organization.

II. Specific References

5. Dennis, Wayne. A description and classification of the responses of the new-born. *Psychol. Bull.,* 1934, **31**, 5–22. See also B. Birns, Individual differences in human neonates' responses to stimulation. *Child Developm.,* 1965, **36**, 249–256.

6. Erikson, Erik H. The roots of virtue. In J. Huxley (Ed.), *The humanist frame.* New York: Harper & Row, 1961. Pp. 145–166.

7. Escalona, S. Feeding disturbances in very young children. *Amer. J. Orthopsychiat.,* 1945, **15**, 76–80.

8. Gesell, A., and C. Amatruda. *Developmental diagnosis.* (2nd ed.) New York: Harper & Row, 1947.

9. Goodfriend, M. J., et al. The effects of maternal narcotic addiction on the newborn. *Amer. J. Obstetr. Gyn.,* 1956, **71**, 29–35.

10. Illingworth, R. S. Common difficulties in infant feeding. *Brit. Med. J.,* 1949, **2**, 1077–1081.

11. Kessen, William. Research in the psychological development of infants: An overview. *Merrill-Palmer Quart.,* 1963, **9**, 83–94.

12. Kunstadter, T. H., et al. Narcotic withdrawal symptoms in newborn infants. *J. Amer. med. Ass.,* 1958, **168**, 1008–1010.

13. Montagu, Ashley. *The human revolution.* Cleveland: World Publishing, 1965.

14. Mussen, Paul H., and John J. Conger. *Child development and personality.* New York: Harper & Row, 1956.

15. National Center for Health Statistics. *The facts of life and death: Selected statistics on the nation's health and people.* (Rev. ed.) U. S. Dept. of Health, Education, and Welfare, 1965.

16. Odenwald, Robert P. *Your child's world from infancy through adolescence.* New York: Random House, 1958.

17. Pratt, K. C. The neonate. In L. Carmichael (Ed.), *Manual of child psychology.* New York: Wiley, 1954. Pp. 215–291.

18. Ross, S., et al. Sucking behavior: A review of the literature. *J. genet. Psychol.,* 1957, **91**, 63–81.

19. Schwartz, Philip. *Birth injuries of the newborn.* New York: Hafner, 1961.

20. Tredgold, A. F., and K. Soddy. *A textbook of mental deficiency.* (9th ed.) Baltimore: Williams & Wilkins, 1956.

21. Van Blarcom, Carolyn C., and Erna Ziegel. *Obstetrical nursing.* New York: Macmillan, 1957.

22. *Vital statistics of the United States: 1965.* Vol. I. 1967.

Part 4
Infancy

Although many developments during infancy are preconditioned by intra-uterine growth, a great deal of behavioral differentiation results from external stimulation and the parental approach to child care. Unlike other mammals, man's prolonged infancy exposes him to the hazards of extreme parental dependence. Internal and external influences set a pattern that will continue to affect the individual during later phases of life.

Throughout infancy rapid growth occurs in the physical, sensorimotor, emotional, language, and cognitive areas. Middle infancy is marked by gains in control over large muscle groups and various parts of the body; later infancy is characterized by the acquisition of locomotion and speaking facility, abilities which serve as communicators of personality qualities and traits. Increasing self-awareness and ego formation are usually accompanied by a marked resistance to parental control and strivings for autonomy.

Developmental tasks of infancy include learning new modes of locomotion, learning to take solid foods, establishing daytime toilet control, learning to communicate by gestures and words, as well as learning to relate emotionally to parents, siblings, and other persons in the home environment. At the beginning of the third year, foundations are laid for further development in most aspects of the human self-organizing system.

MIDDLE INFANCY

Middle infancy extends from the time when the infant begins to make satisfactory adjustments to the tasks of gratifying his biological needs until the time when he takes his first steps independently and begins to use speech as a means of communication. For the majority of children, this happens at the thirteen- to fifteen-month level; for some, later; for others, earlier. Throughout middle infancy, the developing individual depends almost wholly upon parental care for gratification of his needs. The middle stage of infancy is marked by rapid physiological, emotional, and sensorimotor developments and by substantial increments in height and weight. It is also the phase of intense learning of new modes of behavior.

MOTOR DEVELOPMENTS AND CONTROL

The infant's control of the large muscles and other parts of the body increases to a significant extent in middle infancy. Since muscle control is governed by cephalocaudal as well as proximodistal sequence, the balance of head movements is established before trunk and extremities reach the same level of development. Crawling allows for some movement at five months; creeping and standing are often acquired at ten months. At six or seven months, the baby is able to grasp, hold, and manipulate small objects and put them into his mouth. He observes objects and persons best when they are in motion, and such perception may be lost when they cease to move. The span of attention gradually lengthens. Motor activities increase the baby's ability to satisfy his curiosity and partially to enhance rising cognitive and social interests, the advancement of which is a major characteristic of the later phase of infancy.

Charlotte Buhler [1] explored daily cycles of routine behavior in several groups of American and Austrian infants during the first year of life. Figure 8–1 is based on a Viennese group at one month (N=7) and one year (N=5) of age. It is noteworthy that experimenting, absent at the one-month level, occupies 63 percent of the waking time of a one-year-old [1, p. 143]. With the theoretical interpretation of her data, Buhler introduced the concept of *maturational* sequence—the idea that the order for the appearance of specific patterns is the same for all individuals (but the time of appearance varies from person to person). Using a different approach, Arnold Gesell and H. M. Halverson [10] made a cinemanalytic study of a single infant from the 15th to the 235th day of age in his home environment. The film depicted most of his behavior within this period of time. The investigators hypothesized a gradual and progressive trend in growth from week to week.

Accumulated experiences form the basis for conditioned and refined responses to persons, objects, and situations that earlier failed to produce emotional or social reactions. One example of emotional reaction is crying. By the time an infant is six months old or older, crying is often caused by external irritations, such as excessive or abrupt handling, or by physical restraints. There are also psychological causes, such as a desire for attention or a fear of something new. In many cases, crying decreases at this stage to mere fussing or vocalizing. Previously the small infant cried because of an internal stimulus or need, such as discomfort or pain within the digestive system, and as much as two or three hours of the day was spent crying.

Achieving the power to move by creeping is a significant accomplishment for a baby. Now he can reach the objects and persons attracting his attention. His helplessness decreases and his perceptual field is enlarged as he observes his surroundings from many possible points of view. If he is kept continuously in a playpen, perceptual deprivation is likely to occur. At eleven and twelve months, exploratory activities increase considerably and consume close to one-third of the infant's time, unless the environment is very simple and presents insufficient challenge. A stimulating home provides ample opportunities for developing eye-hand coordination. It is beneficial for the infant to have toys and other safe objects available for his manipulation.

Arthur T. Jersild [4, pp. 16–17] has reported on experiments with infants under two weeks of age in which external irritations were produced and the infants' reactions were observed. The experimenters held the babies' noses

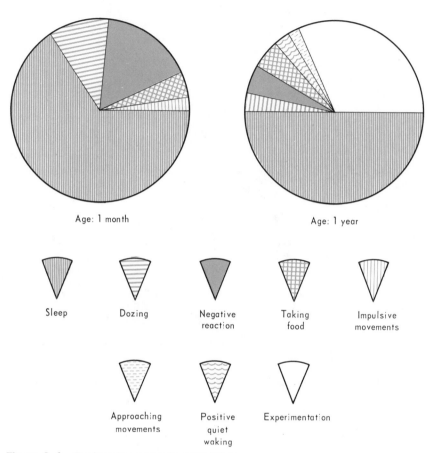

Age: 1 month   Age: 1 year

Sleep   Dozing   Negative   Taking   Impulsive
                                reaction   food   movements

                Approaching   Positive   Experimentation
                movements   quiet
                                waking

Figure 8–1   Typical day cycles in early infancy.

and restrained the babies' arms.   When the babies' arms were restrained, only a few gave evidence of rage or resistance.   When the babies' noses were pinched for five to fifteen seconds so as to prevent breathing, the most frequent reaction was an attempt to withdraw by pulling the head back and arching the spine.   There were practically no attempts at self-defense by waving the arms or any demonstration of anger.

A recent comparative study of motor and mental development [7] based on 1,409 infants from twelve metropolitan areas, ages one to fifteen months, shows no significant differences in revised Bayley's scales' scores between boys and girls, firstborn and later-born.   Nor was parental education, socio-economic status, or geographical location a significant determinant.   Figure 8–2 indicates no differences between whites and Negroes on the mental scale,

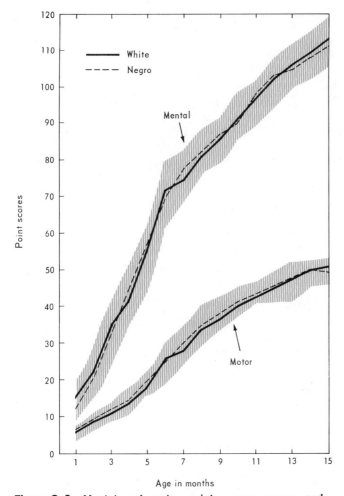

Figure 8–2 Mental and motor point scores: means and
± SD (Standard Deviation) for months 1–15. (Nancy Bayley. Comparisons of mental and motor test scores for ages
1–15 months by sex, birth order, race, geographical location, and education of parents. *Child Develpm.*, 1965, **36**,
379–411. By permission.)

but during the first twelve months the Negro infants score consistently above
whites on the motor scale. As in prenatal development, a great uniformity
in early postnatal growth is suggested. Early forms of behavior, whether
perceptual and adaptive abilities or motor skills, are very similar for the
majority of infants.

LEARNING NEW RESPONSES

The protoplasmic sensitivity of the first weeks of life, when no distinction is made between the self and the non-self, constitutes the morphologic-reflex organization—a basis for accommodation to the object and assimilation to the subject. The progress of this encounter with the surroundings works in the dual direction of externalization and internalization, for example, the acquisition of perceptual experience and of awareness of the operation itself [12, pp. 355–357]. Sensitivity to light, sound, odors, and other stimulation is present from birth. Sense activity produces early perceptual experience, which is the basis for primary learning. Therefore, one would not "leave the child alone to grow up," as John B. Watson suggests, but carry him around to provide sufficient amounts of sensory data for information processing and the perceptual organization of reality. Sensory data nurture the mind. The sensorimotor experience becomes more meaningful as the sensory input is more adequately translated into perceiving and feeling, leading to preference for activities and experiences that more directly serve biological and emotional ends. As experiential retention increases, the infant recognizes his mother by her way of handling him. He also recognizes foods by their color and smell. Distinct reactions to all the members of the family are acquired later. Gradually likes and dislikes are stabilized and lay the foundation for the development of attitudes.

Learning takes place as interpretation of what has been perceived increases. Perceptual refinements further differential responsiveness. The perceptual differentiation depends upon the amount of exposure to learning materials. By approximately ten months of age, the infant should have a repertoire of movements, sounds, and other self-expressive devices to enable him to imitate others with some success. Imitation of others, especially of the mother, father, and older siblings, is a dynamic incentive to further development of language, emotions, and interests. These achievements lay the foundation for other peculiarly human activities. With progress in this stage of development, the sensorimotor coordination improves, and the newly established motor patterns allow for a thorough exploration of the surroundings and expansion of the infant's world. As this phase progresses, the need for stimulation intensifies, and greater curiosity is shown toward novel objects and situations.

During middle infancy the infant begins to detect various nonverbal forms of communication. Although he cannot speak or comprehend the meaning of what is spoken by others, he perceives and interprets many occurrences around him. He learns to attach meaning to gestures, tones of voice, and the movements adults exhibit. The infant's apperceptive function is naturally limited in accuracy, and it is hypothesized that he experiences difficulty in appraising the particular meanings and implications of many of his observations. He senses his own needs and possibly sees his mother as a major contributor to his experience. If the mother shows considerable difficulty in recognizing some of the baby's expressions and reactions, it may be inferred that the baby has as much or more difficulty in understanding her responses. The infant's capacity to learn helps him to utilize various types of action after the first few months of life. Drawing his mother's attention to his needs by means of his vocalization is one of the first actions he learns to perform. When he is in his mother's arms, crying stops and many discomforts become tolerable. Crying for attention is often observed at about six months of age, and sometimes as early as the three-month level.

EMOTIONS AND NEEDS

Emotional growth during middle infancy is rapid and manifold. Its initiation is due to maturation and environmental conditioning. As the infant begins to understand the meaning of things and relationships more clearly, he is able to react with an emotional tone proportional to his depth of perception. Diffuse excitement and mass motion in response to any strong stimulation, which is present at the neonatal level, later develops into a variety of expressions of feeling. The basic feelings, such as anger, rage, fear, delight, and affection, arise in the early months of life and assume important self-expressive and self-assertive roles.

Some specific emotions can be seen early in life. One of these is distress, which may be provoked at an age as early as three weeks in some infants. Annoyances caused by bathing and dressing arouse distress and crying in the infant. As the baby grows older, he meets with attempts by people to restrain him, and being unable to comprehend all aspects of such situations, he is quickly aroused to anger. By the time the infant is nine months old, he becomes angered by his own limited ability to do as he wishes. An older infant who succeeds in pulling himself to a standing position may become angry and begin to cry when he is not capable of doing it again. A young baby expresses his anger in a generalized way, perhaps by throwing things or just crying and kicking; but as his comprehension develops, his anger is directed at whatever object he perceives as the source of his annoyance.

Fear is an emotion experienced less often than anger by babies because the incidents that cause fear occur less frequently than do the daily annoyances that incite anger. Generally, fear is caused by stimuli that startle the baby. Sudden noises, strange objects or persons, objects associated with pain or sudden removal of support tend to arouse the emotion of fear, depending somewhat upon the child's comprehension of the situation. A baby reacts to fear by crying, withdrawing, or seeking refuge in the arms of his mother. Fear is learned, often by conditioning. John B. Watson and R. Raynor [13] give an excellent example of this fact in an experiment in which a baby was exposed to a furry animal. At first, "Albert," the baby, had no fear of the animal, but when he reached for it, the experimenter made a loud noise behind him. This sequence of events was repeated several times, and each time the baby showed greater signs of fear. It was further observed that the fear was transferred to other furry objects.

Pleasant emotions also are seen in babies, two of which are satisfaction and delight. In the small baby, satisfaction is the result of physical contentment. As the baby grows older, he is pleased by being tickled or talked to or played with by another person. The young baby expresses his joy by cooing or smiling, while the older baby laughs aloud. The older baby derives great joy and delight from accomplishing a difficult task, such as turning over, raising himself to a standing position, or climbing upon a piece of furniture. He may express his pleasure by kicking, running, and jumping.

Affection is another of the pleasant emotions, and it can be seen by the eleventh month. At this time the baby gazes at another person's face, kicks, smiles, waves his arms, and shows in other ways that he is not indifferent to those whom he loves. From about the twelfth month on, the baby becomes more selective in giving his affection. Members of his family are the prime objects of his love, though he may be readily attracted to strangers after he becomes accustomed to them. At about this age the baby stretches his arms toward the loved one and pats and plays with the loved one's face. Inanimate objects also may be objects of the baby's affection. The child's affections grow the more often he comes in contact with people who are kind to him. The important principle concerning the development of affection is that an individual must be loved in order to learn to love. Lack of affection causes a baby or child to withdraw into himself; too much affection, "smothering," may lead the child to become self-centered and narcissistic. A baby probably learns to love others before he learns self-love.

Many new emotional responses are learned through imitation of other children and adults, especially during late infancy. The mother's expression of fear in meeting a stranger or reacting to a storm are situations not merely observed by the infant but also introjected by him. Emotional behavior is "contagious"; it readily spreads from person to person. Generally the infant exhibits a strong tendency to react affectively in expressing his needs and desires. Affective responses also accompany many trivial deprivations, delays, and signs of his own inadequacy. Muscular tension and crying are the usual responses to intense stimuli and emotions.

A baby's needs become progressively more numerous and complicated as he develops physically, mentally, socially, and emotionally. Besides the conditions essential for survival, he also needs opportunities to explore new objects and situations, to test his own abilities, and to express himself. The baby's social needs are met in the family circle where he makes his first contacts with other human beings. Here he receives encouragement and stimuli for self-expression. When the baby has opportunities to use his abilities as an individual, he acquires a security that becomes the basis for further development and achievement.

LANGUAGE FOUNDATIONS

Speech is an ability of paramount importance. It involves learning many vocal expressions through observation and practice. Language is the chief vehicle by means of which man communicates his needs, ideas, feelings, and desires to other individuals. Speech is a stimulus to behavior; it evokes responses in others, and it is a response to many interpersonal situations. Speech is helpful in making and maintaining contacts with others. A silent situation is usually uncomfortable and anxiety-provoking. Except for some infrequent cases, the neonate possesses all the equipment and potential needed for the acquisition of the various forms of language and speech communication. The laryngeal activity of sound-making is pleasurable to infants and children alike.

During the first four months of life, vocalization consists of cries and sounds caused by spontaneous movements of air through the vocal cords. As a rule, during the fifth month the infant achieves some voluntary control over the flow of air through these cords and begins to produce "explosive" sounds. As soon as his control over the speech mechanism is improved, rhythm is introduced. This form of vocalization is referred to as *babbling*, or lalling. Like crying, babbling is a preliminary to speech and is used extensively from six to ten months of age. The infant seems to derive great pleasure from listening to his own sounds, the quantity and quality of which increase until at about the one-year level *baby talk* begins. Babbling, as well as baby talk, is produced by combining vowels with consonants, such as "mah," "bah," "hah," "ugh," etc. Baby talk implies a certain refinement of these sounds, including a clearer duplication and, although inaccurate, greater imitation of adult articulated sounds, closely resembling certain words and phrases. The accurate imitation of words produced by others is a major step toward speech. Two other major steps include the understanding of gestures and the association of the articulated sound with its meaning. Considerable progress in both steps is usually observed by the eleventh month.

At present, it is generally agreed that the infant responds to and understands gestures long before he is able to comprehend words. Pantomimes and various expressive movements often accompany vocal expressions and supplement them. The infant points to objects long before he can ask for them. Usually it is not until the age of about four years that the individual learns to combine words in complete sentences. The need for expressive movement is then progressively reduced, but it can never be fully abandoned. It remains a modifier that amplifies communication.

For the purpose of articulation and diction, speech organs continue to improve in efficiency throughout infancy and childhood. Ability to modify the passage of air, using movements of tongue, lips, teeth, and soft palate to produce most sounds, is sufficiently advanced by about the one-year level. As a result, rapid developments in speech occur early in the second year. Jean Piaget [12] has observed: "The infant with a good phonemic storehouse is likely to become the child with a good lexical storehouse."

Early forms of communication, such as crying, and movements of the eyes and face precede the formal steps of socialization, but to a large extent they intertwine. At the two-month level, the baby turns his head in the direction of a human voice and shows relaxation when soft music is played. At the three-month level, the infant responds with a smile to his mother, and he may cry in order to secure her attention. At the eight- to ten-month level, the infant makes another distinct step in relating himself to others: he reacts appropriately to friendly, affectionate, angry, or scolding expressions. At this age he recognizes familiar persons and welcomes their approach; he exhibits signs of fear and eventually cries when strangers approach or watch him closely. At the one-year level many babies respond when spoken to. This is a source of joy to parents, who are frequently surprised by new types of reaction. It has to be kept in mind, however, that the recipient of a message decodes and transforms it according to his own individual life experience and readiness to respond [2, p. 176].

PLAY AND REALITY

A playful attitude and curiosity mark the infant's approach to reality in most of its aspects. As the infant grows and matures, his desire to handle objects in his environment also grows; this includes parts of his body. From the age of four months on, it is good for the infant to be provided with rattles and rubber animals, and later with household articles that are solid and large enough not to be swallowed.

With progress in sensorimotor coordination, cognition, and imagination, simple forms of object manipulation are abandoned for more complex and goal-related activities. Regularities in manipulation patterns begin to appear toward the end of middle infancy and set the stage for advancement in the infant's differential approach to his surroundings. At the ten-month level, for example, many babies make the important observation that objects fall down and produce noise. For some time they enjoy this discovery by allowing their toys, spoons, and foods to fall. Various play activities train the child's senses and initiate and promote his insight into the fundamental laws of nature. Experiential enrichment is of great importance at this early stage of life. What Charles Wenar calls "executive competence" is attained in many activities during this stage [14]. Increased ability and skill undoubtedly result from play activity.

HEALTH AND ADJUSTMENT

During middle infancy, most of the homeostatic mechanisms increase in efficiency, and their original lability and fluctuation following birth tend to decrease. Trivial variations in temperature, diet, or other external conditions become less disturbing to the basal metabolism, hydration, or the rate of heart beat. Throughout infancy the somatic equilibrium continues to show considerable variation. The same applies to diet.

An infant's appetite may vary greatly from meal to meal; however, the healthy infant is likely to compensate for nourishment loss at another feeding. Nutrition is an aspect of health that is still misunderstood by some parents. If any baby is above standard weight, the parents conclude that he is healthy, whereas in reality he may be in need of certain nutritive materials, such as iron and vitamins. It is frequently the overweight babies who succumb to upper respiratory infection.

Infancy is noted for various disturbances in health and difficulties in adjustment. The latter depend upon the parents, who themselves may not have received sufficient infant care. A mother who is tense and anxious while feeding her baby transmits this emotional disturbance to the baby, who in some manner senses his mother's uneasiness and also becomes tense. This tension may cause the baby to have digestive disturbances so that at times he cries extensively and even refuses to eat. Sensitivity to colds and fever at times take serious forms and lead to eczema, earaches, pneumonia, prolonged vomiting, diarrhea, or gastritis. Rapid physiological development, excessive crying, and unsatisfactory care often result in various skin rashes. Heat and allergy rashes are also frequent in middle infancy.

During infancy, body temperature is somewhat unstable and the baby's temperature rises as high as 105 or 106° F when he has an infection. This is often seen when the baby has an upper respiratory infection. Hence, it is important for the mother to know how to take the baby's temperature and how to reduce it. Sponging the baby's body with tepid or lukewarm water, a limb at a time, is recommended in order to maintain the baby's temperature under 104° until a doctor can be reached. High temperatures can cause convulsions and even brain damage. Babies are especially susceptible to infection and should be protected from cold drafts. They should be dressed according to the temperature of their surroundings. Overdressing or over-heating the baby can be just as bad as not dressing him warmly enough.

Vaccinations, especially for smallpox, diphtheria, whooping cough, polio-myelitis, and tetanus, are usually given to babies after they are three months old. Booster shots to continue protection may begin at three years of age. These vaccines have done much to guard babies and young children from the more serious communicable diseases. When a baby or child has been ex-posed to one of the other communicable diseases and the physician fears the disease may be too harmful, he can administer gamma globulin, which will give the child temporary protection and either prevent the disease altogether or lessen its severity. In the United States and other countries, public health departments do much to protect residents against unsanitary food and water which might be the source of disease.

Since approximately ten months of age is the time when creeping or standing is attempted, there should be some anticipation of possible motions to protect the baby from injury. The older baby needs more supervision be-cause he is now capable of creating dangers for himself. The need for pro-tection continues throughout infancy and childhood, although the type and amount will vary from year to year.

QUESTIONS FOR REVIEW

1. Identify some of the motor activities achieved during middle infancy and explain their significance.
2. Describe and evaluate the daily cycle of the one-year-old baby.
3. What are the emotional and social responses that emerge during this stage of life? Discuss fear and anger.
4. Identify several needs of the infant and explain one of them.
5. What are cooing, babbling, and baby talk and explain the differences among them.
6. Define play and indicate its role in middle infancy.
7. What marks the termination of middle infancy? Do other observers distinguish this level of maturity from the preceding and following ones?
8. What do parents have to exhibit and provide during middle infancy for stimulation of genetic potentialities?
9. What can parents do to protect infants from hurts in the late babyhood?
10. Explain what a mother should do when her baby shows signs of high temperature.

REFERENCES

I. Selected Reading

1. Buhler, Charlotte. *The first year of life.* New York: John Day, 1930. A useful source of information concerning language reactions, motor and

cognitive developments, and social relationships at the earliest stages of post-natal life, including tests for the first two years.

2. Frank, Lawrence K. *On the importance of infancy.* New York: Random House, 1966. A comprehensive paperback work on infant developments and related theories.

3. Gesell, Arnold. *Infant development: The embryology of early human behavior.* New York: Harper & Row, 1952. A careful physiological and behavioral study of early development and its organizing forces.

4. Jersild, Arthur T. *Child psychology.* (5th ed.) Englewood Cliffs, N. J.: Prentice-Hall, 1960. A detailed analysis of infancy, including sexual development, infant management, and learning.

5. Pratt, K. C. The neonate. In L. Carmichael (Ed.), *Manual of child psychology.* New York: Wiley, 1954. Chap. 4. A detailed exposition of neonatal behavior and development in most of its aspects.

6. Spitz, René A. *The first years of life.* New York: International Universities Press, 1965. The author's studies of infancy since 1935, with formulation of new insights underlying his total psychoanalytically oriented research on the subject.

II. Specific References

7. Bayley, Nancy. Comparisons of mental and motor test scores for ages 1–15 months by sex, birth order, race, geographical location, and education of parents. *Child Developm.,* 1965, **36**, 379–411.

8. Buhler, Charlotte, and H. Hetzer. *Testing children's development from birth to school age* (translated by Henry Beaumont). New York: Holt, 1935.

9. Eisenson, Jon, J. J. Auer, and J. V. Irwin. *The psychology of communication.* New York: Appleton-Century-Crofts, 1963.

10. Gesell, Arnold, and H. M. Halverson. The daily maturation of infant behavior: A cinema study of postures, movements, and laterality. *J. genet. Psychol.,* 1942, **61**, 3–32.

11. Kessen, William. Research in the psychological development of infants: An overview. *Merrill-Palmer Quart.,* 1963, **9**, 83–94.

12. Piaget, Jean. *The construction of reality in the child* (translated by Margaret Cook). New York: Basic Books, 1954.

13. Watson, John B., and R. Raynor. Conditioned emotional reactions. *J. exp. Psychol.,* 1920, **3**, 1–4.

14. Wenar, Charles. Competence at one. *Merrill-Palmer Quart.,* 1963, **9**, 83–94.

LATE INFANCY

During the last phase of infancy, from approximately fifteen months to two and a half years of age, the infant considerably expands his environment through increased movement, speech, and understanding of fundamental relationships. During this phase the infant achieves greater control over bodily functions and home situations, and infantile helplessness decreases. Newly acquired abilities also play a major role in assisting the development of individual initiative and assertiveness. Awareness of individuality occurs early in this stage. From about two years of age it is marked by expressions of self-reference. Many features of childhood emerge and gradually over-shadow babyhood characteristics. Toward the end of toddlerhood, the infant looks more like a child, yet his maturity level and personality organization remain predominantly infantile, and will not be reorganized until some time during the third year. This is a phase of varied and lively developments, offering rich opportunities for investigation [1; 2, pp. 291–295; 7].

CHANGES IN PHYSIOLOGICAL DEVELOPMENT

In late infancy, susceptibility to a variety of psychosomatic disturbances, in-cluding fever and skin irritations, continues. Physiological growth lessens slightly, although it is still rapid. If during the first year the average infant gained from 14 to 16 pounds in weight and an added 9 to 10 inches in height, the second year will bring an increase of approximately 5½ pounds and 4½ inches [14]. A proportionate increase in weight and height is an important index of development and health.

At the end of infancy the size of body parts is still far removed from the adult proportions they will later assume. The body structure is marked by a very large head since the brain weight exceeds 75 percent of its adult weight, while the lower extremities are short and only slightly developed. This permits the neuromuscular system to mature and lay the foundation for completion of the infant's sensorimotor development and coordination in its phylogenic aspects. Running, jumping, climbing, turning, and balancing skill increases rapidly during the second year. From this time on, facility and speed in performing various motor and play skills will depend chiefly on perceptual maturation and practice. Cognitive development involves perceptual growth, which depends on the adequate functioning of all the human senses, especially those for evaluating distance and depth. Perception is a process of cognitive interpretation that includes both the sensory experience and its meaning and value for the individual. The decreasing structural growth in late infancy permits the child to make more rapid advances in the organization of new behavior traits and the acquisition of many human abilities and skills.

IMAGINATION AND UNDERSTANDING

Interest in and partial understanding of pictures and magazines now emerge and develop at a rapid rate. Whenever booklets are available, the infant makes frequent attempts to turn the pages and seems to enjoy their contents. Many delightful experiences result as he makes associations between pictures and his previous observations of his toys and TV. The first spurt of imaginative growth occurs at this mid-phase. The qualities and activities of living individuals are readily attributed to the inanimate representations of reality. Television programs designed for children, in which birds, dogs, and other animals assume the roles of people, appeal to infants at this stage and serve as stimuli for their imitation, however imperfect this may be. Through imitation the child assimilates language, social behavior, and other forms of complex human self-expression as presented through interpersonal communication and mass media. In our times, learning comes much earlier than it did in former generations.

In her thorough study of infant abilities, Ruth Griffiths [10] developed and used intelligence testing for babies. The study gives evidence that, despite some difficulties in testing the very young, the diagnostic appraisal of mental abilities can be satisfactorily performed and the results are useful as a basis for differential treatment of exceptional children. The Buhler-Hetzer tests

[6] and the subsequent Cattell Infant Intelligence Scale [8], a downward extension of the Stanford-Binet to include subjects as young as three months of age, are also used by experienced examiners for the purpose of appraising various neuromuscular, perceptual, and social abilities in their earliest stages of development.   All infant growth is included in Gesell's *Developmental schedules* [9], based on normative summaries of motor, adaptive, language, and personal-social behavior.   The resulting developmental and intelligence quotients (DQ and IQ) are useful in estimating the child's progress in cognitive growth.

In late infancy cognitive behavior is largely limited to sensorimotor coordinating functions.   The infant does not yet know how to discriminate between effects of his own actions and those of other objects or persons.   He lives in a world without permanent objects and with a shadowy awareness of himself. His behavior organization is prelogical [12].   Appearance of speech and symbolic representation accelerates toward the end of this phase, and search for names and identity commences.

EXPLORATIONS OF ENVIRONMENT

Throughout late infancy, the child eagerly engages in the process of exploring and becoming familiar with his own environment in many of its aspects and with many of its vicissitudes.   Infants make repeated efforts to get anywhere and everywhere, in and out, up and down.   They make use of chairs and other household furniture in order to climb and reach high places in their homes.   Drawers, boxes, cans, and bottles are, whenever possible, opened and their contents examined.   Eagerness to manipulate external objects in every way possible becomes more evident as late infancy advances.

Object-grouping activity observed at the beginning of this phase turns into selective ordering, whereby the toddler classifies and separates small objects on the basis of their differences.   At about two years of age he begins to make simple graphic collections without any verbal instruction or presentation of any pattern.   The mere presence of different small objects is a sufficient stimulus for this discrimination play.

Through grasping, pushing, pulling, sucking, throwing, and banging, the infant stimulates his senses, engages his muscles, and as a result derives much enjoyment, fun, and surprise.   He has a tendency to keep a variety of familiar objects in his possession and use them for old and new activities as his ingenuity inspires him.   Depending on opportunities, neighborhood exploration also advances to a significant extent.   Toddlers need and profit from this type of stimulation.

Using his power of locomotion, the infant slowly increases his ability to estimate distance and depth.   For example, he readily observes a change of line or color, but he needs an accumulation of experience in order to relate these details to distance. Also, he must learn that in many instances a surface continues unchanged even though a color or line has changed. The many difficulties young children have in perceiving depth on the basis of minor changes in line, shading, and object interposition are puzzling to adults since perception of distance and depth seems so natural to them.

At this stage, the infant willingly engages in play with other children if they are ready to contribute the lion's share of cooperation. He may learn to enjoy infants of his own age, especially when such contacts are frequent.

Parallel play and independence in play activity are the first signs of a growing desire for autonomy and greater self-expression in proportion to the infant's own needs and desires. The great variety of exploratory activities in which he engages gives the impression that the age of toddling is well advanced and his reservoir of knowledge greatly enriched. The toddler spends a great deal of time seeking new stimuli the significance of which cannot be fully understood until later.

SEARCH FOR NAMES

Some ability to communicate through speech usually appears during the late stage of infancy. The toddler partially or completely articulates sounds, attaching either the usual meaning or his own to them. He first learns several common nouns, often the names of a few people and things; then several verbs are added. Later he begins to include simple adjectives, adverbs, conjunctions, prepositions, and much later personal pronouns and articles. The single-word sentence is sometimes well established before the infant is one and a half years of age. At this age he begins using phrases and brief sentences. Infant speech is self-centered and is chiefly used to communicate more fully his own needs and desires.

The terms language and speech are frequently used interchangeably even though they denote distinct concepts. First of all, not all sounds made by humans are classified as speech. Vocalizations in the form of cries and explosive or babbling sounds are preliminary forms of linguistic communication.

Two basic criteria should be used to determine the extent to which the infant at this stage is capable of speech: (1) his clarity in pronouncing words and (2) his ability to associate specific meaning with the pronounced sound. Clarity in articulation results from the power to interrupt and modify the sound waves as they pass through the throat, larynx and pharynx, mouth, and nose by intricate movements of the vocal cords, tongue, soft palate, teeth, and lips. Proper pronunciation involves a fine coordination, precise timing, and delicate interaction of these and other organs forming the so-called "speech mechanism." It is not surprising, therefore, that rhythm difficulties are frequent at this stage when basic speech developments are taking place. Knowing the meaning of the words used and clearly associating them with the objects they represent constitute additional evidence of the capacity for speech.

Though baby talk may be understood by parents and others who are in frequent contact with the infant, it usually does not meet the above criteria. Thus, if the baby says "Mama" to every woman, or his association with "bird" or "toy" is general, the specific sound-object association has not as yet taken place. The actual association of articulated sound with particular object or person is fundamentally different from other forms of language shared with certain other mammals. The beginnings of the true speech level are subtle and can be readily misinterpreted by parents and outside observers, including those who are aware of the main criteria. The infant does not readily respond to adults in terms of their requests. This makes it difficult to see whether or not he possesses certain speech abilities.

In the latest phase of infancy, the naming stage usually begins. It is marked by the frequent question "What's that?" The toddler begins to realize that various objects and persons have names, and he wants to know them in order to promote his familiarity with them. As Jean Piaget often points out, this development represents the first major step in a realistic approach to various environmental factors [12]. D. E. Berlyne [5] speaks of "epistemic" curiosity, since the child's responses are aimed not only at dispelling the uncertainties of the moment but also at acquiring knowledge, that is, "information stored in the form of ideational structures and giving rise to internal symbolic responses that can guide behavior on future occasions."

DEVELOPMENTAL TASKS

The late phase of infancy is marked by new developments and skills as the infant becomes more familiar with the home environment. Certain fundamental tasks must be mastered at this time.

1. *Taking solids.* Early opportunities to eat a few solid foods in small quantities and a gradual increase in their variety help the infant to develop enjoyment of new textures and tastes. Otherwise, some children will restrict their choices of foods to such a degree that a balanced diet may become an impossibility. An increasingly competent use of chair, cup, spoon, and dishes is expected, provided the infant has ample opportunity to learn.

2. *Physical control.* The improvement of coordination and neuromuscular control is an important developmental task at this stage, since it gives the child confidence in handling himself in a variety of home situations. A well-furnished home and age-related play materials provide oppor-

tunities for eye-hand and hand-foot coordination. Experimentation with climbing, walking, running, and free dancing plays a part in this. Now the infant has to improve his control over the fine muscle groups.

3. *Understanding communication.* Learning to interpret and use speech is the chief way the child progresses in self-expression and adjustment to other people. It is good for the child if parents take pains to use simple words and phrases distinctly. A correct interpretation of basic concepts, such as "Yes" and "No," "Come" and "Go," and "Take" and "Give," helps the infant greatly in recognizing the dos and don'ts of his environment. It represents the first steps toward further levels of discrimination and personal use of these and related concepts.

4. *Learning toilet control.* Acquiring toilet control is a task of late infancy. Understanding basic concepts and gestures facilitates cooperation in terms of need, procedure, and place. Increased awareness of the function, stemming from neuromuscular readiness, and favorable emotional ties with the mother are key factors in toilet-training success. While some infants at this phase resist bowel-movement regulation, complete sphincter control is frequently attained during the fourth year of life.

5. *Promoting self-assertion.* Self-awareness is a task pertaining more to preschool years than to late infancy. It begins with the discovery of one's individuality, including likes and dislikes, preferences for and relationships with parents, siblings, and others. Acquiring suitable forms of self-assertion is important in fostering the concept of the rights of the individual. Parents, through careful guidance, can help the child attain mastery over obstacles in an efficient manner without displaying a domineering attitude toward him. An insufficient number of contacts with other people at this age may result in shyness and withdrawal during preschool years.

EMOTIONAL AND SOCIAL BEHAVIOR

The basic emotional developments are conditioned by maturation and learning experiences during late infancy. The common affective manifestations at the middle of this stage usually consist of experiences and behavior indicating the existence of various sensory feelings, curiosity, excitement, and several types of fear reaction. The showing of delight and affection, tension and distress, pleasure, laughter, and relaxation, sympathy and compassion, envy and jealousy, and elation and sorrow, as well as a few unclassified reactions, are also included. Early in the third year, signs of an ability to display obstinacy and self-esteem appear. Feelings of inadequacy and conflict, of self-confidence, pride, and admiration, also increase.

At this stage, the affective and emotional life is vivid and spontaneous. Unless punishment is excessively used to inhibit emotional behavior, few if any attempts are made by the infant to control or to restrain emotional response. The expression of an emotional reaction depends largely upon the child's internal state and environmental situation. Parental direction and suppression of his spontaneity in exhibiting emotions are felt in many cases as the stage advances. If the infant is free in his movements, is not hungry or thirsty or sleepy or hurt, most of his reactions are likely to be characterized by pleasantness and easiness; otherwise tension, anger, or temper outbursts are likely to occur, even for trivial reasons. Any kinds of restriction in desires for exploration call forth heightened emotional responses. Generally, emotional tension or disturbances are indicated by restlessness, by nervous mannerisms, such as thumb-sucking, rubbing the head, chest, or genitals, frequent micturition, fidgeting, and excessive crying, by distructive behavior directed toward toys and other objects, and by withdrawal and regression to less mature behavior.

The infant continues to need protection against various dangers which he cannot fully anticipate. Yet his needs for exploration and accomplishment grow, since these are important modes of learning and have to be respected by parents. Exploration often leads to the development of new interests and in this way promotes the personality development of the toddler. Occasionally he cries at night and when ill. He continues to need the close attention of a parent, especially when not feeling well. His habits pertaining to daily routine are fluid and can be easily modified. Freedom for exploration, emotional support, and parental approval are among the most intense needs of this age.

SELF-AWARENESS

The toddler exhibits many signs of his self-consciousness and of personal choice. He readily makes up his own mind and takes initiative in planning play, locating desired food, and getting the attention of the desired person. Self-initiative rises toward the end of late infancy, and parental corrections are objected to vigorously. Very often parents fail to understand the changing personality dynamics of their child when he begins to show awareness of himself as a person, and as a result, they interfere with legitimate modes of self-initiative, learning, and striving for autonomy. While adults have the duty of protecting the infant by stopping activities that may result in infections or injury, for sound personality development they also have to respect in due measure the child as an individual, who has a mind and values of his own. In addition to having his infantile individuality, he is now a child in at least some of his developments and activities. The distinction is this: the toddler is aware of only some aspects of his body and personality; a child is clearly a self-conscious person.

Joseph Church [2, pp. 156—158] shows a child at twenty-seven months of age who has gained much in self-awareness. Benjy is able to express most of his wishes, and he is gradually realizing that yelling for something is less effective than asking for it and saying "Please." Sometimes he will spank himself and say, "Benjy spank," or "Mommy spank," but this is usually when he seems to realize that he is cranky and may be punished. He is still confused about possessive pronouns—uses "my" to mean "your" and has not discovered "mine" at all. Recently, he discovered "No" and occasionally uses it to mean "Yes," but mostly he knows he means "No"—often very vehemently, as a matter of fact. He knows all the large parts of his anatomy and can find them on his animals, doll, or parents. He has taken a renewed interest in looking at himself in the mirror.

QUESTIONS FOR REVIEW

1. What makes the expansion of environmental exploration possible? Under what conditions may neighborhood investigation begin?
2. Indicate the characteristic changes in physiological growth.
3. What are the factors contributing to behavior organization? Explain the parental role in this regard.
4. Describe the toddler's exploration of his home environment.
5. What characteristic language developments occur when the infant enters the speech level?
6. Name the criteria of speech and explain what processes and controls are necessary for speech.
7. Consider the infant's search for names and explain its significance.
8. Name two emotions and describe their manifestations in late infancy.
9. List the developmental tasks of late infancy, and discuss one of them.
10. What are the outstanding signs of self-awareness? Describe infant behavior with this development in mind.
11. In what ways does the infant resemble a child? Identify some of the signs indicating termination of infancy.

REFERENCES

I. Selected Reading

1. Brackbill, Yvonne (Ed.). *Research in infant behavior: A cross-indexed bibliography.* Baltimore: William. & Wilkins, 1964. A catalogue of predominantly empirical studies of normal infant behavior from 1876 to early 1964.

2. Church, Joseph (Ed.). *Three babies: Biographies of cognitive development.* New York: Random House, 1966. A cross-referenced study of two girls and a boy recorded by their mothers, all following an identical observation schedule, devised by the editor, stressing intellectual growth and learning.

3. Jenkins, Gladys G., et al. *These are your children.* (3rd ed.) Chicago:

Scott, Foresman, 1968. Chap. 3. Late infancy discussed and vividly illustrated as the age of the toddler.

4. Meyers, C. E. New trends in child study. *Child Study*, 1966, **28**, No.
110, 3–30. Since the age of greatest sensitivity in childhood is from five or
six months to two or three years, infants need much sensory input during
this period.

II. Specific References

5. Berlyne, D. E. Curiosity and exploration. *Science*, 1966, **153**, 25–33.

6. Buhler, Charlotte, and H. Hetzer. *Testing children's development from
birth to school age* (translated by Henry Beaumont). New York: Holt, 1935.

7. Caldwell, Bettye M., et al. New issues in infant development. *Ann.
New York Acad. Sci.*, 1955, **118**, 783–866.

8. Cattell, Psyche. *The measurement of intelligence of infants and young
children.* New York: Psychological Corporation, 1940.

9. Gesell, Arnold. *Developmental schedules.* New York: Psychological
Corporation, 1949.

10. Griffiths, Ruth. *The abilities of babies: A study of mental measurement.* New York: McGraw-Hill, 1954.

11. McCarthy, Dorothea. Language development in children. In L. Carmichael (Ed.), *Manual of child psychology.* (2nd ed.) New York: Wiley, 1954.
Pp. 492–630.

12. Piaget, Jean. *The construction of reality in the child* (translated by
Margaret Cook). New York: Basic Books, 1954.

13. Sampson, Olive C. A study of speech development in children of
18–30 months. *Brit. J. educ. Psychol.*, 1956, **26**, 194–201.

14. Watson, E. H., and G. H. Lawrey. *Growth and development of children.* Chicago: Year Book Medical Publishers, 1954.

PERSONALITY FOUNDATIONS
DURING INFANCY

In the first two years of life an infant develops greatly and increasingly begins to react as a whole person rather than as a mere reflexive organism producing somewhat isolated stimulus-elicited responses. In order to understand him in terms of his emerging personality, he must be viewed in his total behavioral capacity. Appraising the human individual as a personality involves an integrative approach to the psychological study of development and behavior. Infant personality refers to a cluster of potentialities for biopsychic activity and tendencies in behavior toward certain traits and habits. In appraisal, attention is focused on motivation and the emerging behavioral style of life.

This chapter describes briefly the infant's endowments at birth and gives a detailed analysis of trait, attitude, and habit formation, discusses parental management of infants, and explains how parents' attitudes toward their children have a major influence on the early forms of behavior organization. Several major theories of personality development are also included.

NEONATAL POTENTIAL

Each neonate enters the world with numerous innate capacities, potentialities, and assets, as well as needs and liabilities. These behavior constituents are at first largely latent, but many of them develop during early phases of life. A number of them will not receive sufficient stimulation to be actualized, while others will be suppressed by external pressures at their embryonic levels of development. Interaction among internal needs and emotions and environmental factors lays a foundation for personality development very early in life. Innumerable complexities within the individual, as well as varied types of environmental stimulation, give rise to distinct personality patterns for each infant.

With the exception of an extremely handicapped neonate, the infant begins life with the following basic equipment: physique, temperament, intellectual endowment associated with a capacity to learn, and a potential for individualization. No two individuals have identical genetic materials, even with respect to proteins or ribonucleic acids, although the heredity and early physical environment of identical, or monozygotic, twins are often assumed to be the same. Chapter 4 presented an analysis of the external factors explaining why, regardless of circumstances, the environments of all infants, including identical twins, are different in many aspects. As a result of specific environmental events and pressures from the internal constituents of growth, the variation among neonates is magnified as the infants grow older. New tendencies, traits, and features, stemming from inborn capacities and their organizational qualities, emerge. The multiple and the rapid developments of the first two years of life have already been discussed in the two preceding chapters.

During infancy, changes in sensitivity and in adjustment to various environmental factors begin to take form as distinct patterns of reaction. By the third year, all the major personality qualities and traits have become more closely interrelated. This is particularly due to the child's increased self-awareness, which is now developing at a considerable rate into a system of self and a pattern of relationships with others.

DEVELOPMENT OF TRAITS

There are two major styles of reaction in young infants. A large number of infants show good adaptability, moderate sensitivity, and relaxed, easy-going behavior. They are seldom emotionally upset by normal internal and environmental changes, for example, getting wet, waiting for or taking in food, falling asleep, or experiencing natural temperature changes. Another group of infants is more reactive and excitable. Each new influence and manipulation, for example, being laid down, having a diaper or shirt changed, being put in a different position, or waiting to be fed, causes emotional tension and crying.   Later modifications and refinements of these two approaches to life greatly influence the pattern of personality organization, especially in terms of adjustment and development of self-defenses.   These approaches are the beginnings of fundamental traits and attitudes.

Personality patterns and traits shown during the early years of life tend to develop further and attain a relatively persistent structural status [24, 31, 34].   Madorah E. Smith [31, p. 179], in her study of six siblings of the same family as children and adults, found many traits for individual adults to be significantly consistent with their traits as children.   Fifty years later, the traits appraised as most consistent were affection, ambition, attractiveness, brightness, carelessness, irritability, jealousy, nervousness, quarrelsomeness, and determination.

Later developments of basic patterns and traits are more an expansion and supplement rather than a metamorphosis.   They are evolutionary rather than revolutionary.   Apparently one of the fundamental explanations why the first two or three years are so crucial for later well-being is that the developments of those years form the foundation for structural growth of personality.

The early phase of infancy seems to be the "embryonic stage" of personality formation, during which a number of major abilities appear.   The later phase elicits many peculiarly human developments, such as speech, imagination, and concept formation.   The years of infancy are not only a very critical period for later personality development, they are the most formative for the growth of a child's personality because pattern-setting occurs at this time.

ROLE OF PARENTAL ATTITUDES

Parental influences upon the child are far-reaching; the hereditary, constitutional, social, and cultural qualities of the parents are the most potent conditioning factors in the life of the child.   The parents' level of emotional acceptance of the child and their resulting attitudes toward him play a leading role in laying the foundation for the type of personality the child will develop.

The infant has intrinsic needs for close human association, for gentle and affectionate handling, and for direct protection against common dangers and undesirable influences.   Ordinarily, his mother and father are best suited to help him attain gratification of these needs and to counteract various security-disturbing stimuli, for, because of his helplessness and inaptitude, he is incapable of promoting his own security.

With a favorable child-parent relationship, the parents are likely to be the two dominant human models when the process of identification starts at approximately three years of age.   Long before this, the parents' emotions, attitudes, habits, and other behavior patterns have been taken in, whether resistance was exhibited or not. The extent and quality of the ability to identify with other persons and to relate to them is closely and largely determined by the nature of the relationships within the family during these early years of life [5, p. 175].

Parents' attitudes toward their children may range from affectionate acceptance to hostile rejection, immoderate indulgence to carefree neglect, excessive pampering to extreme lack of mothering, autocratic dictatorship to licensed permissiveness, multiple pressures toward acceleration to distinct nonchalance.

The myriad complexities of behavior in the parents and others who surround the child inevitably tend to elicit from the child a particular behavior pattern and to direct him into it. Thus the infant acquires the means and techniques by which to gratify his needs that those around him approve. Within the family matrix, a child also acquires tendencies to desire or fear certain objects and situations, and learns what to do and what to avoid doing. Such learning, in turn, gives direction to sundry components of his emerging personality. Later the child learns reasons for the dos and don'ts that the parents have established. The effects and implications of different approaches used by American parents in rearing children are studied in *Patterns of child rearing* by Robert R. Sears and others [30]. This is a major work, based on a sample of 379 mothers, that appraises factual data on child-management practices.

David M. Levy's study of *Maternal overprotection* [21] provides classical illustrations of reinforcement of specific traits in children by dominant or submissive mothers. Dominant mothers, by their extensive use of control and punishment, tend to create submissive and dependent traits in their children. An experimental study by Halla Beloff [9, pp. 169–170] shows that anal traits exhibited by the mother are substantially related to the child's acquisition of an "anal character," marked by parsimony, orderliness, pedantry, egoism, desire to dominate, and related features. These and many other studies [4, 14, 15, 16, 24] illustrate how infantile experiences can have noticeable effects in later life. For example, reinforcement increases the strength of the oral drive, and coercive toilet training heightens separation anxiety and magnifies negativistic behavior [11, pp. 41–42].

A dominant trait of the mother is likely to persist from one phase to another. Cleanliness is an example of such a trait. If a mother feels compelled to clean a child's hands repeatedly, after two or three years he begins to realize his mother's appreciation for clean hands. As a result he begins to wash his hands more and more often. He will frequently expose them after washing for his mother's approval. By the end of childhood, a deeply entrenched habit will have been developed, which may give rise to compulsiveness and become a form of anxiety expression later in life. This anxiety may also be expressed as a fear of bacteria when the child learns of their existence. If stressful experiences are encountered, the anxiety expands and affects other aspects of life. It may be expressed in religious fears in which the child, perhaps by then grown up, feels guilty over infrequent hand washing; he therefore feels obliged to wash his hands frequently, in spite of their apparent cleanliness, lest he should displease God and incur punishment.

A mother with a tendency toward perfectionism uses a variety of means to rush the child into achieving things of which he is not yet capable. A self-defensive attitude will be formed by the child in his attempts to adjust to his mother's pressure and impatience. Thus, in many obvious and subtle ways, the mother's own style of life produces particular responses in the child until they ingrain themselves, and he develops a habit which can be both advantageous and disadvantageous to each of them.

The effects of a satisfied need for affection are deep and pervasive. Arthur T. Jersild [19, p. 894] stresses the fact that love enters into and greatly affects the quality of the total environment and conditions its relationship with the child. "A basic and all pervasive feature of parental love for a child is that the child is liked for his own sake; he is viewed as something valuable per se; he is respected as a personality in his own right. The child who is loved for himself is free to be himself." He is then in a position to experiment for himself and to learn to mold his own self in terms of his natural endowments and gifts.

INDIVIDUATION OF RESPONSES

The latter part of infancy is marked by individuation of responses, feelings, and attitudes. As the emotions of self-sufficiency and self-esteem emerge, self-initiative increases, and the child's resistance to parental commands and suggestions becomes magnified. "No, no!" and "Johnnie don't!" are frequent expressions of the two- and the three-year-old child. The developing child gradually realizes that he is an individual with a mind of his own. He can make choices and has desires of his own. From this point on, he continually plans his activities and uses strong emotional outbursts to demonstrate his opposition to any interference on the part of parents, siblings, and other children. Dawdling, stubbornness, and contrariness seem to constitute the nucleus of postinfantile self-assertion. The peak of negativistic behavior occurs early in the third year.

Negativism in children represents a kind of fundamental conflict at the critical periods of self and personality organization. The third year is one of the first critical years in human development because at this age the self-system emerges as a directing force. One of the major and noticeable principles of development is that, when any new ability appears, it is practiced vigorously for some time until it is well learned. The same applies to self-organization. Personal likes and dislikes, as well as tendencies toward specific foods and drinks, activity and rest, now become self-related and therefore are powerfully defended against all threats and barriers. While at first this intensified negativism does not seem to make much sense, it soon becomes integrated with the needs and desires of the emerging personality. Thoughtful and partially permissive handling of this negativistic behavior by parents is a prerequisite for adequate self-development and personality integration in the child. David P. Ausubel [8], Heinz Remplein [26], and others consider negativism not merely as a developmental necessity in promoting individuation but also as a distinct phase of self-development. Negativism seems to typify an awkward stage of transition from the helplessness, docility, and dependence of infancy to the relative autonomy and partial self-reliance of a preschool child who can feed, bathe, and dress himself with little assistance, who can plan his own amusement and activities and utilize a variety of means for his own goals, and who can go alone to play with the neighborhood "kids."

Generally, in acquiring new responses the child uses the discovery approach. He goes through a variety of steps in exploring the object or situation. Whenever his exploration is blocked, he looks for parental assistance with what he is doing. Simultaneous and subsequent questioning aids him to further unravel the intricacies of the world he lives in.

When parents provide opportunities for the infant to choose toys, food, and clothes, they contribute to his desire for self-regulation. They should guard themselves against perfectionism and strictness, particularly in inconsistent discipline. Parental and social influences which contribute to the child's experimentation, planning, and active participation in family, neighborhood, and community life promote the development of his individuality and selfhood. Under adverse circumstances the suppressive effects of over-restriction will produce emotional strain and tend to unbalance behavioral controls. The human individual operates as a self-organizing, self-directing, largely self-repairing and self-stabilizing open system, which becomes progressively patterned after and aligned with the culturally established dimensions of his environment [15, p. 178].

HABIT FORMATION

Another fundamental capacity closely allied to personality growth is the early appearance of the ability to form and revise habits. Already during the first phase of infancy and, especially in the second, habit formation extends to practically all aspects of the child's activity. Any regularity, system, or order introduced by parents readily molds natural tendencies into habitual patterns.

Once the habit is established and practiced for some time, moderate resistance is shown to any attempt to change it.

New developmental processes accompanied by new abilities and skills offer sufficient opportunities for modification of the old habits and formation of the new ones. Since an infant possesses a very limited number of ready-made response systems for gratifying his needs, it is his task to acquire many new and socially acceptable techniques for the expression and satisfaction of hunger, thirst, elimination, curiosity, and other drives. Usually, newly acquired techniques and skills are extensively used and therefore become habituated. The repertoire of habits increases with each passing month and year. As a result, original behavior abates.

INFANT GUIDANCE

Parental treatment of the infant either forms a basis for security and growth or handicaps both. A desirable and secure relationship between parent and infant is marked by genuine acceptance and love. Unconditional acceptance of the infant as he is helps the parent to avoid all extreme forms of interaction and assists much in the establishment of a harmonious balance: the infant is loved but not overprotected; the parent is firm but not domineering. Infant management is flexible but not too permissive. The parent makes efforts to satisfy the infant's needs adequately but refrains from indulgence. The last three decades have been marked by a general decrease in the severity of infant training and an encouraging trend toward tolerance of the infant's toilet controls and autoerotic impulses. Parents are beginning to understand more fully than their forebears that young children are soft and pliable beings who profit from fairly lenient rearing practices.

Although the potential for personality development exists from conception, the core of personality structure seems to solidify when the neonate begins to respond to external stimuli and to experience further learning. Infants seem to be predisposed toward exhibiting and developing certain traits partly because of their awareness of parental reactions to them as persons and partly because of the unique constitutional qualities and features that contribute to more or less distinct behavioral tendencies. These constitutional factors, in turn, are determined by heredity and the prenatal environment. The reinforcing and inhibiting influences of various environmental factors are obvious yet difficult to measure.

The infant's inner forces, leading to a variety of developments and to a gradual self-realization, may be suppressed, inhibited, and distorted if his fundamental needs for acceptance and love, protection and respect are not understood and gratified. The way the mother or her substitute approaches and reacts to the infant is one of the first lasting influences contributing to differential responsiveness (appropriate and particularized, not generalized, responses) on the infant's part. The mother's attitude is therefore a major factor in the formation of not only the foundation but the later surface dimensions and traits of personality.

During late infancy, the parental "yes" and "no" are the beginnings of the semantics of morality. The child also begins to look for "go" and "stop" signs. It is better for him to feel the safety of limits than the "hurt" of an unbounded reality. Even if not fully understood by the toddler, verbal directions are a good start for child management. They allow for communication at a distance.

Adjusting the home to the older infant is a major task for parents. The toddler needs a great deal of sense stimulation; he takes initiative and "gets into things" because of his endless exploration. Various precautions are therefore necessary. Evelyn Duvall's Family development [13, pp. 202–206] presents a detailed treatment of such household arrangements. The child's safety and freedom for activity are, however, much more important than any damage to furniture or other objects. Valuable objects must be placed out of reach. Old or dispensable objects can often substitute for the more fragile ones the child may ruin or damage. Toys, fixtures, and other items must be large and strong enough not to be swallowed or easily broken. Tools, knives, forks, and also insecticides, paints, medicines, and various cleaning compounds mut be locked up or placed out of reach. Low electric outlets should be capped and, when possible, fenced off with heavy furniture so the toddler cannot insert his tongue or a piece of wire into them. It is a wise precaution to have gates at the top (and bottom) of the stairs, allowing the toddler to roam freely about each story of the house. By careful placement of objects emergency treatment for injuries can be prevented. However, there will always be some minor bruises, cuts, and bangs to be taken in stride. For example, within a one-year period our neighbor's child tipped a corner cabinet over herself, drank from a gasoline can, and ran into a bicycle.

Various growth processes can be disturbed by any strong and lasting fear or hostile reaction that may condition the individual, for the sake of safety, to encapsulate himself in one particular phase of maturity or even press him to regress. Parents have a responsibility to exert their own resourcefulness in making the need to grow seem more attractive than the choice of fixation or regression [22].

Neglect of parental responsibility may have powerful repercussions on many later developments. Parents may, for example, show little concern when a child lags behind in performing a developmental task. A mother may not care that her two-year-old infant does not make progress in eating new solids and may continue providing "baby foods." As a result, feeding difficulties may arise and plague the family for years. This undesirable behavior of the infant which could have been readily corrected in the second year becomes more generalized and expands into resistance to other developmental tasks. Difficulties in adjustment thus increase with the years. The child's dressing himself is another example. The mother may continue doing something that the infant is capable of doing himself; in this way she deprives the growing child of his early initiative and acquisition of skill. The child may then have a problem when he enters school by failing to learn something that contributes to his adjustment.

Personality foundations laid during infancy are wholesome only when parents are aware of and satisfy their infant's somatic and psychosocial needs, and when their care is affectionate and their guidance is gentle. As time goes on, parents can promote the child's development by providing appropriate stimulation for emerging qualities and traits. They should play with the infant and provide age-related educational toys, specially designed to foster sensorimotor and cognitive development as well as to give the infant frequent opportunities for self-expression. Such positive social encouragement enables the infant to express his individuality fully and to take the initiative in learning to interact effectively with the various external objects and situations constituting his milieu. Under such circumstances the individual personality becomes organized in terms of his own potentialities and functions at his optimum level of performance.

THE EMERGENCE OF A SELF-CONCEPT

Early in the second year, the infant becomes aware of his own bodily organs, some of their functions, and his capacities in performing simple tasks. Soon he learns to differentiate clearly between his own organism and various objects in the environment. Inner needs and organically aroused desires are distinguished from objects and conditions that can gratify such wants. If the infant is liked and respected as an individual, he will easily progress in awareness of his abilities and will seek opportunities to use them.

The child's self-awareness plays a leading role in organizing and unifying needs, motives, and incentives. As the infant gains control over his motor functions, he begins to manipulate various environmental objects to an increasing degree. For William Stern [34, pp. 471–475] the rising ego consciousness is first of all a desire-filled, emotional experience of the organism, meeting with obstacles and boundaries in fulfilling his needs and desires. He recognizes the presence of self-willed behavior in the fifteen-month-old infant's attempts to accomplish little tasks. A toddler may demand things not even in sight in order to repeat activity he engaged in days before [34, pp. 443–447].

Throughout the latter part of infancy, the self continues to establish the order of priority among the infant's activities, feelings, goals, and desires. Unless some kind of powerful interference or pressure reverses the trend, motives and actions are determined by this hierarchy of wishes and desires. The power to draw from one's own resources for self-directed experiences expands with the following months and years.   John E. Anderson [7, p. 416] goes one step further when he concludes that the child "is very much a creature in his own right, moving through his own experiences and creating his own world."   More and more frequently as the infant grows into childhood and adolescence, he makes decisions in terms of his own self.

THEORIES OF PERSONALITY DEVELOPMENT

Most major theorists, including Freud, Jung, Lewin, Piaget, Watson, Hull, and Sears, assume the predictability (and even determination) of human development and behavior, and attempt to interpret human life as an orderly process, yet all have found many obstacles in predicting the order for even a single aspect of growth.   The core determinant of human action is variously located: inside the organism (sexual processes and urges for Freud; intellectual comprehension for Piaget) or outside it (stimuli and situations for Watson and Hull), in the past (Freud, Jung, and Sears) or in the present (Lewin and Piaget).

The results of most developmental studies are often inconclusive with regard to the antecedents of behavior and are frequently obscured by a lack of conceptual clarity.   Hereditarians such as Franz Kallmann [20] and Amram Scheinfeld [28] and environmentalists such as John B. Watson [35] and Robert S. Woodworth [36] have continued the nature-nurture controversy. The hereditarians propose the theory that personality is determined by inheritance (innate dispositions) and the resultant organismic constitution; the environmentalists would have their students believe that personality is mainly the result of environmental and cultural influences.   In connection with the first theory it may be noted that hereditary susceptibility to a variety of illnesses, including allergies and influenza, as well as personality disorders, is becoming more evident.

The theory of *predetermined* development is consistent with the hereditarian viewpoint.   G. Stanley Hall discussed predetermination in his concept of recapitulation, that is, every human individual passes through the key forms of vertebrate life as he ascends the phylogenetic scale.   When Arnold Gesell speaks of "intrinsic growth" and its normative aspects, he also expresses predetermination through rigid sequences in behavior differentiation with individual differences springing from timing variations among individuals. The parable of the tadpole's tail, in which the hind legs fail to develop if the tail is amputated, embodies an idea of Hall's.   He used it to imply that little

Johnny's "bad" behavior must not be curbed lest in the future some other desirable quality should fail to unfold [35]. Many undesirable forms of behavior can, however, be explained as characteristics of certain phases the individual is going through.

The effects that the environment has on the individual are not easy to assess. Any intense or prolonged experiences during the first years of life may cast the infant's personality into a mold that is difficult to reshape; just as if one branded the infant's body, the stamp endures throughout life [25]. Many carefully designed longitudinal studies are still needed to cast more statistical and conceptual light on the effects of the environment on the individual.

The hypothesis of "critical periods" in childhood development has been raised by several investigators in the field [26, 29, 33]. The main principle is that certain sensitivities and tendencies appear in clusters rather than individually and grow when stimulated by proper influences. If not stimulated during the stage at which they should appear, such traits will not be developed at all. If relevant stimuli are present at an earlier or later level, such developments also fail to occur. It may be inferred that when a fundamental development does not take place any advanced development within the same dimension is impossible. Hence, a lack of emotional and behavioral identification between the mother and her baby handicaps the baby for later identifications with other individuals of female sex. Lack of identification with the father impedes later identifications with males.

The theory of critical periods has gained support from studies of the case histories of sociopathic and psychotic cases. Complete or partial deprivation of human intimacy is very frequently reported in these histories. Several studies also yielded considerable evidence concerning the possibility of developmental arrest of emotional and social-moral sectors of personality in favor of antisocial and other less desirable growth trends [10, 12].

Although there is great flexibility in behavioral development, three kinds of critical-period phenomena have been discovered. These involve optimal periods for infantile stimulation, for the formation of basic social relationships, and for certain optimal periods of learning [29]. As noted in Chapter 2, Myrtle B. McGraw [23] made deliberate attempts to modify performance by giving one of a pair of possibly identical twins (Johnny and Jimmy) special training. She concluded that there are critical periods for human learning that vary for different ontogenetic (but not phylogenetic) functions or activities.

Since Sigmund Freud [17, p. 43] postulated the psychosexual stages of development (oral, anal, phallic, and genital, each of which is divided into early and late periods), many psychologists and psychiatrists have expressed belief in the great importance of these stages and periods for later personality structure. Personality traits, it is believed, are determined by gratifications or frustrations of early forms of psychosexual expression. Freudian hypotheses have given impetus to numerous studies, some of them affirmative and some negative. It is difficult, for example, to obtain experimental evidence validating Freud's theories of infantile omnipotence, the Oedipus complex, or the oral character. Infantile *omnipotence* refers to Freud's belief that the first concept of oneself emerges as a consequence of lack of external demand upon the infant and also of the readiness of parents to respond to and satisfy the infant's needs as soon as they are manifested. Viewing the idea from another angle, one realizes that the full dependence of infants on their parents can scarcely stimulate an image of omnipotence or reinforce it if it is already formed. The psychoanalytic emphasis on the determining power of the infant's early feeding treatment in the formation of such adult characteristics as pessimism or hostility finds little empirical support. It contradicts a better-supported hypothesis that specific feeding and management methods have various psychological influences on different children [25].

Freudian psychoanalysts assume that during the early phase of infancy a considerable amount of the baby's activity consists of the taking in of nourishment and affectionate care, centered around the oral zone. The retentive and the later active or expulsive orality—biting, spitting out, and masticating—may be partially inhibited through lack of objects of gratification. If conflict and anxiety become fixated at this level of psychosexual development, an orally motivated character ensues. It is further hypothesized that such a person will continually seek oral gratification in a variety of forms, for example, excessive interest in and compensatory activities with food and drink, or potent verbal activity characterized by a sharp tongue, verbal aggression, and sarcasm.

The great majority of theories of personality development assign a leading role to the events and experiences of infancy [4, 7, 16, 17, 21, 27, 34, 35]. As the infant develops his capacity for perception and retention, certain images of his parents appear and stabilize. If, in the mind of the child, his parents are a source of protection, affectionate care, and security, the subsequent positive experiences will help contingently, that is, in consequence, to engrave favorable images and characteristics. Conversely, when early experiences of an unpleasant kind predominate, the perception of parents as threatening and punishing agents will be fixated. Many positive experiences would be needed to alter or transform these original impressions [31].

The Freudian doctrine of personality types maintains that personality is largely determined by the first five or six years of life, during which social occurrences are the decisive factors. Parents have practically unlimited opportunities to "duplicate themselves" in their children and to develop either desirable or deviant personality traits and features. Many cognitive and emotional disorders result from infant mismanagement. Despite his early biological orientation, Freud disregarded heredity as a leading factor in personality development and considered infant management and preverbal experience as fundamental for adult trait and symptom formation.

Since fear is a universal response of infants and children, intense or frequent displeasure or frustrating situations associated with parents will tend to stimulate fearfulness and insecurity. This would negatively affect the total parent-child relationship, the fundamentals of which are established during the early phases of infancy. The affection and attention-seeking of the fearful infant will be exaggerated and difficult to gratify. Hence, anger, temper tantrums, jealousy, and hostility reactions will become predominant as the child grows into the preschooler. John B. Watson [35] feels that if this kind of negative relationship is imprinted upon the mind of the infant it will block the responsiveness of the child to parental discipline and later to societal controls. Later attempts by parents to facilitate the formation of sound habits and desirable attitudes will be less effective. Poor training by parents during the late stage of infancy and early childhood will lead to various forms of aggressive behavior or undue dependence and a feeling of inferiority. These traits then become dominant qualities of individual reactivity and ego defense. Referring to the emotional patterns of life, Watson [35, p. 43] stated:

> At three years of age, the child's whole emotional life plan has been laid down, his emotional disposition set. At that age the parents have already determined for him whether he is to grow into a happy person, wholesome and good-natured; whether he is to be a whining, complaining neurotic, an anger-driven, vindictive, overbearing slave driver; or one whose every move in life is definitely controlled by fear.

All the conditions and situations that foster insecurity and promote undesirable intrafamily relationships interfere with the personality development of the child and in some instances predispose him to specific patterns of a maladaptive or deviant nature. Most psychologists and psychoanalysts agree that once such a pattern is stabilized, long-term reeducative or reconstructive psychotherapy is necessary to "correct" the past and to stimulate interest in more adaptive goals and to fortify the ego.

Toward the end of infancy, the individual progresses greatly in his ability to exercise control over the basic skeletal muscle groups and to respond directly to the simple requests of his parents and siblings. Because of this positive attitude, this is the ideal time to begin toilet training. Fifteen to nineteen months of age seems to be the most favorable period for undertaking this task. Bowel control is frequently achieved before the infant's second birthday, while complete bladder control is established about one to two years later. Two basic conditions underlie this significant accomplishment: neuromuscular readiness and no undue strain in the emotional ties with the parents. Within several months after bowel control is achieved, the infant usually learns to use the toilet facilities himself with only occasional assistance from his mother.

Many American parents are too eager to establish toilet control at a noticeably earlier age than is indicated above, and earlier than parents in most other cultures or nations. Psychoanalytic and psychiatric literature points out that in doing so they expose their children to unnecessary strain and conflict, which foster excessive negativism, stinginess, cleanliness, orderliness, obstinacy, and compulsive traits [6, 9, 11, 14]. Psychoanalytic theory emphasizes the close relationship between various types of feeding and toilet control and early libidinal cathexes (need-satisfying attempts), as well as the subsequent patterns of personality organization. Margaret A. Ribble [27] reported on the importance of the mother's motivation in breast feeding and implied that some digestive disturbances are linked to bottle feeding. This, however, has not been validated by other studies [11, 30]. Any intensified frustration leads to a disturbed personality pattern and to difficulty in overcoming early patterns of behavior. This disturbance may persist throughout life. It causes many individuals to act as if situations which have long since disappeared are still in existence.

Of considerable importance are Erik H. Erikson's views [2, pp. 247–274] on the crises of human development. He assumes that each stage of childhood growth has a core problem or conflict. It has to be sufficiently resolved in order to lay the groundwork for orderly and vigorous personality development in the subsequent stage. The earliest conflict involves *trust* and mistrust, during the first or oral-sensory stage of life. The defense mechanisms of introjection and projection appear at this time. Introjection, resulting from trust, occurs when the person attributes outer realities to himself and tries to incorporate them, while by projection inner difficulties are seen as external.

Autonomy versus shame and doubt is the core conflict of the muscular-anal stage that follows the oral-sensory stage of life. Eventually the eighth stage of maturity is reached in late adulthood with its core problem of ego integrity versus despair, concluding Erikson's ages of men. Each crisis successfully passed is conducive to further growth. Each successive stage provides opportunities for new solutions to previous dilemmas, making self-improvement possible. This theory has improved upon the Freudian approach to personality development. All eight developmental crises are seen as universal, yet the cultural situation defines the exact nature of the problem. Although man lives by instinctual forces, the culture legislates concerning the proper use of these instinctual forces [3, pp. 16–18, 23–27].

The Freudian matrix of human development, based on the child-mother-father triangle, in which the child's adjustment and personality structure depend chiefly upon the ways his instinctual needs are met by parents, was revised by Robert R. Sears as a *dyadic* model. The child relates to a single person at a time. His development occurs within the dyadic relationship; most stimulus-response (S-R) sequences are based on mother-child and father-child dyads. For Sears, behavior is the product of S-R learning, reinforced by gratification of organismic needs. During the early years of life, parents are the chief agents of reinforcement. Child-rearing practices determine a child's development and adjustment. A child's inherent desire to learn and a mother's urge to do right create a dyadic situation in which the proper thing to do is decided. Personality is a product of a "lifetime of dyadic action which modifies the individual's potential for further action" [3, pp. 144–154].

A major study by Robert J. Havighurst [18] has provided us with a list of developmental tasks or specific achievements which a subject should be capable of performing at particular phases of growth and maturation. These developmental tasks include the acquisition of the physiological structures necessary for the attainment of specific abilities and skills. An individual learns skills best when he has reached a certain level of neuromuscular, emotional, and cognitive development. For example, a child will acquire the skill of walking when his musculature is sufficiently developed and when he has mastered the prerequisite skills, such as standing and balancing himself. Mastering age-related developmental tasks includes proper adjustment demands, as well as personality integration.

Self-preservation, achievement of physiological equilibrium, and adjustment to the demands of external reality are tasks of the neonatal phase. Control over large muscle groups and overcoming helplessness are some of the tasks of middle infancy. Learning verbal self-expression and fundamental concepts of the physical and social environment and acquiring toilet control are those which ought to occur in late infancy. The satisfactory completion of the developmental tasks of infancy lays a wholesome foundation for growth and maturation in childhood and later periods. Generally, infancy establishes a pattern of adjustment for all later periods of life, during which new developments and revisions are less frequent.

QUESTIONS FOR REVIEW

1. What are the major internal and external factors that lay the foundation for human individuality?
2. Name and illustrate several possible reactions of the infant toward environmental stimuli.
3. Describe several traits and indicate the fundamental relationships between traits and habits.

4. Why are parental attitudes toward and treatment of an infant important for his development and personality growth?
5. Explain the role habits play in personality development.
6. Describe the role of learning in personality formation and development.
7. In what way are assertiveness and negativism related to advanced levels of personality organization?
8. Explain the emergence of the self-concept and its effects on the individual.
9. Evaluate critically the theory of predetermined development.
10. Explain the critical-period hypothesis and present supporting data for it.
11. Describe Sears' theory of dyadic relationships and compare it to the Freudian triangle of child-mother-father.

REFERENCES

I. Selected Reading

1. Baldwin, Alfred L. *Theories of child development.* New York: Wiley, 1967. Discusses theories of developmental psychology from early naïve propositions to the currently accepted theories (Piaget, Freud, Lewin, and Werner), including the sociological systems of Parsons and Bales.
2. Erikson, E. H. *Childhood and society.* (2nd ed.) New York: Norton, 1963. A psychoanalytically oriented work that deals with the period of childhood in a genetic frame of reference. Social conditioning processes are treated in detail. Many sociocultural problems are discussed, including reports of Hitler's childhood and Maxim Gorky's youth.
3. Maier, Henry W. *Three theories of child development.* New York: Harper & Row, 1965. A fairly comprehensive study of the theoretical and research contributions of Erikson, Piaget, and Sears with their applications.
4. Spitz, René A. *The first years of life.* New York: International Universities Press, 1965. A collection of the author's studies of infancy since 1935. It includes new insights based on his research on the subject.
5. Witmer, Helen L., and Ruth Kotinsky (Eds.). *Personality in the making.* New York: Harper & Row, 1952. A presentation of The Fact Finding Report of the Midcentury White House Conference on Children and Youth by many experts from a variety of fields.

II. Specific References

6. Abraham, K. *Selected papers on psychoanalysis.* London: Hogarth, 1927.
7. Anderson, John E. Personality organization in children. *Amer. Psychologist,* 1948, **3**, 409–416.
8. Ausubel, D. P. Negativism as a phase of ego development. *Amer. J. Orthopsychiat.,* 1950, **20**, 796–805.

9. Beloff, Halla.   The structure and origin of the anal character.   *Genet. Psychol. Monogr.*, 1957, **55**, 141–172.

10. Bender, Lauretta.   Psychopathic conduct disorders in children.   In R. M. Linder, *A handbook of correctional psychology.*   New York: Philosophical Library, 1947.

11. Bernstein, Arnold.   Some relations between techniques of feeding and training during infancy and certain behavior in childhood.   *Genet. Psychol. Monogr.*, 1955, **51**, 3–44.

12. Cleckley, H.   *The mask of sanity.*   (2nd ed.) St. Louis: Mosby, 1950.

13. Duvall, Evelyn M.   *Family development.*   (2nd ed.) Philadelphia: Lippincott, 1962.

14. Eissler, Ruth S., et al. (Eds.).   *The psychoanalytic study of the child.*   Vols. I-XXIII.   New York: International Universities Press, 1945–1968.

15. Frank, Lawrence K.   *On the importance of infancy.*   New York: Random House, 1966.

16. Freedman, Daniel G., Charlotte B. Loring, and Robert M. Martin.   Emotional behavior and personality development.   In Yvonne Brackbill (Ed.), *Infancy and early childhood.*   New York: Free Press, 1967.   Pp. 427–502.

17. Freud, Sigmund.   *Three contributions to the sexual theory.*   New York: The Journal of Nervous and Mental Disease Publishing Co., 1910 (originally published in 1905).

18. Havighurst, Robert J.   *Developmental tasks and education.*   (2nd ed.) New York: Longmans, 1952 (originally published in 1948).

19. Jersild, Arthur T.   Emotional development.   In L. Carmichael (Ed.), *Manual of child psychology.*   New York: Wiley, 1954.   Pp. 833–917.

20. Kallmann, Franz.   *Heredity in health and mental disorder.*   New York: Norton, 1953.

21. Levy, David M.   *Maternal overprotection.*   New York: Columbia, 1943 (paperback reprint, New York: Norton, 1966).

22. Maslow, A. H.   Defense and growth.   *Merrill-Palmer Quart.*, 1956, **3**, 36–47.

23. McGraw, Myrtle B.   *Growth: A study of Johnny and Jimmy.*   New York: Appleton-Century-Crofts, 1935.

24. Neilson, Patricia.   Shirley's babies after fifteen years: A personality study.   *J. genet. Psychol.*, 1948, **73**, 175–186.

25. Orlansky, H.   Infant care and personality.   *Psychol. Bull.*, 1946, **46**, 1–48.

26. Remplein, Heinz.   *Die seelische Entwicklung des Menshen im Kindes- und Jugendalter.*   (7th ed.) Munich: Reinhardt, 1958.

27. Ribble, Margaret A.   *The personality of the young child.*   New York: Columbia, 1955.

28. Scheinfeld, Amram. *Your heredity and environment.* Philadelphia: Lippincott, 1965.

29. Scott, J. P. Critical periods in behavioral development. *Science,* 1962, **138,** 949–958. See also Sidney W. Bijou, Ages, stages, and naturalization of human development. *Amer. Psychologist,* 1968, **23,** 419–427.

30. Sears, Robert R., Eleanor E. Maccoby, and H. Levin. *Patterns of child rearing.* New York: Harper & Row, 1957.

31. Smith, Madorah E. A comparison of certain personality traits as rated in the same individuals in childhood and fifty years later. *Child Developm.,* 1952, **23,** 159–180.

32. Stagner, Ross. Homeostasis as a unifying concept in personality theory. *Psychol. Rev.,* 1951, **58,** 5–17.

33. Stendler, Celia B. Critical periods in socialization and overdependency. *Child Developm.,* 1952, **23,** 3–12.

34. Stern, William. *Psychology of early childhood.* New York: Holt, 1930.

35. Watson, John B. *Psychological care of infant and child.* New York: Norton, 1928.

36. Woodworth, Robert S. *Heredity and environment.* Social Science Research Council Bulletin No. 472, New York, 1941.

Part 5
Childhood

As distinguished from infancy and puberty, the period of childhood covers three maturational levels: early childhood, middle childhood, and late childhood. Significant social and cognitive developments, as well as changes in personality and behavior, occur at each of these levels. During the preschool years amazing progress is made in oral self-expression, fantasy, and cognitive and emotional differentiation. Because of the appearance of moral and religious ideas, the development of social interaction, and the expansion of play activities, the child reacts in many new ways to environmental stimuli and situations. More individual differences appear as the young person develops his endowments and selectively utilizes his environmental opportunities.

As intelligence and independence develop, the child is ready to enter school. There he meets and interacts with a teacher and other children of his age. After two or three years of such relationships, he becomes more at ease with his peer group. Parents and other adults begin to notice new traits and attitudes appearing as a result of these away-from-home ventures. The advancing years of childhood lead to more numerous and intimate peer identifications. The child's intellectual grasp of reality is also deepened and magnified. He begins to develop insight into parental and peer characteristics and into his own motives for acting as he continues to grow in knowledge of his physical, social, and cultural environment.

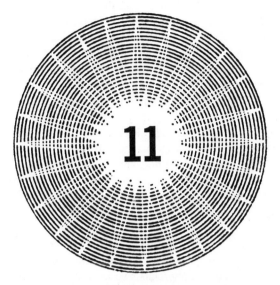

PRESCHOOL AGE

The period of preschool childhood begins at about two and a half and extends to the age of five or six. Developments during this stage are influenced by the partly active and partly passive processes of earlier periods. The child's ability to take in the outside world, his activities, his cognitive assimilation, and his increase in self-awareness, all influence this preschool period. The uniqueness of his feelings and responses already indicates the type of personality he will have. At this stage the child learns to protect himself against common dangers. In frightening and unpleasant situations, instead of crying, he often expresses his emotions verbally. Behavior that is self-centered and emotionally toned, self-awareness, and effective oral self-expression are three outstanding characteristics of the preschool age.

PSYCHOMOTOR CONTROLS AND PLAY ACTIVITIES

Throughout the preschool period, the rate of physiological growth lessens. The child now has finer motor controls and can engage in more physical activities than he could before. In the early days of this phase, he can efficiently leaf through a book or magazine, build a tower of nine or ten large blocks, take care of his toilet needs, and respond to simple requests of his mother. The child can climb, stand on one foot, dance, sing, run, stop wherever necessary, and go unaided up and down stairs, alternating his feet. In his creative expressions he tries to draw vertical and horizontal lines and to identify "things." Whatever the child does he performs it with increasing ease, expertness, and speed and with a purpose. Complicated psychomotor patterns, such as ABC writing, piano playing, skating, and swimming, can be acquired gradually if properly introduced and if the child's attention and effort are sustained. Facility in performing basic and specific motor skills leads to rhythmic activity and gracefulness, which begin to develop at about the mid-point of the preschool phase [14, p. 76]. Group singing and ball playing now appeal to the child, and he eagerly practices to increase his skill.

The preschool child appreciates being noticed and shows delight in whatever he accomplishes. He proudly displays his performance in order to receive attention or praise. Although his "products" are crude, the value of his experience is great. Therefore, the child deserves recognition and encouragement.

During preschool childhood, play activities become increasingly creative and dramatic as the child's imagination develops. In imitating other children, adults, television programs and commercials, various make-believe situations are enacted using dolls, clay, miniature furniture, trucks, balls, human figures, animals, soldiers, and household tools. It is good for the child to initiate activities according to his interests and imagination. His equipment must be not only age-related but varied enough not to restrict his play activities, since he needs spontaneous play. He must feel free to explore his world as a whole, as well as to seek out parts and details in order to gain understanding of his environment and of himself [4, 13].

Under ordinary circumstances the child usually balances strenuous physical activities with passive play. But the young child sometimes needs direct parental regulation in order to avoid exhaustion, especially when visitors are present. The preschool child is a great show-off, and his need for attention is difficult to satisfy. Parents must not allow the child to completely dominate their time, and yet they must fulfill his need for attention and acceptance.

DIFFERENTIATION OF EMOTIONS

Following the child's entrance into the preschool stage, emotional experience undergoes a significant reorganization and a further differentiation. New feelings and emotions continue to emerge. The depth and range of developing emotions affect the child's personality. During this period self-centered emotions appear, such as shame, guilt, and remorse; self-confidence or inferiority is established, and personality-centered attitudes of a social, aesthetic, moral, and religious character are acquired [14, p. 154].

Fear, which is evoked by anything unusual, is a common affective reaction of the preschool child.   As self-awareness increases, so do personal sensibility and vulnerability to fear, even though unfamiliar objects become more acceptable than before.   The child realizes that animals and things which he may have feared are not harmful; but he now learns of many remote and imaginary dangers, such as giants, kidnappers, ghosts, accidents, and death. Fears of getting hurt, of animals, of deep water, of being alone, and of the dark disturb the child, and his imagination tends to increase his awareness of the unusual and terrifying [9, 16].

Anger and *temper* outbursts are frequent during the years of early childhood.   Any unsatisfactory discipline, any deprivation of his needs or desires, any conflicts or frustrations reinforce these reactions.   Some children experience anger or temper outbursts without any provocation, while others show a capacity to tolerate a considerable amount of thwarting or interference. Affective outbursts help children gain the attention they seek.   By temper tantrums children can gratify their whims if parents yield to them for the sake of peace.   Many situations provoke anger: (1) various kinds of deprivation, (2) restraint and improper punishment, especially under emotional excitement, and (3) frustration of a child's freely chosen activity or wishes [14, p. 151].   The beginning of an illness, tiredness, a restless night, a condescending parent, or a strange visitor, all dispose children to anger.

> *Tommy* was an emotionally disturbed boy of four years.   When things were not going as he pleased, he would fly into such a rage that his parents were frightened.   He would pound his head against the wall or hold his breath until his face turned blue and he fainted.   His parents, however, reacted with anger and disgust, which gave Tom the attention he sought, but also embittered and confused him.   Parents ought to look for opportunities to demonstrate affection and genuine acceptance whenever the child is showing his better self.

Envy and *jealousy* are other frequent emotional experiences of the preschool child.   If a child is interested in an object, he wants it until something else gains his attention.   A tendency to collect such objects is characteristic of this age.   Thus, the child becomes envious if his peers take his "treasures," or even if they want to play with them.

Because of his smallness and relative helplessness, the child craves affection from the persons he loves.   As a result, he is keen to notice any attention or favor his parents show to somebody else, especially to his peers. When he is jealous he tries to regain the central role by displays of anger and immature behavior, resorting to helplessness, self-punishment, and hostility. The peak of jealously in childhood comes between three and four years of age.

The need for *affection* is more than a feeling; it is a fundamental human need.   Many psychologists, psychoanalysts, and psychiatrists stress the importance of receiving maternal affection and gentle care during the early years of life [6, 14, 19, 20]. René A. Spitz [20] found that the child's survival apparently depends on the level and frequency of human contact. Where this affectionate contact is inadequate, the infant may die with no apparent medical cause. Mental, developmental, and psychological well-being are furthered by the affectionate care and loving attention of parents and other adults. Parental feelings and attitudes toward a child greatly influence his development and adjustment.

The need for emotional *security* is another basic need in childhood. Generally the child experiences a sense of security when his parents and siblings gratify his needs and treat him as a desired member of the family. Parental expectations must be in harmony with the child's ability and readiness to respond. In most situations, parents should use the positive approach of encouragement, rather than prohibition or correction. The child wants to be respected as a person with a right to do things his own way. An unconditional acceptance of the child as he is strengthens his security and confidence.

Coexperiential emotionality is important in interpersonal relationships at this age. Sympathy, for example, denotes an identification with another's sorrow or pain and a desire to assist him. Empathy refers to an identification with another's emotional state. Compassion is a more developed ability to respond to another's sufferings and problems. How much progress will occur in developing these emotions depends on the parents' own ability to express them. Coexperiential emotions help the young person to understand others and enter more fully into the family group. Later these emotions permit better interaction with other individuals and identification with the child's peer group.

TASKS IN SPEECH DEVELOPMENT

Speech at the preschool age is a valuable means of self-expression and interpersonal adjustment, and the child now makes rapid progress in its use. A child's skill in speaking affects his personality development, accumulation of personal knowledge, and socialization. With continued progress there is a gradual disappearance of infantile forms of speech, such as incomplete sentences, lack of rhythm, slurring, and lisping. C. Van Riper's *Teaching the young child to talk* [23] is an illustrated, easily understood work dealing with speech tasks and problems. It offers many useful suggestions for educating a child to speak more effectively. The ways in which many language skills develop in children between three and eight years of age is traced through experiments by Mildred C. Templin [22]. Figure 11–1, based on a sample of 480 children in Minneapolis, illustrates progress in articulation during the preschool and early school years. A sharp rise in accomplishment takes

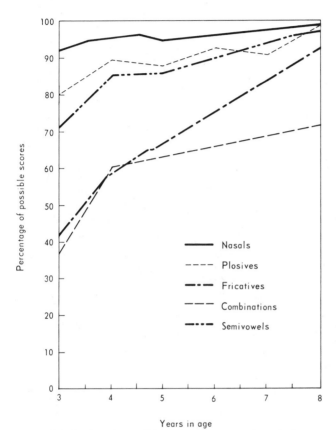

Figure 11–1   Total possible scores on nasals, plosives, fricatives, combinations, and semivowels. (Mildred C. Templin. *Certain language skills in children, their development and interrelationships.* Minneapolis: University of Minnesota Press, 1957. P. 39. By permission.)

place between three and four years of age, but progress is slower during later years.

Speech progress at the preschool age centers around seven interrelated tasks: (1) improving pronunciation and diction, (2) expressing needs and relating experiences, (3) understanding the speech of others, (4) combining words into sentences to express thoughts, (5) using all the parts of speech, (6) increasing conversational skill to secure attention, and (7) building a vocabulary. It is clear that all of these tasks are interrelated—no specific one should be emphasized to the detriment of another. Unless the child is emotionally or socially disturbed, he continues to improve his speech. Many preschool children often have difficulty in enunciating *th, j, r, s, z, h, g,* and

Table 11–1. Mean length of sentence in spoken language as shown in fourteen investigations
(Number of words per sentence)

Author and type of study	Date	Group	N	Age											
				1½	2	2½	3	3½	4	4½	5	5½	6	6½	9½
M. E. Smith:[1] One-hour conversations in play situation. Miscellaneous cases. Not discrete age groups	1926	Boys	64		1.3	2.2	3.3	4.4	4.1	4.8	4.7				
		Girls	60		2.2	2.4	3.5	3.8	4.4	4.7	4.6				
		All	124		1.8	2.2	3.4	4.3	4.2	4.7	4.6				
McCarthy: Representative group. Fifty responses with adults	1930	Boys	67	1.0	1.4	3.2	3.1	4.2	4.3	4.6					
		Girls	73	1.3	2.1	3.1	3.8	4.4	4.4	4.7					
		All	140	1.2	1.8	3.1	3.4	4.3	4.4	4.6					
Day: Representative group of twins. Fifty responses with adult	1932	Boys	79		1.3		2.5		3.0		2.9				
		Girls	81		1.7		2.5		3.0		3.5				
		All	160		1.5		2.5		3.0		3.2				
Shirley: Fifty responses with adult. Longitudinal infant study	1933	All	23		1.7	2.7	4.2	4.5							
Fisher: Gifted group. Three 3-hour samples in play situation	1934	Boys	35		3.4	4.7	5.0	8.4	6.9	10.1					
		Girls	37		3.9	4.8	6.3	5.6	7.6	8.3					
		All	72		3.7	4.8	5.6	6.9	7.2	9.5					

Source: Dorothea McCarthy. Language development in children. In L. Carmichael (Ed.), Manual of child psychology. (2nd ed.) New York: Wiley, 1954. Table 5, pp. 546–549. By permission.

[1] Data from M. E. Smith's 1926 study have been recomputed from raw data presented in the appendix because of discrepancies between her Tables I and XII. Actually based on 124 records from only 88 children.

		N											
Howard:[2] Triplets	1934 All									3.0			
M. E. Smith:[3] Miscellaneous cases. Overlapping in child-child and adult-child situations	1935a All	305	1.2	1.8	2.5	3.5	4.3	4.6	4.9	5.0	5.1		
	Boys	153	1.2	1.5	2.4	3.3	4.3	4.4	5.0	4.9	5.4		
	Girls	152	1.3	2.0	2.6	3.8	4.2	4.7	4.9	5.0	4.7		
	All with adult	198	1.3	2.1	2.8	3.6	4.8	5.1	5.6	6.1	5.7		
	All with child	107	1.1	1.6	2.4	3.4	4.0	4.3	4.6	4.6	4.8		
E. A. Davis: Representative groups. Fifty responses with an adult	1937a Singletons Boys	86									4.4	4.7	6.0
	Girls	87									4.4	5.4	7.0
	All	173									4.4	5.0	6.5
	Twins Boys	83									4.5	5.5	6.3
	Girls	83									4.4	5.3	6.1
	All	166									4.4	5.4	6.2
	Only Boys	49									4.7	5.1	7.4
	Only Girls	48									5.6	5.9	7.2
	All	97									5.1	5.4	7.3
M. E. Smith: Bilingual groups in Hawaii. Fifty responses at play with children	1939 All	1000	1.9			3.0		3.4		3.6		3.7	

[2] As reported by E. A. Davis in *The development of linguistic skill in twins, singletons with siblings, and only children from age five to ten years.* Minneapolis: University of Minnesota, 1937.

[3] Data from two situations have been grouped in the analysis according to sex.

Table 11–1. Mean length of sentence in spoken language as shown in fourteen investigations—(continued)

Author and type of study	Date	Group	N	Age													9½
				1½	2	2½	3	3½	4	4½	5	5½	6	6½	7	8	
Young:	1941	Relief boys	20			2.8	3.0	3.9	4.2	4.3	4.5						
Regular nursery school and relief nursery school cases. Large samples. Four situations		Relief girls	17			3.1	3.7	4.3	4.4	4.6	5.0						
		Regular boys	20			3.3	3.6	4.4	4.9	5.0	5.2						
		Regular girls	17			3.4	4.1	4.8	5.1	5.4	5.9						
		All boys	37			3.1	3.3	4.2	4.6	4.7	4.9						
		All girls	37			3.3	3.9	4.6	4.8	5.0	5.5						
				1½	2	2½	3	3½	4	4½	5	5½	6	6½	7	8	
Shire:	1945	Boys	150											5.0			
Fifty responses with adult. First-graders from 3 parochial schools		Girls	150											5.7			
		All	300											5.4			
Hahn:	1948	All	116											6.9			
Short samples (median 70 words) with adult. 80% upper and middle class																	
Short samples (median 48 words) in 1st grade. "Share and tell" situations same group as above			116											10.4			

Study	Group	N				
Anastasi and D'Angelo: 1952 Fifty responses. Matched Negro and white groups from mixed and unmixed neighborhoods. Lower socioeconomic levels	Negro boys, mixed	14	4.53			
	Negro girls, mixed	11	4.48			
	All Negroes, mixed	25	4.51[4]			
	White boys, mixed	15	4.39			
	White girls, mixed	10	4.75			
	All whites, mixed	25	4.53[4]			
	Negro boys, unmixed	11	4.60			
	Negro girls, unmixed	14	3.86			
	All Negroes, unmixed	25	4.19[4]			
	White boys, unmixed	11	4.58			
	White girls, unmixed	14	4.85			
	All whites, unmixed	25	4.73[4]			
Templin:[5] 1953a Fifty responses with adult. Representative group	Boys	120	5.35	6.73	7.34	7.25
	Girls	120	6.11	6.35	7.16	7.85
	All	240	5.74	6.53	7.26	7.55

[4] Means for total groups combined computed from data supplied in A. Anastasi and R. D'Angelo, A comparison of Negro and white preschool children in language development and Goodenough Draw-A-Man I.Q. *J. genet. Psychol.*, 1952, **81**, 147–165.

[5] Figures made available by the courtesy of Dr. Templin. When the complete study is published, data will be presented for 480 cases from 3½ to 8 years.

ch, in this order. When the child begins to use all the parts of speech, he enters the level of adult speech. Frequently this occurs about the age of four. The average vocabulary at this time includes about three hundred words which the child uses easily and about fifteen hundred other words which he partially understands [14, p. 81]. This shows that the ability to use words and combine them into sentences lags considerably behind the ability to understand and respond to them. The child responds with comprehension to a verbal request long before he can repeat the words spoken to him. In many ways he demonstrates an understanding of terms of speech long before the language is a part of his vocabulary.

Comprehension is one of the easier skills to develop; however, the preschool child tends to take what is said to him literally. Because he usually accepts only one meaning per word, he can misinterpret parental and adult communication, including some affectionate gestures toward him. These can frighten or anger him as he interprets them word by word. The ability to recognize several meanings, to abstract, to see analogies, and to understand humor or metaphor are difficult tasks for the young child. He begins to acquire these skills only as he approaches school age. Facial expressions, gestures, and development of emotional rapport help refine the child's interpersonal communication.

The most noticeable increase in vocabulary occurs in the early part of the preschool age and then gradually levels off. In addition to the increasing use of nouns and verbs, which dominate the infant's speech, the child also begins to use other parts of speech. The number of words per sentence increases fairly rapidly. Many four-year-olds can use almost complete sentences of three to seven or more words. As Table 11–1 indicates [11, pp. 546–549], the increase in the length of the sentence spoken is about one word per year.

One of the most revealing early experimental investigations of vocabulary formation is that of Madorah E. Smith [18]. The study, published in 1926, estimated the average vocabulary from the ages of one to six. The findings indicated that at one a child understands 3 words, at eighteen months 22, at two years 272, at three years 896, at four years 1,540, at five years 2,072, and at six years 2,562. The most obvious increase occurs between the ages of eighteen months and three years. The Smith method of vocabulary assessment measures the breadth, rather than the depth, of the child's verbal understanding.

Since the young child learns principally by imitating other people, he readily accepts the pronunciation and speech pattern of those in his immediate environment. It is important, therefore, that correct speech and diction be used by parents and others with whom the child communicates. Television is also becoming an important factor in the development of communication. Children of large families seem to develop speech habits more slowly than those from families with only one child or a few children since the former depend more heavily on their siblings. Another factor influencing speech development is the socioeconomic status of the family, which creates either a stimulating or a dull background with many or few educational opportunities for the child.

In bilingual families there seems to be no detrimental effect on the child's speech development provided his intellectual capacity is average or better; since each language is taught correctly, undesirable emotional attitudes that would make the child resistant to one of the languages are not involved. When a child is mentally retarded, learning a single language is a practically insurmountable task and a second one becomes an additional obstacle. Many mentally deficient children never reach the full-sentence stage.

FANTASY AND INTELLIGENCE

The growth of imagination, which began in late infancy, reaches a peak during the years of preschool childhood. At that time children show much interest in make-believe activities in which they personify and portray their past adventures, television plays, and adult activities. Home and family, doctor and patient, cowboys and Indians, all are represented by the use of dolls, household tools, toys, and miniature figures. The incident of Washington and the cherry tree is repeated in a variety of contexts. Children are also stimulated and amused by their contacts with neighborhood children and adults, as well as with animals. They may organize parties and drink from empty cups, eat at an empty table, and sell, buy, and exchange their toys. All these activities are accompanied by much self-centered conversation, showing off, and attempts to amuse others and influence their physical and social environment.

Imagination can be stimulated by reading children simple stories, such as "Peter Rabbit," "Little Red Riding Hood," "Hansel and Gretel," "The Five Chinese Brothers," "The Three Bears," and "The Story of Little Black Sambo." The Little Golden Book of Fairy Tales is an excellent anthology for stimulating the imagination.

During the preschool age there is a noticeable expansion of intellectually geared curiosity, the desire to know and conceptualize, and attempts to act in accordance with thought-out conclusions. The first intellect-oriented question "What's that?" is now vividly supplemented by the further frequent questions: "Why?" "How?" "What for?" The child begins to understand and appreciate the purposes various objects serve, what makes things work, and where they come from. It is good for the child if parents and other adults answer such questions adequately and in this way form correct concepts and attitudes because the child needs an accumulation of workable knowledge before he begins his formal education. Impatience and irritability with the child's frequent questioning is interpreted by some children as rejection. A recent study shows that hostile mothers have sons who score high in intelligence in the first year but have comparatively low IQs from four to eighteen years of age [5]. Question-and-answer learning is intellectually stimulating and eliminates much trial and error. G. L. Fahey's study [8] estimates that questioning accounts for 10 to 15 percent of the preschool child's conversation. He suggests further investigations to determine the meaning and implications of the child's questioning activity. Recently, D. E. Berlyne and Francis D. Frommer [7] reported two experiments in which 180 Canadian children from kindergarten through grade six were exposed to series of stimuli consisting of stories and pictures and invited to ask questions after each item. Novel, surprising, and incongruous items elicited more questions than others, supporting Berlyne's theory of *epistemic* (cognitively critical) curiosity. Generally, questioning increased with age, indicating a higher sensitivity to informational gaps and a need to relieve uncertainty raised by incongruity.

An accumulation of various patterns and skills is largely a result of opportunity. Most of the concepts acquired by the child result from his communication with others. Native intelligence cannot be evaluated since test results depend in part upon the amount of knowledge acquired through interaction with the environment or with persons and objects in it. "The more a child has seen and heard, the more he wants to see and hear" [13]. The Montessori teaching method, which uses visual material appealing to preschool children and makes provision for self-corrective matching, is helpful for most children and is greatly needed by culturally disadvantaged children of preschool age. Only a rich environment offers the child opportunity for obtaining stimulation of all modalities and satisfies his nearly inexhaustible curiosity by looking, listening, touching, poking, sniffing, and feeling.

PROGRESS IN SOCIALIZATION

The infant's social interest centers on his parents. Their acceptance satisfies his desire to interact with others. Beyond this, social interaction is casual or environment-enforced as in the case of a large family. The infant experiences a threat whenever a parent, especially his mother, leaves him, and he thinks of her absence frequently despite the substitute's effort to entertain him. The preschool child, however, begins to show much interest in individuals of his own age. He begins to care less when a parent is leaving, provided other individuals try to entertain him. Group life becomes more appealing to him. He shows some eagerness to learn group activities and to assume roles in group situations, especially during his fifth and sixth years. Parallel play is readily abandoned for the sake of associative and cooperative play as soon as the child becomes acquainted with others. Yet if the amount of time spent with others is too long, tears, quarrels, reproofs, and occasional minor injuries often become a common part of social interaction, demonstrating the need for direct adult supervision to reduce speed in play and to avoid poor manners.

Parents have a challenging responsibility to provide opportunities for early social experience with peers. It is their task to stimulate adjustive and co-operative behavior through verbal instruction and direct control. They may have to moderate the child's desire to dominate, to secure the limelight, and to be excessively possessive, all of which interfere with progress in socialization. When parents do their part, social progress is satisfactory, since the child of four and beyond has a strong desire to please the adult and to find a companion for himself. Generally, a dyadic relationship prevails throughout the preschool stage. The child relates effectively to one person at a time, but exposure to groups contributes much to an increase in his social motivation. Intimate associations with others teach the child to take the point of view of another person and see events through his eyes. This ability is an important step in the child's social development.

MORAL AND RELIGIOUS EXPERIENCE

The preschool child has ample opportunities to recognize the limitations of his behavior. Because of parental conditioning, he sees some activities as desirable while others are regrettable. Moral behavior is simply "doing what is right." But "what is right" for the child is determined largely by his parents and older siblings.

Jean Piaget recognizes restraint and cooperation as two different types of moral experience and behavior evoked by interpersonal situations. Situations of restraint force conformity to parental demands until these responses become habituated, while cooperation fosters mutual agreement, motivating the child to want to conform. The young child tends to change rules according to his momentary dislike for them, while the older child accepts established rules. When the rule of reciprocal cooperation replaces the rule of adult restraint, it can be considered a moral act [12, p. 62]. In more obvious situations, the moral sense of right and wrong gradually deepens unless parents are unwilling to use proper instruction and example. Moral conduct is fostered mainly by a deepening awareness of fundamental moral concepts. The understanding of moral concepts is closely related to intellectual maturation and emotional identification with the values and ideals suggested. In stimulating the child's awareness of moral values and virtues, parents must guard against a preaching attitude, a "Do as I say, not as I do" philosophy. At the preschool age, the child can be taught principles of honesty, justice, and fair play.

Religious experience often begins through observation of others' actions, such as the sign of the cross or a short prayer before meals. By using religious articles and explaining any questions about them, parents can provide another opportunity for religious experience.   By taking the child to church parents help him sense the awe-inspiring atmosphere of religious experience [15].

By five or six, the child is capable of understanding most fundamental religious concepts, such as the idea of God as Creator and heavenly Father, the meaning of prayer, of heaven and angels, of hell and devils.   Fear-inspiring information, however, should be minimal.   Illustrated stories of the life of Christ and other Bible stories can provide material for further growth in religious knowledge.   The child's curiosity and natural openness to many religious experiences aids him in acquiring moral guides and understanding the purpose of right behavior in human life [14, pp. 82–83, 205–208].

SELF AND PERSONALITY DEVELOPMENT

Although personality development begins in infancy, the preschool years contribute much toward its differentiation in new traits, attitudes, and habits.   In fact, at this time the child develops swiftly in all aspects of human growth. The various personality factors operating within him are highly affected by environmental stimuli.   In his home, teaching and learning go on from the moment he wakes until all is quiet at night.   In a sense, learning goes on even then.   What is learned in the home shapes the child's personality and attitudes.

The effectiveness of adult approval or disapproval in modifying children's behavior is shown by Harold W. Stevenson's review of about fifty reinforcement studies [21].   Praise expressed by a smile and a few encouraging words does wonders.   Since the young child is consistently exposed to the social stimulation of his parents, other children, and other adults and establishes strong interactional ties with them, his natural tendencies are molded by them.   Through reinforcement, the earlier responses grow stronger and become a foundation for later trait, habit, and attitude formation.   Parents promote maturity by showing pleasure with and rewarding the relatively mature responses to everyday situations, including frustrations.   Conversely, if they accept any of the immature habits of the child and respond favorably to them, they lessen his incentive to grow.

At the preschool stage of development, the child's beliefs, attitudes, and traits are also significantly affected by his association with neighborhood children and any other individuals he meets.   If any major difference with others exists, for example, regarding discipline, conduct, or language, it may create some kind of coarse association and form a basis for an undesirable attitude.

Preschool training may lack moral and religious instruction.   It may disregard cultivation of positive emotions and sentiments, and miss providing for more mature companions. It may even omit stimuli for the development of an attitude of self-worth. Any such omission, however, handicaps progress in wholesome personality development and disposes the child to feelings of inadequacy and maladjustment to reality. Attitudes of dependence or inferiority may result and plague the child now and during adolescence and adulthood.

Whereas the infant's awareness extends to various environmental objects, persons, and some aspects of his own individuality, the preschool child soon becomes self-conscious in a general way and rapidly progresses in self-organization. His traits, attitudes, and habits are incorporated into a personal self-system, a new frame of reference for the assertion of his personality. The self perceives, knows, and judges in terms of its own qualities, characteristics, roles, and interpersonal relationships. Arthur T. Jersild [10, pp. 179–180] explains self as a composite of thoughts and feelings which constitute a person's awareness of his individual existence, characterized by perceptual, conceptual, and attitudinal components. "As a child matures, his selfhood is the sum and substance of his own existence as a human being."

Beginning with the preschool age, the child's conception of himself guides his behavior. Psychologically, then, he becomes somewhat removed from his environmental context and from other persons. Sometimes he stops to think or to delve into his feelings or relationships with others. By disregarding many objects and persons, he restricts his psychological frame of reference. Some children when punished or angered run to their rooms or closets and sob quietly or chew their fingernails for as long as three or four hours. Such preoccupation with self is frequently overcome by a desire for social interaction. As he thinks, the child discovers that he has a "secret" to tell someone he loves. If what he tells is a slight untruth, the preschool child should not be reprimanded for dishonesty since he is merely experimenting with his developing abilities and cannot distinguish between sensory perception and imagination.

The child recognizes his abilities and limitations through the appraisal of others. He perceives his environment, examines it, and draws his own conclusions. Loss or change, from a haircut or tooth extraction, for example, or a major change in a parent's physical appearance, often stimulates fear and deep concern about self-identity and the identity of others close to him.

The child of five or six consolidates most of his new developmental gains and usually integrates them according to his particular personality pattern. If this occurs, he becomes a more secure and self-reliant individual, who is able to adjust to his problems and to tolerate deprivation and anxiety. Indeed, many findings support the view that personality in its basic structure is largely set, if not determined, during early childhood [14, pp. 216–218; 17].

QUESTIONS FOR REVIEW

1. Name some of the motor controls attained during the preschool years and indicate some of the basic implications of these achievements.
2. What are the functions of recreation? What provisions are needed to encourage play activities?
3. Indicate some of the differences between toy play and make-believe play.
4. List and describe the emotional developments that occur during preschool years. Explain the need for and role of parental affection.
5. Enumerate and describe the major tasks of speech development.
6. What are some of the questions frequently asked by children? Why should parents answer the child's questions carefully?
7. What social tendencies have to be encouraged at the preschool age? Why?
8. What are the indications that the preschool child is susceptible to moral and religious experiences and concepts?
9. Of what value is parental teaching? Explain why teaching should not be delayed until school age.
10. Indicate some signs of the child's self-awareness. How does self-awareness affect child personality?

REFERENCES

I. Selected Reading

1. Landreth, Catherine. *Early childhood: Behavior and learning.* (2nd ed.) New York: Knopf, 1967. A categorical presentation of various kinds of behavior, including problems inherent in the study of behavior and stressing environmental circumstances and interpersonal communication.
2. Mussen, Paul H., John J. Conger, and Jerome Kagan. *Child development and personality.* (2nd ed.) New York: Harper & Row, 1963. A major work on various aspects of child growth and behavior.
3. Rand, Winifred, et al. *Growth and development of the young child.* (6th ed.) Philadelphia: Saunders, 1958. A text on early stages of development, stressing physical growth and parent-child relationships.

II. Specific References

4. Almy, Millie. Spontaneous play: An avenue for intellectual development. *Child Study,* 1966, **28**, 2–15.
5. Bayley, Nancy, and Earl S. Schafer. Correlations of maternal and child behavior with the development of mental abilities: Data from the Berkeley growth study. *Monogr. Soc. Res. Child Developm.,* 1964, **29**, Ser. No. 97.

6. Bender, Lauretta. *Aggression, hostility and anxiety in children.* Springfield, Ill.: Charles C Thomas, 1953.

7. Berlyne, D. E., and Francis D. Frommer. Some determinants of the incidence and content of children's questions. *Child Developm.*, 1966, **37**, 177–189.

8. Fahey, George L. The questioning activity of children. *J. genet. Psychol.*, 1942, **60**, 337–357.

9. Hagman, E. R. A study of fears of children of preschool age. *J. exp. Educ.*, 1932, **1**, 110–130.

10. Jersild, Arthur T. *Child psychology.* (5th ed.) Englewood Cliffs, N.J.: Prentice-Hall, 1960.

11. McCarthy, Dorothea. Language development in children. In L. Carmichael (Ed.), *Manual of child psychology.* (2nd ed.) New York: Wiley, 1954.

12. Piaget, Jean. *The moral judgment of the child.* New York: Harcourt, Brace, 1932.

13. Piaget, Jean. *The origins of intelligence in children* (translated by Margaret Cook). New York: International Universities Press, 1952 (originally published 1936).

14. Pikunas, Justin. *Fundamental child psychology.* (2nd ed.) Milwaukee: Bruce, 1965.

15. Pikunas, Justin. Growth in value motivation during childhood. In J. R. Sasnett (Ed.), *Values colloquium II: Value motivation and conduct.* Pasadena, Calif.: The Religion in Education Foundation, 1968. Pp. 21–30.

16. Pikunas, Justin, and Joellen Clary. Fears in normal and emotionally disturbed children. *J. psychol. Studies*, 1962, **13**, 157–164.

17. Scott, Leland H. Personality at four. *Child Developm.*, 1962, **33**, 387–311.

18. Smith, Madorah E. An investigation of the development of the sentence and the extent of vocabulary in young children. *Univer. Iowa Stud. Child Welfare*, 1926, **3**, No. 5.

19. Sontag, L. W. Dynamics of personality formation. *J. Pers.*, 1951, **1**, 119–130.

20. Spitz, René A. The psychogenic diseases in infancy: An attempt at their etiologic classification. *Psychoanal. Stud. Child*, 1951, **6**, 255–278.

21. Stevenson, Harold W. Social reinforcement of children's behavior. In Lewis P. Lipsitt and Charles C. Spiker, *Advances in child development and behavior.* Vol. 2, pp. 97–126. New York: Academic, 1965.

22. Templin, Mildred C. *Certain language skills in children: Their development and interrelationships.* Minneapolis: University of Minnesota Press, 1957.

23. Van Riper, C. *Teaching the young child to talk.* New York: Harper & Row, 1950.

MIDDLE CHILDHOOD

The period of middle childhood extends from the age of about five to nine or ten. The milestones in this phase of development are: (1) readiness for school and the actual entering of school, (2) the broadening of intellectual horizons, (3) a keener interest in the peer group, (4) a growing independence from parents, (5) gains in resilience, (6) an increase in moral and religious motivation, and (7) improved self-identification.

As middle childhood begins, there exists a certain physical imbalance caused by the continual loss of baby teeth, emergence of the first permanent molars, and a greater susceptibility to colds and infectious childhood diseases. Passive withdrawal, dawdling and impulsiveness, increased excitability and inconsistency, oscillation and conflicts characterize the motivational tendencies of the average six-year-old. Within a few months, these tendencies lessen, and the child becomes less demanding and more sociable.

PLAY ACTIVITIES

Since height and weight change slowly, the child is able to gain vigor and balance in sensorimotor operations. Control over the large muscles is perfected, while control over the small muscles is moderately advanced. Since the child has much energy, he is constantly in motion, but he also becomes somewhat cautious. Active play, such as running, playing ball, riding a bicycle, jumping rope, or swimming, can be so intensely absorbing that the child continues to near exhaustion unless adults direct and restrict his activities. Water, sand, and mud play can involve both boys and girls of this age for hours.

Boys are very interested in constructive play in which they can use simple mechanical devices—hammer, knife, scissors, and keys. Bricks and blocks, boxes and beads, pegboards, and picture puzzles also are stimulating materials for construction. Both boys and girls enjoy drawing, one of their finest means of self-expression. As the child matures, his drawing takes on a definite form, color, and accuracy. Coloring and finger-painting also appeal to the child at this age, especially when he is emotionally upset. Many children begin saving objects they like; they enjoy collecting coins, coupons, marbles, stamps, and comic books. Accomplishments bring great satisfaction, and the child now longs for the appreciation of others. Adult interest in the child's achievements easily stimulates further activities.

SCHOOL ENTRANCE

Many factors continually shape the personality of the preschool child; in individual cases they vary both in kind and in degree. Some exert a considerable influence at a certain age and then decline as new influences appear. By the time the child enters school, he has been exposed to many family influences and to physical and social experiences in his neighborhood. From his parents he has received his first training and education, which outside contacts enriched. He has met many other adults and children who have influenced his emotions and motivation. Through these contacts with parents, other adults, and neighborhood children and his experiences in kindergarten, the child builds up response patterns and attitudes in regard to school activity.

It is an important day for the child when he leaves home for the first time to begin the first grade. His separation from the confines of his home and neighborhood is exciting and often frightening. Once he has left his little world of loved ones he may not return until the school day has ended. Yet, on the whole, the average child eagerly anticipates entry into school and exhibits a certain maturity of behavior as a result of his kindergarten attendance.

Because the child's education has already developed considerably, the school will act as a supplement to the family in promoting the child's intellectual, social, and personality development. Beyond that, the school situation is unique in many ways. Here for the first time, the child is entrusted daily to another adult and relates with a large group of peers, most of whom are unfamiliar at first. He will spend a large part of his day in this group situation, and his abilities and social adjustments will be challenged. From this point of view, the child entering school is a typical beginner. Going to school is successful only when the child is ready to make satisfactory adjustments to the novel aspects of school life. His success or failure depends on his level of maturity, which implies mastery of preschool tasks, including separation from parents and readiness to assume school responsibilities.

The child's mental ability and his social preparation influence his school adjustment. His mental ability depends on cognitive development and on progress in doing things for himself. Intellectual maturation can be moderately advanced by educational activities at home, and abilities and skills are enriched by opportunity and encouragement. Praise for attempts to dress himself, for buttoning clothes, and for putting on shoes works virtual miracles in the child's mastery over his apparel. His success in these simple daily activities helps to establish feelings of adequacy and a desire to do things for himself.

The child's preparation for school also includes his frequent exposure to social play situations, in which he is taught to assume roles and to cooperate with others. His ability to interact well with other children is usually indicative of a proper emotional development and control over fear and anger.

Language skills, too, are directly related to a child's education. A school child must be able to communicate his needs, thoughts, and experiences. His intellectual curiosity is verbalized by "How?" and "Why?" These and similar questions indicate the child's level of understanding, as well as the subject matter in which he is most teachable.

Before entering school, the child's interests have been self- and parent-centered. Not much in the way of sharing has been experienced unless the child has learned from other members of the family to give and take. Emotional impulsiveness and other forms of self-assertion have typified many of his responses, while cooperation has been restricted to dyadic relationships with his parents. As was said in Chapter 4, the child likes to relate to a single person at a time.

Let us examine some of the fundamental situations and tasks that determine whether an individual child has a sufficient reservoir of experience on which to rely for making new responses at school.

In the school situation the child must function without family support and must learn to accept not only authority outside the family group but competition also. Teacher-child interaction and group dynamics are more complex than the interpersonal relationships experienced at home and in the neighborhood. At school, for example, there is no escape from the regular demands of the teacher. Moreover, the class often acts as a corrective factor. The child must fuse his behavior into the group pattern or face the rejection and aggression of the class. If a child's appearance or behavior differs greatly from that of other children in the group, he is likely to become a scapegoat for the more aggressive children. A child's acceptance by the group is conditional, while at home he may have been unconditionally accepted without making a contribution of his own. A schoolchild has indeed new adjustments to make and new material to learn.

A good primary school corrects many misconceptions acquired at home, promotes openness to the world, introduces the complexities of human nature and interpersonal relationships, and prepares the child for his lifelong career of learning. The changing functions of the school and the teacher, the need for higher education, and the forces influencing curricula at all levels of education are well presented by various authors in the sixty-fifth yearbook of the National Society for the Study of Education [2].

In modern culture, school experience is an indispensable supplement to home training and education. The school sparks the child's curiosity. It creates situations for learning subjects of vital importance in his life. To a great extent, school relieves parents of educational tasks and provides them with rest periods and a chance to objectify their relationships.

Cecil V. Millard [4, pp. 6–8] questions whether the typical first-grade environment is compatible with the inevitably stormy beginning of a new developmental phase. For one thing, many children now at school, owing to the cultural demand for compulsory school attendance, are not prepared for it either in their maturational level or in their psychosocial development. For another, "Even under the best of circumstances the inability of first graders to behave consistently will result in much confusion."

In school adjustment, most six-year-olds often appear to be regressing rather than progressing in knowledge and behavior. In kindergarten, for example, a child may write the alphabet without apparent difficulty, yet in the first grade he may make the letters backwards. One day he may read a few lines in a story and on the next fail to recognize any of the words. Because of his immaturity in social relations, he will often make mistakes since he is confronted with more problems than he can solve. His errors often alternate from one extreme to another. He becomes either insistent and aggressive or meek and hesitant, or he may attempt tasks beyond his potentialities. In school and on the playground, he has the urge to win, to conquer, and to subdue.

Physiological instability and the new demands of school produce moderate to severe strain for six-year-olds. Explanatory and illustrative material from *Mental hygiene in the classroom* [14, p. 48] describes the entering of school as a period of stress. First-grade teachers know that each year at least one beginner will cry, try to run home, refuse to participate in group activities, or cling to his mother when she brings him to school. The reasons for this type of behavior vary; one child may not be accustomed to a group, while another has a fear implanted by an older child or adult through stories of punishment a teacher may inflict.

> Andrew, an only child who has just entered school this fall, is causing his teacher much concern. He cries, does not play with others, and runs home when he can.
>
> Among the possible reasons for his behavior are these: (1) he has been overprotected at home; (2) he is not very well; (3) he is naturally stubborn.
>
> Assumption that the child is naturally timid or stubborn is a mere evasion of the problem. The judgment that the child is ill is probably wrong, for when a child is really ill, he exhibits other symptoms that can be recognized by adults. The first possibility seems the most likely. Adaptation to school is difficult for beginners, especially if they have had few playmates of their own age and if they have been overprotected.

When the child enters school, he may learn for the first time that certain ethical principles and standards must be respected in order to secure full acceptance and status within the group. At school he is trained to observe rules, to accept discipline, to play fairly, to assist others, and to respect his teacher. The previous goal of securing acceptance at home is now amplified to include gaining the teacher's favor.

For the child, the teacher is a mother substitute. Daisy Franco's study [11] shows that children tend to see their teacher in terms of qualities and traits they attribute to their mothers. During childhood, this transference shows considerable stability.

The school teacher is, however, more than a mother substitute; he (or she, as you prefer) creates and maintains an atmosphere conducive to learning. He helps children meet their new academic and social demands. Studies indicate that pupils prefer teachers who can present subject matter clearly and elicit enthusiasm for learning, who are well-balanced and even-tempered, fair and consistent, well-groomed, democratic, and helpful. Because of the teacher's importance in the socialization of children and the development of their intellect, it is a matter of growing concern that well-adjusted adults be selected as educators. Since teaching is a legally regulated occupation, requiring academic competence and having its own professional organization which sets standards of competence, it is a profession comparable to law or the ministry. The occupational prestige of the school teacher is slowly rising. In a list of ninety occupations, the teacher ranked 34 in 1947 and 27.5 in 1963 [13].

A teacher's guiding influence is vast. He must use his imagination, a friendly enthusiasm, and a playful spirit to live partially in a child's world and to enter into the feelings, attitudes, and emotions he desires to develop in the class. He must make personal efforts to be alert, compassionate, and well-balanced. Self-confidence and poise, high moral standards, a sense of humor, and leadership are other personal qualities which the effective teacher needs. The teacher is responsible for every situation that emerges in the classroom. He must encourage projects and activities that will reap satisfying results and discourage those in which success cannot be anticipated. He guides children to form their goals and to plan, execute, and evaluate their performance. He needs a genuine interest in and love of children, knowledge of child development, and good training in educational methods and skills.

The child has the capacity to evaluate—he likes and appreciates some things, types of behavior, and events and dislikes others. *Valuing* is an ever-increasing quality of his total behavior, often a very decisive feature. Robert L. Brackenbury [8] assumes that no teaching and learning occur without some transmission of values, since education is teaching children to behave as they do not now behave. The real question is: What values are children taught? In school, attitudes toward universal and contemporary issues are manifested both overtly and covertly. "If a teacher makes every effort to hide his beliefs, will his students learn to think for themselves or will they learn that their teacher apparently thinks it does not matter what one thinks or whether one thinks?" Indifference, even apathy, is the logical consequence of instruction that is sterile because of its neutrality [8].

Since childhood is a series of "coming out of enclosures and taking new risks and meeting new and exciting challenges" [17, p. 36], for most children school is neither all drudgery nor all play. During the first year in school, the child's abilities are magnified and expanded in many directions because new stimuli and new subjects are introduced and reinforced by the group reaction. The child is given tasks and projects which, for accomplishment, demand planning and persistence. For superior accomplishments he is praised by the teacher and admired by the other children. This fosters a sense of achievement, of pride in his own ability, and ultimately promotes self-confidence. The child is then ready to master new and more difficult problems.

Through group interaction and the performance of routine duties and tasks, the child develops a certain amount of freedom and self-reliance. Yet he has frequent opportunities to experience the need for companionship and the desire for assistance, which promote the process of socialization. As the child's experience broadens, he learns to work for more remote goals and in this way contributes to his own education. It is readily seen, from what has been said, that going to school is one of the great milestones in the life of any child.

INTELLECTUAL DEVELOPMENT

In a series of books and articles, Jean Piaget, an outstanding Swiss psychologist, pioneered a major theory concerning the child's cognitive development, already outlined in Chapter 5. The middle years of childhood were studied intensively. By means of systematic, firsthand observations and ad hoc experiments (experiments not planned in advance), he gained factual data about language development, the process of thought, and concepts of various aspects of reality. At the Maison des Petits in Geneva, Switzerland, Piaget and his associates recorded most of the speech of a number of children for a month and supplemented their free talk with questions to test the validity of the hypotheses suggested by earlier observations. The findings show a very high frequency of egocentric speech for the group of children aged three to five, and significantly lower for the group aged five to seven. From about seven on, the speech of children becomes sociocentric [18, p. 257]. Egocentrism prevents children from seeing points of view they have never experienced. Children deal efficiently with situations they believe are true.

When Piaget asked children, "When you go out for a walk, what does the sun do?" the responses indicated a conviction that the sun followed the children constantly. Some of the children believed that the sun watched over them or looked to see if they were good or naughty. Children of eight began to doubt the idea that the sun followed them. Only much later, however, were they ready to accept the theory that the sun stays in the same place all the time [17, pp. 214–219].

Many apparently obvious relationships also are not clearly recognized by children. This is illustrated by Piaget's observation that in Geneva children aged eight said they were Genevan yet denied being Swiss, although they stated correctly that Geneva is in Switzerland [18, p. 122]. The ideas and images children acquire differ significantly from ideas acquired later in life. Two recent publications, research articles based on Piaget's theory of cognition, deal with children's ideas in the elementary school period [19, 20].

A monograph based on the Harvard Growth Study [10] and a later reanalysis of this data by E. L. Cornell and C. M. Armstrong [9] offer some insights into children's intellectual development and indicate also how these findings apply to educational guidance. The desirability of classifying pupils by their growth patterns rather than by chronological age is brought out. A child whose IQ is 130 "grows" mentally 1.3 years of MA each year, while a child with an IQ of 70 "grows" 0.7 years of MA each year. Certainly these two children have different degrees of readiness for learning when they enter school at six and later on in their school careers [9, pp. 199, 202].

The amount of knowledge the child acquires outside the home rises sharply during middle childhood as the teacher's influence is felt. As the child grows and learns to adapt himself to an ever-enlarging environment, he acquires increasingly abstract concepts and becomes increasingly objective and, consequently, less self-centered. The middle phase of childhood reaches its end as the child grows into peer society and embraces its values.

DEVELOPMENTAL TASKS

A boy or girl in middle childhood has at his command most of the human qualities and abilities, and many are already specialized into skills. As new areas for application of these skills are presented, the child must be ready to meet the challenges that arise. Most children are sufficiently confident and aggressive to use their early years of education at home and in school in an effective way.

1. *Recognizing one's social role.* To develop and maintain effective relationships with parents, peers, and others, individual differences and idiosyncrasies must be recognized. The child is curious about others and their social roles. He is attracted to individuals who support him and develops loyalty to them; he also tries to come to terms with others who are seemingly antagonistic toward him. He is eager to acquire behavior and manners appropriate to his roles and sex and learns to relate himself to the roles of others.

2. *Emotional control.* The five- to ten-year-old has greater control of his feelings, emotions, and drives than the toddler, perhaps because he begins to see the necessity for control. He finds acceptable ways to release the energies of negative emotions and thus makes his personality more attractive. A balance between readiness to help and to be helped is often established before the completion of middle childhood.

3. *Knowledge of school subjects.* Learning the fundamentals of school subjects, such as reading, spelling, writing, and arithmetic, is crucial in middle childhood. The child's ability to utilize expanding intellectual powers reaches science-oriented proportions. Because he is interested in practical applications of the knowledge acquired, the child tends to ask endless questions of his parents and teachers.

4. *Physical fitness.* The child needs vigorous physical activity. Although the kind and amount of physical activity needed varies, all children must have some vigorous exercise during which most muscles, especially those of the torso and limbs, are strenuously exerted. For physical fitness, children "must have from four and a half to six hours daily vigorous muscular exercise" [15, p. 56]. Unfortunately, many school children today are driven to school by parents or take the bus. After they return home the same way, there are additional sedentary activities, such as homework and television. In winter, early darkness and the cold keep them inside. These children are disadvantaged through no fault of their own and are deprived of their right to acquire sound bodily growth and to improve bodily endurance, both of which are necessary for promotion of their health. Physical fitness also helps a child improve his appearance and gain self-esteem.

GROWING INTO CHILD'S SOCIETY

During middle childhood advanced socialization among peers begins to take place. The child's desire to participate in peer-group activities is usually strong. Whenever groups of children assemble in the neighborhood, playground, or classroom, they soon form lines of association and interaction. Socially cooperative activity comes into prominence. Occasionally quarreling, rivalry, and fighting break out, but generally the child attempts to adjust to others. As the social interaction progresses, the child assumes various roles, often parallel with his interests and abilities. He realizes that in order to be accepted he must act in a prescribed manner. Many children show great appreciation for their playmates, they are pleased and secure in an admiring group, but they resist the efforts of others to join them, especially if the would-be joiners are younger children. Some of the decisive factors in the matrix of attraction and rejection are linked with security in the home environment, common goals and interests, common values and attitudes, friendliness, and resourcefulness.

Rudeness, loud talking, tattling, and the tendency to blame others are some of the self-protective dynamics of insecure children. These are their ways of seeking to maintain their self-respect when they fail to participate well in groups. Such children usually need satisfaction of their most immediate emotional needs so that they may begin to strive for more successful group contacts.

From the earliest stages of his life, an infant's behavior is in many ways influenced by siblings, first by older brothers and sisters and later by the newcomers to the family circle. Among many studies of the family, James H. S. Bossard and Eleanor S. Boll's *The large family system* [7] gives much information concerning the effects of siblings on each other. This empirical study of sixty-four large families identifies eight particular roles assumed by siblings: the responsible one, the popular one, the socially ambitious one, the studious one, the family isolate, the irresponsible one, the sickly one, and the spoiled one [7, pp. 205–221]. The *responsible* one is often the firstborn child, who learns early in life to assume responsibilities for himself and for those younger. Parents often take advantage of him to help younger children and, in this way, further stimulate his growth in responsibility.

The process of assuming roles is influenced by the family constellation and the child's emerging personality type. Role acceptance is usually related to the child's self-concept. In a small family first identifications with a role are influenced by parents, when they assess, interpret, and weigh the child's behavior: "Let's keep little Zeke inside, he catches flu each time he goes out." In a large family, siblings attribute roles to each other; they help parents set distinct roles for each child. Children seize upon differences in appearance, abilities, traits, and idiosyncracies to distinguish one sibling from or contrast him with another. With various degrees of gratification, many children accept the roles attributed to them. Sometimes such distinguishing features help a child to stand out as an individual. Some children reject certain roles and show deep resentment toward those who emphasize them. Any form of adjustment to one's specialized role within the family is, in some ways at least, the key to one's status orientation.

At home children develop their basic orientation to life; here they learn to adhere (or not to adhere) to moral standards and religious ideals. In many good homes the children develop a sense of values and morality which endure throughout their lives. It is good if school and personal interactions with neighbors reinforce this value fiber, otherwise slight or intense conflicts may occur. The family is thus a workshop for developing a lasting character, while the community exerts a major modifying influence.

As the child matures, the need for companions grows stronger, and toward the end of middle childhood, the child approaches the "gang age." Group identification and sentiments of pride, loyalty, and solidarity become powerful drives toward social intimacy in late childhood. The next chapter will deal extensively with group life.

MORAL KNOWLEDGE

The expansion of intellectual horizons and peer interaction are two factors that provoke questions concerning morality. The ability to distinguish between right and wrong gradually deepens. It can be applied to many situations if the child's inquiry is supported by instruction in moral concepts and principles. Otherwise, it remains precarious and at times confusing. The self-initiated practice of moral virtues, such as honesty, justice, and fortitude, is reinforced if moral education is given. Doing good for the sake of others also begins to be appealing. The child shows a desire to please first his parents, siblings, and a few close friends, then expands his interest to include persons and groups with whom he is only slightly associated.

The child's striving for approval and praise grows with age. Fairness becomes a leading virtue, as, about the age of nine or ten, the child recognizes more fully than before the needs of others. At this age also, playing games and doing things according to established rules and regulations becomes important. When disciplinary action is necessary, the child will tend to accept any punishment as long as he realizes he deserves it. He is now sensitive to public criticism and reproof because this is a threat to his social prestige. "Losing face" pulls a child down and often sparks feelings of inferiority or hostility.

GROWTH OF SELFHOOD

With increased independence from parental supervision and daily contacts with a large peer group and a teacher, a child has ample opportunities to develop a realistic self-concept. A schoolchild's self-appraisal is largely based on the appraisals given by parents and teachers, siblings and peers. Parental estimation, whether favorable or not, may be somewhat one-sided. If it is negative, the child's self-concept will necessarily be distorted by a lack of self-acceptance and by emotionalized self-assertion; later, intra-aggressive tendencies will begin to be generated, resulting in an internal conflict. This situation is somewhat relieved when relationships with others become more expansive and objective.

Growth in selfhood is only in part autogenous (self-generated). Much of it is elicited by others with whom the child identifies himself. The child's efforts to correct his behavior and conceal disapproved traits also influence self-growth. Any improvement or expansion of self-regulation is a sign of increasing ego strength unless it involves repression of strong drives. In such a case, internal conflict develops and increases tension.

A child's self-control often begins outside himself. He starts to curb his impulses to please his parents. He will inhibit one of his drives when he sees he will be punished. A child is very clever in winning recognition or praise. His parent's or teacher's sensitivity in responding to his efforts encourages desirable traits and attitudes.

Most children can adjust well to others and can accept reasonable obligations. Their flexibility in motivation and behavior is helpful to them. One can assume that a child is well adjusted in the middle and late phases of childhood if an affirmative answer can be given to the following questions [12, p. 9]: Does the child have reasonable control over his emotions? Does he play well with other children for long periods? Is he helpful to siblings and classmates most of the time? Is he achieving near his capacity? Can he be depended upon for simple chores and homework?

Parental direction of the activities of an eight- or nine-year-old often helps the child establish internal control. Through external control he acquires new habits and skills. Without some environmental conditioning the child's endowments are neglected, and undesirable and maladjustive reactions may take root. Extensive conditioning, however, severely lessens the child's initiative, increases his dependence, and stunts his curiosity. If restricted, the child cannot fully utilize his native endowments and later adjustments and developments of self-direction become too difficult for him to seek. The dependent child has little confidence in his drives for autonomy and self-reliance.

QUESTIONS FOR REVIEW

1. What changes mark the entrance of a child into middle childhood?
2. What are the typical play activities and interests at this stage of development?
3. Indicate some abilities and skills that are necessary for school adjustment in the first grade.
4. What are the key functions of the teacher in grade school?
5. Identify and describe the major findings of Piaget's studies on the reasoning and language of children.
6. Explain the teacher's role in the child's emotional and social adjustment.
7. What personality factors operate in group acceptance and peer companionship?
8. According to Bossard and Boll, what roles do siblings in large families tend to assume?
9. What often handicaps the child in his peer relationships?
10. Under what conditions are moral principles and virtues best assimilated by children?
11. Identify the developmental tasks of middle childhood and explain one of them.
12. How does appraisal by peers affect the child's self-acceptance?

REFERENCES

I. Selected Reading

1. Gesell, Arnold, and Frances L. Ilg. *The child from five to ten.* New York: Harper & Row, 1946. A presentation of developmental trends, interests, activities, and adjustments year by year, based on the authors' observations and records of children's growth and behavior.
2. Goodlad, John I. (Ed.). *The changing American school: The sixty-fifth yearbook of the National Society for the Study of Education.* Chicago: University of Chicago Press, 1966. The second part of the sixty-fifth yearbook of the society, this work includes studies by twelve contributors. It analyzes the current school situation and the various forces molding it.
3. Hawkes, Glenn R., and Damaris Pease. *Behavior and development from 5 to 12.* New York: Harper & Row, 1962. A book on the school child in our society, including his problems and guidance.
4. Millard, Cecil V. *School and child.* East Lansing, Michigan: Michigan State College Press, 1954. An analysis of the child's development in terms of the first six grades; age-related problems and problems of adjustment are presented and illustrated by detailed case histories.

II. Specific References

5. Berlyne, D. E. Recent developments in Piaget's work. *Brit. J. educ. Psychol.*, 1951, **27**, 3–5.

6. Blatz, W. E. Psychological analysis of children in the first three grades of school. *Educ. Dig.*, 1958, **23**, 40–43.

7. Bossard, James H. S., and Eleanor S. Boll. *The large family system.* Philadelphia: University of Pennsylvania Press, 1956.

8. Brackenbury, Robert L. Values: Developing through education. *Child Fam.*, 1966, **5**, 51–61.

9. Cornell, Ethel L., and Charles M. Armstrong. Forms of mental growth patterns revealed by re-analysis of the Harvard growth data. *Child Developm.*, 1955, **26**, 169–204.

10. Dearborn, Walter F., et al. Data on the growth of public school children. *Monogr. Soc. Res. Child Developm.*, 1938, **3**, No. 1.

11. Franco, Daisy. The child's perception of "the teacher" as compared to his perception of "the mother." *J. genet. Psychol.*, 1955, **107**, 133–141.

12. Gesell, Arnold, and Frances L. Ilg. *Infant and child in the culture of today.* New York: Harper & Row, 1943.

13. Hodge, Robert W., P. M. Soegel, and P. H. Rossi. Occupational prestige in the United States, 1925–1963. *Amer. J. Sociol.*, 1964, **70**, 286–302.

14. Joint Committee on Health Problems in Education, et al. *Mental hygiene in the classroom.* Chicago: American Medical Association, 1948.

15. La Salle, Dorothy. *Guidance of children through physical education.* (2nd ed.) New York: Ronald, 1957.

16. New York State Education Department, Mental Health Committee. *Removing blocks to mental health in school.* Albany, N.Y., 1954.

17. Piaget, Jean. *The child's conception of the world* (translated by Joan and Andrew Tomlinson). New York: Humanities Press, 1951 (originally published in 1929).

18. Piaget, Jean. *Judgment and reasoning in the child* (translated by Marjorie Warden [pseud.]). New York: Humanities Press, 1952.

19. Piaget, Jean, and Bärbel Inhelder. *L'image mentale chez l'enfant.* Paris, France: Presses Universitaires de France, 1966.

20. Sigel, Irving E., and Frank H. Hooper (Eds.). *Logical thinking in children: Research based on Piaget's theory.* New York: Holt, 1967.

21. Wallach, M. A., and N. Kagan. A new look on the creativity-intelligence distinction. *J. Person.*, 1965, **33**, 348–369.

LATE CHILDHOOD

Most children reach late childhood, or preadolescence as it is also called, at approximately nine or ten. The years of late childhood are marked by an increasing growth of critical thinking, by theoretical questioning about causes and effects, by resistance to adult opinions, and by emotional identification with peers of one's own sex. Interests and activities begin to reflect the child's sex more closely than before. Late childhood is further characterized by substantial gains in emotional self-control and greater readiness on the child's part to assume responsibility for his own actions. The peak of childhood development is now reached. This is accompanied by a strong drive for self-expansion and adventure, as the child strongly feels his strength and skill. Late childhood ends as pubertal changes begin to develop.

The preadolescent is strongly motivated by the influence of his peer group. On the other hand, parental and other adult control subsides. Time and again parental controls are weakened by the child's social group life. While a younger child does not notice parents' moods and foresee their probable responses, most older children know how and when to get privileges from them. They cleverly play upon the feelings and sentiments of either parent. When younger, they saw their parents as all-seeing and all-knowing, but now the dethroning process is about complete. This can be very disturbing to a parent who does not understand the change taking place in the child's social standards and expectations. The preadolescent often rejects what grown-ups consider to be good manners; at times he criticizes almost everything and everyone, lacks consideration for parents, and often behaves boisterously. Adults find such conduct difficult to overlook. Nevertheless, the child needs the warmth of a harmonious home, where he can heal the wounds inflicted on his self-esteem by some of his classmates and peers. In times of trouble, whether he or someone else has caused it, he needs the emotional support of his parents. He longs to be fully understood when the fruits of growing up turn a little bitter.

In relation to his siblings, the preadolescent is impressed by older brothers and sisters, while he sees younger children as inferior and tries to avoid them in his ventures. Squabbling and rivalry among siblings are unavoidable. The preadolescent may be friendly one minute and as scrappy as an alley cat the next. Occasionally he seems to derive sheer delight from embarrassing, bullying, or tormenting others, yet seldom are these persecutions carried to an extreme. Sibling support and companionship are often sought, as pre-adolescents readily gang up against their parents. Individual differences among children, including siblings, are intensified and interests and activities reach a peak of diversity in late childhood.

In any family with school-age children sufficient and effective communication is a problem. Although the family is dispersed much of the day, a good start in the morning is important. Mother and father alike must "forget" the quarrels and unpleasant remarks of yesterday and show bright and encouraging faces toward their children each day, for it must be recognized that family life serves as an "emotional reconditioning center" for all its members [10, pp. 277–280]. A child who comes "home from his rigorous day in the classroom and playground full of . . . pent-up emotions" is likely to take them out "on the first available member of the family." From time to time this is to be expected. Sometimes feelings will explode as children annoy each other and begin quarreling, even fighting. Preadolescents as well as other people need occasional opportunities to express their rising emotions, even to the point of breaking ties with opponents. A resourceful mother can do much to restore the disturbed lines of family communication, especially if she takes time to evaluate the needs of the whole family. It is very important that family members share their feelings and thoughts. Only when the communication system within the family is restored can parental love flow through and remove the "waste products" of everyday living with children.

NEW HORIZONS OF UNDERSTANDING

By the end of the fourth grade, the child has acquired some competence in the fundamental skills and abilities that are necessary for further, more advanced learning. Most children are now ready for a more complex curriculum, and their interest in extracurricular activities also increases noticeably. The fourth grade is often the first grade in which the child must use abstraction and judgment, in addition to retention. Arithmetic, science, and social studies begin to demand more than memory work. Therefore some children progress rapidly, while others begin to have difficulties. When this occurs, it is important that the less able children should not be left with a completely frustrating sense of defeat. A teacher may therefore encourage such children to improve their own accomplishments rather than compete against more gifted students.

After the fourth grade the child is ready to read independently, to deal with fractions, to refine his sense of history, to abstract and generalize, to notice individual idiosyncrasies. He has little difficulty understanding explanations, whether these concern moral, social, or cultural matters. Now the child often develops interests and ideas of his own. These result from his previous experience and present thinking and are elicited by companions, movies, and mass media. The child is eager to learn more about his immediate environment, his country, other nations, and the universe as well. Interests in and knowledge of world history, geography, and the secrets of nature gradually gain in depth and understanding. His motivation to master new skills and techniques is dynamic and consistent. Often a ten- or eleven-year-old will spend the entire afternoon with a chemistry kit, an interesting book, or a hobby. He works hard to increase his knowledge and his feeling of accomplishment. Much time is spent in group games and projects, athletics, and other social activities, which now take precedence over schoolwork and time spent with parents.

The progressive-education policy of passing a slowly developing child to the next grade level, and not detaining him in a grade he has failed, may place serious obstacles in his development of academic and social self-assertion. Children who have not acquired the knowledge and skills of previous grades have little foundation upon which to be eager and interested in more advanced and complicated subjects. In some children of a sensitive nature fear, worry, insecurity, and feelings of inadequacy may be stirred up and generate anxiety which, in turn, may disturb their physiological and emotional lives.

The policy of promotion is beneficial for the child's social integration, since group identity, it is believed, plays a key role in the child's security, promotes his feelings of adequacy, and contributes substantially to his emotional growth and adjustment. The question is whether promotion outweighs the undesirable consequences of academic failure and failure in other school activities. Such social promotion may lead to more serious academic deficiencies later, from which further emotional problems could germinate. In general, repeating a grade at the primary level can fortify the child's academic foundation; later, however, the social maladjustment that results from failing a grade will hinder scholastic progress anyway. Ungraded primaries, in which each child progresses at his own rate, and may take two or three years, eliminate the shame and stigma attached to nonpromotion.

PEER LIFE

During preadolescence boys and girls are eager to join others of their own age, sex, and status. They readily develop emotional attachments and are proud of their friends and the groups to which they belong. Group play, team games, and seasonal athletic activities are very appealing at this age. Everyone feels obliged to assume a role assigned by others and to contribute to the preferred group activities. Obedience to a leader and conformity to basic group standards is generally necessary for complete acceptance. Children are attracted to groups by common interests, standards, and ideals.

Peer companionship is so urgently needed and so constantly sought that many children come to school mainly to play with their companions. Often two or more children with similar needs or interests form an attachment, for they understand each other's desires and derive satisfaction from their friendship. Preadolescent groups offer opportunities for the development of deep interpersonal friendships and for identifications with selected members of the same sex. Generally, in preadolescence, if not before, the child finds a particular friend to confide in and with whom he can share his conflicts and problems. Such a friend becomes one of the major influences in his life.

Groups at this age are frequently homogeneous; members of the opposite sex are rarely included in the more compact and emotionally toned groupings. Generally girls engage in fewer group activities than boys. Their groups are small, consisting of three to five girls. Usually they meet at the home of one of the girls, since parents generally grant less freedom to girls than to boys.

Engaging in exciting adventures is often one of the objectives of the boys' groups. Much depends on the leader's initiative. The boy who surpasses other group members in strength or achievement in preferred activities usually assumes leadership of the group. Awareness of the likes and dislikes, of the interests and social ideals of other children adds much to this leadership potential. Competition and cooperation run high during preadolescence and must be satisfied. A child often develops an intense drive to surpass others, including his friends. Motivation to make a showing for himself in order to gain approval or prestige is dynamic. When rivalry between groups is involved, he is likely to exert himself as much for "his side" as for personal recognition. Competition has both advantages and disadvantages for older children. In competing, a child may discover capacities within himself that he had not otherwise realized.   It also helps him to discover the limits of his abilities and efforts.   On the other hand, competition will become harmful when an inferiority feeling results or when it makes many other children unhappy.   In addition to leadership, friendliness, enthusiasm, daring, and originality are other qualities highly valued by children.   It is not unusual for a child tending to delinquency to become a leader and to persuade an entire group to follow his ideas and engage in some type of delinquent behavior.

The strength of group identification increases as the child grows older. He begins to transfer some of his emotional identification from his parents to his companions.   Since peer ties are marked by loyalty and solidarity, group life places its imprint on the personality of the child, and parental influence gradually declines as the group influence becomes stronger.   Naturally these two influences operate simultaneously in molding children's attitudes and interests.   Under desirable circumstances parental and group influences reinforce each other.   More often, however, they clash, at least in some ways, and cause conflicts and anxieties within the child himself.   As participation in a peer society increases, resistance to adult standards and guidance seems to be reinforced.

In a group situation the child is less inhibited than he is in the home. Therefore, some undesirable tendencies may develop when the support of others is secured.   Group activities also may become so time-consuming that a child finds it difficult to complete his schoolwork or becomes negligent of his home responsibilities.

Gangs result from many spontaneous efforts by children to form groups able to meet their needs for self-expansion and security.   Some gang activities are cloaked in the language of a code and other secrecies.   Acceptability depends to some extent on the members' social class, national origin, and residential district.   Gangs in the lower socioeconomic neighborhoods may have fights, and encounters with law enforcement agencies may also arise. Nevertheless, through gang activities, a child receives important training in group dynamics and social relationships which he could not obtain successfully from adults.   Peer cooperation is fostered, as well as communication skills.

It has been suggested that "gang spirits" can be channeled into supervised clubs for children sponsored by schools and adult organizations.   Admittedly Boy Scouts, Girl Scouts, and Camp Fire Girls exert a powerful influence upon the social and personality traits of the child, yet it is questionable whether the adult-sponsored clubs can completely fill the need of the preadolescent to "go it alone."   It is important, nevertheless, that children's clubs and camps ensure (1) sufficient guidance to initiate wholesome activities, and (2) enough freedom to satisfy the child's need for independence in individual and group situations.   When the child learns ethical conduct in an adult-supervised organization, he will probably be guided by these standards when he is on his own.

SEXUAL TYPING

Sexual typing may be understood as a process of intrapsychic identification with those personality qualities and traits that pertain to one's own gender. It begins with a closer identification with the parent of the same sex in early childhood. Most five-year-olds dichotomize people into male and female. A male child labels himself as a boy and likes associating with his father. Girls become more interested in the mother's activities.

For lack of any significant sexual development during the early phases of childhood the young boy's sex awareness increases only moderately. But many older boys are interested in reading about human origins and about interpersonal sex relations. Some interest is also directed toward the father's role in sex. Affective attachments, however, are usually directed toward other boys who have similar interests and needs. Thus, playmates are almost exclusively boys. Similarly, girls' social and emotional ties are directed to other girls.

At the ten-year-old level, the segregation of boys and girls is almost complete. Social contacts with members of the other sex are marked by aloofness, lack of response, mocking, annoying and apparent contempt, and shy withdrawal. The cleavage is pronounced in the later part of preadolescence. Most preadolescents find it difficult to accept members of the opposite sex as companions. Disparaging and deriding members of the opposite sex and ganging up on them occur frequently in late childhood. Play activities and interests also diverge sharply. Boys prefer vigorous and competitive activities —sports, bicycling, hiking, and mechanics. Girls' interests center on clothes, handicrafts, art appreciation, household assistance, and other quiet or sedentary activities. Jumping rope, swimming, and skating are their more active interests.

It is natural for a child to associate with members of his own sex, for through these relationships he learns to identify with his own sex and to adjust to it. Since a girl is expected to show feminine qualities and engage in typically feminine activities, close relationships with other girls help her to meet these demands. Conflict or confusion from contrasting pubertal urges are thus reduced or avoided. Jerome Kagan [15] distinguishes core attributes of masculinity and femininity. Boys want height and large muscles. They show more independence, athletic activity, and aggression than girls. As compared to boys, girls are conforming, dependent, and nurtural. They want to be attractive and have social poise. The impressions girls feel they make on others influence significantly their own self-concepts.

Occasionally, some preadolescents hesitate to identify themselves with a sex-linked role. During these years and at the time of pubertal changes, some girls strive to be masculine, yet these efforts lessen as adolescence advances. Masculine traits frequently mark a girl who has only brothers and naturally is forced to compete with them. It is advantageous for girls to have understanding mothers and for boys to have fathers who show interest and encouragement. This enhances proper sex-role identifications—a basic necessity for the healthy development of the child's personality.

The child needs two mature sex models, in order to fashion his own sex identity and his later relationships to members of the opposite sex. While dangers of a too close and too deep association with members of the same sex are infrequent, they are possible, especially when cross-parent relationships are poor. If the cross-parent relationship is missing because of death, divorce, or separation, the child is deprived of a model on whom to base the qualities and traits of his sex role.

Probably because of her close association with her mother, a girl's perception of her sex-typed role is more advanced than that of a boy: she is more embarrassed when conversation concerns sex; she thinks often about her future role as a mother and housewife. Somewhat paradoxically, though her interest in boys is aroused even earlier, she usually continues aloofness or scorn during preadolescence. Beyond the facade of indifference, however, she is eager to learn to dance, to develop her social manners and conversational skills. In fact, in many instances she is ready to interact, and uses some means to attract the attention of boys. She now feels capable of adjustments in her social relationships with members of the other sex.

Boys, however, find it more difficult to achieve sex-role identification, and their early relationships to girls are awkward and uncomfortable if not filled with anxiety. The desired sex-role behavior for boys is often defined as something they should not do: to gain in masculinity, they must learn to avoid "girllike" activities. This *divergent* feedback information is a sign that the boy is not progressing satisfactorily toward the correct pattern of masculine behavior. As a result boys are more anxious than girls about their sex-role identification and hold stronger feelings of hostility toward girls [19].

For a man to be masculine and a woman to be feminine is that which makes each an *authentic* human person [7].

SELF-CONCEPT AND PERSONALITY

During preadolescence, the child's self-concept undergoes new developments as his identity becomes increasingly related to his peer society. He attains a new level of self-expression through advanced schoolwork and complex group activities. As the individual reaches the peak of his childhood development, greater harmony exists within himself, often accompanied by a superior ability to apply himself. Feelings of self-respect and optimism are mingled with buoyant cheerfulness and audacity. The child's experiential background has outlined the contours of his self-image. Except where considerable damage has been done to his concept of self-worth, he sees himself as being good and capable of accomplishing his tasks. His own abilities and talents are usually evaluated in terms of school standing, athletics, peer acceptance, and popularity. He is ready to use his powers and prefers activity that tests his ability. He establishes fair standards and desires to perform well. The preadolescent's attitude toward self is, thus, based on an expanded frame of social relationships and performances.

The child has an increased sensitivity to the approval and disapproval of people whom he thinks are important. He is particularly concerned about winning the approval of his peers, and this desire increases throughout late childhood. Because the less skilled child often has difficulty in asserting himself when confronted with new peers, the emotional support of his parents is very important for his self-acceptance and his adjustment to others. The development of some special interest or ability is of much help to him. Encouragement of athletic skill, dancing, or the ability to play a musical instrument usually assists in socialization and personal maturation. Relating oneself to others is very important, especially for girls. Learning the skills of relating successfully to others, as in modes of conservation and etiquette, is helpful in personal adjustment.

Occasional problems in relating to others, parents and peers alike, may give a child the impression that he is changing for the worse. Many parents strongly reinforce this self-devaluation, especially if the child's efforts at self-improvement are not given careful consideration. If encouraged and given opportunities, the preadolescent can capitalize on his own strengths and assets. If, however, the family atmosphere does not allow for shortcomings, he is forced to turn toward the self-defenses of rationalization or denial of responsibility.

The preadolescent's activities and accomplishments are in some way expressions of himself. Various facets of his personality come to light in projective evaluation of his motion patterns in play, art, and social situations. Figure 13–1 reproduces drawings of a house, a tree, and a person by two eleven-year-old boys from the same middle-class environment, attending the same school. The interindividual variety is vividly reflected in all three subjects. When these illustrations are compared with the boys' drawings of the identical subjects at eight years of age [21, p. 265], two impressions arise: continuity and change, with the first overshadowing the second.

Figure 13–1   The same objects drawn by children of the same age.

CHARACTER FORMATION

The stabilization of psychological gains which takes place during preadolescence encourages character development. Character is a configuration of traits that are related to ethical and moral principles and virtues. While character is primarily an inner system of traits, outside factors delay or accelerate its development. Among these factors are consistent parental behavior in regard to values and principles, consistent parental discipline, and a sense of parental moral responsibility.

Most parental behavior affects children either directly or indirectly. Parents who are guided by a definite philosophy of life accept a certain hierarchy of values and act in accordance with it. Often children are taught these values and the value-based ethical principles such as honesty, truthfulness, fair play, loyalty, and personal responsibility for their acts. Emotional identification with their parents promotes assimilation of parental values by children. Adoption of such values and the resultant behavior standards is reflected in many aspects of a child's thinking and acting. A preadolescent usually understands practical necessities and is ready to modify principles or rules to fit circumstances. When social reinforcements complete a child's reliance on values, codification of principles and ideals begins.

By the age of twelve, most children are ready to assume greater responsibilities toward others, such as baby-sitting, safety patrol, or a part-time job. Their identification with a duty or task assigned to them improves as their age advances. Their sense of right and wrong grows in refinement; in fact, many children will not cheat when they are sure of being trusted. As control increases over the impulsive and emotional tendencies, parental and school controls help to develop self-regulation based on ethical and moral principles. Thus the character foundation for adolescence and adulthood is consolidated. Ideally, ethical motivation, when developed by example and religious instruction, reinforces moral sensitivity. The observance of religious practice can encourage the desire to act in accordance with God's precepts. As moral and religious values gain power, they direct the child's behavior toward personally and socially desired goals. Their guidance fosters (as a part of adjustment to reality) a philosophy of life based on religion. Character development is, of course, a slow process, and it continues through adolescence and adulthood.

The following two cases illustrate the important role parents play in the character formation of a child.

> David, the oldest of three children, was fifteen years old and in the eighth grade. For the last couple of years he had been depressed. He depreciated himself, had little motivation toward any specific goal, and seemed incapable of making even minor decisions. Often he seemed to be hostile

and under great pressure—so much so that he frequently trembled, cried, moved around uncomfortably, and occasionally banged his fist on the desk. His thinking sometimes became blocked, and when asked what he had said, he would reply, "I can't remember."

Evidence of deep resentment, if not hatred, for both parents was evident. According to David, there had been years of friction and disharmony in the home, ending in divorce when he was about twelve. His mother was a rather unstable person emotionally. With her children she asserted herself only through anger and tears.

For some time, David and his mother had not communicated with each other. According to David, "the younger kids are getting just like her . . . angry and complacent." He said, "I can't stand being around here no more," and stated that he wanted to get out of the house for good. David wanted to leave home but as yet could see no practical way of doing so. At one time he was ready to leave just as soon as he had sold his "stuff."

Dan spent most of his previous year in the County Juvenile Home. This year he returned to school to "try" a new teacher; the trial lasted only six weeks. His last act was to attack his teacher with a gnarled branch from a nearby tree. Once more he was ushered out by two policemen.

Dan was an "angry boy," and his background points to some of the reasons why. At home he was rejected by his mother, unsupported and occasionally abused by his father. They lived in a poor neighborhood. At the age of ten he was a master of deceit, quick in provoking his classmates and teachers, threatening and cruel to those physically inferior to himself. His delinquency ranged from truancy to acts of vandalism, from foul and lewd language to extortion and sexual attacks on small girls. There was virtually no day without some disciplinary problem in spite of a great deal of patience and kindness shown him by school superiors. His particular talent was turning hopefully bright days into sad ones. Understanding and leniency were not enough, and there were always other children to teach and to guide. Dan made himself difficult to teach by hurting others and at times striking out blindly. Usually he hurt himself as much as or more than others.

PREPARATION FOR ADOLESCENT TASKS

At each stage of development, characteristics of that stage reach maximum expression some time before the period ends. At the age of ten to eleven, the majority of children arrive at their preadolescent maximum and appear to stop for a while. This, then, is a time for efficient preparation for the developmental tasks of puberty and adolescence.

Academic accomplishments are very important for the preadolescent because he needs to be proud of his achievements. His desire to excel increases his efforts. He looks for an area of success, and when he finds one, either in academic or nonacademic fields, he is benefited. If his sense of accomplishment is strengthened, the feelings of inadequacy that readily afflict the nonachieving preadolescent are counteracted. The adolescent defeatist attitude may begin to take root during the years of late childhood. Procrastination at work and aggressiveness in social situations often accompany this attitude. Parents, through encouragement and control, can often correct the situation if they are aware of the importance of achievement in preadolescence.

Peer identification is one of the first antecedents of later adolescent and adult identifications with persons of one's own age. In late childhood, as was stated earlier, close peer associations are usually limited to members of the same sex. The emotional intimacy, however, is a reminder of later identifications. Frequent peer activities in large and small groups lay the foundations for a personally gratifying postpubertal crowd and clique relationship.

As a child becomes readier to respond to the information and suggestion of his peer groups, as the leader or majority rule of the group is followed, the child recognizes alternatives and expands his perspective. Then, in some home or school situations, he insists on acting on his own choice. Peer identification thus represents a major step toward self-reliance. It is noteworthy that a child of twelve or thirteen is occasionally concerned with and projects himself into a new cycle of development that will continue until the twenties. He admires boys who are bold and daring. He wants to be sixteen or eighteen, anticipating the privileges he will enjoy then, especially driving a car.

With adolescent developments and adjustments in mind, specific preparation can be satisfactorily undertaken to form later attitudes, especially toward sex and morality. Fundamentally, this preparation consists of parental instruction and the preadolescent's own learning how to adjust to sexual maturation. Because the school is primarily concerned with intellectual development, the home bears the responsibility for moral, religious, and sexual instruction at this level.

Since in the various phases of childhood, incoherent and incomplete information on sexual matters is bound to be encountered, advanced instruction is needed to correct and complete sex information as it concerns the approaching adolescent and adult phases of life. When to give this instruction depends on many factors, especially the need and interest of the child concerned. The beginnings of pubertal growth in height and weight are a definite indication of such a need because these changes are followed by sexual maturation. Generally, the parent of the same sex should give this instruction. If he feels the task is too difficult for him, it is his duty to find a satisfactory substitute. Teachers, physicians, psychologists, social workers, and clergymen are often well prepared to convey this information. The instruction should center around the oncoming sexual developments and their basic implications. Books by George A. Kelly [16], and J. A. O'Brien [4], as well as pamphlets [8, 12, 13, 20], may be of considerable assistance to the parent and sometimes to the prepubescent himself. Sex instruction should present not only basic information but also healthy attitudes which are essential.   Along with instruction, the major moral implications of sex should be explained.   E. B. Lyman's *Let's tell the whole story about sex* [18] consists of four recorded conversations between parents and their children: how babies are born, menstruation, problems of growing boys, and the marriage union.   These stories are for parents and adult organizations—not for children.   Frank and fairly complete, they consider some of the moral and religious implications of the subject.

Beyond this, most children need explanations of moral considerations in various peer relationships and activities, a clarification of the concept of virtues, and an analysis of the relationships between moral conduct and religious precepts.   Such information fosters the development of conscience, which, in turn, will make it easier to act in accordance with moral principles and virtues. Thus, the foundation of a moral character will be laid and strengthened before the adolescent style of life is set.   Reverent references to religious values and the meaning of religious practices are bound to strengthen religious motivation and assist in making faith the crowning experience of human life.   With moral insight and conscience and with a penetrating religious experience, the young person has the best possible resources to face the tasks of adolescence and adulthood.   In childhood, much depended on what happened in infancy; so, too, in adolescence, much depends on the developments and adjustments of the years of childhood.

QUESTIONS FOR REVIEW

1. How do peer influences affect the child's personality during the late years of childhood?
2. Describe the child's relationship to his parents and to his siblings.
3. How does an individual grow into child society?   Describe the emergence of a gang.
4. What are some of the outstanding goals in child group life?   How are they realized?
5. Describe the child's advances in cognitive development and the resultant interests.
6. Explain the changes in competition and cooperation which occur in preadolescence.
7. In what ways do preadolescent boys and girls differ?   How do boys express their dislike for girls and vice versa?
8. Why are children's clubs and organizations necessary?
9. How are self-identity and self-appraisal modified by parents and by peers?
10. Describe sexual typing and identify factors affecting it.

11. What are the factors promoting character development? How does parental behavior affect the child's character development?
12. What does a child need in order to be prepared for adolescent developmental tasks?

REFERENCES

I. Selected Reading

1. Gesell, Arnold, et al. *Youth: The years from ten to sixteen.* New York: Harper & Row, 1956. A discussion of maturity profiles, gradients, and age trends on a year-to-year basis.
2. Loomis, Mary J. *The preadolescent: Three major concerns.* New York: Appleton-Century-Crofts, 1959. A study of strivings for independence, sexual identification, and school adjustment.
3. Maccoby, Eleanor E. (Ed.). *The development of sex differences.* Stanford, Calif.: Stanford, 1966. A major work on various aspects of psychosexual development. It consists of five essays: three psychological, one anthropological, and one physiological.
4. O'Brien, John A. *Sex-character education.* New York: Macmillan, 1953. An analysis of the role sex plays in character development. The need for and some practical steps toward promotion of sex instruction are emphasized by the book's several contributors.
5. Strang, Ruth. *An introduction to child study.* (4th ed.) New York: Macmillan, 1959. An age-related presentation of child development, its psychology and educational needs. Part 5 deals with preadolescent years.

II. Specific References

6. Bernhardt, Karl S. Sex education. *Bull. Inst. Child Study,* University of Toronto, 1954, **16**, 5–10.
7. Bieliauskas, Vytautas J. Recent advances in the psychology of masculinity and femininity. *J. Psychol.*, 1965, **60**, 255–263.
8. Brueckner, P. J. *How to give sex instructions.* St. Louis: Queen's Work, 1940.
9. Calon, P. *De Jongen* (The Boy). Heemstede, Utig: De Toorts, 1954.
10. Duvall, Evelyn M. *Family development.* (2nd ed.) Philadelphia: Lippincott, 1962.
11. Endebrock, Donald M. *The parental obligation to care for the religious education of children.* Washington, D. C.: Catholic U. Press, 1955.
12. Gruenberg, Sidonie M. *The wonderful story of how you were born.* New York: Doubleday, 1952. (For reading by children.)
13. Hymes, James L., Jr. *The technique of sex information.* New York: Public Affairs Committee, 1949.

14. Johnson, M.   Sex role learning in the nuclear family.   *Child Developm.,* 1963, **34,** 319–333.

15. Kagan, Jerome.   Acquisition and significance of sex role identity.   In M. L. Hoffman and L. W. Hoffman (Eds.), *Review of child development research.*   New York: Russell Sage Foundation, 1964.   Vol. 1, pp. 137–167.

16. Kelly, George A.   *Your child and sex.*   New York: Random House, 1964.

17. Laughlin, Frances.   *The peer status of sixth and seventh grade children.*   New York: Columbia, 1954.

18. Lyman, E. B.   Let's tell the whole story about sex.   A recent album of four 78-r.p.m. records or one 33⅓-r.p.m. record distributed by the American Social Health Organization (1790 Broadway, New York, N. Y. 10019).

19. Lynn, David B.   Divergent feedback and sex-role identification in boys and men.   *Merrill-Palmer Quart.,* 1964, **10,** 17–23.

20. Newland, Mary R.   Sex education in the family.   *The living Light,* Summer 1965.   (Also available from National CCD Center, 1312 Massachusetts Ave., Washington, D. C. 20005.)

21. Pikunas, Justin.   *Fundamental child psychology.*   (2nd ed.) Milwaukee: Bruce, 1965.

22. Redl, Fritz.   Preadolescents—what makes them tick.   In F. Redl, *When we deal with children: Selected writings.*   New York: Free Press, 1966. Pp. 395–408.

Part 6
Puberty

In the earlier levels of growth already discussed, not many of the final characteristics, qualities, or features had yet been manifested in the forms in which they later present themselves in the adult's personality organization and physique. Puberty is the stage of life when adult features and body proportions begin to appear. Through rapid bodily growth at this time adult features of the organism emerge, together with the psychosexual developments needed for full masculinity and femininity. Only by drastic means may some of these normally durable traits be modified or transformed.

Preoccupation with oneself and worry about one's personal adequacy, identity, and social status intensify as the individual undergoes these perplexing and transforming changes leading toward adult qualities and abilities. Achieving self-identity and finding one's place in peer society are pubertal tasks of great complexity. Puberty marks the beginning of adolescent development. It is more than that: most of the transforming changes of adolescence occur within the years of puberty. The following two chapters will deal chiefly with pubertal developments, while the next two will concentrate on occurrences during postpubertal years.

PUBERTAL DEVELOPMENTS

Puberty and adolescence are usually considered transitional stages between childhood and adulthood. Childish behavior and personality diminish at this time, while adult traits and features with their specific masculine or feminine characteristics grow.

CONCEPTS OF PUBERTY AND ADOLESCENCE

Puberty is the beginning of adolescent development. The term puberty comes from the Latin *pubertas,* meaning coming to the age of manhood; adolescence comes from the Latin verb *adolescere,* which means "to grow to maturity." The psychology of adolescence deals with both the pubertal and adolescent phases of ontogenetic growth and ends with the attainment of adult maturity. During puberty, besides physical growth and sexual maturation, intense emotional, social, cognitive, and personality developments occur.

In our Western culture the adolescent period of life has been looked upon and characterized as a time of storm and stress; an age of suffering and frustration; an era of many problems, surprises, and life-determining decisions; a span of intensified conflicts and crises of adjustment; and a stage of alienation from adult society. Viewed from a more positive standpoint, it can be regarded as a stage of search for one's self marked by intimate peer affiliation, romance, and love; by discovery of values, ideals, and full personal identity; by development of personality and character; and by attainment of adult status with its privileges, challenges, and responsibilities.

Usually an adolescent becomes deeply aware of many issues and questions relating to himself and others. He is concerned over his obligations, the expectations of others—especially members of the opposite sex—and his liberty to undertake new experiences and adventures. He must learn to achieve a balance between the pursuit of pleasure and the acceptance of responsibility and service to fellowmen, country, and God. As the adolescent's world enlarges, his mind becomes somewhat attuned to the challenges and opportunities before him.

Growing up involves considerable stress and strain, feelings of uncertainty and anxiety, with many ups and downs before an adult personality pattern begins to appear. The adolescent is deeply sensitive and often appears to be a bundle of contradictions. He often vacillates between feverish activity and idleness, and between childish narcissism and adult altruism. His behavior continues to be marked to some extent by instability and incoherence. He is at times confused with reference to his roles, tasks, and obligations. Surprises and disappointments are frequent. Adolescent living is like a never-ending dream in the dark night where powerful flashes of light occur yet are blinding rather than illuminating.

The experiences that occur in the course of adolescence vary greatly in intensity among individuals, but are similar in various technologically advanced societies. Norman Kiell gives an impressive amount of biographical data in support of his thesis that "the great internal turmoil and external disorder of adolescence are universal and only moderately affected by cultural determinants" [11, p. 9]. For many individuals some of the developmental tasks of this time are unfinished and are carried over into the years of early adulthood.

U. S. youth and its educational needs. Furnishing proper educational facilities and providing occupational opportunities for adolescents and young adults presents a challenge to the nation because their swelling numbers—a result of the record number of births in 1946 and subsequent years—show no sign of abating. (See Figures 14–1 and 14–2.) The early 1960s saw a phenomenal rise in high school and college enrollments. From 1960 to 1965 high schools added over 640,000 students a year to their total enrollment, and colleges averaged increases of nearly 275,000 students each year. The tendency for young people not only to complete high school but to continue their education beyond this level augurs well for the future of the nation, which largely depends on the education and guidance opportunities for youth.

Project TALENT [10] was the first major national study of available ability

Millions of children

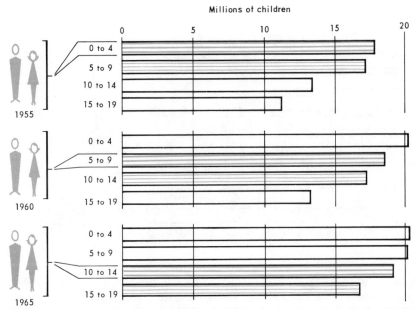

Figure 14–1 Child and adolescent population. *(Children and youth: Their health and welfare.* Children's Bureau Publication No. 363, 1958; and *Current population reports,* series P-25, No. 321, 1966.)

and creativity. This study explored the relations among aptitudes, interests, motivations, and productivity, as well as the effectiveness of various educational programs and procedures for realizing individual potentials. The testing of nearly 500,000 high school students (5 percent of the total high school enrollment) was completed in 1960. Follow-up questionnaires will tell what has happened to the high school seniors of 1960, whether they have gone to college, taken jobs, or changed their earlier plans. Further information and data will continue to be collected from TALENT students one, five, ten, and twenty years after they have graduated from high school.

Donald N. Michael's *The next generation* [13] points to the direction society is likely to take in education; he foresees, for example, separate schools for professionals and technicians, where only superior students will receive the constant attention of teachers, and teaching machines will be utilized to an ever-increasing degree by students not entitled to the attention of professors. This book predicts for the decades to come many other trends and possibilities in education, occupation, and related political issues.

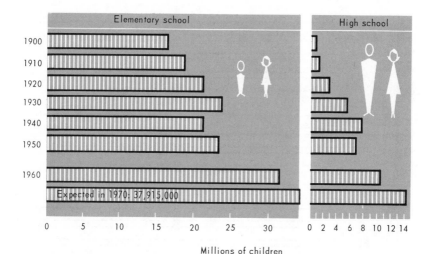

Millions of children

Figure 14-2   Schools are growing.   (Fact Finding Committee, Midcentury White House Conference on Children and Youth. *A graphic presentation of social and economic facts important in the lives of children and youth,* 1951; and U. S. Bureau of the Census. *Statistical abstract of the United States: 1966,* 1966.)

FACTORS PRECIPITATING PUBERTAL CHANGES

Pubertal, or early adolescent, growth consists primarily of rapid somatic maturation and the beginning of a more adult body structure, sexual developments resulting in the active functioning of the gonads, and the appearance of the secondary sex characteristics which then clearly distinguish the mature male and female.   A release of new genetic information in the organizing cells is a fundamental cause of the pubertal growth spurt.   This information produces functional changes in the thalamic-pituitary axis.   For the total cycle of pubertal change a balanced interaction among the cerebral cortex, autonomic nervous system, thalamus, pituitary, thyroid, adrenal cortex, and gonads seems to be required.

On the average, the structural growth occurs between eleven and a half to fourteen for girls, and twelve and a half to fifteen and a half for boys.   This increase depends directly on change in the functioning of the endocrine gland system.   Several endocrine glands participate extensively in these pubertal changes.

The *pituitary* gland, located at the base of the brain, is a master gland which produces hormones for stimulating growth and activity in all other endocrine glands.   The hormonal activity of the pituitary appears to depend largely on stimulation by the hypothalamus and the hormones of certain other glands [18]. The anterior lobe of the pituitary produces several hormones that directly or indirectly function as growth regulators. Somatotrophin (STH), one of the pituitary's growth-promoting hormones, controls the size of the individual and, especially, the length of the limbs. Hyposecretion of the anterior portion of the pituitary causes one to remain childlike in size, while hypersecretion makes growth spurt to giant proportions. Normally the increased activity of the pituitary's anterior lobe in terms of somatotrophic hormone production stimulates increased structural growth of the extremities of the body. Arms and hands, legs and feet, and the nose grow quickly and assume practically adult proportions. At the same time, the heart enlarges disproportionately to the slower increase of the arteries, resulting in increased blood pressure. The disproportion in capacity between heart and arteries and the elevated blood pressure cause many young teen-agers to experience moments of dizziness and general weakness.

Other pituitary hormones stimulate the thyroid (TSH), the adrenal cortex (ACTH), certain metabolic processes, and to a certain extent the blood pressure. In cases of strain or infection, ACTH is produced rapidly and causes the adrenal cortex to speed up its corticoid production. The pro-inflammatory (P) and anti-inflammatory (A) hormones of the adrenals create an organized defense against any invasion by foreign matter. Too many P's, however, may produce more damage than a splinter, bacilli, or other sources of stress [17, pp. 178–181].

Research in endocrynology has verified the existence of a close relationship between the secretion of the pituitary's gonadotrophic hormone and the sex glands: increased secretion of this hormone activates the growth and functional maturation of the sex glands. However, when the gonads—testes in the male and ovaries in the female—reach their maturity, they begin to produce hormones of their own which affect the pituitary's functions, by slowing down its growth-producing secretions, and stimulate the development of secondary sex characteristics.

Another factor influencing structural growth is the *thyroid* gland, located in front of the larynx within the throat region. Its secretion, thyroxin, consists chiefly of iodine (65 percent) and greatly influences metabolism—the nutrition and energy exchange within the organism and related cellular activity—and, especially, oxygen consumption. Poor thyroid functioning without medical care leads to a general retardation of physical and mental development, a condition known as myxedema. Excessive thyroid functioning increases the metabolic rate of the individual, raises the blood pressure, and makes the person excitable, especially when the condition is accompanied by a hypofunctioning of the parathyroids.

The adrenals, attached to the kidneys, increase their functional activity as puberty advances, while the thymus gland, located in the chest anterior to the mediastinum and behind the sternum, grows smaller and deteriorates at about the same time.

Ossification and muscle development play a considerable role in adolescent behavior because physical strength largely depends on the bone and muscle systems. At the age of eight the weight of the muscles approximates 27 percent of the gross body weight; at sixteen years it reaches 44 percent. The greatest increase occurs with puberty. Strength usually doubles between the ages of twelve and sixteen. Recently the average height of young American women rose to 65 inches and their weight increased to about 134 pounds, while the average man measured 70 inches and weighed approximately 150 pounds.

When cartilage is converted into bone at a fast rate, discomforts, cramps, and aches result. While bone development is consistent with the general rate of physical maturation, the speed of muscular growth is influenced by the amount of physical exercise. Muscle growth that precedes bone development is apt to contribute heavily to psychomotor incoordination and clumsiness. Intricate relationships between various enlarged muscle systems and neural extensions, stimulating their activity, add much to the pubertal difficulties in muscle coordination. Muscles become flabby and weak and shrink in size if they are not used for strenuous activities. Recent studies suggest that the average high school student spends only two hours a week in group play or exercise. This is one reason why one-third of the 200,000 pupils tested for the President's Council on Physical Fitness failed, owing to insufficient strength, flexibility, and stamina [12, p. 5].

All the various biochemical and physical changes taking place within him expose the pubertal child to loss of symmetry and grace. This is especially true of boys in social situations. The adolescent's changing body and uncertain movements increase his self-consciousness. He does, however, gradually gain in muscular coordination through his performances in athletics. The emergence of new impulses and desires, especially those related to sexual maturation, bring about motivational and behavioral indecision and even disorientation of a temporary nature. Yet the adolescent begins to search for the meanings and implications of these changes and makes attempts at controlling and integrating them within his expanded self-system. The young teen-ager should be well informed about the major effects of pubertal changes.

SEXUAL DEVELOPMENT

With the exception of the primary sex characteristics, boys and girls are quite similar in their physical appearance during childhood. The increasing difference in appearance during puberty is due to the growth of skeletal and muscular systems, and is especially related to growth of secondary sex characteristics. The development of the testes, the distribution and pigmentation of pubic hair, and changes in voice are the significant secondary sex traits of boys. The young male's high-pitched voice drops approximately one octave. Breast formation from budding papillae to mature breasts and the appearance of pubic hair, broadening hips, and menstruation are the signs of a girl's progress in pubertal growth.

The physical changes of adolescence reach their peak when sex glands achieve structural maturity and begin to function. Aside from wide individual differences, the average age for this occurrence in girls approximates 12.5 years and for boys 14.2 years. The norms depend on the criterion that is being used. The amount of gonadotrophic hormone in the urine, determined by laboratory analysis, furnishes a satisfactory but infrequently used criterion for measuring the level of pubertal development. Another criterion is provided by appraising X-rays of wrist bone structure, for it has been determined that gonad maturation occurs simultaneously with a certain level of ossification. On the basis of skeletal age, developmental norms have been formulated for both boys and girls [7]. The entire process of sexual maturation requires about three years, but individual differences are great indeed. Sexual maturity implies a capacity for offspring.

The onset of sexual maturation in girls is frequently an abrupt phenomenon requiring emotional and social readjustments of an immediate nature. This process is less sudden in boys. Their need for readjustment comes more gradually. The transition from an immature to a mature physical sexuality requires approximately one year. This transition constitutes the peak of pubertal changes. Growth in the reproductive system greatly influences the experiences, attitudes, and behavior of the growing person. The effects of sexual growth on the self-concept and personality are pervasive and cannot be overemphasized.

If a pituitary hyperfunction exists during the years of childhood, pubertal changes occur several years earlier than they are normally expected. In such exceptional cases, the secondary sex characteristics appear, but heterosexual interests do not develop as rapidly. On the other hand, various factors, such as glandular disturbances, poor diet, long illness, or otherwise retarded development, can delay pubertal changes for several years.

Slightly precocious sexual maturation usually has advantages for boys and disadvantages for girls. Since the precocious boy looks grown up, he often secures more popularity and social prestige among his peers than prepubertal boys, but very early puberty often makes the individual unsuited for his own age group, while still unaccepted in older groups. The grown-up boy is often admired by his peers for his physical strength and athletic prowess. Early onset of puberty for girls gives them a growth spurt which makes them larger than boys. Very often this is a decided disadvantage for them.

Delayed puberty results in a small body with less strength than one's faster-maturing peers. The boy may be pressured to withdraw from the group with which he was associated and to compensate by association with a younger age group—a situation often causing the boy to entertain feelings of inadequacy or an attitude of failure. Considering teen-age problems as a whole, it may be concluded that boys who mature late are beset with more problems and troubles than those who mature early. Gifted and intellectually superior children usually undergo puberty changes earlier than the average, and the average begin before the mentally dull and borderline groups. Individual exceptions, however, are fairly frequent.

When pubertal changes appear comparatively early, structural growth is more gradual and regular than in most cases of late growth. If it starts late, growth is often turbulent and less integrated. Rapid acceleration in growth brings with it restlessness, fatigue, and disturbances in motor coordination. In general, pubertal changes appear at a similar age among all races, nationalities, and cultures, but are mildly delayed in northern regions and more rapid in southern areas.

CHANGES IN EMOTIONS AND ATTITUDES

Puberty is a stage of heightened emotionality. The pubertal child begins to experience definite and heightened feelings and undertakes to revise his own attitudes. The great increase in emotional differentiation is apparent in the various moods experienced. The pubescent becomes increasingly sensitive and reacts strongly to events and social situations. While the advanced adolescent is able to control his emotions to a considerable extent, the young adolescent is swept along by the vivid currents of his feelings and sentiments. When aroused, his emotions are frequently out of proportion to the initial stimulus. Attempts to control emotional expressions are frequent but not always successful. The emotionally charged actions closely resemble the heightened negativism and temper seen during the third year of life, at the dawn of early childhood.

Ambivalent feelings are the rule rather than the exception at puberty. The adolescent often experiences contradictory feelings, that is, love and hate, enthusiasm and then apathy, toward the same persons and events. Trivial disappointments may arouse his antagonism without destroying his original feeling of cordiality or warmth. The capacity for keeping affective experiences in harmony seems to be lost.

The effort to achieve social and sexual maturity is probably the most difficult task of the pubertal period. Transference of affection and love from parents to peers, including members of the opposite sex, represents a major change in emotional cathexis. Discouragement and emotional tension are common while this key shift of feelings is occurring. New adjustments at any age are accompanied by heightened affective reactions. Development of new attitudes and integration of new values are parts of a painful process. Lack of preparation for the adolescent role, parental insensitivity and objections, and financial need, all contribute to this state of emotional uneasiness. Such states lead to occasional outbursts which, when not physically discharged, accumulate and interrupt functioning of the sensitive organismic system. As a result, organismic balance and personal health are disturbed, especially if such states repeatedly arise. New self-defense tactics are needed to preserve some kind of balance. Indecision and daydreaming, aggression and discrimination are among the self-defensive reactions often used by adolescents to protect themselves from the threats and contradictions of the social world. The young adolescent experiences great difficulty in finding his place in peer society and culture.

Increased social awareness and a need for intimate peer companionship make an adolescent ready to conform to the expectations of his contemporaries. He takes pains to establish favorable relationships with the various individuals he meets and the groups with which he comes in contact. Full social acceptance is highly desired but for many teen-agers is difficult to attain. Contacts with members of the opposite sex assume higher value and are soon regarded as vital for self-esteem.

Emotional instability is typical at puberty. Strong likes and dislikes prevalent in the group form a basis for attitudes toward classes of people and situations that earlier were matters of indifference. These attitudes, typical of adolescence in pattern, will affect and change personality.

HEALTH AND ENERGY CONSUMPTION

Late childhood is usually a healthy age, but this is not the case when pubertal changes occur. Often the young adolescent feels ill and suffers headaches, bodily discomforts, and stomach pains. He may have little energy for work or even for play, feel tired if not exhausted, or be annoyed by other minor disturbances of a psychosomatic nature. He may experience a generally run-down condition or frequently be bothered by influenza and sore throats or tonsilitis. Sometimes "feeling ill" is used as an escape from duties and responsibilities to which he objects. There are not any severe illnesses specific to this stage and, excluding accidents, few die from adolescent sicknesses.

There are some physiological explanations for the young adolescent's lack of energy and his frequent colds and aches. First of all, the slower growth of blood vessels in relation to the heart raises the blood pressure and creates both strain on the heart and feelings of tension and tiredness. At this phase of accelerated growth a young person should not be pressed into robust activities. Usually, though, the pubertal child feels inclined to expand a great amount of energy, even beyond his capacity. By overexpending himself in sports and late shows and endless unnecessary activity, and often with an inadequate intake of food, the adolescent occasionally develops an enlarged heart or respiratory illness.

Since *smoking* is fairly common among teen-agers today, its detrimental effects on growth and health should be considered. After each cigarette the heart beats faster for about 30 to 60 minutes. This superfluous activity lowers the cardiac reserve. The use of tobacco mildly constricts blood vessels, slowing down oxygenation and effecting the quick loss of breath. Another frequent result of smoking is loss of appetite because of slower than normal stomach movement; eating less may prevent the full nutrition required for growth.. Medical research studies show that nonsmokers have the best records for health and length of life; moderate smokers have poorer records but excel over heavy smokers. Athletes who smoke experience greater difficulty in strenuous competition than do others [12, pp. 212–213; 20].

At puberty the oil-producing glands increase their productivity and result in skin eruptions and acne of various types. Rapid growth, emotional turmoil, and unpredictable eating and activity habits also contribute to skin trouble. Difficulties in social relationships and the resulting conflicts and frustrations are additional contributing causes. Following the completion of major pubertal changes, physical health usually reaches its highest level in late adolescence and early adulthood.

DEVELOPMENTAL TASKS OF PUBERTY

The developmental tasks of puberty are not peculiar to this one period, since most of them extend into adolescence. Some pubertal developments, however, including bodily control, peer identification, social sensitivity, reorganization of personality and self, maintenance of external interests and activity, and progress in controlling impulses, especially sexual urges and emotional moods, though they pertain specifically to this phase, are necessary prerequisites for later adolescent adjustment and achievement.

1. *Bodily control.* Pubescent developments indirectly lead to awkwardness, poor posture, and physical discomforts. Regaining control over the body becomes a continual task for the teen-ager. Constant effort and exercise are necessary to achieve sufficient strength and the control required for mature gracefulness or athletic prowess.

2. *Peer identification.* At puberty the adolescent seems to be confronted with two sets of motives: the prepubertal egoistical ones, which aim to satisfy pleasure-seeking drives, and the social ones by which he strives for affiliation, approval, and interpersonal intimacy. The desire to make a good impression on others, especially on peers of both sexes, becomes intense. The individual gradually learns to adjust his actions to fit the group pattern and strives for total identification with its goals and activities. Achieving success in this developmental task is a major

step in managing to identify oneself socially and emotionally with persons and groups other than parents and family. This ability is crucial for social adjustment during one's later years. Self-identification with models more mature than oneself is also a further step in this direction.

3. *Social sensitivity.* As the young boy or girl becomes more interested in peers of both sexes and seeks their approval, he or she learns more about the qualities and characteristics of others. Acquiring knowledge of others' needs helps the teen-ager improve his sensitivity to the wants, preferences, and expectations of his peers. He is deeply concerned about the impression he makes upon them. Through his manner of speech, his dress, and specific interests, the pubertal child makes many attempts to become a member of a prestige group. He alters his thoughts and opinions to fit group structure and dynamics as well as social conventions to be in good standing with his peers.

4. *Self-reorganization.* A general breakup of child personality structure occurs in the early phase of adolescence. Many new attitudes and interests, such as the changing relation to parents and peers, awakened sexuality and a grown-up body, and new moods and fantasies, lead to a reorganization of the total personality. In the course of this reorganization, the child's attitudes and interests are largely modified or transformed. Many attempts are usually made by the pubescent to prove to himself that he is not a child any longer. Objections to treatment like one are frequently raised if parents or teachers do not recognize his newly developing self-concept.

5. *External interests and activity.* The pubertal child is usually preoccupied with self and frequently engages in brooding fantasy and prolonged daydreaming. Withdrawal into oneself at puberty is a threat to the individual's learning and to his advance in socialization. At this stage he can learn much by activity and participation and by experimenting with his own endowments in order to utilize and assess them for his present and future needs. It is the time for expanding interests in social life and culture.

6. *Growth of self-regulation.* Self-control must be exerted to curb sexual impulses and emotions, especially those which disturb interpersonal relationships, such as anger, temper outbursts, and moods. Forces from without could be relied on for control in childhood, but the pubescent makes efforts to free himself of such dominance and to establish his own internal authority on which he can rely, thus increasing his self-direction and asserting the individuality of his own personality. Growth in self-regulation is also needed for developing skills in interpersonal communication, and gaining in popularity and leadership.

Pubertal development can be summed up by comparing it to a young plant that is starting to grow into the fullness of its intrinsic nature. This period may also remind one of the words of Christ when He said, "Unless the grain of wheat fall into the ground and die, itself remains alone.   But if it die, it brings forth much fruit."   So also the pubescent must figuratively suffer the death of his childhood ways if he is to develop into a fairly adjusted and useful adult.   Puberty is a period of preparation for the serious commitments of later adolescence.

QUESTIONS FOR REVIEW

1. Explain the concept of adolescence.   Give some characteristics of this phase of life.
2. Explain the relationship between puberty and adolescence.
3. What are some typical problems and conflicts arising during pubertal changes?
4. Indicate the role the pituitary gland plays in precipitating pubertal growth.
5. Give some facts about the structural changes within the heart, bone, and muscular systems.
6. Enumerate some reasons for either early or late sexual maturation. Explain the social effects of early sexual maturity.
7. What criteria are used in estimating the level of pubertal development?
8. Name some health disturbances which frequently occur at puberty and adolescence.
9. What emotional changes take place during puberty?   How are emotions and attitudes related?
10. Identify several developmental tasks of puberty and explain one of them.

REFERENCES

I. Selected Reading

1. Cole, Luella, with Irma N. Hall. *Psychology of adolescence.* (6th ed.) New York: Holt, 1964.   A general text on adolescent experience, motivation, and behavior, normal and deviant, including educational applications.
2. Douvan, Elizabeth, and Joseph Adelson. *The adolescent experience.* New York: Wiley, 1966.   A national survey, based on interview data concerning about three thousand adolescents, which discusses social attitudes, masculine and feminine crises, culture, values, and personality integrating themes.
3. Hurlock, Elizabeth B. *Adolescent development.* (3rd ed.) New York: McGraw-Hill, 1967.   A presentation of adolescent psychology in an encyclopedic fashion, documented by a great variety of studies.
4. Jersild, Arthur T. *The psychology of adolescence.* (2nd ed.) New York: Macmillan, 1963.   A general text on adolescence, which emphasizes emotional development, social relationships, and the self.
5. Remplein, Heinz. *Die seelische Entwicklung des Menschen im Kindes-*

und Jugendalter. (7th ed.) Munich: Reinhardt, 1958. Sec. 4. An analysis of pubertal developments and their repercussions on personality.

6. Schneiders, Alexander A. *Personality development and adjustment in adolescence.* Milwaukee: Bruce, 1960. A lengthy treatment of the dynamics underlying behavior, with consideration of physiology, sociology, character, and guidance.

II. Specific References

7. Bayley, Nancy. Tables for predicting adult height from skeletal age and present height. *J. Pediat.,* 1946, **28,** 49–64.

8. Bayley, Nancy. Growth curves of height and weight by age for boys and girls scaled according to physical maturity. *J. Pediat.,* 1956, **48,** 187–194.

9. Dale, R. J. A method for measuring developmental tasks: Scales for selected tasks at the beginning of adolescence. *Child Develop.,* 1955, **26,** 11–122.

10. Flanagan, J. C., et al. *The talents of American youth I: Design for a study of American youth.* Boston: Houghton Mifflin, 1962. See also Schoenfeldt, Lyle F. *A national data resource for behavioral, social, and educational research.* Palo Alto: American Institutes of Research, 1968.

11. Kiell, Norman. *The universal experience of adolescence.* New York: International Universities Press, 1964.

12. La Salle, Dorothy, and Gladys Geer. *Health instruction for today's schools.* Englewood Cliffs, N. J.: Prentice-Hall, 1963.

13. Michael, Donald N. *The next generation: The prospects ahead for the youth of today and tomorrow.* New York: Random House, 1965.

14. Nicholson, A. B., and C. Hanley. Indices of physiological maturity. *Child Developm.,* 1953, **24,** 3–38.

15. President's Council on Physical Fitness. *Youth physical fitness: Suggested elements of a school-centered program.* 1965.

16. President's Council on Physical Fitness. *Vigor: A complete exercise plan for boys 12 to 18.* 1964.

17. Selye, Hans. The stress of life. In M. L. Haimowitz and Natalie R. Haimowitz (Eds.), *Human development: Selected readings.* (2nd ed.) New York: Crowell, 1966. Chap. 23, pp. 170–195.

18. Talbot, N. B., et al. *Functional endocrynology from birth through adolescence.* Cambridge, Mass.: Harvard, 1952.

19. Tanner, James M. *Growth at adolescence.* Oxford: Blackwell, 1964.

20. Vermes, Hal C. *The boy's book of physical fitness.* New York: Association Press, 1961. (Also: *The girl's book of physical fitness,* by Jean C. Vermes.)

21. Zaccaria, Joseph S. Developmental tasks: Implications for the goals of guidance. *Personnel Guid. J.,* 1965, **44,** 373–374.

PERSONALITY
REORGANIZATION

The previous chapter pointed out the numerous developments that occur during puberty. As one might expect, a major personality transformation also begins when the individual enters the early adolescent phase of growth. Personality reorganization is stimulated by structural maturity and functional changes within the glandular and neuromuscular systems.

CHANGING SELF-AWARENESS

When an adult puts on a new suit or any new wearing apparel, it tends to increase his self-inspection, and feelings of adequacy or inadequacy become more noticeable at these times. Similarly, growth or alteration of any part of the organism is likely to promote heightened self-awareness and to stir up attitudes related to one's self-concept. It is therefore not surprising that pubertal transformations within various bodily systems affect the total personality pattern. Growth in body structures and changes in proportion, producing a more adult physique, stimulate changes in attitudes toward oneself and others. New vistas of experience and behavior appear. Feelings of self-sufficiency and self-worth are magnified if growth is consistent with one's ideal, as determined from observation of others who have achieved this growth. Feelings of inadequacy and inferiority emerge or are strengthened if one notices differences and interprets them as deficiencies or abnormalities.

At the transitional age of puberty, the individual is very much concerned about his appearance because he is now more self-conscious than before and capable of more critical self-evaluation. He comes to realize that his appearance will remain, to a large degree, the same for adolescence and adulthood as well. The pinup glamour girl or the Tarzan are often present but impossible to fully realize. Many pubertal children have some difficulties in accepting themselves as they are, especially if others do not seem to accept them as they are. Frequently peers point out undesirable traits or behavioral peculiarities. Any critical remark on the part of companions alters the adolescent's self-acceptance. Nicknames are a teen-ager's tool for marking and noting differences in others, as well as for expressing annoyance over deviations from the standard. Shorty, Spider, Fatty, Butch, Blubber, Squeeky, Whale, Machine Gun, and Beanpole are some examples of nicknaming. If the name is directed toward him and meant to be cutting, the adolescent soon feels out of place.

In addition to the tendency toward self-evaluation, there are other sources of concern that preoccupy the adolescent. Which specific drive or function may attract attention depends to a certain degree on whether the young person is a boy or a girl. The concerns of a teen-age boy are specific to the male adolescent population. Awkwardness due to the rapid growth of limbs and muscles is an early source of adolescent concern. At a later point, speech will be affected too. The lack of control over one's voice and the changes in tone quality result in some embarrassments and occasionally lead to pubescent *reticence,* in certain social situations at least, until control improves. Discomfort and tension periods also occur when full sexual functioning takes place. A boy may be disturbed and sometimes even frightened by nocturnal emissions and the strength of sexual impulses.

Relieving sexual tension by means of masturbation and enjoying a pleasurable experience often result in guilt and, occasionally, feelings of depression in adolescents, especially if they have been taught to believe that this activity is sinful or immoral. Actually, the practice is a common one, which the adolescent usually outgrows if he makes serious efforts to control it. If the youth does not make sufficient effort to gain control over his sexual fantasies and activities, however, the situation may become pathological and result in a perversion of the sexual drive. If a pubescent masturbates excessively without any experience of shame or guilt, his chances to develop normally and to remain a healthy personality are seriously threatened. Excessive masturbation is not a suitable means for expressing or eliminating sexual drive. The parent or counselor should encourage a growth of inner control to help in redirecting some of these sexual energies toward more sublimated and creative goals. Moral convictions on the adolescent's part facilitate achievement of reasonable control, helping to keep his motivation clear.

With strong feelings and strange changes occurring within him, the adolescent naturally experiences great interest in and curiosity over sexual matters. Like every new experience and power, the developing sexual capacity is intriguing and the drive compelling. The boy becomes concerned about the significance and implications of these sexual changes. He seeks to know if his friends have the same experiences. His interest and curiosity are also directed toward members of the opposite sex. Perhaps for the first time in his life, girls strike him as fascinating and exciting individuals, and he begins to seek their company. Sometimes eagerness to associate with them appears almost spontaneously, but more often it develops gradually. Boys and girls begin wondering what it feels like to kiss someone of the opposite sex. If they have not received a favorable picture of the opposite sex in their home environment, however, they may now experience ambivalent feelings and mistrust.

When a young girl first realizes she is beginning to acquire a more mature feminine shape, she may become embarrassed and try to minimize her developing figure. Soon, however, the feminine model as pictured in fashion magazines and other publications begins to appeal to her. Then she begins to strive to enhance her womanly appearance. An unattractive feature or excessive height can be problems of great significance to a young girl. In addition, the menarche (the coming of menstruation) produces some discomfort and tension, worry and fear, especially if the girl has not been fully informed about it in advance. The menstrual cycle during early adolescence is often irregular. Despite the fact that menstruation is a sign of a normal and healthy condition, for many girls it is accompanied by headaches, cramps, lassitude, and a feeling of being ill. Increased irritability or depression are frequently other symptoms of the approaching period. The attitude toward menstruation, often acquired from the mother or some other informant, has much to do with the presence of these or other mild psychosomatic disturbances. Masturbation as a means of securing pleasure may also complicate the general picture of a girl's adjustment at this stage of life. Since girls mature sexually at an earlier age than boys, their interest in members of the opposite sex, usually older than themselves, generally occurs about two years earlier.

The motivational reorganization following pubertal changes is marked by a heightened tendency to show off one's new abilities and to feel great pride in achievements that impress members of the other sex. Emotional sensitivity and strivings for emancipation from home ties are necessary prerequisites for growing into peer society. The anticipation of adult privileges, a more positive attitude toward others, and efforts at self-improvement are also part of the transition from childhood to adolescence.

OUTGROWING CHILDLIKE MOTIVATION

During the pubertal period the young person differentiates himself from his family and neighborhood. He begins to understand personal responsibilities more fully and starts to accept them. It is a great challenge to the youth to strive toward responsible behavior, since as a child he ran away from many of his duties.

The increasing desire to show off one's skill or prowess to others leads the adolescent to participate in individual and group contests. Competitive sports, tasks requiring physical strength, and striving for popularity and scholastic honors are some of the more frequent fields of adolescent self-assertion. Any type of achievement, if acknowledged by others, increases one's feelings of self-importance and adequacy. Any failure is deeply discouraging and motivates withdrawal from the activity. Occasionally, the resulting conflict leads to depression and self-blame, or anger toward and aggression against others. The opposite may also occur; the young man's level of aspiration may become totally unrealistic as he tries to compensate for earlier failure. Perfectionist strivings are not infrequent during puberty and adolescence. These are often marked by repetitive attempts at self-improvement, attainment of a high scholastic standing, and an increase in popularity within peer groups of the community and school.

Emancipation from home ties consists mainly in gaining emotional independence from parents. The earlier feelings of tenderness and affection toward parents during childhood are now readily directed toward individuals of their own age. The young adolescent becomes emotionally and socially distant from his parents, making many attempts to gain and hold the affection, confidence, and esteem of his age group and to seek security in peer identification. The deep-seated adolescent need for exchange of personal experiences, thoughts, and desires is best satisfied by his peers in both dyadic and group situations. Parental claims to intimacy and dependence from the adolescent meet with resistance and resentment, even open defiance. Parental commands and restrictions are often seen as barriers to outside associations and group activities. The adolescent expects and demands consideration on an adult level. Unlike a child, he will not readily compromise. A significant number of adolescents, especially those who mature very early or late, tend to remain somewhat dependent upon their parents, possibly because they are less accepted by their age-mates or lack the skills for success in peer groupings.

Emotional sensitivity increases as the pubertal years pass. The slightest difficulty or disappointment results in increased tension and emotionally toned behavior.   As they continue in sexual and emotional development, boys and girls begin to assume gradually a more positive attitude toward parents and other adults.   This is accompanied by a gradual improvement in their manners and social behavior, with consideration and respect for the feelings of others.   Altruistic sentiments toward individuals and groups appear, yet discrimination also emerges as a strong power in social life.

The adolescent is aware of his inadequate emotional and behavioral control. Yet he exhibits fear in relation to social situations far out of proportion to the circumstances.   His own inconsistencies further complicate interpersonal situations, especially with members of the opposite sex.   He strives to appear grown up and by middle or late adolescence he has learned to take constructive steps toward improving his own self-control and social skills.   A facade of maturity is often established long before the adolescent reaches adult stature.

Childish motivation is not fully outgrown during the pubertal years.   Many earlier traits persist but are enriched by additional features.   Continuity of basic traits and extensions from the original core of personality are concepts supported by recent studies [6, 7, 10].

PUBESCENT FANTASIES

During puberty the final phase of perceptive and imaginative developments occurs.   The adolescent begins to recognize minute aspects and refinements of relationship among various persons and objects.   He enjoys vicarious experiences by means of which he can go to various places, known and strange, and engage in activities without being physically involved.   Frequently, when the pubertal child is exposed to a frustration or disappointment, he tends to compensate by recourse to fantasy.   There he can cope more successfully with threatening situations and events.   Thus, by means of daydreaming, the pubescent transcends the limits of his own powers, and of time and space barriers, and enters upon experiences that otherwise are not attainable by him.   Fantasy is often a means of escaping from current tension, anxiety, and frustration.   One major theme of pubertal reverie is the "suffering hero." Here the adolescent pictures himself as undergoing various trials and persecutions, eventually being vindicated and, in a way, successful.   The "conquering hero" represents another frequent theme of imagination which the adolescent uses for partial compensation.   Boys daydream about adult roles, vocational success, possessions, friends, sexual encounters, homage and grandeur, and a variety of adventures.   Girls daydream about their attractiveness, romances, singing, dancing, and the attention and interest of a handsome boy.

An empirical study by Percival M. Symonds [12, pp. 218–255], based on responses to pictures by forty subjects from twelve to eighteen years of age, reveals that themes of *aggression* (for example, violence and frenzied excitement) and themes of *love* (for example, dating episodes, driving together, and courting) are typical for adolescents. Other frequent themes of adolescent imagination include anxiety, guilt, depression, success, independence, happiness, conflict over good and evil, Oedipus longings and conflicts, and dread of sickness and injury. Apparently the aggressive drives growing out of frustrations at this age are further stimulated by the adolescent's need to assert his independence and to obtain adult privileges. The adolescent is also driven by his need for love, his need for belonging and security, his need to be unconditionally accepted by others, and his need to identify with someone he can admire and thus compensate for the inadequacies which he senses in himself.

The function of daydreaming is obviously to furnish a retreat from self-restraint and criticism. This gives free rein to the operation of underlying needs, drives, attitudes, and emotions. The creation of gratifying and joyful events, though imaginary, serves as a useful outlet as well as an escape from the threatening confines of the present situation. Actually, obligations present in reality cannot be avoided by flights into the world of fantasy. As the years of adolescence progress, the vicarious experiences of daydreaming become more closely related to the individual's reality situation and fuse with his plans and aspirations. Vividly trying to imagine and anticipate coming events helps the individual to avoid a number of mistakes and errors.

COGNITIVE MATURATION

During puberty, in addition to perceptual and imaginative development, the adolescent attains his adult intellectual level. There is a great increase in his ability to comprehend relationships, discern facts and assumptions, abstract what is essential, and use less concrete terms and symbols. The ability to learn—to absorb information and ideas—and to solve problems is near its highest. This is illustrated by the fact that the adolescent attains almost the same scores on intelligence tests as an adult.

The young adolescent begins to feel confident in his mental ability and enjoys intellectual activity. A vivid preoccupation with thinking, experimenting, and generalizing at thirteen or fourteen years of age leads to the acquisition of a theoretical and very critical attitude. His curiosity about existential and sexual problems is accompanied by a desire to seek out satisfactory solutions to the problems he is trying to solve through books and pamphlets. He now wishes to formulate answers of his own rather than rely on parents' or teachers' judgments, dependence upon which was so typical of the years of childhood.

The increased ability to abstract and to generalize is seen in the type of self-expression the teen-ager chooses. He now relies heavily on a conceptual rather than a concrete type of analysis.   Less tangible relationships and roles are recognized.   Branches of science and philosophy begin to interest him. He can direct his attention to the scientific objectives of astronomy, cosmology, ethics, aesthetics, logic, and metaphysics.

At fourteen to fifteen years of age, many adolescents fully acquire formal thinking (i.e., consider most of the possible combinations in each case) and propositional operation (i.e., combine various empirical associations on which multiplicative classes are based in many possible ways).   Now they handle most of the formal operations, including disjunction, incompatibility, and various forms of implication and exclusion successfully and are able to set up experimental conditions for verifying their simple assumptions.   At this age the adolescent can successfully apply general principles to most specific situations.   While deduction of hypotheses appears to be easy at this level of development, success in experimental induction, based on the variation of a single factor with the others held constant or equal, is difficult [9, pp. 334–342].   Being able to verify his assumptions experimentally contributes greatly to his confident approach to problems and to a further development of cognitive efficiency.   A detailed analysis of formal, propositional, and experimental operations at this age may be found in Bärbel Inhelder and Jean Piaget's book *The growth of logical thinking* [9].

RELIGIOUS REEVALUATION

Puberty is usually the time when the individual reevaluates the values and ideals of his religious system.   Childhood concepts, beliefs, and practices are minutely examined in the light of abstract and propositional thinking.   In many cases, doubts pertaining to some of the secondary tenets or to practices arise.   This is especially true for individuals whose previous religious instruction was incomplete or lacked careful developmental planning.   Many adolescents are not exposed to religious education commensurate with their level of understanding and feeling.   Additional higher-level religious instruction is definitely needed during early adolescence.   Modern counselors in religion should be available to settle the doubts the individual has about his relationships to God and Church and his moral obligations.

The influence of the peer group at this time is great.   If the individual associates with persons of little or no religious training or belief, his own beliefs may be shaken.   Parents, too, have a part to play during this period.   By explaining the beliefs they hold as adults, they help the adolescent to realize the role religion plays in adult life, thus giving his earlier beliefs new meaning.   Church and school also ought to contribute to the spiritual development of youth.   Reading religious books and magazines may be helpful in gaining depth in religious faith.

GROWTH CHANGES AND ADJUSTMENT

A reorganization of motivation in the direction of individual resourcefulness at puberty, with a consequent growth of that quality, is a prime factor in initiating changes in behavior and in influencing subsequent adjustment. It would seem logical to hypothesize that as skills and abilities increase, the level of adolescent adjustment will improve. Actually, the opposite usually occurs. Most young adolescents are less adjusted than they were during the late phases of childhood. Even those adolescents who seem to apply their newly attained powers and skills well usually meet barriers and obstacles and suffer from discouragement and frustration. Both those engaged in active ventures and enterprises and those showing much withdrawal and passivity meet with personal problems. During this transitional phase of life discouragement and difficulty seem inevitable. Most adolescents, however, still strive to have a good time in spite of their situation. Usually this involves friendships with members of the opposite sex. Since attractions are based on good looks and personality, the competition makes difficulties almost inescapable.

The ever-increasing complexity and competition built into America's technology-minded society constantly introduce new difficulties into adolescent adjustment. This is one of the reasons why adolescence, as a time of preparation for adult tasks and obligations, is a relatively long period in our culture. At present, on the average, it takes nearly eight years to make a transition from childhood to adulthood.

The self. In the context of peer identifications the adolescent's self continues to evolve. Moreover, the boundaries of the self expand as the individual strives to integrate his physical strength and drives with his cognitive abilities. The young teen-ager exerts a real zeal in advancing his abilities and expanding his skills, interests, and activities. His attempts to concentrate largely upon his own experiences and thoughts lead him to perceive new meanings and implications for the growth of the self. The impact of the cultural and technological environment, although somewhat reduced by pubertal introspectiveness, also produces changes in self-identity. The world is opened before him by all the various mass-media communications. He views the world with both the bewilderment and the enthusiasm that the programs elicit.

The adolescent is keenly aware of his feelings and reactions. His deep introspection and observation create a new perspective. Although his grasp of life is not completely adequate, he feels capable of many self-initiated activities, thus establishing new interpersonal relationships. Boarding schools, summer camps, and travel offer valuable means for increasing knowledge and self-reliance, which are needed to enhance social confidence. Moral and ethical sensitivity is an added dimension, which provides a position for self-identification with others. The pubescent is unsure of his personal identity until a network of relationships with peers is acquired. This is especially true for the girl, who often sees herself through the communications of peers.

ILLUSTRATIVE CASE SUMMARIES

Three case summaries from a work by Lawrence K. Frank and others [2, pp. 214–215, 247–248, 284–285] have been selected to point out the prepubertal, pubertal, and postpubertal levels of personality functioning as revealed by means of projective testing.*

Prepubertal: Constance

On the surface, Constance appears rather well adjusted without serious difficulties (R, TAT, HH, FD). However, this is probably due to conformity to the demands made on her, and for it she pays the price of overregulation, constant restraint, and politeness (FD). She plays the role of the happy child her parents seem to expect of her (R), but it is accompanied by resentment, restlessness, and dissatisfaction (FD) and a desire for expansion (HH). Temper outbursts are possible, and she feels guilty about her aggression (FD).

Constance is ambitious and has high aspirations (R, FD, G), but this seems to be at least partially a result of environmental pressure toward accomplishment (HH). While she has good intellectual capacity (R), her fantasy is rather infantile (TAT, HH). She is not able to achieve on a level with her ambitions, which results in tensions and anxiety (R, HH but no indication of anxiety on TAT) and loss of spontaneity (R, FD). The limited imaginative range (TAT) may also be an expression of this. She forces herself to do things that are more impressive and attractive than she can do in a natural way (HH). At times she is rather evasive (FD, R). Actually, Constance is quite childish and dependent (R, FD). There are strong attachments to a protecting home environment (R, FD), feelings of insecurity (HH, FD), and marked ambivalence about growing up (G, FD). She is frightened, lacking in confidence, and self-conscious (FD). Her fear of aloneness and her need for parental love are too strong (G) for her to loosen the parental bonds. There is much egocentricity (G) and emotional immaturity (TAT). While she has a good capacity for outside stimulation and is socially oriented (R, FD, HH), she is too uncertain (FD) to be able to form social relations on a mature level (HH). Her social needs seem to be primarily for admiration and approval (R, FD), and she is quite exhibitionistic (R, FD). The motive of even her forced intellectualization is to please and to obtain social prestige (G).

Although her identification is basically feminine (R, HH, FD), there seems to be some wavering in regard to the sexual role and possibly some masculine protest tendencies (R, FD). There is strong yearning for acceptance by her father (FD), and her desire to satisfy him by acting like a boy may help to explain the masculine protest elements (FD). He seems to symbolize a mighty power in comparison with whom she feels small (HH).

* The projective tests used are referred to by the following abbreviations: Rorschach method—R; Thematic Apperception Test—TAT; Drawing of the Human Figure—FD; Horn-Hellersberg drawing test—HH; and graphology—G.

Pubertal: Barbara

Barbara is a bright girl (FD, G, R) from a relatively sheltered home (FD). She is quite self-absorbed (G, FD), engaged in an attempt to understand herself (HH). Still quite dependent (FD), she seeks security (HH) and self-assurance (G). She has a strong interest in furtive means of pleasing (G). She appears shy (R, G), passive and subdued, without real aggression. However, the TAT indicated lively affect, possible aggression, and tomboyishness; the FD found indications of aggression; and the HH found that she was receptive to her inner urges but did not know how to relate them to social demands and rules.

Barbara feels that the environment is aggressive, and she is suspicious (G), fearful, distrustful, and cautious (R) in her dealings with it. She has become quite skillful in avoiding conflict (G). She becomes evasive and withdraws (R), avoiding issues, arguments, and definite attitudes (G). In short, she avoids friction by avoiding depth (G). This type of defense may partially explain the apparent passivity found in the Rorschach, without excluding the more intense emotional life, perhaps existing on a deeper level and fairly well controlled, that was found on the TAT. Although she shows a capacity for affection (TAT), she is not demonstrative (R). She is unwilling to form deep attachments (G) or experience strong emotions (R) which might be threatening to her. Similarly, her sensitivity (R, TAT, HH) is also used for the purpose of self-protection (G, HH). She has a capacity for much more outgoing behavior (R), but she spends enormous effort in keeping unconscious content under rational control (HH). She tends to escape into daydreams (R) to relieve the tension (R, FD, HH); at times, however, she may be very outspoken and tactless (G). The FD found indications of ambition, while the TAT found only the barest suggestion of desire for worldly achievement. The apparent discrepancy here may be related to family demands for success. At any rate, concentration on school work is not easy for her because of her own inner problems.

Barbara seems to be rather discouraged (FD, TAT), feels inadequate and awkward (FD). There is a fair amount of anxiety present (FD, R, G, HH), and she seems somewhat sad (FD) and depressed at times (TAT). There is a good deal of ambivalence about growing up (FD). Her childhood is a little too comfortable for her to leave readily (FD, R), and she is frightened by adulthood and confused about her future goals (FD).

Barbara's home appears to be adult dominated (FD), with possible friction between the parents (TAT). The mother is probably dominant, and Barbara identifies with her (FD, TAT). There is also rivalry with a sister (FD). She appears to be superficial, perhaps as a result of attempts to contain her vitality (TAT).

Questions of physical maturity are most acute (HH), and there is some sexual wavering (FD, G) and conflict (HH). The TAT gives evidence of more than usual sexual maturity, connected with real feeling, while the Rorschach indicates that she seems to be waiting and does not yet show much warmth. On the whole, the picture is one of control; her curiosity (HH) and heightened sexual feelings are restrained (FD), and she tends to withdraw from sexual situations (FD). She would like to postpone the solution of the sexual problem (HH). There is also sexual shame (R) and guilt over masturbation. She is definitely feminine (G), and there is no evidence of rejection of her sexual role (R), but she readily entertains thoughts of being like a boy (FD). Apparently she envisages the boy's role as more acceptable to her father, more compatible with her ambition, and connected with fewer restraints (FD). Her overmodesty is apparently a reaction formation related to her strong display needs (FD, R, G), and she also seems to be afraid of rejection (R).

All in all, the picture seems to be that of a girl whose problems are typical for her age period and economic group (R, FD, TAT) and who is handling them reasonably well now (R, G). Her capacities will enable her to grow into an adult without too much difficulty (G) although the transition into adulthood will probably be somewhat prolonged (R, FD).

Adolescent: Jean

Jean seems to have had a happy childhood (HH) and a protective home environment (R, TAT). Her family relationships have been secure, and she considers the world a kind and friendly place (TAT). But in a typical adolescent manner she is vacillating between dependence on her family (TAT, G) and being irritable and critical of them (G), struggling for independence in a somewhat defensive manner (G).

Her sound family life (FD) seems to have provided the basis for her emotionality (FD, G, TAT), her capacity for wholehearted participation (HH), and her underlying optimism (TAT). However, her independence has been delayed (R) so that she remains emotionally tied to family tradition (G). Independence appears painful (R) and threatening to her (FD, R, TAT), and a good deal of uncertainty results (FD). She is anxious about the future (HH) and seems in conflict about marriage and a career (FD).

At the present time, she is restless (FD) and unstable (R) with fairly frequent mood swings (FD). She is rather excited and agitated and tends to overreact (R). Her anxiety and tension result in some restraint (R), and her fear of rebuff (FD) results in emotional caution (R, G). Since her control is so precarious (R), occasional temper outbursts can be expected (R, FD).

Jean also has feelings of self-consciousness (HH), inadequacy (R), insecurity (R, FD), and fear (R, G). These seem to intensify her needs for dependency (FD) and affection (TAT). She seems intensely afraid of loss of love, and from this is derived her tendency to introject those whom she loves (G).

At this point, Jean feels that there is a good deal of aggression directed against her, and, although basically unaggressive, she responds with defensive aggression.

Her present introversive swing (FD), with its narcissistic dreaminess (G), its probing and self-absorption (FD), is undoubtedly a reaction to an escape from her inner and outer problems, for she has both the capacity (R) and the need for social participation (FD), and her approach is essentially an emotional one (TAT).

Jean is well endowed (HH), and has a highly original (HH, FD) and integrative (HH) intelligence, but she is not fully employing these resources (HH). She lacks confidence in her achievements (FD), and tends to be oversensitive to criticism (FD). She is not an "intellectual" (TAT); at this point she would like to substitute sensual and affectional life for intellectual achievements (FD). It is perhaps for these reasons that she projects her ambitions on to her future husband (FD, G) while wanting protection for herself (G). In contemplation, Jean is driven to extremes of relaxation (FD); there are moody retreats into romanticism and sentimentality (FD). (On the TAT, however, girlish romanticism was conspicuously absent.) There is no real depression (FD), but Jean's fantasy life seems to absorb her more productive energies (R).

Jean is quite conscious of her body (FD) and probably somewhat unhappy about her figure (FD). Her tendency toward body exhibitionism is repressed (FD). She feels inadequate and insecure in the sexual area (R), and she is conflicted and disturbed about her sexual future (FD). Her strong sensuous desires are inhibited (G). While there seems to have been feminine awakening (HH), it has not yet found its own personal expression (HH) and her affection is not yet clearly channelized in a mature heterosexual direction (FD, TAT). Jean is interested in bringing up a family, the maternal side of femininity (HH, FD), perhaps because of her close affiliation (TAT) and identification with her mother (G). She seems to have a strong but ambivalent attachment to her father (G) and to see him chiefly in the role of a protector (R). It is interesting that that is also the role which she projects for her future husband (G). Her relationship to her brother may also be fraught with ambivalence, since the TAT gave evidence of unusual affection for him, while the FD found suggestions of rivalry.

Jean is basically sound (FD, HH) and well equipped (R). Her disturbances and conflicts are typical of adolescence (FD), and her adjustment is good (TAT) within its limitations (G).

Additional case studies and more detailed analysis of those mentioned may be found in the Frank monograph [2]. Similar information about adolescent boys may be procured from Urban H. Fleege's work [8]. Fleege used questionnaires to obtain material pertaining to adolescent problems, conflicts, and maladjustments. A recent national survey of three thousand American teenagers [1] revealed a number of changes in adolescent social relationships and their expectations which will be discussed in detail later.

QUESTIONS FOR REVIEW

1. What are some outstanding causes for increased self-awareness in young adolescents?
2. Mention one of the common problems of early adolescent life and explain its influence on the concept of self.
3. Why does a child's motivation have to be revised during adolescence? Why are slight modifications unsatisfactory?
4. Why is emancipation from parents necessary?
5. Why are close peer associations desirable at this age?
6. List some themes of pubertal daydreaming. Make an attempt to explain why such themes are frequent.
7. Describe the nature of intellectual development during adolescence.
8. What does a pubescent need to further his religious development?

What factors promote deeper religious interests during the adolescent level of life?
9. Explain how changes in motivation and ability affect the self and personal adjustment.
10. What are some characteristic attitudes of the pubescent toward himself?
11. What makes case history accounts useful material in studying pubertal or adolescent personality?

REFERENCES

I. Selected Reading

1. Douvan, Elizabeth, and Joseph Adelson. *The adolescent experience.* New York: Wiley, 1966. For note, see References, Chap. 14.
2. Frank, Lawrence K., et al. Personality development in adolescent girls. *Monogr. Soc. Res. Child Developm.,* 1951, **16,** No. 53. Child Development Publications, 1953. Interpretation of findings and suggestions for schools and youth agencies on the basis of projective data applied to 100 prepubertal and 100 adolescent girls, with several cases presented in detail.
3. Harsh, Charles M., and H. G. Schrickel. *Personality: Development and assessment.* (2nd ed.) New York: Ronald, 1959. Chapters 7 to 9 pertain largely to personality development during puberty and adolescence.
4. Strang, Ruth. *The adolescent views himself.* New York: McGraw-Hill, 1957. A work from the adolescent's viewpoint rather than adult interpretation.
5. Whalen, Richard E. Sexual motivation. *Psychol. Rev.,* 1966, **73,** 151–163. The author's theory of sexual arousal is explained, with illustrations, along experimental lines.

II. Specific References

6. Bronson, Wanda C. Central orientations: A study of behavior organization from childhood to adolescence. *Child Developm.,* 1966, **37,** 125–155.
7. Carlson, Rae. Stability and changes in adolescent self image. *Child Developm.,* 1965, **136,** 659–666.
8. Fleege, Urban H. *Self-revelations of the adolescent boy.* Milwaukee: Bruce, 1945.
9. Inhelder, Bärbel, and Jean Piaget. *The growth of logical thinking from childhood to adolescence* (translated by Anne Parsons and Stanley Milgram). New York: Basic Books, 1958.
10. More, D. Developmental concordance and discordance during puberty and early adolescence. *Monogr. Soc. Res. Child Develop.,* 1953, **18,** 1–127.
11. Rubé, P. The inner world of adolescence. *Amer. J. Psychother.,* 1955, **9,** 673–691.
12. Symonds, Percival M. *Adolescent fantasy.* New York: Columbia, 1949.

Part 7
Adolescence

This is a period of life in which sexual, emotional, and social self-realization on an adult level is achieved. Personal abilities and aptitudes are well established and can be appraised more adequately than before; liabilities and deficiencies, however, begin to stand out as problem behavior. School performance is one of the indicators of the direction trait formation and occupational interest will take. The adult begins to take shape as the total number of interests narrows and the few that will be dominant in his life style intensify. Much growth, but also much ambivalence, turmoil, and oscillation, as well as trial and error, take place before the individual adopts his adult pattern of life. Adolescence is a critical age, at which many life-determining decisions are made.

Adolescence is a time for further inquiry into questions such as "Who am I? What do I want to be?" There is a many-sided search for personal identity as the adolescent envisions himself in various adult roles. The adolescent explores adult activities and selects what is suitable for himself [13]. Adolescent maturation is a highly personal task, and the individual must deal with it himself. At best, others can aid him in this undertaking only by showing understanding toward his behavior and experiences.

THE DYNAMICS OF ADOLESCENT BEHAVIOR

Adolescent motivation emerges from pubertal developments and experiences which, in turn, were preconditioned by the individual's background, his resources, and childhood experiences. Sexual, emotional, cognitive, social, and moral developments in each individual stand out as sources of later dynamic trends and behavioral tendencies. Each adolescent's individual needs, interests, attitudes, and problems spring from them.

In the early part of adolescence, even a strong enthusiasm or a heightened interest for something wanes quickly and is replaced by other interests, sometimes antagonistic, sometimes peculiar, but always totally absorbing for some time at least. In the later phase of adolescence, some attractions, interests, and preferred activities become firmly established through practice and gain in depth and stability. These are closely related to the individual's endowments and gifts, his status and environmental opportunities. Less oscillation and more consistency is shown as the years of adolescence pass.

ADOLESCENT NEEDS

With pubertal changes the hierarchy of needs and need derivatives is revised if not transformed. On first sight, adolescent needs appear to be the same needs as those of the adult.   Closer observation, however, reveals marked differences.   Motivational development in terms of needs involves many subtle shifts of emphasis throughout infancy, childhood, and adolescence. During the early phase of adolescence the climax of these changes occurs and there is a gradual stabilization of the adult pattern.

Needs, interests, and desires are most complex during adolescence.   Gratification of *somatogenic* needs, such as needs for oxygen, nutrients, and fluids, is necessary for the maintenance of organismic functioning.   Besides these primary requisites for physical survival, there are the locomotive and sensory drives that affect behavior and evoke new traits.   Children are curious to see and touch; even more so are the adolescents.   They are eager to approach and learn new objects and subjects.

What many individuals desire and appreciate most is their growth in sexual maturity.   On screen or stage, when a boy of ten sees skirts flying up, this is just funny for him, but when a boy of fifteen sees the same scene, his sexual drive is likely to become activated.   The arousal may not disappear with passing of the stimulus.   At this age girls' legs are a source of fascination for many boys—not mere curiosity.   Most boys become attentive to the sexual aspects of girls and women.   Kuhlen and Houlihan's study [19] suggests that the intensity of the heterosexual interests of puberty and adolescence for the present generation is considerably greater than in past decades.   A comparison of 700 sixth, ninth, and twelfth graders of 1942 to 2,061 students of the same grades in 1963 shows greater heterosexual interest for each grade of the 1963 sample.

The human drives activated by needs create forces that cause the individual to approach or avoid certain objects.   Kurt Lewin [20], describing the attractive or repulsive character of drive-stimulating objects, uses the term *valence* to illustrate the type of field that is created.   An approach reaction results from a positive valence.   An object that stimulates an avoidance reaction is said to have a negative valence.

The *psychological* dimension of human existence generates need for affection, security, independence, and moral integrity.   Sociogenic needs include group acceptance, identification, participation, and recognition.   Cultural enrichment, intellectual understanding, and moral commitment also belong to the total structure of human needs.   Evidence of a hierarchy of needs may be observed in the later part of adolescence as a definite order of exigency begins to appear.   Any need the individual is deprived of usually gains in motivating power.   Lack of love, for example, heightens the need for affection.   When not successful, the individual compensates by overeating, hoarding, reveries, or other undesirable forms of behavior.

As the adolescent develops, his abilities and skills enable him to gratify successfully fundamental and derived needs.   The social structure and culture in which each adolescent finds himself provide some media for satisfying these needs; yet a poorly endowed or a handicapped adolescent at times finds it almost impossible, in spite of effort, to maintain a satisfactory gratification of his needs or compensate for the lack of gratification.

It is good to keep in mind the fact that the adolescent is not always aware of his individual needs or of a suitable manner of gratifying them. For example, only a careful medical examination reveals the need for certain vitamins or hormones, and only a thorough psychological examination indicates a lack of affection and love which is the underlying reason for excessive eating and the resulting obesity.

Certain emotional and social needs affect the adolescent greatly and have far-reaching effects on his behavior and personality. A brief analysis of some of these needs will shed some light on the adolescent pattern of dynamics and the accompanying drives, interests, and desires.

The need for *novel experiences* is a major motivational force driving the adolescent toward activity and self-involvement. Anything not as yet experienced attracts the youth. His curiosity to explore and to live his life fully is practically insatiable. The adolescent is eager to join various groups, to plan and make trips; he is interested in adventures and new activities. Everyday experiences often appear monotonous, and the desire to escape into something sensational grows with the advancing adolescent years.

The need for *security* is another strong motivational force. During adolescence, security is greatly determined by the person's estimate of himself—of his power and worth, his social status, and his moral integrity [6, p. 166]. Security depends upon an attitude of self-confidence and self-control, which, in turn, result from the satisfaction of emotional and social needs. Social acceptance plays a major role in gratifying emotional needs. The adolescent feels secure in his pursuits or engagements when he is emotionally supported by his parents and especially by his peers. Because of their earlier failures, many adolescents lack adequate self-confidence. Consequently, their expectations are clouded with anticipation of danger and threat. Because of an ambivalence in his views and judgments, it is often difficult for the adolescent to make decisions. He tends to experience opposing desires and to waver between needs for support and independence, selfishness and altruism, conformity and a desire for individuality. Such experiences create feelings of inadequacy and, in turn, feelings of insecurity. Adolescent security is furthered by affectionate acceptance, concern, and tolerant consideration by parents as well as enthusiastic acceptance into peer groups. The experience of intimate friendships is also important [8, p. 42].

The need for *status* extends to family, peers, school, and community. The adolescent has a strong desire to be appreciated by his parents as he is, to be accepted with his idiosyncracies, and to be dealt with on an equal and friendly basis. The very natural wish to share experiences with his peers is fundamental for establishing status within his limited society, trying everything in his power to be attractive to and on very friendly terms with members of both sexes. Moreover, the adolescent wants adult rights and privileges. Desire for status influences him in school and other institutions with which he comes in contact. Membership insignia and clothes are used as external signs of his particular status. Most adolescents make efforts to achieve some control in the school and community according to their own needs and abilities. Finding a place in peer society and later in adult society is, each time, a milestone in adequate socialization.

The need for *physical* and *social adequacy* is a pressing one, and the young adolescent seeks to feel fully accepted by his reference groups. If he does not, self-defenses become intensified and make practical adjustment difficult. With lack of social acceptance, tensions and conflicts are bound to arise; these, in turn, elicit strong anxieties and feelings of inferiority and gradual withdrawal. The loner broods over the aggressiveness and injustice of others. In this way, leanings toward hostility and destruction begin, and violent assaults against others or oneself can result.

Related to the need for physical adequacy is the need for *self-identity* [13]. The adolescent is very often engaged in an active search to discover what he is or what he ought to become. Frequently, the adolescent girl wants to be told directly how people feel about her. She may feel pressed to ask a friend how her clothes look and whether she is acceptable to the other sex. She needs reassurance in order to accept herself as she really is. Through peer evaluation and help the adolescent gets a picture of himself, or at least how others view him.

In the search for identity and standards, many adolescents show contempt for the values of their parents and adult society. Stealing, gang fights, superfluous use of pep pills and other drugs, sexual experimentation, drinking, and truancy may be attempted during the transition from childhood to mature adulthood, especially during this late phase of development.

Although teen-ager years are characterized mainly by transition and change, some basic attitude configurations survive throughout childhood and adolescence. In her recent reexamination of the Berkeley Guidance Study data, Wanda C. Bronson [10] postulates fairly salient and enduring *central orientations* (patterns of attitudes), originating from genetic material, physical-physiological events, and early interpersonal experiences. The central orientation determines the limits for the hierarchy of responses favored by the organism despite shifting developmental pressures. A core group of forty-five boys and forty girls representative of the Berkeley population from age five to age sixteen was repeatedly rated for a variety of behavior traits. The greatest degree of persistence and centrality was found among three dimensions: withdrawal-expressiveness, reactivity-placidity, and passivity-dominance. Reserved-withdrawn versus expressive-outgoing and reactive-explosive versus placid-controlled are styles of behavior related to the first and second dimensions.

There are distinct areas of concern for adolescent boys and girls, even when the concepts used do not differ. Elizabeth Douvan and J. Adelson [12, pp. 343–350] feel that "the key terms in adolescent development for the boy in our culture are *erotic, autonomy* (assertiveness, independence, achievement), and *identity.* For the girl the comparable terms are the *erotic,* the *interpersonal,* and *identity.*" The girl's concerns with identity and the erotic differ greatly from the same concerns of the boy. The development of interpersonal ties—the sensitivities and values of intimate associations with other individuals—forms the core of the girl's identity, while the masculine identity "focuses about the capacity to handle and master nonsocial reality, to design and win for oneself an independent area of work which fits one's individual talents and taste and permits achievement of at least some central personal goals." For the girl the erotic consists mainly of winning and maintaining love, but the boy is exposed to "turbulent instinctual struggles." Most adolescents, however, experience a strong desire for one another's company. This is often accompanied by strong emotional currents and sexual stirrings leading to love and sexual intimacy. Most overt sexual approaches are not sanctioned by adults nor approved by the majority of adolescents. Masturbation, however, and other alternative outlets are used by a large percentage of boys and a minority of girls.

Boys and girls alike show a strong interest in the future, an interest that is somewhat realistic among boys, but more idealistic among girls. Characterizing adolescents of today, Elizabeth B. Hurlock [18] attributes to them (in her own words) compulsion to follow the herd, preoccupation with status symbols, irresponsibility, anti-work, anti-intellectualism, unacceptable new values, disrespect for elders, disregard for rules and laws, and unrealistic levels of aspiration. She feels that permissive child education as well as permissiveness in the entire American culture is responsible for the new breed of "inferior" teen-agers.

DEVELOPMENTAL TASKS OF ADOLESCENCE

The powerful desire to grow and to mature in order to secure acceptance into peer and adult society and culture is a mark of late adolescence. With time the adolescent acquires a clearer awareness of what is expected of him. Robert J. Havighurst [16, pp. 33–71] was probably the first to enumerate distinct developmental tasks for adolescence. Achieving new and more mature relations with age-mates of both sexes, selecting and preparing for an occupation, developing intellectual skills and concepts necessary for civic competence, preparing for marriage and family life, and acquiring a set of values and an ethical system as a guide to behavior are the major tasks of the adolescent.

Several developmental tasks pertain mainly to the middle and late phases of adolescence:

1. Accepting one's adult physique and its various qualities as something final and self-related.
2. Attaining emotional independence from parents and authority figures.
3. Developing skill in interpersonal communication and learning to get along with peers and other people individually and in groups.
4. Finding human models with whom to identify. This is a basic step for achieving self-identity.
5. Accepting oneself and relying on one's own abilities and resources.
6. Strengthening self-control from within, based on a scale of values and principles or *Weltanschauung*. This implies satisfactory answers to such questions as "Who am I?" "Why am I?" and "What kind of a person would I like to be?"
7. Outgrowing infantile, puerile, and pubescent modes of reaction and adjustment.

A person's ability to find sources and means of gratification for his needs and to master age-related tasks is the key sign of his general adequacy. A great deal of exploration and learning are necessary to move ahead toward self-realization. Luella Cole [3, pp. 4—9] arranged adolescent goals into nine maturational steps: general emotional maturity, establishment of heterosexual interests, general social maturity, emancipation from home control, intellectual maturity, selection of an occupation, suitable use of leisure, a philosophy of life, and identification of self. Table 16—1 shows fundamental steps in adolescent maturation. This table includes some of Cole's formulations in a modified version. The period of adolescence is a time of continual movement from the puerile level of maturity to that of adulthood.

MOTIVATIONAL TENDENCIES AND LEADING INTERESTS

A major characteristic of most needs, abilities, interests, and other driving tendencies is their activity-stimulating power, which results in a variety of experiences for the adolescent. In order to survey correctly motivational tendencies and interests as they pertain to adolescence proper, and to understand their role in the life of adolescents, these dispositions first have to be classified into major categories and then subdivided into typical individual interests and resulting activities.

Those tendencies and interests which center around self-fulfillment are best identified as *personal interests*. Other activities, although personally moti-

Table 16–1   The developmental goals of the adolescent period*

From	Toward
Social and emotional maturation	
Social awkwardness	Social poise and gracefulness
Slavish imitation of peers	Interdependence and self-esteem
Superiority strivings and intolerance	Tolerance and feelings of adequacy
Parental control	Self-control
Feelings of uncertainty about oneself and others	Feelings of self-acceptance and sociability
Anger, temper tantrums, and hostility	Constructive and creative expressions of emotions; refinement of moods and sentiment
Growth in heterosexuality	
Acute awareness of sexual changes	Genuine acceptance of sex
Identification with members of the same sex	Interest in and association with peers of opposite sex
Relationships with many possible mates	Selection of a mate
Cognitive maturation	
Desire for universal principles and final answers	Need for explanation of facts and theories
Acceptance of truth on the basis of authority	Demand for substantial evidence before acceptance
Many interests and concerns	Few, stable, and genuine concerns
Subjective interpretation of situations	Objective interpretation of situations and reality
Weltanschauung—Philosophy of Life	
Behavior motivated by pleasure and the like	Behavior based upon duty and conscience
Indifference toward ideologies and ethical principles	Interest and ego-involvement in ideologies and Christian ethics
Behavior dependent on reinforcements	Behavior guided by moral responsibility and ideals

* We have drawn heavily on "Goals of the adolescent period" as presented by Luella Cole with Irma N. Hall in *Psychology of adolescence* (6th ed.), New York: Holt, 1964, pp. 4–9.

vated, are other-centered and directly involve the participation of other individuals.   Group activity is a fundamental means of expressing such tendencies.   Other- and group-centered interests can be referred to as *social interests*.   The remaining interests, involving various cultural areas such as literature, education, science and philosophy, law, the visual arts, music, and the theater, can be grouped as *cultural interests*.

These areas of interest merge in some activities.   For example, the adolescent's desire for recreation may be seen as personal interest, yet various forms of recreation are often social in character, and a preference for a particular form of recreation is largely determined by environmental opportunities and cultural preferences.   A person's interests are a good indication of the personality structure and the level of development as well.   Interests change with age and stage, yet one can strongly suspect that the adolescent's maturity and his adjustment are related to his interests and interest-related activities.

Personal interests

During pubescence the adolescent's introspective and egocentric tendencies intensify.   His concern for himself is often far greater than that which he feels for parents, siblings, and companions.   At times he is suspicious of others, and his relationships to them are strained and distant.   This is a time when many personal interests begin to crystallize and take form.   The boy is strongly motivated to demonstrate his autonomy and sexual adequacy, utilizing all he recognizes as masculine qualities and prerequisites for recognition as a man.   Likewise, the girl begins to feel she must assert her femininity, acquire an attractive appearance, and improve her personality.   At this time there are many personal interests, preoccupations, and problems.   Several of them are vital to the adolescent and are selected here for analysis.

Interest in appearance.   During adolescence, concern over physical appearance, including concern about physical features such as face, chest, arms and hands, feet and legs, and bodily measurements, stand out as a major dynamic factor.   This interest includes voice and hair, clothes and ornaments, and the use of cosmetics.   By his own experience, the adolescent learns that personal appearance plays a major role in social acceptability or lack of it, especially with members of the opposite sex.   To be accepted or to gain popularity, the adolescent must make his appearance conform to patterns and expectations set by adolescent and adult society.   Since social needs and drives are powerful, the young adolescent is very anxious to obtain the approval of others.   Hence, his attention is often focused upon himself.   He examines critically his size and proportions, hair, and other aspects of himself in order to compare favorably with others of his age and maintain a sense of adequacy. If he finds a deviation, even a minute one, he becomes concerned and worried. This concern is often so pronounced that teen-agers, especially girls, prefer to undergo considerable inconvenience and discomfort in order to correct their deficiencies. Some withdraw from group activities to avoid being exposed to unfavorable remarks and intensified feelings of inferiority or rejection. With meticulousness the adolescent pays attention to every possible aspect of appearance, especially clothing. Since the post-pubertal physical appearance is almost adult and resists change, the adolescent has to learn to accept and adjust his feelings and attitudes toward it. Most aspects of physical appearance must be accepted as they are. Yet some obvious facial deformations can be corrected through plastic surgery.

Changes of fashion and style tend to produce additional worries as the adolescent learns about them through the channels of advertising, television, and magazines. To increase in charm is almost an obsession with many adolescent girls. Abnormal height, overweight, or a poorly developed figure are among the more frequent feminine problems. Being shorter than average, too small, or too heavy are characteristics feared by the male adolescent. Wanting to appear handsome is one of his preoccupations when masculine qualities begin to impress him.

Complexion worries and problems are quite frequent. Rapid growth, emotional turmoil, and conflicts are often accompanied by acne and other skin eruptions. While it is difficult for a boy to cover up pigmentation and skin disturbances, girls can use creams, rouge, and powder to their advantage. Adolescent girls spend a great deal of time before the mirror trying to achieve an attractive complexion. They apply mascara to make their eyes appear deeper and more colorful. Much interest is also paid to the general hygiene of the body, including dental care, control of perspiration, and manicure.

The changes that occur at puberty affect vocal quality significantly in both the male and the female voice as the speech-productive organs undergo final modification. When the pitch of voice lowers at a fast rate, the voice cracks. Difficulties with voice control are common among boys, whose voices drop nearly an octave. In girls the change is much more moderate, and it is not likely to cause embarrassment. Realizing that attractiveness depends not only on appearance but also on the modal qualities of their voices, girls in particular strive to acquire pleasant voices.

Appearance is much affected by apparel, jewelry, and other ornaments. The teen-ager has no difficulty in realizing the role clothes play among his peers and in society at large. In order to attract attention, the adolescent tries to be very selective in his choice of clothes. Styles and fashions of the season are quickly adopted. A desire for novelty and surprise is an important factor in adolescent choice of clothing and ornaments. Usually by the time he has taken on the characteristics of an adult and has discarded those of the teen-ager, he has acquired skill and good taste in the selection of attractive clothing. Then he begins to prefer less flashy colors and learns to harmonize them better. By the end of adolescence most individuals feel secure enough to abandon conformity in dress and hair style.

Self-regulation. Even among children there is a great satisfaction in being able to take care of oneself. The desire for self-direction usually becomes stronger as puberty nears completion and is one of the most outstanding traits of the adolescent. It manifests itself as a continually rising pressure to break away from existing bonds and dependence upon others. The need to speak one's own mind and to assert one's personality becomes strong after the onset of pubertal changes. Various forms of self-assertion, including aggressiveness in defense of one's own status, become prominent and sometimes lead to friction between young adolescents and their parents. Differences of view in regard to selection of activities and companions, education and vocation are frequent factors in the parent-adolescent disputes. Many young adolescents begin to feel estranged from their parents for this reason. Feelings of being misunderstood and a desire to leave home arise if parents rely solely on their own experience or authority in maintaining restrictions and inflexible views. Many boys and girls find it difficult to achieve their vital right to self-regulation.

Parents and educators who tend to overemphasize their own advice, preferences, and controls have difficulty in realizing the importance of self-direction and self-reliance in the development of the teen-ager. The adolescent's desire for a spending allowance to use as he chooses and for privacy regarding telephone calls and mail, as well as his wish to have a room of his own, are disregarded by some parents. The adolescent feels hurt and distrusted when he is questioned about where he has been and what he has done. This overprotective practice of parents may be well intended, but the adolescent must be allowed to make some errors as he strives to act on his own. Through them he gains experience which he can rely on later. Adolescence is the proper time to gain independence from parental influences and controls.

Vocational preference. Vocation is another major area of adolescent concern, especially on the part of boys. At this phase of life, the individual understands the general need for a vocation. An adolescent is often aware of the vocation he would like to pursue, but as is typical of the adolescent phase, he is not mature enough to make a serious choice. Elizabeth Douvan and Joseph Adelson's empirical findings [12, p. 342] show that "for the most part the jobs boys choose represent modest advances over their fathers' position, and they are jobs with which the boys have had some personal contact." However, over half of the total sample of boys ($N = 1,045$) named a professional or semiprofessional job they hoped to fill, while only one in fourteen thought his future was in semiskilled and unskilled work. A considerable number of adolescents are confused about vocational possibilities and the education needed for them.   A significant minority of the boys in this sample did not have any clear vocational plans.

If a vocational choice is made too early, the selections have to be altered and rethought later.   Public opinion surveys related to careers generally reveal a dissatisfaction among the majority of factory workers and a minimum of discontent among professionals.

Practically all studies on adolescent occupational preferences show a very high percentage of adolescents selecting professional vocations.   This points to a lack of adequate self-appraisal because many of those selecting professions will not qualify for them [23].   Interest in glamorous and prestige occupations must be replaced by interest in practical occupations related to ability and economic resources.   Achieving satisfactory occupational status contributes to economic security and personal independence.   It is usually accompanied by improved adjustment and a mature adaptation to adult expectations and ability to marry and set up a home.   Vocation and marriage are the two last milestones initiating adult life patterns.   Marriage is the vocation for the majority of girls.   As a result, girls' career needs decline as marriage plans come into view.   Vocation is the major area of achievement for boys, marriage—for girls.

Daydreaming.   Fantasy is one of the universal forms of adolescent self-expression and escape.   A strong drive for new experiences and adventures finds partial gratification in this form of preoccupation with self.   In daydreaming, imagined activities and the vicarious experiences following them usually fuse elements of past events and future anticipation.   The more vivid an imagination one has, the more dramatic his fantasies of his relationship to people and to the world will be.   A noticeable feature of teen-age daydreaming is the dreamer's feeling of importance, which otherwise is very questionable during this period.   Since puberty and adolescence is a time of insecurity accompanied by feelings of inadequacy, guilt, and inferiority, owing to adult restrictions, school requirements, and real and merely imagined deficiencies and transgressions, escape into the realm of fantasy is a major source of relief.   This withdrawal into a world of one's own creation offers compensation for many unpleasant realities.   The formulation of a self-ideal is gradually fashioned by these leaps into the future.

For some adolescents self-expression in dreams and reveries becomes too frequent and turns into a deeply entrenched habit of retreating from situational demands.   Excessive daydreaming prevents the individual from exercising initiative in the utilization of actual opportunities to engage in the constructive learning activities that are necessary for the development of abilities and skills.   *Pubertism* is a term used to label this mentally unhealthy attitude of frequent readiness to submerge oneself in fantasies that have little relation to reality. Ultimately, they promote neurotic and psychotic tendencies. Some adolescents, though possessing good endowment, cannot properly utilize their potential. They continue brooding and living in their reveries instead of making any realistic attempt to outgrow the pubescent mode of life. Usually day- and night-dreaming subside as a person takes practical steps toward the attainment of the higher levels of maturation characteristic of late adolescence and early adulthood.

Need for literary and creative self-expression. Communication with oneself, or self-reflection, precedes and often supplements advanced forms of communication with others. As self-centered baby talk precedes the acquisition of a common language, so imaginary and literary notions precede advanced forms of adolescent interpersonal communication. Literary and other forms of creative self-expression are fairly common among adolescents who experience a strong desire to convey their feelings and ideas about personally significant events and to keep a record of them. Desire for self-expression in art is probably as common, since many adolescents experience impulses of pictorial or plastic creativity as well.

Diaries, letters, poetry, short novels, musical compositions, and autobiographical incidents in the form of short stories based on real life represent typical modes of expression at this phase of life. A need to confide in an intimate friend is dynamic, but many teen-agers do not as yet have such close friends or do not trust them enough to share all their personal hopes and concerns. Formulating one's inner experiences and problems and putting them on paper can be a substitute for intimate friendship. The diary often becomes the first silent confidant, to whom many secret desires, behavior problems, and ambitions can be told without reproach or embarrassment for the writer. It also serves as a repository for these experiences, feelings, and thoughts which adolescents consider very important and want to treasure.

The writings of puberty and middle adolescence are primarily signs of emotional growth and cognitive maturation rather than indications of literary talent. From a psychological viewpoint, adolescent writings are equivalent to autistic forms of conversation. The tension of self-expressive drives finds a relief from the feelings of isolation experienced in this phase of intensified psychosocial development. Keeping a diary may become a habitual activity, and in some cases it will not be abandoned with the attainment of personal maturity but continue into adulthood.

In 1928, Leta S. Hollingworth [17, pp. 189–190] and, in 1932, Charlotte Bühler [11] concluded that diary writing and similar forms of literary preoccupation were typically the activity of adolescents with superior intelligence. This, however, may not hold true for the present day. A higher degree of introversion during adolescence also seems to be indicative of vivid fantasy and creative productivity during the mid-phase of adolescence. Writing as a means of self-expression is used more often by girls than by boys.

Watching movies and television plays of a dramatic and romantic type and reading novels and stories from "real life" have similar ventilating effects on adolescent emotional tension and partially satisfy the need for novel experiences.

Recreational activities.   Play is the child's principal form of recreation. During the course of pubertal developments, child-play activities are largely discarded as the need for amusement and relaxation increases.   Frequenting motion pictures, watching TV, reading magazines, papers, and books, listening to music, and making collections—stamps, coins, records, etc.—are some typical forms of early adolescent recreation.   Summer and winter sports, athletic and creative activities, trips and youth gatherings, dates and dancing parties are additional teen-age diversions.   Membership in various clubs not only satisfies the adolescent's social needs but provides recreational opportunities.

Other personal interests include attempts at *self-improvement,* aspirations for exceptional *accomplishment,* and acquisition of high *status symbols.* These are consistent with the adolescent strivings for perfection.

Social interests

The social tendencies and activities of the adolescent are largely determined by his family attitudes, sex, personality, degree of introversion, and environmental opportunities for social interaction.   A bright, extroverted adolescent has more social interests and friends than a dull individual, whose interests will also be different.   An introvert is usually satisfied with fewer friends than an extrovert.

In social contacts and in relating to others the adolescent tends to show a number of tendencies, such as resistance to adult authority, discrimination against "inferiors" and "isolates," emotional intimacy with chums, and concern over heterosexual relationships.   Adolescent social interaction can be classified according to: (1) interpersonal communication, (2) dating, (3) group activity, and (4) interest in helping others.

Interpersonal communication.   As the years of adolescence continue, interpersonal communication expands in varying degrees, depending on individual personalities.   Extroverted persons are eager to establish interpersonal communications to share their experiences, feelings, attitudes, and thoughts with their peers, while introverts concentrate on preoccupations of various kinds a much longer time before establishing similar forms of self-expression in personal matters with their companions.   Compared to the extroverts, the introverts' communication remains relatively restricted.

Sharing personal experiences is a fundamental requisite for adolescent adjustment.   Many teen-agers appear irritable and in low spirits when they are separated from their companions.   When the adolescent is alone for a long while or far away from his close friends, conflicts and problems increase. Long letters, and telephone calls usually satisfy his need for personal communication and are often adequate substitutes for dates.

Generally adolescents choose activities that offer opportunities for conversation. The desire to communicate personal opinions is often so strong in the adolescent that he is incapable of following any systematic procedure for talking in turn. Even in places where conversation is disturbing, such as movies or high school classes, whispering is frequent. Much leisure time is spent with friends lounging around corner drugstores—another outlet for conversational self-expression and social interaction. In late adolescence small group conversations are usually quite free and frank.

Adolescent topics of conversation center around (1) boy-girl relationships, (2) athletic events and individual performances, (3) movie and TV stars, (4) sex and morals, (5) parents and teachers, (6) money, clothes, and status symbols, and (7) reading. Individual opinions generally receive a hearing by the group. Disagreements are infrequent and usually of little consequence. In most interpersonal communications there is a strong desire to be understood and appreciated.

Discussions with peers serve to improve the teen-ager's communication skills as well as to generate new interests and attitudes, to broaden viewpoints and to amplify general knowledge, thus greatly enriching his personality. Discussions prepare the ground for peer identification and emotional intimacy. All of this communication promotes maturity and the development of social skills and graces.

Dating is the chief means for establishing close relationships with members of the opposite sex. Since urges toward heterosexual friendship exist, dating is used by the adolescent as a means of testing his popularity with selected members of the cther sex. As soon as emotional acceptance by the partner occurs, dating tends to become steady. Going steady offers security because the need for a companion is satisfied. Table 16–2 enumerates the traits a teen-ager looks for in his steady date.

Frequent dating leads to situations where sexual exploration and intimacy are experimented with. Usually the boy tries to get as much as possible and the girl yields as little as possible. The girl is expected to set the limit, and the boy is expected to conform. Boys usually value girls who are adamant, although college ethics seem to be undergoing many changes. Group outings and double dating are best for most of the adolescent years. Otherwise dating moves too fast toward steady dating, and the adolescent misses opportunities for varied experiences and a sufficient range of acquaintances.

In steady dating the partners are exposed to the dangers of early sexual intimacy. By frequently dating the same person an intimacy that would seem inappropriate to one or both parties on the first or second date appears quite

Table 16-2   Traits desired for a future mate and for a companion

| | Percentage | |
Traits	Boys	Girls
Future mate		
Desires normal family life with children	77	87
Knows how to budget and manage money	62	75
Is approved by my parents	56	74
Is independent of his or her parents	45	64
Has interests similar to mine	49	48
Has ideals similar to mine	46	52
Has a job	9	93
Knows how to cook and to keep house	79	15
Is as intelligent as I am	27	42
Is started on a professional career	8	42
Companion		
Is dependable, can be trusted	92	96
Takes pride in personal appearance and manners	89	90
Is considerate of me and of others	84	95
Shows affection	84	85
Acts his (her) age, is not childish	77	87
Has a pleasant disposition	77	84
Is clean in speech and action	72	82
Mixes well in social situations	51	59
Does not use liquor	49	49
Is popular with others	46	42

Source: Purdue Opinion Panel. Youth's attitudes toward courtship and marriage. *Report of Poll No. 62,* 1961. (Based on two thousand high school boys and girls.)

natural since it is the result of gradual advances over a long period of time [22, p. 374].

The girl should be aware of the sexual significance of bodily contact with a boy, especially in privacy.   While a girl usually does not experience erotic sensations from sitting very close to her date, placing arms around each other's waist, or many forms of necking, boys often become sexually aroused and interpret such permission as submission to sexual advances of a higher degree of intimacy.   Sometimes sexual aggressiveness becomes uncontrollable as the boy's impulsiveness is heightened.   By permitting hugging and kissing, girls invite petting, and by permitting petting, they are drawn toward intercourse [22, p. 325].

Group activity.   A major means for the development of manners, social graces, tact, and adolescent social attachments is group activities and parties.

Preadolescent interest in the group reawakens in a new form in postpuberty, when the individual has achieved physiological and sexual maturation. His group interest now includes members of the opposite sex. With very few exceptions, girls and boys enjoy gatherings and group activities because such occasions offer opportunities to mingle with their peers, to play various games, and to assume new roles. Dancing suddenly becomes an important skill. The interest of girls in adolescent parties starts about two years earlier than that of boys because girls mature earlier. The interest of boys is often handi-capped by their lack of confidence and skill in taking the initiative for conver-sation and dancing.

Teen-agers prefer informal gatherings of their own without adult participa-tion. Any formal procedure in the adult sense of the term is tension-producing and offers little recreation to them. Semiformal parties close on an informal note. Adolescents like careful planning of their parties. A great deal of attention is given to details, such as what refreshments are to be served, how furniture has to be rearranged, what records to play, and particularly with girls, what clothes to wear. Heterosexual association during parties is an-other milestone in the total process of socialization.

Herbert A. Bloch and Arthur Niederhoffer [9] analyzed and interpreted adolescent group activities in terms of rites, rituals, and delinquency in primi-tive and modern settings. Developmental needs and their relationships to present-day community and culture were also appraised. The findings indi-cate that ritual and stereotyped behavior do occur in the more subtle adoles-cent activities and play a decisive role in promoting feelings of security and a sense of adequacy.

Interest in helping others. Interest in helping others is usually dynamic throughout adolescence. It seems likely that the adolescent's sensitivity to the needs of others is related to his own problems and difficulties. His friends' problems are treated as his own, but even a stranger in need or dis-tress arouses concern in the adolescent. Most adolescents are capable of identifying themselves with a man or a group in distress, becoming ego-involved, and often throwing themselves enthusiastically into any necessary action. Altruism and charity permeate a major part of their activities and often outbalance the tendency to discriminate. Severe social injustice and oppression of persons, nations, races, or religions call forth an urge to assist the victims and a drive to reform the existing evils.

In applying his powers and resources to helping others, the adolescent is ready with advice and service and occasionally is prepared to sacrifice him-self. Many social services attract their attention. Since the teen-ager is quite naïve in some respects persuasive speakers can arouse their energies for radical causes as well. Without the total dedication of the youth of those times, the success of European Communism, Nazism, and Fascism could not be explained. Youth fell prey to advanced .propaganda techniques. Moreover, the extremist, with his ideology of upheaval and transformation, seems to have a specific appeal to adolescents. The desire for an ideal society can be appealed to and readily directed toward changing the environment: home and school, community and nation, and the world at large.

Cultural interests

In the course of his maturing interests, the adolescent begins to evaluate the various facets of Western and American culture. As a result, views and concerns relating to education, religion, science and philosophy, reading matter, entertainment, law, and politics emerge and grow as development advances. Strong cultural concerns are more closely related to early adulthood than to adolescence, but their appeal depends on the amount of stimulation in these fields the individual has received and his responsiveness to it.

Education. Education is a process in which the adolescent is deeply involved. Not only does it account for a major portion of his daily activity, it is also the sphere in which he experiences his rapidly expanding intellectual and social skills. The curriculum, teachers' personalities, school-group relationships, and extracurricular activities are all factors affecting him directly.

Because curricula differ from one school system to another, because his powers of inquiry and reasoning advance rapidly, and because he frequently displays considerable idealism, many important issues arise for the adolescent. To what extent, for example, should purely academic subjects be studied, especially when such topics are not directly related to vocational aspirations? What is the responsibilty of the school with regard to giving the individual special training in a trade or preparing him for a profession? What duty, if any, does the school have to teach certain fundamental value concepts? What emphasis should education place upon the development of personality traits and social skills? How should different subjects be taught for maximum effectiveness? What are the traits most necessary and desirable for a teacher? These and many other questions arise in the adolescent's mind as he continues his education.

Because of his tendency toward idealism and perfection, together with his difficulty in perceiving many practical considerations, youth often expresses bitter criticism of modern educational systems and educators. In many cases, to be sure, such criticisms are not without merit. However, the questions raised, the answers proposed, and the personal reactions to teachers and school provide significant information regarding the personality dynamics and level of maturity of the individual. Male students frequently show rebellion against school rules because of their strong need for independent thought and activity. Coupled with this is their tendency to truancy. On the other hand, frequent attempts to assist teachers and identify with them are also seen. Some idealistic adolescents seek to introduce various reforms within the school, even in regard to its educational philosophy. The magnitude of the problem of reconciling the conflict between school-oriented tasks and personal desires, however, is clearly revealed by the studies of the 1950s. They indicate that approximately half the young people in this country possess a moderate to strong desire to discontinue their education before state law permits. However, satisfaction with occupational choice depends in large part on continuation of education. During the 1960s the teen-ager's awareness of the importance of education increased noticeably. Chapter 18 includes further discussion of education and vocational pursuits.

Religion.   Religion penetrates all aspects of human life—personal, social, economic, and cultural. The presence or lack of it is a major motivational factor during adolescence. Religious reevaluation occurs at this time, and the majority of adolescents respond sensitively to religious values. They may question or worry about some religious issues, since these are variously explained by representatives of the many faiths practiced in our country. Morality, ethics, religious obligations, and teachings concerning marriage and birth control are important issues to youth.

Although most adolescents believe in God and life hereafter, doubts are common regarding some passages of the Bible, dogmas of faith, and the value of prayer and other practices. The transition from the religious ideas of childhood to a mature acceptance of religious values and practices is not a smooth one. Yet in many cases religious reevaluation is a gradual process rather than an abrupt and deeply emotional change as in cases of conversion. If a deep and abiding faith is developed, it has emotional, moral, and cognitive constituents, and it affects the individual as a whole. Religious maturation is often achieved at the college level, especially when education favors the development of a spiritual philosophy of life. Religion can be the basis for a very comprehensive and unifying philosophy since it identifies the goals and relationships of the individual during the present life and relates them to a life of happiness hereafter as the chief goal for which to strive. For many adolescents, then, religion can be the source of ideals and goals. When its values and principles are clearly comprehended and accepted by an individual, it motivates and directs his behavior. Moreover, it enables the adolescent to evaluate his experiences and conduct and to recognize their ultimate meaning for him as a morally responsible individual.

Science and philosophy.   Science, as well as philosophy, appeals to the adolescent as his intellectual capacities approach the adult level. The adolescent often imagines science and science-oriented philosophy to be a source from which he can derive final answers to his questions. Scientific source books and encyclopedias are sometimes regarded as major affirmations of human wisdom.   Adolescents often consult these references in order to gain information.   Naturally they often fail to realize that progress in science only results in new issues and questions and that scientific knowledge at best only approximates the truth but usually does not reveal it.

In late adolescence the ability to conceptualize and theorize increases noticeably.   However, because of the adolescent's inexperience, and the changing trends in both science and theology, knowledge and revelation often appear to him to be in conflict.

It has to be kept in mind that philosophies often give rise to ideologies. Hedonism, as the doctrine of deliberate pleasure-seeking, and stoicism, as cold-blooded endurance of adversities, have been embraced by millions through the centuries.   The economic and class doctrines of Karl Marx and Nikolai Lenin and the later versions of Communism have imposed codes of ethics on about one-third of the world population today, with extreme suppression of all other systems.

Reading matter.   Reading matter affects youth in many ways, and an adolescent's choices in this field tend to reveal his thoughts and areas of interest. Books, magazines, and pamphlets commonly read by adolescents also show their level of learning.   The popularity of sex magazines among adolescents seems to indicate their lack of discernment.   The lives of famous historical personalities and literary figures, however, also rank high with a significant number of adolescents.   Even though not living today, these subjects offer adolescents models on which they can pattern their own self-concepts.

The reading and works of art to which adolescents are exposed offer them much material for vicarious experience and recreation.   At the same time advertising evokes many new desires.   In this way it becomes a source of conflict and frustration since adolescents often lack the money to indulge their whims as they are encouraged to do by the advertisements in the magazines they read.

Entertainment.   Entertainment basically serves the purposes of distraction and recreation.   It usually includes the fine arts, music, and the theater, ballet, radio, TV, motion pictures, and athletic activities.   While the adolescent's interest is directed toward most of these activities, absence of environmental facilities and his own limited purse usually restrict his participation to two or three areas.   Adolescents need a variety of entertainments to absorb their energies and develop their talents.   A balanced repertoire of such activities furthers the cognitive and social growth of the individual.   Since many entertainments are social in character, they afford opportunities to the adolescent to increase his confidence and popularity with members of both sexes.

Law.   State laws and community ordinances limit the antisocial activities of the adolescent.   Since the teen-ager had no say in the establishment of the laws or law-enforcing institutions, he is likely to disregard and come into conflict with some of their regulations. A law may encroach upon the free expression of his aggressive tendencies. Adjustment to laws and regulations is a slow process for adolescents who fail to realize that not even the most primitive societies can afford to act entirely on impulse. The intricacies of social intercourse in a highly specialized industrial society require regulations and law enforcement in order to preserve order and to protect the rights of the individual.

Speed regulations are especially offensive to young drivers, especially when their moods run high. Consumption by minors of prohibited alcoholic beverages is another common law violation, since the adolescent wants to have the privileges of the adult. Yet the protective value of these regulations is important for the welfare of adolescents as well as society as a whole. The questioning of legal authority, so common at this stage, is evidence of the male adolescent's continual search for expansion of his independence.

Politics. Politics, another area of culture, affects the adolescent and draws his attention to political and diplomatic affairs that concern his country and its relations with other nations. The teen-ager is often curious about elections, international conferences, reforms, coups d'état, wars, and revolutions. Travel usually stimulates his curiosity about other cultures and nations and promotes world interest instead of provincial isolation. The recent rise in student protests over academic and civil rights and Vietnam is a sign of the political awakening of our American youth.

In studying adolescent motivation, one should bear in mind its dual source, which includes frequent and powerful promptings from within and the situational stimuli of the adolescent's social milieu, both of which mold and direct his energies and drives into adequate or inadequate patterns of activity and experience. The following chapter on personality development will elaborate upon this concept.

QUESTIONS FOR REVIEW

1. Explain several psychogenic needs and indicate their valences during adolescence.
2. How do human needs relate to the development of adolescent interests?
3. List several developmental tasks of adolescence and discuss one of them. What might result if necessary developmental tasks are not mastered during adolescence?
4. Enumerate several person-centered interests. Select one for detailed discussion.
5. Discuss social interests. Explain one of them as it applies to the different phases of adolescence.
6. What are frequent topics of adolescent conversation?

7. Which cultural areas evoke adolescent interest and concern? Analyze one cultural area in detail. Relate it to the present-day adolescent population.
8. What role do interests and activities play in the adjustment of an adolescent?
9. Identify several forms of entertainment and indicate the adolescent's interest in them.
10. Give reasons for the teen-ager's resistance to laws or ordinances.

REFERENCES

I. Selected Reading

1. Ausubel, David P. *Theory and problems of adolescent development.* New York: Grune & Stratton, 1954. A study of adolescence emphasizing the development of ego and personality and including a number of significant deviations.
2. Bier, William C. (Ed.). *The adolescent: His search for understanding.* New York: Fordham, 1963. A fairly comprehensive selection of original articles on social relationships and the self-concept of the adolescent.
3. Cole, Luella, with Irma N. Hall. *Psychology of adolescence.* (6th ed.) New York: Holt, 1964. A well-revised edition dealing with physical, intellectual, emotional, social, and moral developments during adolescence, including educational applications.
4. Hurlock, Elizabeth B. *Adolescent development.* (3rd ed.) New York: McGraw-Hill, 1967. A study of various aspects of growth, as well as analysis of factors in personality development.
5. Rosenberg, Morris. *Society and the adolescent self-image.* Princeton, N. J.: Princeton, 1965. Self-esteem, as an independent variable, is related to various neighborhoods. Its presence in the upper class, its lower level among minority groups, and a lesser degree of self-esteem among girls than among boys are discussed. Five thousand subjects from ten New York high schools were studied.
6. Schneiders, Alexander A. *Personality development and adjustment in adolescence.* Milwaukee: Bruce, 1960. Chaps. 8 and 10 to 14. An exposition of interests, values, and related motivational factors.

II. Specific References

7. Amatora, Sister M. Expression of adolescent interests. *Genet. Psychol. Monogr.,* 1957, 55, 173–219.
8. Blatz, William E. *Human security: Some reflections.* Toronto: University of Toronto Press, 1966.
9. Bloch, Herbert A., and Arthur Niederhoffer. *The gang.* New York: Philosophical Library, 1958.

10. Bronson, Wanda C.   Central orientations: A study of behavior organization from childhood to adolescence. *Child Developm.*, 1966, **37**, 125–155.

11. Bühler, Charlotte. *Jugendtagebuch und Lebenslauf.* Jena, 1932.

12. Douvan, Elizabeth, and Joseph Adelson. *The adolescent experience.* New York: Wiley, 1966.

13. Erikson, Erik H.   Identity and the life cycle. *Psychol. Issues,* Monogr. No. 1 (New York: International Universities Press), 1959.

14. Frank, Lawrence K., and M. Frank. *Your adolescent at home and in school.* New York: Viking, 1956.

15. Harris, Dale B.   Life problems and interests of adolescents in 1935 and 1957. *School Rev.,* 1959, **67**, 335–343.   Also in *Child Developm.,* 1959, **30**, 453–457.

16. Havighurst, Robert J. *Developmental tasks and education.* New York: Longmans, 1952 (originally published in 1948).

17. Hollingworth, Leta S. *The psychology of the adolescent.* New York: Macmillan, 1928.

18. Hurlock, Elizabeth B.   American adolescents of today—a new species. *Adolescence,* 1966, **1**, 7–21.

19. Kuhlen, Raymond G., and Nancy B. Houlihan.   Adolescent heterosexual interest in 1942 and 1963. *Child Developm.,* 1965, **36**, 1049–1052.

20. Lewin, Kurt. *Principles of topological psychology.* New York: McGraw-Hill, 1936.

21. Smith, Ernest A. *American youth culture: Group life in teenage society.* New York: Free Press, 1962.

22. Staton, Thomas F. *Dynamics of adolescent adjustment.* New York: Macmillan, 1963.

23. Stevenson, R. M.   Occupational aspirations and plans of 443 ninth graders. *J. educ. Res.,* 1955, **49**, 27–35.

PERSONALITY DEVELOPMENT AND ADJUSTMENT

Personality structure is influenced by the development and maturation of the physical, sexual, emotional, social, and moral qualities of the individual. There is interaction among all of these factors, and each one directly or indirectly influences the person's approach to his environment. Consistency in the response repertoire is what is referred to as personality.

The major aspects of personality—the physiological, emotional, social, and cognitive elements—exhibit drives and needs that must in some way be gratified before further development and adjustment can take place. Physically, a child or adolescent needs nutrients and exercise for somatic development. Emotionally, a child and adolescent need affection and security. Socially and intellectually, the child needs opportunities to affiliate with others and to develop skills that require constant stimulation and experience for competence. All of these areas of development are at various times a source of conflict for the individual, the solution and mastery of which lead the individual to a greater degree of maturity and adjustment. A system of traits, attitudes, interests, habits, and activities forms slowly as a result of the many experiences the child meets, and the qualities and characteristics he exhibits tend to give the personality a certain observable pattern of behavioral consistencies.

Adolescence is a significant phase of personality development and integration. A fully mature personality is possible only when all the major areas of growth have had an opportunity to develop toward their maximal capacity. It is of paramount importance that an individual successfully complete each successive level of development if a sound, integrated personality is to be attained. The personality patterns established during childhood are modified during adolescence when new factors and experiences enter the individual's life.

Briefly, some of the new factors and experiences that appear in adolescence and alter personality are (1) adult physique, (2) sexual maturation, accompanied by new drives and emotions, (3) greater self-awareness, resulting in a heightened desire for self-direction and a reevaluation of standards, aims, and ideals, (4) the need for companionship with emphasis on heterosexual friendships, and (5) numerous conflicts arising from the adolescent's transition from childhood to adulthood.

Relative stability in motivation is reached during the years of early adulthood, when the individual has found his place in society and has gained control over his feelings and himself. Some people never reach full maturity in all the dimensions of personality.

Lack of personality development can be the result of having a low biological and cognitive endowment or remaining too long in any one of the childhood or adolescent stages of development because of insufficient stimulation for growth and adjustment. Immaturity usually includes lack of initiative in searching and experimenting and therefore slow or little development. Any fixation restrains flexibility and learning, and so lowers the accumulation of personality resources. Some minor difficulties in adjustment during childhood, when not corrected, are responsible for more serious problems and antisocial behavior which may appear in adolescence. Early deprivations, frustrations, and conflicts make lasting impressions, which later produce anxiety and withdrawal or hostility and destructive tendencies.

ABILITIES AND ASPIRATIONS

No two adolescents have equal endowments or potentialities, be they physical or cognitive, nor are acquired abilities and skills the same for all teen-agers. Aspirations formulated during the early phase of adolescence are usually high. Many young persons are striving toward goals and achievement levels that are unrealistic in view of their actual endowments and acquired abilities. Adolescents' goals and ambitions are comparable to neurotic and prepsychotic strivings. If their aspirations are not sufficiently realistic, they repeatedly fail and experience deep disappointment and even despair. This is often accompanied by feelings of inadequacy tinted with depression or defeatism.

The conflicts and disappointments that result from overestimation of the teen-ager's abilities may be constructive or they may cause him to form a deviant evaluation of himself and society. When conflict and strain increase, hostility and aggressive tendencies accumulate and may lead to rebellion against societal regulations and, especially, against those in authority.

Many adolescents and young adults have difficulty in discarding unattainable, too idealistic goals. Poorly developed ego and insufficient self-understanding contribute partially to a distorted self-concept. Sometimes parents pressure the adolescent into striving toward goals he lacks the ability to achieve. Adjusting aspirations to abilities and skills is essential in avoiding situations of severe conflict and in promoting personality integration. Professional counseling is often necessary to solve these and other conflicts that arise during adolescence.

The adolescent's personality develops as he becomes better acquainted with his real self, its assets, and its liabilities. This inner life is explored by a magnified self-awareness and a tendency toward reflection. Questions begin to arise concerning phenomena and events that were wholly accepted before. The adolescent reevaluates himself, his feelings, beliefs, desires, and joys. He also considers his companions, parents, teachers, education, and the very world itself. Many objects and situations now appear in a new light. He ponders over his future and his place in society, his relationship to God, and his moral and religious obligations. He is concerned with his current situation and the problems of adjustment arising from his inconsistent emotional responses, which are unpredictable and likely to lead him into some interpersonal troubles. He is gradually learning the importance of utilizing his intellectual powers in his attempt at personality organization. Increasingly consistent behavior is the major index of personality development.

Adolescent personality growth is also marked by progress in social behavior toward peers of both sexes and adults as well. The desire for regular companionship with a member of the opposite sex and interest in the adult pattern of social interaction are signs of personal maturation. Vicarious exploration of interpersonal relationships through movies, biographies, and fiction gives way to a more realistic approach as notions about marriage and family life appear. Girls, and to a lesser degree boys too, begin to think about qualities desired in a prospective life partner. Gradually their heterosexual associations and friendships become more selective.

The young adolescent depends upon his close companions for support and encouragement, since at times it seems that these associates are the only people who fully understand him. Their capacity for empathy and understanding is strengthened by their experience of similar changes, conflicts, and trials. Quite frequently, peer approval is sought to the point of causing conflicts with parents and other representatives of authority. The adolescent's selection of emotionally and morally mature friends and reference groups is highly desirable since the standards and values of the peer group have a strong and lasting influence on each of its members. Generally, adolescents who are raised in a morally acceptable and emotionally mature environment will tend to seek friends of this type—they desire fewer kicks springing from vicarious or delinquent experiences.

VALUES, ATTITUDES, AND IDEALS

Values result from the ability to perceive worth and importance. From a psychological point of view values refer to "meanings perceived as related to self" [4]. The commerce between the adolescent and his environment is marked by a valuing transaction. The adolescent likes and appreciates some ideas and events more than others. There are persons, objects, and situations that are considered worth having. Deep in his heart he craves love from certain people and possibly fears being swallowed up in the crowd [17].

Viktor E. Frankl of Vienna introduced a very useful concept, the "will to meaning"—an intrinsic desire to search for meanings and to experience them. This term finds a specific application in the adolescent's quest for values and virtues during this period of heightened experience. The self is not merely the core of personality; it is also central in one's search for personally meaningful standards and ideals.

Before adolescence begins, some values and attitudes have been accepted by the child and preadolescent. If emotions and opinions are adequately developed, an adolescent's response to external values will be magnified during the later part of adolescence. By repeating personal responses to values and ideals as these are demonstrated by his peers and other significant individuals, an adolescent alters his earlier convictions and develops new attitudes.

There is common agreement among experts in the field that values, attitudes, and ideals act as powerful organizers of behavior as soon as the adolescent begins establishing them for himself. Through experience, the adolescent is able to establish his own hierarchy of values and to set standards based on these values. He should not, however, rely solely upon his own abilities in this task; he should seek help from his parents, teachers, and counselors. With this help he can properly set his goals and ascertain the means necessary to attain them.

As has been pointed out, a primary source of information concerning meaning and values is the social environment of the adolescent. Values and meanings are taken in from significant persons such as parents, teachers, and peer-group leaders. Peers begin to rank high as an adolescent strives to free himself from excessive parental and adult influences. Occasionally, life-determining decisions result from intimate talks with close friends. In the advanced years of adolescence, societal and cultural norms and expectations gain substantially in their conditioning power.   Peers and other social agents praise and reward certain forms of behavior; they censure and punish others. In line with the former, the individual tends to develop positive approach values; and with the latter he tends to develop negative avoidance values [20].

In a survey of changing values among American college students in the 1950s Phillip Jacobs [12] reported a weakness of fiber.   About three-fourths were "gloriously contented, both in regard to their present day-to-day activity and their outlook for the future."   They hoped to realize their personal desires by conforming to the conventions of the business world, not crusading against racial segregation or injustice, but accepting nondiscrimination when it comes. They did not wish to have an influence upon public policy or governmental affairs.   They regarded college education as desirable because it gave them a vocational preparation, social status, and enjoyable recreation.   Their aspirations were primarily for acquiring material possessions.

Gordon W. Allport [4] maintains that our national values, although about the finest mankind has ever formulated, are deteriorating badly.   Unless Judeo-Christian ethics are revitalized, "our youth may not have the personal fortitude and moral implements that the future will require."   Alexander A. Schneiders [3, p. 186] believes that "perhaps the most effective way of helping adolescents to develop a value system is for parents and teachers to provide *models* of behavior and right thinking for young people," since the adolescent's thinking is greatly affected by those around him.   Many adolescents' problems can be traced to the fact that our society has no set hierarchy of values, and the young people are unable to understand the importance and place of moral and spiritual values in their lives.   Many do not include them in their attempts at growth and adjustment.

In public educational policies the ultimate source of value or sanction often remains unidentified.   An illustration of this is found in the work of the Educational Policies Commission of the National Education Association of the United States and the American Association of School Administrators [16, pp. 18–30].   The commission has acknowledged the supreme importance of individual personality development as the basic moral and spiritual value in American life.   If this is so, continues the commission, the other leading tenets include these:

1. Each person should feel responsible for the consequences of his own conduct.   Moral responsibility and self-direction are marks of maturity.
2. The human mind should be liberated by access to information and opinion.
3. Excellence in mind, character, and creative ability should be fostered.
4. Each person should be offered the emotional and spiritual experiences that transcend the materialistic aspects of life.

But how to "transcend the materialistic aspects of life," and acknowledge the fact that "the individual personality is supreme" is still a problem for the adolescent, teacher, and parent since the authors fail to give concrete sugges- tions for putting the advice into practice.   Too often education leaves the adolescent to act on his own resources.   It is difficult for him to solve educa- tion and culture-reinforced conflicts.   When no hierarchy of values is formed and traditional values are rejected, the emptiness youth experiences is often replaced by poor substitutes since mankind abhors living in a vacuum.   This may be partly responsible for the rebellion that adolescents find themselves experiencing.   The principle of equal rights sometimes conflicts with their quest for personal achievement and self-gratification.   The development of a full human nature implies a religion-oriented scheme of values.   The school should provide a foundation for his value system.

Although the teaching of values should permeate the entire educational process and all the school's resources should be used to teach moral and spiritual values [16, pp. 55, 60], implementing this would probably meet with many serious obstacles.   The same applies to the demand for "the public school to teach objectively any religious creed" [16, p. 77].   Confusion is bound to result if the assumption is made that American education must be derived from the "moral and spiritual values which are shared by the mem- bers of all religious faiths."   Despite the rise of the ecumenical spirit, the major American faiths probably differ too much to agree on a common course for teaching religious living.   A basic course suitable to all faiths would be much too vague to be of any significance to the individual student.   A course in religion, it is felt, would present a number of controversial issues without offering concrete guidance.

Two further references may shed some light on the issue of religious edu- cation as seen by the Educational Policies Commission:

> To omit from the classroom all references to religion and the institutions of religion is to neglect an important part of American life.   Knowing about religion is essential for a full understanding of our culture, literature, art, history, and current affairs.   That religious beliefs are controversial is not an adequate reason for excluding teaching about religion from the public schools [16, pp. 77–78].

> The Commission comes to the conclusion that the public schools will con- tinue to be indispensable in the total process of developing moral and spiritual values, and that they can and should increase their effectiveness in this respect [16, p. 100].

Teaching religion in schools is probably a crucial factor in the development of a moral character.   Why should religion be more isolated than geography or social sciences?   The more religious ideals and principles can be integrated into the curriculum, the more meaningful this aspect of daily living will be for its students.   This is one major advantage of private and church-related education.   However, just because public schools are not sectarian and their teaching of a common course in religion is not feasible, should educators feel they can completely disregard the need for religious education?   A method has been found in the public school system for teaching controversial issues in social and other sciences; then there should also be a plan for teaching religion whereby each student could receive instruction in his own faith.   One satisfactory solution is offered by several public school systems that have a released-time program in which children are dismissed early one day each week to attend religious classes at a nearby parochial school, church, or synagogue.   Donald N. Michael [15, p. 107] predicts that the debate over the proper values for youth will be carried on by parents and leaders for at least the next twenty years.   "It will be an intense debate and a partisan one, since we will continue to be unclear about the kind of world we want and what education we wish to emphasize for those ends."   Further insight into the problem of religious versus nonreligious education can be gained from several other sources [11, 19, 23].   Leo R. Ward [24] suggests teaching What Believers Believe as the first step in an approach to a course in the ideas and values of the major American faiths.

Adolescent attitudes.   The formation of adolescent attitudes is greatly determined by the home environment.   The experiential background, race, nationality, and religion of the parents, as well as their socioeconomic class, all have a significant influence upon the adolescent.   However, he is most directly influenced by peer opinion, evaluation, and concern.   While most adolescents strongly resist a great deal of influence, they appear almost defenseless against the values, standards, and morals of their peer reference groups.   Under the surface appearance of great variety, there are several general and permeating attitudes that mark adolescent behavior in our society.

Emancipation from the home accompanies the marked increase of abilities during puberty which favors autonomy and increased self-direction.   As home conflicts continue to arise, the adolescent breaks away from various forms of parental influence and control.

Self-direction is not only a goal for which the adolescent strives but also a prerequisite for attaining adult status.   In early and middle adolescence, the major effort is toward freedom from parental control.   Only when this is satisfactorily achieved can the task of liberating himself from peer-group domination be begun.   Both of these sources of external influence must be subordinated to direction from within before the years of adolescence expire.   Emancipation and self-regulation are the main elements of adolescent masculine crisis.   While the adolescent tends to resist parental direction, the peer group is usually seen as a supportive influence.

The adolescent increasingly expects and demands the privileges of an adult.   Important among these are the use of the family car, the selection of his own clothes, resistance to a curfew, and permission for late television viewing. These are problem areas in the adolescent's striving for a fuller autonomy. Although it is true that the adolescent's demands may not be in keeping with his level of maturity, it is also true that some parents try to maintain their authority and exercise control over their children's lives beyond the proper age.

If decision-making is not allowed, the adolescent will be ill-equipped as an adult to direct his energies and talents toward worthwhile goals. More immediately, his need for independence will be severely frustrated, and this frustration will foster the development of negative attitudes toward parents and authority in general. The limits on the adolescent's sphere of self-direction must be increasingly widened the moment he shows the desire to assume responsibility. The parents' judgment and experience must guide them in determining the limits of the adolescent's autonomy. Since the adolescent's attitudes toward himself, his family, and peers are changing rapidly, parental understanding and discreet guidance can do much to help shape these attitudes into healthy, morally and socially accepted ones.

During the time of pubertal changes, and in middle adolescence, individuals are particularly inclined toward *prejudice*. This can be traced to several factors. First of all, the volatility of emotions is extremely high during this period. Emotional reactions are often far out of proportion to their stimulus because of the changing physiological, cognitive, and social dimensions of personality. Emotional control is often low and inadequate because of lack of personality integration. The heightened sensitivity of the adolescent at this stage often results in feelings of insecurity and inferiority. These feelings are intolerable to the individual, and attitudes of hostility and prejudice toward other groups may be utilized as an ego-defense dynamism. Using scapegoating and projection, although so doing minimizes tensions for the adolescent, is a form of maladaptive behavior that hinders rather than helps the individual in his progress toward maturity and adjustment.

Adolescents at this stage of development are easily influenced by the attitudes of others, particularly their peer group. If one member, especially the leader, has strong feelings of prejudice, these undesirable attitudes will easily be assimilated by the others.

Along with the prejudice of youth comes *alienation,* a more recent problem among college students on large campuses. A sense of personal identity and moral values is lost in the mass of students and the dearth of personal interaction with influential adults—parents and professors alike. Frequently deterioration of beliefs and morals is accompanied by depersonalization and loss of standards.

Hedonism and bureaucracy, the experience of rootlessness and loneliness, all lead to mass alienation. "The alienated person is not only out of touch with other persons but also out of touch with himself" [8]. Kenneth Keniston [13] feels that excessive cultural homogeneity and uniformity prepare the soil for developmental estrangement as one becomes less and less able to apply himself creatively and feels pressed toward criticism and repudiation of society and culture. Alienation is now chosen by youth in large numbers as its basic stance toward society [13, p. 3]. Apparently there is a rising estrangement from both *ordo socialis* and *ordo divinis.*

The following is a case abstract which points to defective foundations in an adolescent's personality formation.

> John is a tall, rather handsome high school senior, aged seventeen. He is currently in a home for boys, having been placed there by a juvenile court for several violations of the law, ranging from truancy to car theft.
>
> John has an extremely negative attitude toward authority and also has difficulty relating to the other boys. He often causes disciplinary problems, and has no interest in conforming to what is expected of the boys.
>
> Although John has an above-average intelligence, he lacks the motivation to settle down and apply himself. He has an almost complete lack of tolerance for frustration, and is extremely impulsive. Throughout his school years, he has often clashed with teachers and school authorities.
>
> John's early home life is largely responsible for his problem. His father, an alcoholic, punished him severely for real or imaginary infractions of rules. John's mother, on the other hand, was too lenient, and admitted that John too often had his own way with her. John feels that his father was no good, and is to blame for his problems.
>
> John's adjustment to life is precarious in pattern. The outlook for him is not promising since he lacks satisfactory relationships with others and his negativism is deeply internalized.

HETEROSEXUAL RELATIONSHIPS

A marked heterosexual interest appears at the age of thirteen or fourteen in girls and at about fifteen or sixteen in boys. This interest and curiosity are closely related to the individual's sexual maturation, which occurs at puberty. Girls wish to attract the boys' attention and vice versa. A desire to make social contacts and find companionship also appears at this age and continues to increase as the years of adolescence pass. Since most schools are coeducational, young people make a variety of contacts with members of the opposite sex during their school years and learn about the opposite sex's characteristics and interests.

In the middle stage of adolescence, which is marked by a strong interest in members of the opposite sex in general rather than in any single individual, group activities have a strong appeal. Boys are curious about "anyone wearing a skirt," and girls are interested in "anyone wearing trousers"; this phase is therefore marked by a girl-crazy and boy-crazy attitude. Toward the end of adolescence, the heterosexual interest begins to center on one particular person of the other sex. When one or two romances fail, the girl tends to become cautious and more selective before "falling in love." With adult maturity sex drives and erotic sentiments fuse into a single and powerful force of motivation, leading toward an increased desire for associating fully with a chosen one and a desire for marriage.

During middle, group-conscious adolescence, dating is frequent. Observation and a deeper insight into overt personality traits of the opposite sex result. If the impressions are positive, they stimulate affection and love, referred to as infatuation, puppy love, or "love at first sight." These teenagers are not as yet emotionally and socially mature enough for a long-term intimate association. Through their expectation of finding an ideal companion, they are readily "hurt." Envy, jealousy, and arguments occur and result in antagonistic emotions. The breaking up of each intimate cross-sexual association causes feelings of inadequacy or depression and sometimes a total reappraisal of the self-concept. Many adolescents experience five or six romantic attachments before they marry. Teen-age marriages resulting from infatuation or puppy love show the highest divorce rates because most teen-agers are not yet mature enough to choose properly and to assume full marriage responsibilities.

ADOLESCENT CONFLICTS AND PROBLEMS

Adolescent behavior often has a surface appearance of gay and carefree activity marked by rollicking antics and enthusiasm for living. Beneath the shiny veneer of adolescent self-expression, however, the trained observer detects marks of the anxious thoughts and the uncertain cares of young persons undergoing a decision-making and problem-solving period of development. In learning to adjust to his own changing body and motivation, assailed by some irrational drives and desires, the adolescent is struggling within himself. Life is offering new goals and views, and he is becoming increasingly aware of new relationships with parents and peers. Problems in adjusting spring from many sources, including new abilities and urges, feelings of love and hate, restlessness and discouragement, adult needs and childhood limitations. Table 17–1 shows fifteen leading adolescent problems and interests and their changes from 1935 to 1957 and 1967. Money, mental hygiene, and sex adjustments ranked highest as personal problems in 1967 for adolescents in the Detroit area. Sex adjustments, money, and personal attractiveness were the foremost problems of interest for the same sample.

During adolescence conflicts arise from a variety of causes. Difficulty in gratifying emotional and social needs is one of them. The need for new experiences to meet the demands of newly acquired drives, abilities, and skills is an urgent one at this time of rapid and many-faceted developments.

Table 17–1 Ranks of adolescent life problems and interests: 1935, 1957, and 1967

Issues	As personal problems						As problems of interest					
	1935		1957		1967		1935		1957		1967	
	Mean rank	Rank of mean	Mean rank	Rank of mean	Mean rank	Rank of mean	Mean rank	Rank of mean	Mean rank	Rank of mean	Mean rank	Rank of mean
Health	6.61	2	8.9	12.5	7.79	11	6.1	2	6.7	1	6.09	4
Sex adjustments	10.0	15	8.9	12.5	5.09	3	9.3	12	7.1	7	3.84	1
Safety	8.6	12	9.6	14	8.30	15	8.5	10	9.5	12	8.18	14
Money	6.5	1	6.4	2	4.39	1	7.6	7	7.4	9	4.63	2
Mental hygiene	8.5	11	7.6	5.5	5.06	2	9.2	12	8.8	11	6.89	7
Study habits	7.1	4	5.7	1	5.31	4	9.0	11	9.6	13	7.81	12
Recreation	8.3	10	10.1	15	8.08	14	5.2	1	6.8	3	7.04	9
Personal and moral qualities	7.2	5	6.9	3	5.84	5	7.6	7	7.2	8	6.25	6
Home and family relationships	8.2	8.5	8.0	7	6.39	6	8.4	9	6.8	3	7.36	11
Manners and courtesy	7.9	7	8.1	8	7.98	12	6.9	4	8.6	10	7.21	10
Personal attractiveness	7.0	3	7.3	4	7.99	13	6.8	3	7.0	6	6.01	3
Daily schedule	9.2	14	8.5	11	7.63	10	10.4	15	11.2	15	9.25	15
Civic interests, etc	8.7	13	8.2	9	7.05	8	9.4	14	9.8	14	8.03	13
Getting along with others	8.2	8.5	8.3	10	7.42	9	7.6	7	6.8	3	6.19	5
Philosophy of life	7.5	6	7.6	5.5	6.47	7	7.5	5	6.9	5	6.95	8

Sources: Percival M. Symonds. Life problems and interests of adolescents, *School Rev.*, 1936, **44**, 506–518; Dale B. Harris. Life problems and interests of adolescents in 1935 and 1957, *School Rev.*, 1959, **67**, 335–343; Sharon Kroha and Justin Pikunas. Adolescent life problems and interests in 1967 (a study in progress; N=424).

Curiosity increases and dissatisfaction with the daily routine and ordinary situations leads youth to seek thrills and the sensational. At times great risks, including conspicuous disregard for law and convention, are incurred. Although the needs for personal development and approval are common to all individuals, their great amplitude and power in the adolescent make them especially strong sources of conflict and dissatisfaction. The keen desire of adolescents to associate with others results in cliques, clubs, fraternities, sororities, and other formal and informal groups. Intensified group activity often interferes with school and home responsibilities. Conformity to the accepted standards of speech, dress, and manners suppresses individuality.

The tough-minded extrovert may openly rebel against parental pressures or social regulations. The tender-minded introvert may attempt to escape his dilemmas by retreating into reverie. The need for erecting a shell of ego-protective dynamisms rises as personal hurts continue occurring. A lack of emotional balance, fluctuating high and low spirits, exhibitionistic tendencies, and restlessness are frequent features of adolescent motivation. External situations, such as quarreling parents, nagging and teasing by a member of the family, having to attend school, and being misunderstood by a friend or rejected by the peer group, add much fire to the internal stress. Regression to a puerile level of adjustment or aggressive resolutions resulting from the inner strain may occur almost spontaneously. A lack of proper recreational facilities for the key adolescent interests—social, athletic, and creative—also blocks release of tension.

The adolescent has a complex personality, and many conditions contribute to his search for status and for gratification of his basic and acquired needs. Frustrations and conflicts are practically inevitable and bring the need of in-trapsychic self-defense into focus. The thwarting of drives and impulses related to the satisfaction of underlying needs is closely related to the rise of emotional dynamics. Affective responses arise when internal or external limitation, inhibition, or obstruction of a drive or desire occurs. The growing intensity of the drive increases the probability of violent and disorganized behavior directed against the sources of deprivation.

Ambivalence

Ambivalence springs from the presence of antagonistic feelings toward the same object or situation. The young adolescent is often torn between admiration and denial, attraction and repulsion, frenzied activity and idleness. His bipolarity of emotion and thinking points to a lack of harmonious fusion among his various psychobiological drives. This is especially true when the sexual drive becomes involved before sexual and emotional maturity is attained. Lack of perspective and moderation seem to reinforce the states of doubt and ambivalence. Frequently adolescents (and some adults) lack the ability to make important decisions by themselves. Often their closest friends make decisions for them. With progress in character formation there is a decline in the intensity of ambivalent tendencies.

Self-defenses

The advanced level of adolescent development allows for the acquiring of numerous self-defensive responses. By means of various self-defenses the person attempts to reestablish a temporary balance between internal superego regulations and external stimulants and pressures. They are compromises between internal needs and reality.

The excessive use of defense mechanisms that are persistent modes of individual behavior resulting from interpersonal relations can have disintegrating or isolating effects [22, pp. 102–109]. They are gradually incorporated into the self-system of a growing person before he is able to assess their full consequences or implications. His perception of the world becomes clouded by his personal drives and inhibitions and these techniques for coping with them. Some of the more frequently used dynamisms are compensation and substitution, rationalization and displacement, introjection and projection, and repression and reaction formation. Friedrich Nietzsche and Sigmund Freud are the original formulators of most of them. The ones most commonly employed by adolescents will be briefly discussed here.

Rationalization is a dynamism that appears in the early years of childhood and occasionally continues throughout life. It is an attempt at self-justification by finding reasons to excuse oneself from criticism or punishment. The actual facts in a situation are misinterpreted by the individual in order to protect his own self-concept from the adverse opinion of others.

Projection refers to a dynamism by which personal weaknesses and undesirable qualities and traits are attributed to other individuals and other external sources. Undesirable elements of the self are unconsciously treated as though they existed in another and not in one's self. For example, traits of dishonesty and hostility are often projected; when this occurs, lying and aggressiveness are seen by the individual as characteristics of others against which he must protect himself.

Any evidence of return to an earlier, less mature level of functioning is referred to as *regression* rather than as a situational response. When an individual is exposed to a frustrating or anxiety-provoking experience, his mature manner of adjustment may fail. Avoidance or some more primitive reaction is used to protect the self, and if the source of frustration or stress is not removed or resolved, this response pattern, properly called regression, becomes habitual. The level of regression is judged by the level at which one functions or in terms of the number of years a person's behavior and interest regress. When regression results in the use of infantile ways of handling needs and problems, this level of self-defense is referred to as *infantilism*. When the adolescent's behavior can be characterized by a frequent need of assistance, extreme dependence, and inability to delay the gratification of his needs or desires, he is displaying an infantile level of functioning.

Neurotic tendencies

Fierce and prolonged conflict situations cause some adolescents, especially those who have experienced childhood trauma, to suffer mental disturbances and an inability to integrate their personality into a sound functional system. As a result, anxiety intensifies and forms a basis for a neurotic pattern of behavior marked by chronic symptoms. Of the various forms of neurosis, the adolescent appears to be most susceptible to conversion reactions, anxiety attacks, and obsessive-compulsive reactions. In more extreme cases of maladjustment, psychotic reactions, such as hebephrenic or catatonic schizophrenia, may result.

Insistent, irrational ideas or actions which the subject often recognizes as illogical, but which he nevertheless attends to because of the reduction in tension that they bring, constitute *obsessions*. As obsessions intensify, they are partially released in various forms of compulsive behavior. Obsessive-compulsive reactions afflict a significant minority of adolescents. The tension brought about as a result of trying to ignore or suppress these urges is almost unbearable to the individual. The underlying cause of this behavior is usually a deep sense of inferiority or guilt that creates tension and expresses itself symbolically in the persistence of the same ideas and behavior.

Adolescents often experience guilt over the processes and urges that arise as a result of pubertal changes. Sexual arousal and expressions, as well as menstruation in girls and nocturnal emissions in boys, sometimes produce guilt that in some cases leads to obsessive-compulsive responses. This is especially true when knowledge of these phenomena is incomplete or lacking, or when negative attitudes toward matters pertaining to sex have been deeply instilled.

Frequent and unnecessary hand washing is a compulsion usually resulting from a deep sense of guilt, often attributed to sexual factors. This guilt may be caused by fear of the future. That is, the hand washing or any other compulsion may be an immediate defense or an attempt to prevent actions that the adolescent fears he or she will commit.

Obsessions are irremovable ideas that often plague a person's consciousness and seriously disturb his efficiency and adjustment. The content of these ideas may be almost anything; fear of insanity, sexual fantasies, or hatred for parents or members of the opposite sex. These ideas easily arise in adolescence, in part because of a lack of success in heterosexual attraction, the need for independence from parents, and an abundance of sexual stimuli. A lack of complete sexual information or the concomitant moral instruction necessary for satisfactory sexual adjustment, overprotective or dominating parents, and lack of self-knowledge, all contribute to obsessions and consequent maladaptive behavior in adolescence. If discovered early enough, obsessions or compulsions can be successfully treated. But often they are not made known in time, and persist throughout adolescence and into adulthood. In these cases long-term psychotherapeutic treatment is necessary, and its success is less certain.

Anxiety is an unrealistic and unpleasant emotional state in which threats and dangers to the life of the person are vividly anticipated. It is out of proportion to any stimulus and is often undifferentiated and diffuse. Adolescents, because of the multitude of adjustments and decisions that they must make, and because of their level of maturity and lack of experience, are an easy prey for this type of emotional disturbance. The tensions resulting from physiological changes, lack of confidence in themselves, and the indecision and ambivalence in many areas of their lives readily lead to the experience of intense anxiety. When these tensions and strains accumulate, anxiety attacks may be the result.

A person experiencing intense anxiety becomes terrified, sweats profusely, and his heart palpitates. This state of near panic usually subsides in two or three hours. Some attacks are detrimental to both the physical and functional well-being of the adolescent. They produce as much intense physiological excitation as do fears or phobias, and mentally they are even more debilitating than fear in that the anxiety-producing stimulus is not a specific object or event which can be dealt with or from which the adolescent can flee. On the contrary, the adolescent does not know what he is afraid of, or what catastrophic event is going to take place; rather, the fearful feelings attach themselves easily to any forthcoming event. Yet when the event has passed, the anxiety is only slightly lowered and it takes little time before another situation arouses it.

Calm and deliberate reassurance is often of great help in allaying anxiety. If the adolescent can be convinced that his fears are shared by others, and that others are surmounting these fears and adjusting satisfactorily to new situations in spite of them, he may be helped. If the anxiety is deeply rooted in the personality, then counseling and psychotherapy may be needed to help the adolescent rid himself of this affliction. A person showing these symptoms can be considered a neurotic if anxiety attacks occur periodically. This is not the case if a single attack takes place during the final examination period or a similar situation of intense strain.

Conversion reactions are essentially a symptomatic externalization of inner conflict and anxiety that are usually not recognized by the individual. The conflict is usually of such a nature that it is unacceptable to the conscious mind and its tension is expressed in physical symptoms. These symptoms may be of many types: anesthesia, writer's cramp, hysterical paralysis, or neuromuscular convulsions. There is no organic basis for conversion symptoms. They are not physically or neurologically caused. Rather, they are purposeful, unconsciously adopted methods of resolving conflict and reducing anxiety. Unconsciously cardiac disturbances, severe pain, or nausea are utilized by some adolescents as fair and honorable methods of escaping stress situations.

Conversion reactions, one of the most common of the neuroses, are usually found in individuals who have habitually reacted to reality in an evasive or escapist way. A strong reliance on defense dynamisms is also a usual part of the individual's past. Additional difficulties result in various types of conversion.

Adolescents, because of their lack of personality integration, absence of pertinent experience, and other related factors, resort to this type of maladjustment in order to relieve their conflicts. Antagonistic tendencies, such as the need for independence and the duty to love and obey parents, may be another contributing factor. A combination of strong moral precepts and sexual fantasies can produce conflicts unacceptable at the conscious level. If the adolescent is unprepared for his new needs and urges, they may be repressed, but remain dynamic, and after accumulation, express themselves in conversion symptoms.

The prevention of conversion reactions begins in childhood. The individual must be taught to face reality and deal with problems as they arise. Once a pattern of evasion and escape is built up by the individual, the problems and conflicts of adolescence prove too much for an already precarious adjustment. Dealing with these problems after such a pattern has taken hold is difficult, because the individual is usually unwilling or unable to bring the conflict to the surface where it might be understood and dealt with effectively.

Delinquent trends

Delinquent trends are often the resulting reactions to continual deprivation and frustration and prolonged lack of success. "Battered" children often become aggressive teen-agers. Some adolescents tend to respond to situational deprivation by verbal or physical aggression. Aggressive behavior involves some form of attack, such as using abusive language, or provoking and striking another person. According to N. R. F. Maier [14, p. 101], when a frustrated person strikes another individual, he is doing so not to remove him as an obstacle or to injure him, but because he is frustrated and too tense. Removal of the obstacle or injury is secondary. In some instances, the immediate response to frustration is an increase of self-control and toleration of the situation, yet the suppressed aggressive tendencies pile up and are likely to show themselves later. Thus, various aggressive reactions are only temporarily delayed, compressed, disguised, displaced, or otherwise deflected from the original source. John Dollard and Neal E. Miller [5] assumed that frustration is always accompanied by some form of aggression. Granting the probability that some aggressive energies can be compensated for, or sublimated and constructively expressed, it may be expected that during this period of increased conflict and frustration some adolescents will turn to delinquent activities as a means of discharging aggression.

Many books and magazines, motion pictures and TV shows emphasizing sex and violence, when not balanced by moral education and an integrated family life, contribute greatly to delinquent activities. Some of the most common delinquent activities will be discussed. *Truancy* is a form of withdrawal from school reality in order to avoid subjectively unpleasant tasks in the classroom. It is one of the most common delinquent activities and often precedes other forms of delinquency. Uncontrollable misbehavior at home and at school and offenses against others and society are other typical forms of adolescent delinquency. For some adolescents, however, conflicts and the resulting frustrations can serve as valuable assets for the building of ego strength and character, and for the development of more mature reasoning power and personal judgment. This frequently happens when the adolescent has the advantage of a good home.

Cheating and stealing at home and at school, destruction of property, association with "rough gangs," and a tendency to get involved in fights are typical forms of delinquent behavior resulting from frustration and tension. In the school situation, refusing to submit to the regulations of the teacher causes added difficulties. In many instances, adolescents steal articles that they cannot even use as an indirect expression of dislike which they hesitate to manifest as overt aggression because of a fear of punishment. When control against aggressive impulses is inadequate, cruelty and sex offenses also occur.

SEARCH FOR ONESELF

The adolescent's capacity to draw upon his own resources, to reason for himself, and to act upon his own decisions grows in proportion to his progress toward an adult level of functioning. The adolescent advances in self-discovery by way of three interrelated steps: (1) search for human models, (2) choice of principles and ideals, and (3) formulation of a philosophy of life based on a value system. A favorable and mature understanding of oneself can be achieved by channeling one's energies and dynamics according to a more mature and well-structured personality model. Despite the perfectionistic tendencies of adolescence it cannot be assumed that all youth necessarily pick out good models. Much depends on their drives and emotions, their needs and goals, and their environmental and school circumstances. To a large extent, this is a subconscious process.

In respect to social attraction and identification, the stage of puberty is a somewhat disoriented period in adolescent life. The personality structure of the child, including its self-identification, is becoming lost. The emergence of a new structure takes time. In order to bring himself out of this confusion and the difficulties arising from considering what to do and what not to do and deciding what must be learned or achieved, the adolescent's attention is directed toward peers and young adults who appear to embody some or most of his sensed or partially assimilated values and ideals. Some identification with their attitudes, views, and behavior occurs, and some stabilization of his motivation is established. Any deep identification with another individual may become a foundation for a life pattern.

Hill's study [10] of 8,813 children in Alabama shows that 54.7 percent of older urban children select for their idols and ideals famous historical figures and persons in the public eye. People in their immediate environment—parents, teachers, and acquaintances—also rank high: 35.1 percent. Since considerable changes occur at the adolescent level, similar studies are necessary for the assessment of current adolescent identifications. Television and motion-picture stars are often imitated by the adolescent of this generation. The Beatles were popular in the early sixties, the Monkees in the middle sixties. Who can predict the characteristics that will appeal to the next generation?

Toward the middle of adolescence, a high level of abstract and symbolic thinking is developed. It enables the teen-ager to draw many inferences and comparisons. Therefore, when he sees and admires the conduct of some individuals, he also recognizes the ethical principles and at times the hierarchy of values behind such actions. This, of course, greatly helps him in assimilating the principles and ideals by which he wants to live. Principles and ideals, when assimilated, result in greater stability, because they serve as guides toward goals and as standards for objectives accompanying the goals.

The latter part of adolescence is a phase during which a pattern of adult life is formulated and embraced. This pattern of life is greatly influenced by events and occurrences of childhood and puberty and the types of identifications made with adults. The value of character and Weltanschauung can hardly be overemphasized as prerequisite for harmonious adult functioning.

WELTANSCHAUUNG AND CHARACTER

The process of acquiring a rational design for living is a part of character formation. Character, in psychology, refers to the acquired system of motivational tendencies that enable a person to react consistently to moral values and issues. Consistency of behavior and conduct are external signs of gains in internal character structure.

Late adolescence is a major phase of character development, which is largely influenced by a person's experiential background and the direction his own dispositions, endowments, abilities, and other resources take. Character has its roots embedded in early childhood experiences in which the parents' influence is very strong. Psychoanalysts assume that the foundation for a person's character structure is well laid by the age of five or six years. Other childhood experiences that affect character are conflicts encountered by the child, such as repeated failures in school which may lead to truancy, dishonesty, and contempt for authority. A lack of fundamental necessities, such as food and clothing, may lead the child into habits of stealing. Pleasurable and satisfying events also affect character development and usually promote desirable character traits if the pleasure is lawful and not excessive. The type of neighborhood and its mores and standards also make an impression on character as the child tends to assimilate what he is exposed to. Responsiveness to what is good must be reinforced throughout childhood in order to foster an appreciation of moral principles and ideals.

In *Children who hate* [18], Fritz Redl and D. Wineman describe their work with children ten years of age and younger whose personality and character were warped by their social environment. These children had become so accustomed to rejection and hate that they could not love or were afraid to love. After a year or more in an atmosphere of kindness and patience, these boys still retained most of their hostile attitudes and destructive behavior.

One can still say that the final determiner of character is the individual's disposition in spite of what the environmental background might have contributed. This can easily be seen in cases where siblings or twins are reared in the same environment and have similar family influences, yet habitually react very differently to practically identical situations. One child, for example, becomes submissive when corrected by his parents; the other child becomes angry and resentful. Individual dispositions would seem to account for many differences in a person's reaction pattern.

During adolescence, autonomy and self-control become major forces of character development. Strivings for independence, combined with the realization of approaching adulthood, make the adolescent weigh carefully his behavior, abilities, and weaknesses with the future in mind. He searches for meanings and goals and decides what kind of person he wants to be. He considers the ethics of his society and community, morality, religion, the wishes of his parents, and the attitudes of his friends. He attempts to use self-control in cultivating the traits he desires. While self-control necessitates personal effort, self-appraisal depends largely upon the estimation of others. Occasionally the casual opinions of peers, parents, and others greatly disturb a youth. After considering the views of others, an individual consciously or unconsciously undertakes self-evaluation and, possibly, alteration. Personality and character greatly reflect the adolescent's self-concept. The search for self often completes itself with the design of moral character.

Gains in ego strength seem to be related to the development of moral character. In *The psychology of character development* by R. F. Peck and Robert J. Havighurst [2], the psychologists' ratings of ego strength based on interview and projective tests of a small city's adolescents correlated significantly with total moral character scores as rated by schoolmates, teachers, and other adults ($N=35$, $r=.69$). In the same study Peck and Havighurst formulated a character typology chiefly based on the moral dimension. They distinguished amoral, expedient, conforming, rational-conscientious, and rational-altruistic types. The highest level of moral maturity is represented by the *rational-altruistic* type who displays a stable set of values and principles by which he is guided. Such an individual is highly concerned about the welfare of others. In direct contrast is the *expedient* individual who is self-centered and wants to gain his own ends, yet avoids disapproval. The *rational-conscientious* type is rigidly guided by an internal standard of right and wrong.

During adolescence the teen-ager begins to develop a philosophy of life. The majority of adolescents construct their Weltanschauung on the basis of religion. Most Christian denominations offer a comprehensive authoritative perspective for a sound philosophy of life. Large numbers of persons adopt an ideology in which the state and nation take the place of God and religion, while others attempt a plan of life based on other philosophies, such as the *hedonistic* doctrine whereby a person seeks pleasure as an end in itself. Because of the conflict and confusion within our present culture, the process of Weltanschauung formation usually extends well into the years of adulthood, or the general life orientation remains unformulated altogether. The adolescent's progress in personality and character formation indicates his approach to an adult level of maturity. The next chapter will attempt to define signs indicating personal maturity at the postadolescent level of life.

QUESTIONS FOR REVIEW

1. How is adolescent personality development related to (a) developments during childhood, and (b) social adjustment?
2. Why do many adolescents set unrealistic goals and aspirations for themselves?

3. Discuss some relationships between personality and the self.
4. Which are the key sources from which an adolescent assimilates values and attitudes?
5. In what way do heterosexual relationships change after puberty?
6. Identify some major difficulties in teaching moral values and religion in school.
7. Identify and describe several sources of adolescent conflicts and problems.
8. Define anxiety and explain its effects on adolescent adjustment.
9. Give some reasons for delinquent tendencies and explain one of them.
10. What processes and activities indicate progress in self-discovery?
11. Explain what is meant by a philosophy of life and how it influences adolescent behavior.
12. Define character and indicate some major internal and external factors which influence its development.

REFERENCES

I. Selected Reading

1. Havighurst, R. J., and H. Taba. *Adolescent character and personality.* New York: Wiley, 1949. A study of the development of various personality and character traits in a typical American community.

2. Peck, R. F., R. J. Havighurst, et al. *The psychology of character development.* New York: Wiley, 1960. A major study of character and ethics, including a new character typology.

3. Schneiders, Alexander A. *Adolescents and the challenge of maturity.* Milwaukee: Bruce, 1965. A good source for adolescent guidance. Covers needs, problems, family relationships, counseling, and the search for maturity at this age.

II. Specific References

4. Allport, Gordon W. Values and our youth. *Teachers Coll. Rec.,* 1961, **63**, 211–219.

5. Dollard, J., et al. *Frustration and aggression.* New Haven, Conn.: Yale, 1939.

6. Engel, M. The stability of the self-concept in adolescence. *J. abnorm. soc. Psychol.,* 1959, **58**, 211–215.

7. Frank, Lawrence K., and M. Frank. *Your adolescent at home and in school.* New York: Viking, 1956.

8. Gersten, Walter M. Alienation in mass society: Some causes and responses. *Sociol. soc. Res.,* 1965, **49**, 143–152.

9. Gesell, Arnold, et al. *Youth: The years from ten to sixteen.* New York: Harper & Row, 1956.

10. Hill, D. S. Personification of ideals by urban children. *J. soc. Psychol.*, 1930, **1**, 379–393.

11. Inch, Morris A. The American heritage and teaching about religion. *Rel. Educ.*, 1964, **59**, 400–404.

12. Jacobs, Phillip. *Changing values in college.* New York: Harper & Row, 1957.

13. Keniston, Kenneth. *The uncommitted: Alienated youth in American society.* New York: Harcourt, Brace & World, 1965.

14. Maier, N. R. F. *Frustration.* New York: McGraw-Hill, 1949.

15. Michael, Donald N. *The next generation: The prospects ahead for the youth of today and tomorrow.* New York: Random House, 1965.

16. National Education Association and American Association of School Administrators, Educational Policies Commission. *Moral and spiritual values in the public schools.* Washington: National Education Association of the United States, 1951.

17. O'Neill, Hugh P. *The concept of personal value.* Detroit: University of Detroit Press, 1966 (an eight-page pamphlet).

18. Redl, F., and D. Wineman. *Children who hate: The disorganization and breakdown of behavior controls.* Glencoe, Ill.: Free Press, 1951.

19. Report of the Commission on Religion in the Public Schools. *Religion in the public schools.* Washington: American Association of School Administrators, 1964.

20. Seidman, Jerome M. Psychological roots of moral development in adolescence. *Cath. psychol. Rec.*, 1963, **1**, 19–27.

21. Staton, Thomas F. *Dynamics of adolescent adjustment.* New York: Macmillan, 1963.

22. Sullivan, Harry S. *The interpersonal theory of psychiatry.* New York: Norton, 1953.

23. VanDyke II, Paul, and John Pierce-Jones. The psychology of religion in middle and late adolescence: A review of empirical research, 1950–1960. *Rel. Educ.*, 1963, **58**, 529–537.

24. Ward, Leo R. Religion in the public schools: Symposium II. *Rel. Educ.*, 1964, **59**, 446–447.

Part **8**
Adulthood

Achieving adult status is the main task of the second decade of life. Each level of development has made significant contributions to it. Each aspect of growth has served as a foundation for adulthood's traits, superiorities, and shortcomings. While childhood and adolescence will be outgrown, adulthood must be kept for the rest of life. Becoming adult is a process that involves choosing a vocation, selecting a life mate, and integrating the civic and cultural structure and dynamics of the society in which the person is to function.

Adult maturity comes with the consolidation of personality structure, development of character, and self-actualization, especially as they are related to the vocational role the individual will assume. The following chapters in this section will attempt a presentation of the psychosocial aspects of maturing and living the early, middle, and late levels of adulthood.

ACHIEVING ADULT STATUS

With the mastering of the developmental tasks of adolescence and the integration of acquired abilities and skills into a smoothly functioning system, the person becomes an adult capable of mature behavior. There is still a need, however, for the adjustment which a person continues to acquire and perfect during the early years of adulthood. Childhood and adolescent experiences provide the developmental matrix within which the forces and abilities that will determine the adult pattern of behavior are organized. The thrust to the future becomes more powerful as the individual approaches adulthood.

Without a continual willingness to learn and to act, and without a satisfactory store of knowledge and skills, a sound pattern of adult living will not be acquired. Without sufficient interests and incentives, learning loses its efficiency. For the teen-ager accomplishments without peer approval or praise tended to lose meaning. A strong sense of personal adequacy and self-reliance must be established before the individual can effectively explore the various areas of human endeavor. A maximal use of abilities and skills is possible only when the individual is not disturbed by anxiety or fears, and is capable of being realistic about his assets and liabilities. Any undue emphasis on liabilities and deficiencies acts as an impediment to adult adjustment. The ability and the willingness to assume adult activities and responsibilities must be implanted within the adolescent as he approaches his

twenties.   Balancing daring aspirations with endowments, abilities, and assets is also important in promoting integrity and adjustment.

OVERCOMING IMMATURITY

The ability and the desire to respond in mature ways under varying circumstances is an important adult developmental task.   A mature response implies
the overcoming of puerile and pubescent tendencies and vicissitudes.   Frequently seeking help is an indication of helplessness.   Frequent irritability,
moodiness, and emotional outbursts as responses to everyday disappointment
or frustration are adolescent reactions.   Constant search for excitement, fun,
and the sensational are also signs of pubescent motivation.   If a pubescent
level of motivation becomes deeply entrenched within the personality structure of the individual, he will be handicapped in assuming adult responsibilities later.

During the postadolescent years, many learn to exhibit an external "facade
of maturity," but internally they are still frequently moved by anxieties and
by ambivalent feelings.   Time and again, they reject facing their problems and
use fantasy, rationalization, or illness as means of escape from unpleasant
situations and challenging events.   Moodiness and emotional oscillations are
also signs of a preadult level of living.   In the early twenties many individuals
find it difficult to exercise internal controls, yet loss of control may result in
tragic developments later.   The lack of readiness to assume one's sexual role
or an inability to foster deep and permanent human relationships are signs
of immaturity if shown when the individual enters the adult years of life.

Experimenting with various roles and relationships is necessary for the
realization of one's limits and hidden strengths.   Most adolescents enthusiastically enter into new relationships and assume roles offered to them.   They
are eager for intellectual, emotional, and social enterprises that help them to
experience various forms of life as well as job opportunities suited to them.
Certain tendencies toward particular roles and interpersonal relationships
seem to be determined by attitudes acquired about earlier roles during the
years of childhood.   As James H. S. Bossard and Eleanor S. Boll [5] show,
the younger children find some roles already taken by siblings; for example,
one plays the role of the boss, another is good in scholastic performance, and
a third may be the troublemaker most of the time.   Attempts by a younger
sibling to take such roles meet with immediate competition; so the child is
pressed to find roles not yet performed by his siblings.

Adequate development toward an adult level of functioning is often dis-
rupted by continued ambivalence, conflicting drives, and excessive use of self-
defenses.   Frequent use of dynamisms in self-defense, under normal condi-

tions, indicates immaturity and is a barrier to exploring new methods and means for adjustment. Growing persons are destined to be, but never to remain, pubescents or adolescents. As the period of early adulthood continues, doubts about adequacy of the self subside. Suicidal thoughts, and ideas about "being abnormal" or "going crazy," if they have occurred, gradually diminish.

For many individuals there is too much continuity, and too little revision, of early childhood traits and attitudes. A major Fels Institute Study [10, p. 266], based on eighty-nine subjects, summarized its most consistent finding as follows: ". . . Many of the behaviors exhibited by the child during the period three to six were moderately good predictors of theoretically related behaviors during early adulthood." Apart from revisions and modifications of behavior, the threads of continuity show themselves throughout adulthood. If development turns into deviation, parents, community, and society are often responsible for it. "It is not evil babies who grow up into evil human beings, but an evil society which turns good babies into disordered adults, and it does so on a regimen of frustration" [13].

To embrace an adult pattern of life, the individual must surmount most of the significant features constituting the normal profile of an adolescent personality. In a thoughtful article, James A. Knight [11] identifies most of the typical features of the adolescent, such as egocentricity and the reactivation of narcissism, a high degree of ambivalence involving many people and issues, marked indecisiveness on many points, rebellious drive for independence and escape from adult standards and authority, great need for the protective coloration of the peer group, various degrees of anxiety, guilt feelings, and disorganized behavior, the need for freedom and the need for restraints and controls, and omnipotentiality and commitment. Knight emphasizes that it is most difficult for the adolescent to accept his finiteness, for whatever he "does, he is determined to succeed. Thus, he overdoes most everything, and thereby often appears clumsy and awkward." There is much to outgrow and to revise before the individual becomes a full-fledged adult.

ACQUIRING A VOCATION

One of the important steps in the adolescent's striving toward adulthood is in the area of vocational training. Today, because of automation, the percentage of unskilled labor continues to decline. Moreover, most vocational training takes longer than it did in the past, and changes in occupational choices cannot be made without encountering considerable difficulty. For boys vocational choice involves a *vital* decision since it will affect the individual's whole life. The adolescent knows he needs a vocation. He also realizes that a vocation

Table 18–1 Employment and school status: Civilian noninstitutional population 14 to 34 years old: U. S. October 1965
Numbers in thousands

298

Age and sex	Enrolled in school						Not enrolled in school					
		Labor force			Unemployed			Labor force			Unemployed	
	Population	Total	Percent of population	Employed	Number	Percent of labor force	Population	Total	Percent of population	Employed	Number	Percent of labor force
Both sexes												
Total, 14 to 34 yrs	19,324	5,794	35.0	5,360	434	7.5	34,866	23,783	68.2	22,608	1,175	4.9
14 to 17 yrs	13,033	3,023	23.2	2,768	255	8.4	951	561	59.0	459	102	18.2
14 and 15 yrs	6,980	1,108	15.9	1,059	49	4.4	79	25	*	25		
16 and 17 yrs	6,053	1,915	31.6	1,709	206	10.8	872	536	61.5	434	102	19.0
18 to 24 yrs	5,290	2,052	38.8	1,884	168	8.2	13,484	9,570	71.0	8,900	670	7.0
18 and 19 yrs	5,930	971	33.1	862	109	11.2	3,399	2,529	74.4	2,223	306	12.1
20 to 24 yrs	2,360	1,081	45.8	1,022	59	5.5	10,085	7,041	69.8	6,677	364	5.2
20 and 21 yrs	1,378	534	38.8	505	29	5.4	3,613	2,567	71.0	2,379	188	7.3
22 to 24 yrs	982	547	55.7	517	30	5.5	6,472	4,474	69.1	4,298	176	3.9
25 to 34 yrs	1,001	719	71.8	708	11	1.5	20,431	13,652	66.8	13,249	403	3.0
25 to 29 yrs	658	468	71.1	461	7	1.5	10,191	6,770	66.4	6,553	217	3.2
30 to 34 yrs	343	251	73.2	247	4	1.6	10,240	6,882	67.2	6,996	186	2.7
Male												
Total, 14 to 34 yrs	10,572	3,797	35.9	3,493	304	8.0	15,371	14,845	96.6	14,314	531	3.6
14 to 17 yrs	6,613	1,838	27.8	1,657	181	9.8	455	356	78.2	300	56	15.7
14 and 15 yrs	3,546	698	19.7	656	42	6.0	35	14	*	14		
16 and 17 yrs	3,067	1,140	37.2	1,001	139	12.2	420	342	81.4	286	56	16.4

18 to 24 yrs	3,248	1,375	42.3	1,263	112	8.1	5,432	5,162	95.0	4,869	293	5.7
18 and 19 yrs	1,689	611	36.2	536	75	12.3	1,351	1,232	91.2	1,104	128	10.4
20 to 24 yrs	1,559	764	49.0	727	37	4.8	4,081	3,930	96.3	3,765	165	4.2
20 and 21 yrs	839	359	42.8	340	19	5.3	1,394	1,308	93.8	1,227	81	6.2
22 to 24 yrs	720	405	56.2	387	18	4.4	2,687	2,622	97.6	2,538	84	3.2
25 to 34 yrs	711	584	82.1	573	11	1.9	9,484	9,327	98.3	9,145	182	2.0
25 to 29 yrs	483	374	77.4	367	7	1.9	4,660	4,586	98.4	4,482	104	2.3
30 to 34 yrs	228	210	92.1	206	4	1.9	4,824	4,741	98.3	4,663	78	1.6
Total, 14 to 34 yrs	8,752	1,997	22.8	1,867	130	6.5	19,495	8,938	45.8	8,294	644	7.2
Female												
14 to 17 yrs	6,420	1,185	18.5	1,111	74	6.2	496	205	41.3	159	46	22.4
14 and 15 yrs	3,434	410	11.9	403	7	1.7	44	11	*	11		
16 and 17 yrs	2,986	775	26.0	708	67	8.6	452	194	42.9	148	46	23.7
18 to 24 yrs	2,042	677	33.2	621	56	8.3	8,052	4,408	54.7	4,031	377	8.6
18 and 19 yrs	1,241	360	29.0	326	34	9.4	2,048	1,297	63.3	1,119	178	13.7
20 to 24 yrs	801	317	39.6	295	22	6.9	6,004	3,111	51.8	2,912	199	6.4
20 and 21 yrs	539	175	32.5	165	10	5.7	2,219	1,259	56.7	1,152	107	8.5
22 to 24 yrs	262	142	54.2	130	12	8.5	3,785	1,852	48.9	1,760	92	5.0
25 to 34 yrs	290	135	46.6	135			10,947	4,325	39.5	4,104	221	5.1
25 to 29 yrs	175	94	53.7	94			5,531	2,184	39.5	2,071	113	5.2
30 to 34 yrs	115	41	35.7	41			5,416	2,141	39.5	2,033	108	5.0

Source: Special Labor Force Report No. 68. *Employment of school age youth* (A Monthly Labor Review Reprint, July 1966).
* Percent not shown where base is less than 100,000.

is needed for the economic independence for which he is striving. A reconciliation between his ability and his vocational preference must be made at the outset of vocational training.

Many factors must be considered in the selection of a training program, and several decisions have to be made. The question whether or not to continue in high school is one of the early decisions. Despite the fact that a great majority of parents—more than three-fourths—urge their adolescent boys and girls to complete their high school education, over 40 percent of the adolescents in the United States were high school dropouts in 1960.

There are indications that the United States is approaching a realization of the ideal of universal education. Despite increased employment, larger numbers of youths are going to school not only because the population is growing but also because a larger proportion of school-age children continue their education into the high school and college level. Nevertheless, there is a rather sharp decline in school attendance at the age when the law of the state permits withdrawal from school. Probably for this reason a number of states have revised their laws on school attendance, raising the age requirement to seventeen and eighteen years of age. Table 18–1 shows employment and school status by age and sex from 14 to 34 years of age. During the last decade (1955–1965) both the employment rate and the school attendance rate continued to rise with a new high for the latter. Various statistical reports show that, while in the United Kingdom, Germany, France, and Italy less than 20 percent remain in school after the age of fifteen, in the United States even at the age of eighteen more than 45 percent are pursuing education. In the mid 1960s about 40 percent of the U. S. college-age population was enrolled in institutions of higher learning, while the percentages for the same age group in the United Kingdom, Germany, France, and Italy were about 10, 7, 15, and 7 respectively.

Child labor laws, including the 1938 Fair Labor Standards Act and the 1966 Child Protection Act, protect children and young adolescents against work likely to hinder well-rounded development, and increase the adolescents' chances of remaining in school longer. The Fair Labor Standards Act sets sixteen years as the minimum age for work during school hours and for occupations in manufacturing at any time. At present, most states permit working after school hours.

Many young people who withdraw from school feel pressed to take full-time jobs. Part-time employment satisfies students who are partly supported by their parents. Withdrawal from school at times implies hesitation on the part of parents to supply an older adolescent with funds. Availability of jobs is of crucial importance in this connection and will greatly determine whether the individual can find work suited to him and make a satisfactory adjustment to his occupation. The accessibility of trade schools is also an important factor in the acquisition of the technical skills sought by industry.

Bridging the gap between school and work is a significant challenge for youth today.   First of all, young people must be adaptable if they are to fit into the rapidly changing world of employment.   They must be well educated and emotionally prepared for finding jobs consistent with their education and talents.   National Science Foundation studies indicate that nationally, less than half of those in the top third of their high school graduating class go on to graduate from college.   Those who do not go on take jobs below their potential capacity and deprive other young people with less educational ability of the jobs they could have adequately handled.   From 1960 to 1970, 26 million youths will have entered the labor force.   The poorly educated segment of this population will compete with machines for employment on somewhat unequal terms, since the machines being produced today have skills equivalent to a high school diploma.

In the developing cybernated system, potentially unlimited output can be achieved by systems of machines which will require little cooperation from human beings.   As machines take over production from men, they absorb an increasing proportion of resources while the men who are displaced become dependent on minimal and unrelated government measures—unemployment insurance, social security, welfare payments [19, p. 311].

Figure 18–1 shows the breakdown of educational status for employment-seeking youth.

Despite steadily increasing educational requirements for employment, about 30 percent of all youths drop out of school before finishing high school. Moreover, about 40 percent of all students entering college withdraw before

Figure 18–1   Educational   levels   of   employment-seeking youth in the 1960s.   (President's Committee on Youth Employment.   *The challenge of jobless youth,* 1963.)

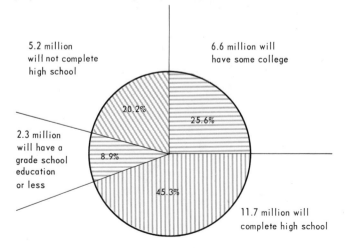

5.2 million will not complete high school

6.6 million will have some college

2.3 million will have a grade school education or less

11.7 million will complete high school

20.2%

25.6%

8.9%

45.3%

completing a four-year program.   Prospects for desirable employment are highly probable only for those who complete college.   As shown in Table 18–1, the fairly high, 1965 unemployment rate for youth with limited education is likely to rise as many occupations for the unskilled decline slowly in the years ahead [20].   It is also noteworthy, that, according to 1963 Census figures, the high school dropout earns only 12 percent more than the eighth grade graduate, while the high school graduate earns 15 percent more than the high school dropout.   The college graduate earns 42 percent more than the high school graduate and 83 percent more than the eighth grade graduate.   Since the American picture of success is related to both education and earnings, school and college are the major stepping-stones for rising above the earlier status.   Investments in education will continue paying big dividends.   Apparently, the teen-agers of today are growing up in an era where only lifelong education will prepare them to profit by the opportunities and advantages of rapidly changing industry and business.

Figure 18–2 indicates that in 1966, 1,247,000 youths and adults were

Figure 18–2 Employment counseling: 1950 and 1966. (Fact Finding Committee, Midcentury White House Conference on Children and Youth. *A graphic presentation of social and economic facts important in the lives of children and youth,* 1951; and Laura M. Kress's letter from the American Personnel and Guidance Association, April 20, 1967.)

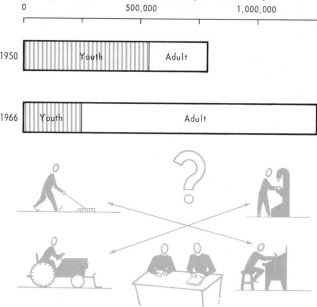

counseled in public employment offices; of these 250,000 were under twenty-two years of age.   Counseling services that included interviews and aptitude testing were given in approximately seventeen hundred local centers of the United States Employment Service in 1950 to an average of 45,000 adolescents per month.

The existence of over 100,000 distinct job choices in the United States makes vocational choice complex.   There is apt to be some trial and error unless a person has formed definite vocational goals based on a realistic appraisal of self and of the requirements of a given occupation.   Limited knowledge of requirements adds stress to the vocational aspirations of many adolescents.

As the percentage of high schools having vocational guidance services steadily increases, it becomes more likely that American youth will choose occupations commensurate with their abilities.   This is chiefly due to vocational aptitude testing.   An adolescent is likely to put considerable value on such testing results since his vocational interests are often confused.   E. K. Strong, Jr. [16] found that only after the age of twenty-five are vocational interests well crystallized.   It is unfortunate that a majority of people, including those who attend colleges, have to make a vocational choice before this age.   During early adulthood, most individuals, frequently after two or three trials and changes, settle down and maintain the same occupation.

The counseling program of the Employment Service was established on a nationwide basis in 1945.   Since the National Defense Education Act of 1960, there has been rapid growth in the guidance services offered by the secondary schools.   In the fall of 1962, there were 36,500 individuals serving as counselors in the public secondary schools.   Most of the school dropouts and at least 40 percent of high school graduates need both aptitude testing and employment counseling [22].   David A. Goslin [9, p. 189] emphasizes the need for assessing ability through aptitude testing.

> As the skills required for most jobs in modern industrial society become increasingly complex, it becomes correspondingly more important that individuals are given responsibilities according to their abilities and aptitudes.   In this respect, the possession of adequate means of measuring the intellectual capacities of individuals is virtually a prerequisite of continued technological advancement.

Goslin estimates that each year between 200 and 250 million standardized ability and aptitude tests are administered in the United States [9, pp. 53–54].

SELECTING A MATE

At the same time that vocational opportunities are attracting the young adult, so are the selection of a spouse, and the establishment of a home.   Despite the fact that these accomplishments involve difficulties and problems, they all contribute substantially to the achievement of adult status and adjustment. Figure 18–3 indicates that the average age for marriage has become lower in the United States; from 1960 to 1965, however, the age remained about the same as in 1950. The usual age difference between men and women narrowed down to approximately two years [23].

In late adolescence or early adulthood, a strong and lasting attraction toward a peer member of the opposite sex occurs. Such attachments are frequently mutual and offer deep ego gratifications. They also promote feelings of adequacy and security in most individuals. The percentage of companionships and romances that lead to mutual love and marriage rises steadily and reaches its peak in the early part of adulthood. The universal desire to love and be loved and feel needed finds its complete satisfaction in marriage. While many persons in the early twenties are sufficiently mature to assume marital and parental responsibilities, a significant number of individuals are not yet ready to assume parental responsibilities. Quite a few who have been damaged in their earlier development by the attitudes of their parents later find the partners they select incompatible. The desire for personal security as well as parental pressures influence some girls to contract a marriage particularly during the later part of young adulthood. Pregnancy is another fairly frequent reason for early marriage. Thus, the voluntary acceptance of this new role can be questioned in many cases of marriage, early marriages in particular.

The time needed to complete adolescent cognitive, emotional, and social

Figure 18–3   Ages of brides and grooms: U. S., 1910–1965. (U. S. Bureau of the Census. *Statistical abstract of the United States: 1966.* (87th ed.) 1966.)

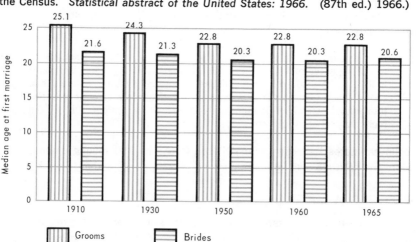

maturation has increased with the complexity of our technology and culture and the rising standard of living.   In American society, completion of pubertal growth no longer implies adult competence as it does in most primitive societies.   During the twentieth century, the duration of adolescence has increased with each generation.   The law of readiness implies a greater delay period before marriage with each increase in the period of adolescence.   Prior to the 1950s, each generation got married at an earlier age.   Apparently many married before they were psychologically ready to do so successfully.   Frequently teen-age marriages are contracted because of pregnancy.   Marriages are often preceded by too short a period of courtship, thus increasing the chances of incompatibilty between the individuals involved.   These inadequate preparations for marriage are contributing causes of discord and separation. Statistics, though incomplete, show that during the first half of the century the rate of divorce was actually increasing from generation to generation. Between 1960 and 1965 each year about 450,000 (481,000 in 1965) divorce and annulment cases were reported in the United States.   The comparable figures for Australia, the United Kingdom, Federal Germany, and France are about 7,500, 31,000, 48,000, and 32,000 respectively.   The rate of divorce in the United States is about three times higher than the rates of the countries just mentioned [20, 23].   Many teen-age marriages are dissolved by divorce. Emotionally immature teen-agers find it difficult to postpone marriage.   In most states teen-agers cannot marry without parental consent, and the laws determine at what age such consent is unnecessary.

Table 18–2   Estimated divorce rates in the United States and Australia
Number per 1,000 marriages

Year	United States	Australia
1900	79	
1901		14.4
1910	83	
1911		13.1
1920	171	
1921		32
1930	196	
1931		50.3
1940	165	
1941		44.6
1950	231	
1951		94.8
1960	206	88.9

Sources: *Vital statistics of the United States: 1955*, Vol. 1; *Demographic yearbook 1965* (New York: United Nations, 1966).

Statistical findings indicate that divorces are more frequent in states with lenient divorce laws; among city families, especially those of lesser education; in the laboring class; and in cases of teen-age and mixed-faith marriages. Table 18–2 shows that divorces per thousand marriages increased from 79 in 1900 to 206 in 1960. Divorces are most frequent within the first few years of marriage.

Frustrations in the expectation of marital happiness often occur on psychological grounds. The dominance relationship is one of them. If both partners have strong tendencies to dominate each other, congruity is difficult to establish. An example of incongruity may also be seen in intense striving for independence on the part of both partners. Lack of similarity in interest and activities presents a major obstacle to the mutual sharing of marital life Doubts about mutual faithfulness evoke jealousy and jeopardize marital sta bility. Finally, ineffectiveness of communication makes other problems insoluble.

PREREQUISITES FOR A SUCCESSFUL MARRIAGE

Georg Simmel's theoretical assumptions [15] and present research by sociologists and psychologists find that race and religion have usually been the most decisive factors in designing males and females as acceptable or unacceptable for courtship and marriage. Experience gathered from thousands of families indicates a difficulty in sharing married life without sharing a basic identity in appearance or in faith.

Similarities in age, socioeconomic background, talents, and acquired abilities contribute to the permanence of a marital relationship. These factors are helpful in promoting mutual understanding and enjoyment of the same activities, especially if love is to be more than infatuation or mere companionship. Table 16–2, page 263, shows traits indicated as very desirable in a future mate by two thousand high school boys and girls. The first group of characteristics suggests that students realize that just physical attraction and affection are not enough for marital success. The second group identifies traits desired in a companion whether marriage is being considered or not.

A dissimilarity between the personality needs of one and the corresponding drives of the other will assist in deepening a relationship beyond the level of mere companionship. For example, persons with high assertiveness tend to be attracted by persons having receptive traits as dominant characteristics of their personality. Persons with strong strivings toward independence fit the needs of those preferring dependence and submission better than persons with similar strivings. Robert F. Winch [24, pp. 96–98, 101–103] originated and presented supportive data for the hypothesis that *complementary* rather than similar need patterns promote marital adjustment. Reciprocity enables the fullest possible personality development within the family structure.   Nevertheless, in terms of basic interests, abilities, and values, it appears that similarity of partners is a major force contributing to marital stability.

Happiness in marriage also depends on the degree of similarity of the partner and one's concept of the ideal mate.   The image of the cross-parent plays a role in building such a concept.   Positive qualities of the mother and other women in his life deeply impress a boy and subconsciously influence his image of the ideal mate.   As the "dream model" crystallizes during adolescence, it begins to act as a definite influence upon the boy-girl relationships that follow.

The selection of a mate is greatly influenced by the individual's popularity among members of the opposite sex and by his attitudes concerning appearance and personality in a life partner.   It has been found that men rank appearance, contiguity of interests, and cheerfulness much higher than women do; to women, intellectual abilities, educational status, and social ease are of prime importance.   Of course, the intensity of love tends to outrank these and many other considerations, especially among young persons contemplating marriage.   When in love, marital partners are usually successful in complementing one another.

Marriage represents a major transition that challenges personal maturity and adequacy.   Personal problems, if present, readily produce family problems.   Growing obligations, an incongruity of leading traits, lack of preparation, and sexual incompatibility are other obstacles to marital adjustment.   Frictions between the parents during childhood, heightened self-defensiveness, and current financial difficulties add much to the discord and unhappiness of many couples.

Ernest W. Burgess and L. S. Cottrell's study [6, pp. 354–361] of 526 couples in the Chicago area, with an average age of 26.1 and 23.4 for husbands and wives respectively, points out the greater significance of the husbands' background over the wives' for adjustment in marriage.   Apparently wives usually adapt themselves much more easily to their husbands than husbands do to them.   The majority of wives attempt to achieve their goals in subtle and indirect ways, while husbands often act directly and impose their expectations and demands on their wives.

This investigation and Lewis M. Terman's [18] of 792 husbands and wives in the Los Angeles and San Francisco areas, with a mean age of 38.8 and 35.8 for husbands and wives respectively, illustrates the importance of the earlier environment of family affection for the later adjustment of adults to married life.

1. Happy marriages of parents are positively related to happiness in the marriage relationships of their children.

2. Close emotional ties with cross-parents and absence of marked conflicts with both parents are also positively related to a person's adjustment in marriage. The child's response patterns in regard to affectional relationships are largely reproduced in adult associations, and
deeply affect the marital relationships.

NEED OF MARITAL COUNSELING

A marriage counselor usually realizes that marital conflicts spring either from
severe incompatibilities or from personal problems of one or both parties.
Lack of maturity is a frequent source of difficulty. A husband, for example,
may continue to be attracted by other women. Jealousy reactions result, and
may remain a permanent obstacle to a mutual understanding. Perfectionistic
strivings on the part of the husband may be expressed in remarks indicative
of dissatisfaction with the wife's actions or an occasional criticism of her
methods of doing routine tasks. Frequently, these lead to more disruptive
arguments and general discord within the budding family structure. Conflict
sometimes is related to previous vocational or other aspirations of the wife,
who regrets substituting marriage for them. The wife's financial demands
and pressure on the husband to achieve a better-paying position are other
sources of disagreement. Generally several undesirable factors or traits work
together to disrupt harmony or make it impossible to establish it. Professional counseling aids familial integration by discovering the underlying factors of discord, and establishing new lines of communication.

Higher levels of education and socioeconomic background or achievement
lend themselves to extensive social participation and adaptability to others, in
marriage relationships as elsewhere. Although sexual and economic factors
are often a source of family friction, they are primarily symptomatic of deeper
causes of marital discord. General lack of preparation and undesirable personality traits, such as impulsiveness, a critical attitude, domineering behavior, and neurotic tendencies often cause family dissension. The belief in
romantic love with the "one and only" tends to produce disappointment and
frustration as well. So-called "sexual incompatibility" is now usually recognized as symptomatic of marital discord rather than responsible for it.

SOCIOCULTURAL INTEGRATION

The pattern of adult society may be unattractive to an individual in his teens
or even in his twenties. Some have a strong desire to continue the life style
set by adolescent peers despite the fact that chronologically they have reached
adulthood. They remain engrossed in typically adolescent activities, and in
other ways oppose what is conventional. They show contempt for authority
through criticism of those directing social and cultural affairs.

The majority of young adults, however, appear to have little difficulty in accepting societal and cultural norms and acting in accordance with expectations based on these guides. The need for self-reliance, however, is still great, and many postadolescents experience anxiety in acting on their own judgment. The need for support from others is not easily discarded, and it takes time to become comfortable amidst the complexities of adult society and culture.

INFLUENCES ON PSYCHOLOGICAL STATUS

Many factors in countless ways affect the status of the adolescent and young adult among his peers and other individuals. Appearance and level of maturity are some of the factors that rank high.

Physique, as it compares with that of peers, is one of the major influences on status. Adolescents and adults differ more in height than children of the same age; the maturing and the physically mature differ greatly in height, weight, and many other quantitative features. To begin with, some individuals, girls as well as boys, begin pubertal transformation at an earlier age than their age-mates. In a typical eighth-grade class many girls are adolescents, while others lag behind in development and are only entering the pubertal phase of accelerated growth. There may be several postpubertal boys in the class, as well as many others who are still children and conspicuously small by comparison. Such a situation is confusing to all the members of the class, since their interests and concerns will differ markedly. Many have blemishes and skin eruptions, in addition to voice changes. Embarrassment and tensions mount when attempts at self-assertion fail more frequently than before. Some are upset by unforeseen sexual phenomena. Doubts about personal adequacy emerge more frequently as their social acceptance decreases. The situation may become grave when they enter high school and find unexpected difficulties in making new friends. Physical appearance is important in the attraction of friends throughout life.

Intrafamily frictions often develop as the adolescent girl desires to become womanly and charming by the use of cosmetics and women's dress and the adolescent boy tries to show his manliness by attempting to smoke and to drink. Selection of friends, late evening social life, money, and the use of the family car are frequent points of a teen-ager's conflict with his parents. The atmosphere of the home, its educational and socioeconomic level, and its morale, all have a major bearing on the total family relationship.

Within cities families with similar income and status tend to live near each other. This then creates certain general attitudes and an atmosphere related to the class of people in the neighborhood. The adolescent has many advantages in some districts and experiences deprivation in others. Lack of recreational facilities is often one disadvantage, presence of delinquency is another. With his limited resources, the teen-ager must cope with these disadvantages. His status is affected and modified by cultural influences as well as by the personal factors. Whether he is a master of his own driving forces or is a mere responder to outside influences and situations greatly depends on the opportunities he receives to develop himself.

In the modern nexus of culture and scientific advance, excessive reliance on science is common. Science is often seen as the road to all knowledge. There is danger of a partial or complete exclusion of other key ways of knowing, such as religion, philosophy, and the arts. Lack of perspective results, which, in turn promotes compartmentalization and denial of important dimensions of reality. As a consequence, personality development may remain incomplete in its structural aspects with a lack of maturity marking many responses.

Personality growth usually continues throughout early adulthood, and, in some respects, it progresses until the end of life. If ordinary developments have taken place in childhood and pubertal conflicts have been resolved, self-direction and objectivity increase.

It is advantageous for the maturing person to capitalize on the preceding phases of development. The genuine smile of infancy; the curiosity and experimentation of the preschool years; the affiliative trends and vivid emotions of childhood; and the zest for adventure, courage, and idealism of adolescence —all may be incorporated into a complete adult personality. During the years of adulthood, much should be modified and added to it. Personal initiative for achievement, continuity of effort, sensitivity to the needs of others, and foresight in planning are all needed for an adult style of life. Self-reliance comes not only from identifying with human models but also from religion, philosophy, social sciences, and the arts. It will be supplemented by information and counsel gained from other adults of good character or professional competence.

GUIDING THE MATURING PERSON

Few would argue against a need for continued adolescent and early adult guidance, yet not many would agree on an exact approach. Since the adolescent is no longer a child, parental and educational demands should be different from those placed upon a child. Several ideas should be kept in mind in attempting to clarify an adolescent's need for guidance. First, an adolescent is in a state of rapid development. This development is pervasive and encompasses practically all dimensions of his personality. Whenever there is change or reshaping in progress, any unexpected influence can deform it more readily than if it were to occur after an adolescent has acquired an advanced level of personality organization.   Some influences may therefore be incongruous with what has been developed up to this age.   The maturing person's past experiences and controls must also be respected.   He usually needs many good influences to support him in his strivings for a higher level of self-realization.   Lawrence K. Frank points out also that "the best preparation for tomorrow is to live adequately today, to deal with today's requirements so as to be able to go forward without too much 'unfinished business' " [8].

Modified *informed permissiveness* seems to be the best approach in helping adolescents and young adults alike, especially in the complex situations of modern life.   Since the adolescent's desire to learn often runs high, his attention is usually satisfactory or good, and he will benefit from information about alternatives in a permissive atmosphere.   A positive attitude toward granting freedom of expression and choice usually appeals to the adolescent. Permissiveness is not necessarily indulgence; approval of alternative actions is not implied.   Permissiveness is modified by the adolescent's needs and tendencies, about which the guidance worker, parent, teacher, counselor, or camp leader secure competent information from reliable informed sources before starting.   Without proper guidance growing into adulthood is not a process of enlightenment or certainty.   Percival M. Symonds's intensive study [17, p. 206] of a small sample of young adults (N=28) shows that "their maturing was on the whole a blind, trial-and-error process."

It is important that proper guidance be available to all growing persons who need information and advice.   The maturing person should be encouraged to come out of himself and to accept greater responsibility in making decisions for his own advantage and that of his family.   Finally, in guiding maturing persons Goethe's maxim must be taken seriously: "If we take people as they are, we make them worse.   If we treat them as if they were what they ought to be, we help them become what they are capable of becoming."

QUESTIONS FOR REVIEW

1. What adolescent achievements indicate a readiness to enter adulthood?
2. Why should an adolescent experiment with various roles?
3. Why do ambivalence and self-defenses often indicate a lack of maturity?
4. What is the role played by vocational preparation during adolescence?
5. List and explain some major factors operating in the vocational choice of a maturing person.
6. What does education have to do with vocational choice?
7. Enumerate several factors contributing to marital happiness.   Analyze one of them.

8. List factors contributing to marital friction and explain two or three of them.
9. Which are the traits seen as very desirable for a future mate by (a) boys and (b) girls?
10. What are some major influences affecting maturational status? Explain some implications of one of them.
11. What kinds of parental guidance and counseling does a maturing person need?
12. Why does an adolescent need increased permissiveness from his parents?
13. Name some fallacies in regard to adolescent guidance found among (a) parents, (b) educators.
14. What are some profitable modern means for guiding the maturing person?
15. Explain how an adolescent develops self-direction from within.

REFERENCES

I. Selected Reading

1. Bier, William C. (Ed.). *Marriage: A psychological and moral approach.* New York: Fordham, 1965. A volume in the Pastoral Psychology Series, No. 4, dealing with preparation for marriage, adjustment to growth, and breakdown in marriage by over twenty contributors.
2. Fishbein, M., and E. W. Burgess. *Successful marriage.* (2nd ed.) New York: Doubleday, 1955. A comprehensive work on personal and other factors involved in the marriage relationship.
3. Moore, Bernice M., and Wayne E. Holtzman. *Tomorrow's parents: A study of youth and their families.* Austin: University of Texas Press, 1965. An extensive Texas study of nearly 12,900 high school students, comparing their attitudes toward and concerns about themselves, parents and teachers, authority, mobility, freedom, etc., in the life situations of youth.
4. Wattenberg, William W. *The adolescent years.* New York: Harcourt, Brace, 1955. Chaps. 6, 8, 12, 18, and 19. A lively discussion of the foundations of adulthood.

II. Specific References

5. Bossard, James H. S., and Eleanor S. Boll. Personality roles in the large family. *Child Developm.,* 1955, **26**, 71–78.
6. Burgess, Ernest W., and Leonard S. Cottrell. *Predicting success or failure in marriage.* Englewood Cliffs, N. J.: Prentice-Hall, 1939.
7. Crites, John D. Measurement of vocational maturity in adolescence. *Psychol. Monogr.,* 1955, **69**, No. 595.

8. Frank, Lawrence K.   Personality development in adolescent girls. *Monogr. Soc. Res. Child Developm.,* 1951, **16**, No. 53.

9. Goslin, David A.   *The search for ability: Standardized testing in social perspective.*   New York: Russell Sage Foundation, 1963.

10. Kagan, Jerome, and H. A. Moss.   *Birth to maturity.*   New York: Wiley, 1962.

11. Knight, James A.   The profile of the normal adolescent   *Ann. Allergy,* 1967, **25**, 129–136.

12. McAllister, Robert J.   Role expectations in marriage.   In William C. Bier (Ed.), *Marriage: A psychological and moral approach.*   New York: Fordham, 1965.   Pp. 151–158.

13. Montagu, A.   *The direction of development.*   New York: Harper & Row, 1955.

14. President's Committee on Youth Employment.   *The challenge of jobless youth.*   1963.

15. Simmel, Georg.   *The sociology of Georg Simmel* (translated by Kurt H. Wolf).   Glencoe, Ill.: Free Press, 1950.

16. Strong, E. K., Jr.   *Vocational interests of men and women.*   Stanford, Calif.: Stanford, 1943.

17. Symonds, Percival M., with A. R. Jensen.   *From adolescent to adult.*   New York: Columbia, 1961.

18. Terman, Lewis M.   *Psychological factors in marital happiness.*   New York: McGraw-Hill, 1938.

19. Triple Revolution, the Ad Hoc Committee on the; Ferry, W. H., et al. The triple revolution.   In A. E. Winder and D. L. Angus (Eds.), *Adolescence: Contemporary studies.*   New York: American Book, 1968.   Pp. 308–321.

20. United Nations.   *Demographic yearbook 1965.*   New York: 1966.

21. U. S. Dept. of Labor.   *Counselor's guide to occupational and other man power information.*   1965.

22. U. S. Dept. of Labor.   *Counseling and employment service for youth.* 1963.

23. *Vital Statistics of the United States: 1965.*   Vol. I.   1967.

24. Winch, Robert F.   *Mate selection: A study of complementary needs.* New York: Harper & Row, 1958.

THE CONCEPT
AND CRITERIA OF MATURITY

The "miracle" of structural growth and functional maturation continues for almost two decades before the human individual begins to approach sectorial and global maturity. As we have seen in Chapters 5 through 18, the total process of development is marked by many aspects and factors, steps and particular tasks. Maturation, as was pointed out in Chapter 3, refers to the emergence and particularly to the increase of functional abilities and powers ultimately leading to maturity.

In growing up, the organism and personality reach, and begin to operate upon, successively advanced levels of maturity. It is good to bear in mind that an adult acts at a top level of unfolded abilities only when the situation calls for it, for example, in a political debate among civic leaders. When the same adult finds himself among children, he may speak simply and act in a somewhat childish manner. The teacher often has to use a lowered level of self-expression to make himself understood or to initiate activities based on child-group interests. Responding to a situational demand, he merely faces reality and acts appropriately; this naturally does not mean that he regresses into immature forms of behavior. Ability to act at a child's level is very helpful in showing full understanding of children.

At times children and adolescents strive for maturity as modeled and illustrated by their parents and other adults. A girl of five, for example, puts on lipstick, speaks about marriage, and in many other little ways indicates her desire to become a person like her mother. A young boy may try to step into his father's shoes and enact "Father" by assuming some aspects of the parental role or by showing preference for adult interests and activities.

The major effects of heightened maturation are: (1) expanded ability in learning, (2) higher efficiency of performance, and (3) recognition of meaning and value. The mature person is, then, characterized by his readiness to utilize his reservoir of abilities and skills to achieve desired self-expression and accomplishment. Maturity, ultimately, refers to the adequacy and completeness of integration; it is a stage at which human capacities and personality traits are not merely developed but functionally integrated. The mature individual experiences increased freedom in applying his powers, abilities, and skills to attain his goals and objectives.

STUDIES ON MATURITY

A survey of psychological and related literature indicates that the process of human maturation is a typical subject of developmental psychology. Furthermore, it is analyzed in volumes on personality and mental hygiene. Maturational orientation seems to be adequately presented in the works of Alfred L. Baldwin [7], Arnold Gesell [11, 12, 13, 14] and especially Douglas H. Heath [4] and Phillip Lersch [5]. Recently, Kaoru Yamamoto [29] summarized theories and criteria of a closely allied concept, the healthy person. This is an individual who lives fully at his point of development. At the same time he is becoming—changing himself and his environment to attain the next level of maturity and equilibrium.

Lersch develops a complex developmental structure of the mature personality. Fundamentally, this structure is characterized by two interpenetrating operational strata, conceptualized as "endothymic ground" and the "I"-related or personal superstructure. The former is derived from the Greek *endon*, meaning within or internal, and *thymos*, meaning emotionality as a frame of experience. Endothymic processes make individual life deep, resourceful, and creative. The "I"-related function refers primarily to self-regulation in the light of reason and volition. Thus it performs the function of marshaling and directing endothymically elicited energies into the pursuit of rationally defined goals and aspirations. Maturity is attained by advanced development of the personal superstructure, especially when it is integrated with the endothymic ground.

Gordon W. Allport [1] devotes a chapter to the mature personality. He outlines maturity primarily in terms of extension of the sense of self, warm relating of self to others, emotional security, self-objectification, and a unifying philosophy of life. Louis P. Thorpe and W. W. Cruze [28, p. 613] identify maturity as "a goal toward which most children and adolescents constantly strive." They identify the mature person as "one who has attained physical maturity and who, at the same time, has developed certain attitudes, interests, and ambitions which differ considerably from those characteristic of childhood and adolescence" [28, p. 594]. Evidence of maturity is seen in sectorial maturation of various developmental aspects [28, pp. 604–612].

Many writers on maturity [3, 20, 24, 25, 28] present data on physical, sexual, emotional, and social maturation, but fail to integrate the data in terms of personality so as to see fully its interpersonal significance. In recognizing the great need for a concept of psychological maturity, in the late 1940s H. A. Overstreet [20] noted that past contributions have been leading to this "master concept of our time" which is "central to our whole enterprise of living." This situation still prevails today. The concept of maturity remains an open-end task for future research.

In a recent empirical study Douglas H. Heath [4] observes that the maturing person effectively integrates experience into a changing but reasonably stable structure and maintains his stability and identity in the face of extreme or adverse internal or external transformations. Development, when uninterrupted, leads to maturity and psychological health, marked by increased ability to tolerate frustration and deal constructively with strain and conflict. Heath considers maturity and psychological health synonymous and feels that this is the case with most professional workers in the field.

TESTING MATURITY

Dissociation of many segmental maturities and the designing of measures to appraise them separately provide the gauge often used in testing maturity at the present time. This method will produce at best questionable results unless it is supplemented by a synthetic correlation of the data. Other indexes of maturity may be attained by means of laboratory evaluation of several bodily systems. For instance, X-ray records of the wrist indicate the development stage of ossification. Laboratory analysis of the amount of gonadotrophic hormones produces an index of sexual maturity. In addition, psychometric tests, for example, intelligence tests, show the level at which certain cognitive abilities function.

The Vineland Social Maturity Scale [9] is another example of the sectorial approach. This scale is constructed on the model of the Stanford-Binet and is designed to appraise social adequacy. The items are grouped into age levels—from early infancy to the age of thirty years—representing progressive personal-social maturation and adjustment in terms of self-help, self-direction, locomotion, occupation, communication, and socialization. Answers by the subject or one who knows him well are converted into an age-related interpretation.

In scanning Arnold Gesell's normative scale of maturation from one-year-oldness to sixteen-year-oldness [12 to 14], one cannot fail to observe the increasing complexity of understanding and behavior, of communication and interpersonal relationships. According to Gesell, developmental diagnosis "is a matching of observations and of norms. When the matching is guided by ample clinical experience, it has the validity of true measurement" [11, p. 8]. Following his directions the examiner obtains a developmental quotient (DQ) [11, pp. 111–117]. This quotient is based on the ratio between maturity of motor, adaptive, language, and personal-social behavior and the chronological age of the subject. The four behavior aspects are defined and tested on Gesell's developmental chart [12]. The Buhler-Hetzer tests [8] use a similar approach in the appraisal of the early developmental status of behavior differentiation.

Multidimensional evaluations of personality factors may also come from the application of projective techniques, especially if the Rorschach method, the Thematic Apperception Test, or the more complex drawing techniques are used by experts in projective psychology. Among the newer measures, the Stephens Categorization Tasks [26] and Pikunas Graphoscopic Scale [21] may be mentioned. Categorizing ability taps the resources of learned material as well as the cognitive processing as the individual faces tasks of this nature. Both tests have been applied but still need further exploration [17, pp. 100–104].

THE CRITERIA OF MATURITY

Another approach in appraising the level of maturity is offered by means of the global criteria of maturity, more hypothetical yet sufficiently useful for the purpose of practical evaluation.

Differential responsiveness. Intellectual development and, in particular, various avenues of learning enable the child and the adolescent to expand and improve his understanding of the many realities of life, their dimensions, and their relationships. The child's early forms of exploration and his subsequent modes of questioning and reading are important means for his acquisition of knowledge. The variety of experiences to which the growing person is exposed contributes substantially to the extension of familiarity with the many details of his environmental and cultural matrix. A child may discover that certain types of antisocial behavior, such as unwillingness to share or attempts to dominate, lead to unpopularity with his playmates. As a result, the child learns to control such aspects of behavior for the sake of preserving friendships. Holding other factors equal, some adolescents deliberately introduce a single behavior variable such as flirting or sulking and test the reactions of others, thereby employing a form of experimental procedure and reasoning.

An insatiable desire to gain knowledge and to acquire a variety of skills, supplemented by formal education, serves as a motive to increase and refine a person's judgment and discriminating abilities, enabling the individual to give a fluent verbal description of a concept. The range of vocabulary and the use of compound sentences bespeaks with some clarity a person's discriminatory ability. While some individuals reach a very elevated level of discrimination, many others remain at various lower levels. Therefore, the level of discrimination and accuracy serves well as a criterion of maturity. A vocabulary test with words having many meanings and connotations, including the abstract and symbolic, may be used as a direct measure of differential responsiveness. The relationship between popular or usual and original or unusual responses on the Rorschach test may also serve the same purpose.

Lack of differential responsiveness on the part of youths and adults is frequently indicated by certain popular misconceptions, such as those of the similarity of doctor and physician, teacher and instructor. For a certain student, anyone who lectures is a "professor" or anyone of the faculty may be unqualifiably referred to as "Mr." Similarly, reference to "doctor" will be associated with the medical profession only. All musical performances may be identified as merely melodies or songs, and all female dancers as ballerinas.

To face reality in all its aspects, anticipation and prediction of future action based on past experiences and experiments cannot reach an adequate level without progress in responding to various specific factors and circumstances. By way of illustration, let us suppose a small child was pushed down by a young boy. If the child does not perceive this incident as a specific situation, he may tend to expect similar aggressive acts by other boys, thus exhibiting a lack of differential response. Progressive improvement in sensitivity and refinement of conceptual interpretation constitute a sine qua non in such a process. Accumulation of a variety of experience and knowledge represents a capital gain for feelings of adequacy and self-reliance. Maturity of response in various situations depends on previous experience and the range of one's information pertaining to each situation.

Interdependence. Growth in autonomy and independence from significant persons in an individual's life is a kind of psychosocial weaning. Many steps are involved in this process.

Late infancy and preadolescence are characteristic in this respect. At about the two-year level a new attitude becomes dominant, which is marked by excessive resistance to parental control and suggestion, stubbornness, and attempts at contrary behavior. The infant begins to feel he has a mind and will of his own and starts to exercise them. On the other hand, the pubertal adolescent transfers his emotional affiliation from his parents to peers. This gain in independence is a major sign of maturation, yet the youth may remain fully dependent on a clique or his "best friend" and feel lost when separated. In approaching maturity, however, the adolescent must break away from his severe dependence on the peer group in particular and "peer culture" in general in order to integrate himself into adult society and culture as a self-reliant individual.

In the late years of early adulthood, a person will not reach a satisfactory level of autonomy if, for example, he as a husband is now dominated by his wife or children, or if she as a wife is largely subjected to her husband's likes and whims. Thus, a mere transference of dependence cannot be an indicator of maturity. To view this matter from another angle, complete independence can only be attained as a form of extreme autocracy or withdrawal from reality. For example, a schizophrenic is independent from outside influences.

In order to reach a high level of maturity, a balance between dependence and independence must be established. Hence, a process of change from the passive dependence of infancy and childhood to the creative interdependence of the adult stage, and to ultimate reliance on a will higher than one's own, one's parents', or one's peers'—namely, on the will of the Creator of man—points to genuine maturity. Continual interdependence is possible only through the ability to love and direct this all-penetrating emotion in varying degrees to various values, individuals, and objects. Marriage, for example, requires an interdependence of the partners through love. If this love cools, one or both partners depend less upon the other, but as they become more independent the integration of the family suffers. The lack of compromising agreements between employer and employee and also between nations exemplifies the uncertainty of interdependence resulting from abuses of justice and charity. Love furthers maturity, and maturity shows the works of love. An experienced psychiatrist has stated, "The more love is the driving factor in life, the more integrated the personality will be" [27].

Participating activity. Without personal and active engagement, little can be performed or learned. Much passivity, spectatorship, and "letting others do it" restrict initiative and the constructive use of energies which, if not utilized, lead to physiological tension. Experience with children shows that they frequently enjoy being challenged and usually work at the top level of their ability, while adolescents and adults often refuse to cooperate with many such opportunities. Activity that challenges major motor and cognitive abilities should become a daily engagement, producing enjoyment and fun. Self-gratifications are impossible without constructive or creative participation in various spheres of activity. A satisfactory self-knowledge, active engagement of an individual's abilities, and experimentation with potentialities help him to mold himself into a human model closely allied to his individual nature.

Foresightful application of knowledge and experience. In the process of formal and personal education, self-examination should take place so as to improve discrimination in terms of what is worth knowing and how this knowledge is applicable. To foster broadmindedness, the individual needs to study alternatives in order to expand his perspectives and vistas in an overall evaluation of various implications and possible consequences. The mature person establishes the locus of evaluation firmly within himself. Following the phenomenology of Edmund Husserl and Marx F. Scheler, Carl R. Rogers [23] emphasizes "a letting oneself down into the immediacy of what one is experiencing, endeavoring to sense and to clarify all its complex meanings." Overviews or summary evaluations preceding important decisions are likely to enable one to perceive danger signs relative to oneself and others, and may considerably improve the predictability of events. This, in turn, will facilitate making better choices and acting on the basis of long-range goals, rather than relying on short-term advantages or satisfactions.

Communication of experience. Development of the ability to verbalize and satisfactorily relate experiences, especially those which are emotional in character, provides an additional predisposition to personal adequacy and adjustment. Apparently many adult individuals continue to have difficulty in conceptualizing and communicating emotional aspects of their personal experiences. This is a frequent observation of psychotherapists. Hence, as the individual grows up and matures, he has to make progress in vocabulary, diction, and effective interpersonal communication, and he must be able to establish some close interpersonal relationships which will offer satisfactory opportunities for this kind of self-expression. It is also a task of the adult to advance to a more abstract and conceptual yet stimulating level of communication.

Sensitivity to the needs of others. Infants and children are sensitive to their own needs and interests. Their behavior forcefully indicates their presence or absence. A young child is likely to cry excessively when he misses either an enjoyable person or a pleasing object. Yet the needs or interests of their siblings or parents are readily disregarded, if felt at all. A child takes away a new toy given to his sibling and indicates little awareness of his cry. An adult need has to be presented in a particular way in order to make it understood by a child. When the mother is being examined by a physician whom the child recognizes as a doctor, his concern grows. It may be interpreted that the fear elicited grows less on a basis of identification with the mother and more from an expectation by the child that he will be examined thereafter.

Sensitivity to the needs of others gradually develops during childhood but does not reach any depth before adolescence. The adolescent preoccupation with self is usually transformed into an examination and consideration of others. This observation of others often leads to deep insights relative to the needs of others. Yet an adolescent's activities for the gratification of others' needs are frequently interrupted by the emergence of his own acute desires. Behavioral priority for his own needs usually prevails. A young adult may, however, attain a level of control that permits his continual service to the needs of others. Estimation of others' wants improves with maturity, and responses are less often interfered with by reappearing egoistic considerations. Versatility in relating to others greatly expands in late adolescence and early adulthood.

Sensitivity to the needs of others tends to decrease with advancing age. In old age, self-concern deepens and usually constricts the direction of personal interest in others. Then the needs of others are often disregarded and forgotten in favor of preoccupation with self and gratification of the individual's own drives and inclinations.

Dealing constructively with frustration. One of the major signs of maturity is the increasing ability to delay the gratification of psychological needs and to control or tolerate considerable amounts of disappointment, deprivation, anxiety, and frustration in general. In recalling and examining past frustrations, one should draw positive lessons for future activities and investigate the possibility of prevention where possible.

The adolescents' standards and ideals, on the one hand, and drives of emotional and sexual character, on the other, often do not readily fuse into an integrated and consistent behavior pattern; therefore, disillusionment and conflicts occur which, if intense, are likely to disturb the individual in a variety of ways and situations. As the adolescent becomes better able to cope with and solve these conflicts, he advances toward the attainment of maturity.

Adequate capacity for self-control. A satisfactory handling of affection, emotion, and sexual and other impulses has to be achieved during the stages preceding adulthood. The personal direction of life energies toward well-chosen activities and goals and adequate standards of conduct signifies self-regulation and character. These, in fact, are the signs of maturation of a higher order. A tense, ill-tempered, envious, suspicious, and hostile person is both uncontrolled and immature. Throughout life each level of development is marked by additional controls. These restraints reach a peak in early adulthood. One must learn to express oneself without hurting others or oneself.

Willingness to assume responsibilities. A young adult has to develop his abilities and advance his readiness to assume personal responsibilities pertaining to his status, duties, and obligations. Progress in anticipating and in setting long-term objectives has to be shown during the years of adolescence and early adulthood. Frequently willingness to assume responsibilities involves sacrifice and courage on the part of the young person. He must learn to overcome fear of failure, disregard feelings of disgust or apathy, and ignore comments from his peers when his responsibilities must be met and solved in a rational manner before he can develop a personality that is reliable in fulfilling duties.

Character. During the years of childhood, adolescence, and adulthood, the individual is exposed to a variety of societal, cultural, and moral factors and has a long-term task in integrating his behavior with them. Since moral maturation is often misunderstood or neglected, some clarification is needed in this area of development. Moral maturation commences when a child begins to show some obedience to the dictates of his conscience and when it becomes his own judge in the daily activities and organization of living in general.

Progress in moral maturation is marked by an increase of freedom to choose the good; yet selection of the bad is not excluded. Habitual choice of the good points to moral maturity, and it is an ideal for adolescent and adult alike. Hence, the morally mature person guides himself and is largely self-determined. In order to induce control over his instinctual urges, impulses, and undesirable emotions, he utilizes various brain mechanisms and neuro-muscular systems. An individual may use self-control by substitution, whereby he replaces an unacceptable thought or desire with a more accept-able one, or by suppression, whereby he forces a thought out of conscious-ness by distraction. The individual may use neuromuscular control by refusing to give vent to an impulse, such as refusing to strike someone when he is angry. In such use of control, self-imposed principles and values take prece-dence over his own convenience and gratifications in satisfying biological or emotional drives [19]. When a number of ethical and moral principles are assimilated and start acting as effective behavior organizers, man begins to evidence character, which is one of the ultimate indicators of advanced ma-turation and of adult personality.

Self-reliance. Adequacy in facing novel situations improves as the person gains self-control through his past training, education, and other influences and begins to profit from them. Achievement of success in dealing with present situations promotes the feelings of self-sufficiency and self-worth. Such feelings inflate the ego, and as a result, the individual will hesitate less in applying his own resources. Consequently, the organization of the individ-ual's energies for various life activities becomes a smooth process. A person is neither mature nor self-reliant if he seeks excessive assistance from others or if he expects or unduly requests privileges. Maturity, rather, implies con-siderable independence from others and primary reliance on oneself.

Harmony. Ludwig Klages [16, pp. 310, 337] originated and Heinz Rem-plein [22, pp. 415–417] elaborates on the concept of the *niveau* of person-ality. A high niveau is seen in the similarity between a personality and a piece of art filled with experience of life, originality, and compositional equilibrium between *Seele* (vitality) and *Geist* (rationality). The latter channelizes the energy toward constructive goals and objectives. Harmony implies integrity and its maintenance of internal order under both normal and stressful conditions.

Weltanschauung. "Unifying philosophy of life," Gordon W. Allport's term [1], or "rational design for living," the phrase employed by Magda B. Arnold and J. A. Gasson [2], both refer to an important criterion of a mature person. Allport comes to the conclusion that "an integrated sense of moral obligation provides a unifying philosophy of life whether or not it is tied to an equally developed religious sentiment" [1, p. 304].

Acquiring a religious belief and practicing it offer the means for a fundamental integration of human experience since belief conveys meaning and value to all human activities. Philosophies with a lesser frame of reference are incapable of performing this. The famous analytical psychologist Carl G. Jung, after many years of clinical practice, came to the realization that, unless a patient seeks and regains a religious outlook, psychotheraphy is signally unsuccessful [15, p. 265]. Karl Stern, a psychoanalyst, also tells us of this important relationship. "In my experience, lack of religious faith or loss of faith has often proved to be a serious indication of a disordered person" [27, p. 283]. John A. Gasson [2] emphasizes love of the Creator of men as the final remedy. "In the actual and active loving of God, the person finds himself in the most suitable condition with respect to himself, with respect to his environment, and with respect to inner tendencies. 'For those who love God all things work together unto good.' " Hence, the rational design for living representing the Christian hierarchy of values tends to establish a coherence between the natural and supernatural, between the person's self-imposed ethical principles and his religious experience.

DEFINING THE MATURE PERSON

A mature person structures his environment and is able to perceive himself and others correctly. He has acquired a personal identity and integration of his total personality. In the process of living he attains the developmental tasks for his level of life and develops an ever-increasing number of abilities and skills for coping with the present and the future.

In terms of the previously presented criteria and their basic implications, a mature individual is a person of chronologically adequate physiological, sexual, cognitive, and ego development who:

1. Has the ability to respond differentially in terms of his needs and the outside factors operating in his situation;
2. Channels his tensions, impulses, and emotions into constructive behavior, and directs his behavior toward achievement of positive long-

term goals, yet retains the basic sensitivity, openness, emotional driving strength, and the high degree of satisfaction and enjoyment of late adolescence;

3. In reference to his parents and peers, establishes interdependent patterns of relationships, and is able to impress and influence them and to maintain his role and response with flexibility;

4. Is satisfied by and derives enjoyment from his status and occupation; continues to develop and expand a reservoir of abilities, skills, and viewpoints; learns to recognize his own assets and limitations; and seeks compromise and creative solutions;

5. Is at home with reality in most of its aspects; has learned to relate effectively with persons of all ages and see himself and others with respect, humor, and patience;

6. Values and considers the alternatives and consequences of his actions; finds ways of contributing to his community, his nation, and humanity;

7. Feels whole and satisfied with himself and his own design for living, and is committed to his assimilated values and ideals.

In terms of later adulthood the mature person is the one who has incorporated into his self-structure the Eriksonian attributes of trust, autonomy, initiative, industry, identity, intimacy, generativity (creative productivity), and integrity. His dynamic yet integrative pattern of adjustment makes him capable of working effectively and loving wisely.

MAJOR IMPLICATIONS

It is well to notice that the criteria of maturity presented above are related and overlap to an appreciable extent and that therefore, for practical estimation, one needs only three or four of them to come to expedient conclusions when a particular person is under consideration. The criteria need to be considerably modified for a child or an adolescent. Moreover, any strict application readily leads to a perfectionist interpretation. Human strivings for a higher level of integration, consistency, adequacy, and progress in maturity during adulthood do not make them perfect; mediocrity usually prevails. There is always much to be desired in terms of human potential for creative and integrative activities when closely observing the spectrum of interpersonal, intergroup, and international behavior. Gardner Murphy's *Human potentialities* [18, pp. 129–137, 243–252] points to many possible extensions of creative activity into new dimensions and fields by developing and applying powers inherent in the "three human natures," namely, biological, social-cultural, and that of creative understanding.

Maturity and adjustment.   These two attributes of life appear to be inseparable. Without satisfactory progress in maturation, adequate adjustment to oneself, to others, and to culture is inconceivable. Age-related maturity is a determining disposition toward proper responses and relationships, even when situations involve frustration, deprivation, or other adversity.

There is, of course, no one-to-one relationship between circumstance and response because adjustment has a broad frame of reference and involves the interaction of factors that may make mature responses impossible; for example, a drunken husband with sadistic tendencies and lacking moral motivation is an individual to whom wife and children may not be able to adjust, yet the lack of such adjustment cannot serve as a sign of the wife's immaturity.

It is conventional to indicate that maturity promotes mental health and general welfare since it safeguards the individual from prolonged conflicts and anxieties. It provides stimuli for familial and communal improvements because a mature individual acts as a corrective influence, in some ways at least.

QUESTIONS FOR REVIEW

1. Analyze the process of human maturation in the light of adolescent developments and then explain its end product, maturity.
2. List several studies emphasizing maturation and maturity. Discuss one of them.
3. Identify two or three measures for testing maturity and evaluate one of them.
4. How well is the concept of maturity defined and accepted as a subject of developmental psychology?
5. List several sectorial indexes of maturity. Select and examine one of the global criteria of maturity.
6. Explain the relationships between reason, conscience, and moral maturity.
7. How does independence contribute to personal maturity? What is the relationship between interdependence and adult maturity?
8. In what ways does a philosophy of life or a rational design for living promote maturity?
9. What are the outstanding characteristics of a mature person? How will such a person cope with the problems and adverse situations in his life?
10. Indicate some relationships between (a) maturity and adjustment, (b) maturity and mental health.

REFERENCES

I. Selected Reading

1. Allport, Gordon W. *Pattern and growth in personality.* New York: Holt,

1961. Chap. 15. Extension of the self through security, self-objectification, and the unifying philosophy of life is discussed.

2. Arnold, Magda B., and John A. Gasson. *The human person.* New York: Ronald, 1954. Person and personality from the broad Christian point of view are discussed through consideration of various disciplines, and the need for spiritual life is stressed.

3. Cole, Luella. *Attaining maturity.* New York: Rinehart, 1944. Sectorial maturational processes and indexes of maturity are presented with case illustrations.

4. Heath, Douglas H. *Explorations of maturity: Studies of mature and immature college men.* New York: Appleton-Century-Crofts, 1965. A systematic research monograph exploring the meaning of maturity and testing it on a small sample of college students.

5. Lersch, Phillip. *Aufbau der Person.* (7th ed.) Munich: Barth, 1956. The structural growth of temperament, personality, and character qualities and traits and their interaction are thoughtfully presented. Stratification of organizational levels is an essential feature in approach.

6. Mounier, Emmanuel. *The character of man* (translated by Cynthia Rowland from Traité du characteur, 1942). New York: Harper, 1956. A condensed translation of a comprehensive volume on character which stresses common and unique personality features and their relationships, as well as factors influencing them.

II. Specific References

7. Baldwin, Alfred L. *Behavior and development in childhood.* New York: Holt (for Dryden Press), 1955.

8. Buhler, Charlotte, and H. Hetzer. *Testing children's development from birth to school age* (translated by Henry Beaumont). New York: Holt, 1935.

9. Doll, E. A. *The measurement of social competence.* Minneapolis: Education Test Bureau, 1953.

10. Gesell, Arnold, *Gesell developmental schedules.* New York: Psychological Corporation, 1949.

11. Gesell, Arnold, and Catherine S. Amatruda. *Developmental diagnosis.* (2nd ed.) New York: Harper & Row, 1947.

12. Gesell, Arnold, and Frances L. Ilg. *Infant and child in the culture of today.* New York: Harper & Row, 1943.

13. Gesell, Arnold, and Frances L. Ilg. *The child from five to ten.* New York: Harper & Row, 1946.

14. Gesell, Arnold, et al. *Youth: The years from ten to sixteen.* New York: Harper & Row, 1956.

15. Jung, Carl G. *Modern man in search of a soul* (translated by W. S. Dell and Cary F. Baynes). (2nd ed.) New York: Harcourt, Brace, 1953.

16. Klages, Ludwig. *Grundlegung der Wissenschaft von Ausdruck.* (7th ed.) Bonn: Bouvier, 1950.

17. Morrissette, Pauline. The use of categories by bright, normal, and subnormal preadolescent girls on the Pikunas Graphoscopic Scale and the Stephens' Categorization Tasks. Unpublished doctoral dissertation, University of Oklahoma, 1967.

18. Murphy, Gardner. *Human potentialities.* New York: Basic Books, 1958.

19. Odier, C. *Les deux sources consciente et inconsciente de la vie morale.* Boudry, Switzerland: Baconnière, 1947.

20. Overstreet, H. A. *The mature mind.* New York: Norton, 1949.

21. Pikunas, Justin. *The Graphoscopic Scale: Manual.* Detroit: University of Detroit, 1969. (Mimeographed.)

22. Remplein, Heinz. *Psychologie der Persönlichkeit.* (2nd ed.) Munich: Reinhardt, 1956.

23. Rogers, Carl R. Toward a modern approach to values: The valuing process in the mature person. *J. abnorm. soc. Psychol.,* 1964, **68**, 160–167.

24. Saul, L. T. *Emotional maturity: The development and dynamics of personality.* Philadelphia: Lippincott, 1947.

25. Smith, Elliot D. The attainment of maturity. *Pastoral Psychol.,* 1957, **8**(71), 25–32.

26. Stephens, Wyatt, *A comparison of normal and subnormal boys on tasks requiring the use of selected categories.* Published doctoral dissertation, University of Oklahoma, 1963.

27. Stern, Karl. *The third revolution.* New York: Harcourt, Brace, 1954.

28. Thorpe, Louis P., and Wendell W. Cruze *Developmental psychology.* New York: Ronald, 1956

29. Yamamoto, Kaoru. The "healthy person": A review. *Personnel Guid. J.,* 1966, **44**, 596–605.

DEVELOPMENTAL TASKS
OF EARLY ADULTHOOD

Following the conflict-ridden stage of adolescence, the individual in our society is faced with yet another problem, that of integration into adult society
and culture.   The challenges and responsibilities that must be met and accepted are many, and the possible hindrances to satisfactory adjustment and
development are varied.   The responsibility for participating in local, religious, fraternal, and political organizations, for voting intelligently, and for
keeping informed on national and international issues is becoming more and
more mandatory if the young adult is to take his place in adult society as a
peer.   This chapter attempts to analyze the major developmental tasks and
problem areas in the early adult years.

ACHIEVING INTERDEPENDENCE AND RESPONSIBILITY

Among the criteria of maturity mentioned in the previous chapter are achievement of interdependence and willingness to accept adult responsibility.
These are two of the most crucial attributes in distinguishing an adult from
a child or adolescent.   The task of becoming interdependent and responsible

is especially important in the emotional, social, and economic areas of life. Each of these areas will be examined separately.

Emotional

Emotional interdependence may be understood as a progression from parental and peer dependence to relative autonomy. In other words, although maintaining close emotional ties to others, the individual becomes less susceptible to anger or despair when others disagree or are displeased with him than he was as a child. Emotional autonomy is the most important and the most difficult interdependence to achieve. The young adult must arrive at a level of affective development in which his emotional needs are best satisfied by peers rather than by parents. Too strong an attachment to one or both parents will create severe problems, especially in marital adjustment. If an individual derives his greatest satisfaction from pleasing his parents or from being with them rather than with his peers, particularly of the opposite sex, his emotional development is retarded or distorted.

In most cases, the individual begins to free himself from emotional dependence on his parents during preadolescence. The increased social life of adolescence and new friendships with members of both sexes aid in the transference of emotional ties. During this time, feelings toward parents should become more adult in tone. That is, the affection should be coupled with mutual respect, less like the dependent attachment of children. Evaluating decisions and persons in terms of parents' opinions, or acting only with parental approval, are characteristic of an earlier level of social development.

Attaining emotional independence from parents does not imply complete self-sufficiency. Rather, the individual always remains interdependent in relation to others. Affection, security, status, and related needs are satisfied by his marriage partner, his peer group, and even his occupation. The individual, in turn, contributes to the gratification of the emotional needs of others in his family and reference groups.

Emotional interdependence is not achieved by a mere transference of emotional dependency from parents to peers. The young adult who is dependent on his peers as he was on his parents is still far from being emotionally mature. Freedom from parental control, in terms of emotional attachment, is usually recognized by both parents and young adults as a natural step in the growing-up process. However, emotional maturity means a certain degree of freedom from group domination as well. A young adult who feels lost when he is not with his particular peer group, or one whose decisions are dictated by his peers, is still emotionally dependent. Similarly, the husband who shifts his emotional dependence from mother to wife has made little progress toward emotional maturity. Progress in establishing proper emotional ties to others is a comparatively slow process, and the adolescent and early adult years serve this purpose well.

The capacity to love someone other than oneself is another integral factor in adult emotional interdependence. Excessive self-love and the inability to give of self are not only signs of emotional immaturity but also of a personality disorder. A successful marriage demands a giving of self, and one who is incapable of this emotional giving is going to have grave difficulties in adjusting to marriage [1]. Marriage demands a deep and permanent emotional cathexis and self-involvement.

Social

Social interdependence implies primarily the acceptance of the individual in adult society. To permit this, the individual must demonstrate decidedly adult traits and qualities, or despite his age, he will not be treated as an adult. The adoption of mature social characteristics is generally not too difficult, and this criterion of social maturity is met by many who do not strive for leadership.

Some young adults, however, are not satisfied with mere acceptance in an adult group. Having been leaders in their peer groups, they strive for positions of power and prestige in groups or organizations composed of older individuals. Often their attempts meet with rebuff or a wait-and-see attitude. These individuals must understand that in a sense they are on probation, and adults will not, as a rule, grant them positions of leadership until they have proved they are also good followers and are able to contribute something worthwhile to the group.

A young adult should try to contribute to the group and in that way benefit both the group and himself. Volunteering for some of the necessary busywork and performing it well will gain him the respect of the adult group along with a heightened feeling of achievement and confidence in his dealing with his seniors.

A decidedly more difficult task, and one that is allied to emotional maturity, is the achievement of self-direction rather than group domination. The socially mature adult is in large measure inner-directed rather than group-controlled. His decisions and behavior flow from personal conviction based on his own principles, values, and ideals. The group is not a constrictive force binding him with ties of dependency. Decisions of the group which run contrary to the convictions of the individual are not followed by an adult who has achieved social maturity. He has reached the point at which his feelings of personal adequacy and security are such that they do not need constant reinforcement, which implies insecurity or dependence. Communication of one's beliefs is a part of group interaction.

Social interdependence carries with it social responsibilities. To partake of the privileges of adult life, the individual must assume the obligations of an adult. Occupational, educational, civic, and religious areas are but a few of those in which the young adult must assume responsibilities and be willing to do his part.

That many young adults are preparing for their future responsibilities by continuing their education through college training is seen in Figure 20–1. From 1960 to 1965 the college and professional school enrollment rose by 59 percent, that is, from about 3,570,000 to 5,675,000 students, excluding individuals older than thirty-four [8].

Economic

Integration into adult society usually presupposes economic autonomy, that is, being able to support oneself and one's family. This idea, as a rule, precludes living with one's parents, whether or not the individual is economically

Figure 20–1   College enrollment (full- and part-time).   (The American Association of Registrars and Admissions Offices, 1957–1965; *Current population reports,* Series P-20, No. 149, and Series P-25, No. 338, 1966; reports of the U. S. Office of Education, 1966.)

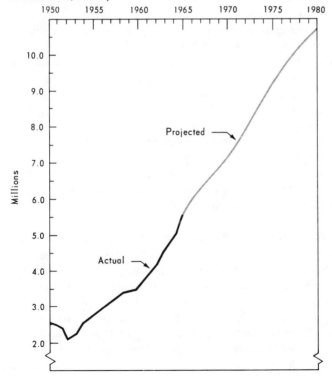

self-supporting. American culture, with its emphasis on additional higher education, makes the attainment of economic independence difficult. Without special training, the number of occupational opportunities is severely curtailed. In order to secure the necessary education for a specific occupation, the individual is, in most cases, forced to prolong his financial dependence on his parents. Parents usually encourage further training and the concomitant extension of financial dependence, and their partial authority over their children is therefore often extended into the mid-twenties. The rising number of federal and other scholarships for graduate studies facilitate financial independence from parents.

The young adult is faced with yet another facet of this problem. To continue training is, in many cases, to postpone marriage. Is the period of marriage postponement "beyond the achievement of physical maturity . . . one of stress and strain, emotional incompleteness, frustration, physical restraint, and intellectual confusion for myriad young people, among whom the college student is one of the most common and most poignant sufferers" as Henry A. Bowman [2, pp. 309–310] pictures it? Probably not, since many young persons are emotionally not ready for an exclusive long-term companionship, still less for parenthood and its responsibilities. Marriage is not a solution for young adolescents who fall into puppy love, but are not ready to assume the contingent responsibilities.

Since the postponement of marriage and family life seems too great a sacrifice to make, many individuals try to combine marriage and further education. The result is, in most cases, a severe strain on the marriage relationship, or an even more prolonged program of training or education because the individual is usually forced to take a job and relegate education to evening classes. The birth of children complicates the already strained situation. This is not to imply that some couples cannot successfully combine marriage and extended training. The fact remains, however, that the first years of a marriage demand from both partners a great deal of cooperation and concentration. Attempts to combine education and marriage put a great strain on both endeavors. However, the great number of stipends and large amount of housing for married students on many campuses encourage such prolonging of education.

Sidney L. Pressey [7] questions the need for prolonged education where half a lifetime may go by before one can begin his lifework. Since the body of knowledge increases at a very high rate, it probably would be better to start professional work earlier and to enter refresher courses and adult programs later to gain timely control over the expanded knowledge.

Young adults form the most educated age group. As Figure 20–2 shows, in 1965 the median of school years completed was about 12.5 for whites and 11.7 for Negroes. During the late sixties, the median continued rising, as

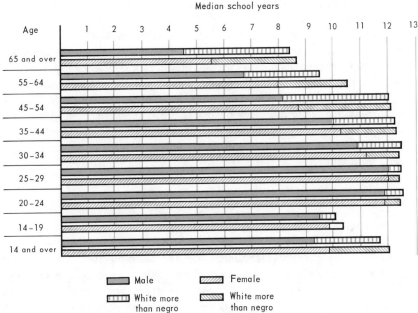

Figure 20–2   Median school years completed: 1965.   (*Americans at mid-decade,* Series P-23, No. 16.   Department of Commerce, 1966.)

percentages of young adult population completing high school and college rose at a fairly sharp rate.

Economic independence demands, along with freedom from financial dependence, an acceptance of financial responsibility.   Young adults, especially in establishing a home, usually must go into debt.   The prompt payment of bills and debts demands a degree of perspective and maturity.   Usually payment of large bills demands some self-denial in the form of putting off other purchases and curtailing entertainment.   However, chronic indebtedness in large amounts is a sign of financial mismanagement and a symptom of personal dependence.

ESTABLISHING THE HOME

Perhaps the largest problem confronting young couples is the establishment of their homes.   The economic, interpersonal, and social problems are many in such an undertaking.   The interpersonal adjustments that must be made will be discussed in the next section.   Other problems are primarily economic. Establishing a budget and adhering to it is a prevalent problem.   However, this may be considered as merely symptomatic of a deeper problem, namely, that many young couples desire at the beginning of their marriage the same standard of living or a higher one than their parents have attained after twenty or thirty years of work.

The distinction between luxuries and necessities is often obscured, and consequently many commodities are acquired which are not really essential. The financial outlay in such cases usually produces a deficiency in the budget in other areas. A certain amount of credit or installment-plan purchasing is usually necessary. In this connection, a common rule of thumb is that indebtedness, including mortgage payments on the home, should in no event exceed 40 percent of the yearly income. A realistic viewpoint regarding their desires as opposed to their income is an essential trait in a young couple striving for maturity.

MARITAL ADJUSTMENT

For most people, marriage is their deepest social commitment. The constructive channeling of forces that did not participate in bringing the two persons together is a task of great magnitude. These forces often start disturbing the marital life before the first year of marriage expires, unless one has high reserves of self-control and flexibility for readjustment. The marital role per se involves the acceptance of another role, that of parenthood. A desire for children by one partner, social expectations that married persons should have children, and accidental pregnancies are some of the factors operating in this regard.

A young married woman is likely to entertain imaginings of "holding a baby in my arms" or "having someone little to love me." She may also want "someone to help me spend the many hours while my husband is at work." The less pleasant aspects of pregnancy, childbirth, and the many sleepless nights when the baby cries or is sick are less likely to come to mind or to impress her deeply at the budding stage of married life. The passing years of married life usually intensify her desire to have children.

Family life involves fundamental learning in each domain of living. This learning advances before and when children arrive. The demands of sharing in daily chores, conversation, and activities, thoughtfulness for others, and respect for their claims and peculiarities become more complex with the addition of each new member to the family. It is impossible to discuss all the possible forms of relationship and interaction that occur within the framework of the family. Excluding extremes, each family represents living in most of its aspects. Family life is a stage of further growth for each member. Friction and rivalry within the total constitution of the family, even between parents, often serves as a necessary "training ground" for learning mature responses and better ways of settling interpersonal differences. The need and opportunity to utilize additional potentialities is often present. As a rule, family living furthers maximal opportunity for personal self-realization. This is less true for the wife and mother who becomes busy with her children and has too little time left for her own education and cultural concerns.

Since both parents come from different familial constellations and often have quite different backgrounds, it is normal that they should have some differences of opinion about the rearing of children. Their attitudes toward children are likely to be different. This constitutes a source of friction in their efforts to train and educate their children. Frequently, a significant difference of opinion appears concerning methods of discipline. Leniency by one parent is counteracted by a strict adherence to certain modes of punishment by the other parent. Then sympathy expressed by the first parent on such occasions makes a child antagonistic to the other parent. The tendency toward egalitarianism in the American family makes the role differentiation between father and mother difficult. As a result, many young persons feel somewhat confused as to how to organize their families and how to share in the care and management of their children [9, pp. 428–429].

Ernest W. Burgess's and H. J. Locke's classification [6, pp. 431–437] of basic factors in marital adjustment includes personality characteristics, cultural backgrounds, social participation, economic status, response patterns, and sex desires. The following six personality variables are listed as contributing to unhappiness in marriage relationships: pessimistic temperament, neurotic tendencies, domineering behavior, inconsiderate attitudes, lack of self-confidence, and lack of self-sufficiency. They assume that differences in cultural background form barriers for effective communication. The romantic response patterns, such as infatuation and "love at first sight," are generally associated with marital maladjustment. They involve notions of affinity for the marriage partner, of supreme happiness in marriage, and of passionate love overcoming all barriers of culture, class, and prudence.

ADJUSTMENTS TO PARENTHOOD

The decision to have children often involves some ignorance concerning the realities of parenthood. Unforeseeable contingencies may later distort the desire for parenthood even more and raise the feelings of rejection and hostility toward the offspring, especially if the child belongs to the sex other than that desired or if he appears to be retarded or handicapped. Since the appearance of tender sentiment and love is likely to occur, a mental conflict of considerable intensity develops with some mothers. Thus, difficulties in adjusting to motherhood are not infrequent. Most young mothers, however, have controls and stamina sufficient to overcome initial burdens, and begin to gain satisfaction as the child develops and exhibits his personality. Their desire to be good mothers usually gains in strength, especially if the husband-wife relationships are satisfactory.

The modern family needs some form of birth control, yet the method to be applied often produces an issue. After giving birth to three or four children in four or five years, most mothers need a longer rest period between pregnancies to prevent biological exhaustion and to safeguard their own welfare.

With many sources as a frame of reference, including fragmentary recollections of their own childhood, young parents begin to associate their role with maintenance of the physical and emotional welfare of their child. Care of his physical needs involves not merely age-related foods and clothes but also many comforts and provision of age-mates and toys for play activity and the education of the child. Emotional welfare of the child is built on many expressions of affection and empathy, of "I know how you feel." Continual love of the child implies frequent help and sympathy in time of trouble, tender handling, and patience with his desires and whims.

General parental attitudes toward children may be identified as indifference, partial rejection, partial acceptance, and fullhearted identification with them.

1. Indifference may be experienced because of difficulties in accepting the parental role, lack of affection and psychological fusion between adult and child environments, and extensive pursuit of preparental interests.

2. Rejection is only exceptionally complete. Frequently it is partial and marked by alternating acceptance and hostile withdrawal into narcissistic gratifications. The ideas of children as intruders and added burdens may stand foremost in the parents' minds. They have to force themselves to accept responsibilities related to child rearing and education. Falling short in this, parents shower their children with toys and gifts, go into occasional spasms of affectionate handling, and in many other ways compensate for their rising feelings of guilt.

3. Partial acceptance is often marked by setting high standards and expecting children to meet them. While children appear to be part of the scheme of the parents' lives and emotional identification often occurs, they are also seen as inadequate, misbehaving, and in need of strict handling and corporal punishment.

4. Fullhearted identification with children is marked by strong emotional ties, by disregard of the child's shortcomings, and by a belief that children are desirable challenges. Parents are ready to do almost anything in their power to promote the child's development and his welfare. Parental activity centers around their children.

The *father's* role, in addition to breadwinning, includes many kinds of assistance and substitution, especially in the area of discipline. It is often the father who begins to feel the growing obligations, and worries about his competence to meet them adequately. The father's responsibilities usually grow as children develop, attend schools, and become adolescents, while gratifications coming from children largely depend on the adequacy of their early training. This, in turn, has been substantially determined by the mother's knowledge of and adequacy in infant handling. Since the mother is the heart of the family, her personality traits contribute to or disturb the total family picture to a greater extent than similar characteristics of the father.

A family's compatibility and ability to act as a unit is tested each time a vital decision has to be made. Buying a new house is one of them. Husband and wife frequently have different ideas about the desired qualities and characteristics of a new house for their family. The ideas presented as to its location, construction or selection, size, style, yard, garage, and financing, all may differ in significant ways. Division of responsibilities and a readiness for tolerant compromises have to prevail in overcoming the obstacles met in striving to possess a home of one's own selection.

Parental attitudes and approaches in child rearing tend to differ in some ways with each child. The *firstborn* child often undergoes "experiments in caring for a baby," resulting from lack of information and experience in managing a child. Advice of other people is sought and followed with relatively little skill. Occasionally the firstborn baby is a victim of a parental overprotective attitude. All his needs and whims are responded to. Experience in dealing with the firstborn proves invaluable when the *second* child arrives. The mother often shows more confidence in herself and less concern about the baby. More often the second child is less often stimulated or even neglected, and many of his whims and cries are disregarded. Difficulties with the firstborn at this time are likely to arise if the second-born gains too much attention.

The *third-born* is not a novelty at all unless the first two were of the same sex and different in sex from the third. His care is more casual and tension-free. Parents have learned to delimit gratification of children's demands. The third and the following children are likely to suffer from this from the very beginning. With the exception of the last-born, they will remain less dependent on their parents and more affected by their older siblings.

The children in the middle are likely to show less maladjustment in their childhood and adolescent years than the firstborn or the last-born. Good adjustment on the part of parents and their adequacy in dealing with the specific needs of each child are key factors in childhood adjustment to the demand of reality.

In adulthood, being a member of a family typically involves sacrifices in personal freedom. When they have a baby or young children, parents are restricted in their private and social life. While most kinds of occupational activities permit the father to be away for a considerable length of time, the mother is obliged to spend most of her time in caring for and entertaining her children. Since the extended family has moved definitely into the past, exclusion of grandparents from most families makes substitution for the mother difficult. Baby-sitting by someone else tends to produce much concern on the part of mother and frequently tones down her outside satisfactions considerably when she takes a "maid's night out" for a social evening or theater.

REMAINING SINGLE

A significant minority of young adults in our culture remain single. Recent years show a slightly declining percentage of the population. The reasons for this vary from one individual to another. Some daughters feel a responsibility for care of their parents, especially if they are aged or infirm and consequently deny themselves possible chances of marriage. Some enter the religious life, which in many cases demands celibacy. For many others, the opportunity for an acceptable marriage never presents itself, since there are fewer males than females in all age groups above eighteen. Shocking disappointments in love resulting in depressive bitterness militate against accepting new intimacies [5, pp. 102–109].

Despite the reasons for remaining single, the individuals who do so face special problems in their adjustment. Their personal adjustment is often difficult, owing to a feeling of *aloneness*, especially if they are not living with relatives. They must perform the "total role" of breadwinner and home manager. The problems of companionship, of receiving love, and of maintaining emotional balance are, for a time at least, acutely felt. Socially they are somewhat out of place in adult gatherings of married couples. Additionally they are often urged by their married friends to reconsider their choice. In many cases, they are the object of matchmaking attempts by well-meaning friends, most of whom fail to realize that many unmarried individuals choose to remain single.

The opportunities for additional education, for community, religious, or fraternal service as well as for personal advancement are, in many cases, greater for single persons than for those with the responsibilities of a family. Whether or not they use their free time for these activities depends on their values and aspirations.

ENHANCING SELF-REALIZATION

During the years of early adulthood, the individual generally comes to a realization of his total nature. The unrealistic ambitions of adolescence have yielded to more practical goals. Self-knowledge in many areas is deepened by the improved reality testing of this period.

Assets and liabilities have been more clearly delineated by occupational experience, and personal qualities have been brought to the fore by the adjustments necessary in marriage. Planning ability has been tested in the reality of family finance, and the individual's ability as a provider is, by now, adequately demonstrated. The interests of the young adult have crystallized somewhat, and his self-concept is more or less stabilized by this time. Reliance on the habitual begins to gain in motivational power.

It is at this stage that the individual is presented with enviable opportunities for self-realization. Unless he faces too many stressful situations, consolidation of the gains made up to this point and a valid assessment of self lead to real progress in applying himself to attainment of his goals. There was a long period of preparation for adult life, now he is much on his own to move ahead and to use his endowments completely. The returns of such diligence and ego-involvement differ greatly from person to person.

SETTING THE PATTERN OF LIFE

Toward the end of early adulthood, the individual is in a position to predict, rather validly, his future and to adjust the pattern of life accordingly. Plans are made for the attainment of some long-range goals, such as educating the children or ensuring financial welfare. The trial-and-error experiences of raising children usually solidify into a definite pattern for guidance of the individuals through childhood and adolescence. The individual's philosophy of life may be altered in the light of experience and in anticipation of future responsibilities. The majority of people settle down during this period of life and the intensity of struggling or meddling subsides.

QUESTIONS FOR REVIEW

1. Discuss interdependence as it is used in this chapter with reference to dependence and maturity.
2. Explain how emotional interdependence is attained.
3. Discuss the problems of attaining economic independence.
4. Present some basic considerations in buying a home.
5. Explain the relationship between emotional maturity and marital adjustment.
6. Discuss some basic factors leading to marital happiness.
7. Characterize some general parental attitudes toward children.
8. Identify some desirable qualities and traits of mothers and father
9. Discuss some major problems of the single person.
10. What developments in early adulthood help to set the adult pattern of life?

REFERENCES

I. Selected Reading

1. Bee, Lawrence S. *Marriage and family relations*. New York: Harper &

Row, 1959.   An analysis of the major factors influencing success in marriage, with emphasis on personality patterns and interrelationships.

2. Bowman, Henry A.   *Marriage for moderns.*   (5th ed.) New York: McGraw-Hill, 1965.   Discusses dating, partner selection, readiness for marriage, adjustments to marriage and family living, divorce, and other aspects of marriage.

3. Clemens, Alphonse H.   *Design for successful marriage.*   (2nd ed.) Englewood Cliffs, N. J.: Prentice-Hall, 1964.   Various aspects of dating, marriage, sex, and parenthood in a presentation consistent with the Catholic point of view.

4. Havighurst, Robert J.   *Developmental tasks and education.*   New York: Longmans, 1951.   Chap. 6.   A summary of the developmental tasks of early adulthood.

5. Reed, Ruth.   *The single woman.*   New York: Macmillan, 1942.   An account of the problems and adjustments that face the unmarried woman, and methods of dealing with them.

II. Specific References

6. Burgess, E. W., and H. J. Locke.   *The family: From institution to companionship.*   (2nd ed.) New York: American Book, 1953.

7. Pressey, Sidney L.   Two basic neglected psychoeducational problems. *Amer. Psychologist,* 1965, **20**, 391–395.

8. U. S. Bureau of the Census.   *Current population reports: Population characteristics.*   Series P-20, No. 149.   1966.

9. Winch, Robert F.   *The modern family.*   (2nd ed.) New York: Holt, 1963.

MIDDLE ADULTHOOD

The middle stage of life begins when a person attains his peak in performing most of the vocational obligations and recreational activities in which he participates. It blends completion of the upward development with an increased integration among motivational tendencies, abilities, and skills. Most types of education and training are finished before one enters this stage. Moreover, vocational, marital, and other related social experiences are accumulated, and the pattern of life is largely set. It is estimated that women enter this phase of life at the completion of about thirty years of life, while men follow suit at about thirty-five. The middle period of life encompasses approximately fifteen of the most productive years of life. It gradually shades into the phase of late adulthood when declines are not fully compensated by recoveries, nor is there further growth of diverse human potentialities.

During middle adult years, most individuals progress in vocational, marital, civic, and socioeconomic areas of living. Consolidation of previous gains also occurs at this stage. The intensity of experiencing life declines as compared to the adolescent and early adult stages of development. Since one's children are becoming adolescents and adults, marrying, and moving away, responsibilities associated with child and adolescent guidance and education reach a peak and start declining. With the increase of life expectancy, some extension of the middle-age span is observed. This extension and shorter working hours offer increased opportunity for self-chosen activities and personality growth.

SOCIOECONOMIC CONSOLIDATION

The adult person is continually ranked by his friends, associates, employer, and neighbors. The status to which he is assigned largely depends on fluctuations and changes in his social traits and personality structure, appearance and performance, as well as on his economic standing.

By the time the individual reaches the middle adult years, his personality has gained in stability, and there is little room for change. Nevertheless, some traits that were barely noticeable earlier now come into prominence. For example, the man of forty-five who suddenly volunteers as a scoutmaster may have had a great deal of civic interest, but had to delay its practical expression until his responsibilities at home and at work permitted. Learning and experience contribute greatly toward the consolidation of previous gains in the personality structure. Some individuals go beyond mere consolidation by exerting considerable personal effort toward optimal development of their talents and potentialities. Throughout these years a noted progress in personality and self-integration are often achieved.

Unlike the personality structure, social traits are likely to fluctuate considerably, largely because the growth of social traits is closely related to gratifications coming from interaction with other individuals and groups. The young adult recently out of school, beginning the busy whirl of his family life, belongs to few clubs and groups, and may barely make his social presence known outside his neighborhood. As the family grows into school age, many adults join groups related to their children's activities, such as the scout leaders, the parent-teacher associations, and the band mothers. Membership in formal clubs or groups reaches its peak at the end of the middle adult years and slowly tapers off with the advancing years of late adulthood. Social confidence and poise tend to rise with the increase of friendships and the development of leadership traits. On the other hand, suspicion and hostility tend to arise when one lacks support in his personal goals or has to compete extensively with others. Interest and participation in civic and political affairs also rise constantly to a peak at about the age of fifty; however, unlike social traits, civic and political activity is maintained at a high level until very old age.

With most persons, economic status improves throughout the middle adult years. This is largely due to progress in vocational standing, seniority rights, and various fringe benefits, on the one hand, and to decreasing capital expenses, such as buying and paying for a house or furnishings and providing infant and child care, on the other. Such expenditures usually burden the years of early maturity but decline at this age. The improving financial situation affords opportunities to acquire articles that promote the comforts of living. Some long-desired luxuries are now procured. Personal satisfaction and a rise in social status often result from obtaining such items.

Progress in occupational standing usually levels off at about forty, if not before. This plateau curbs any noticeable further climbs on the economic ladder. Excluding people in certain fields of business, in certain professions, and in some governmental positions, the economic end and lack of progress in vocational performance is felt by a large majority of the working population. This often is a key factor in self-reappraisal in the late part of this stage, which will be elaborated on in a later part of this chapter.

A minority of less-endowed and emotionally or socially unstable adults continue to have employment difficulties for several reasons. Since they lack a trade or technical knowledge, they represent the unskilled or semiskilled labor force, readily engaging in seasonal and dead-end jobs and changing occupations frequently. They are plagued by intermittent layoffs or unemployment as automation processes and seasonal or general recessions eliminate many job opportunities for the unskilled. Although the ranks of this category generally decrease with advancing age, the total percentage does not change much, in large industrial cities at least, chiefly because of the continuing migration from the South and Southwest. Inability to maintain a job at this age is often reflected in decline of ascribed status. It cuts deep into personal self-reliance, and raises hostile tendencies toward assumed sources of injustice.

HEALTH AND ACTIVITIES

The prime of life does not end abruptly upon entrance into the middle adult years. The body with all its organs and systems continues to function near its optimal level throughout this phase, marked only by very gradual impairment, which often has origins in the earlier years.

Man's most vital senses, vision and hearing, illustrate the above statement most clearly. From childhood the lens of the eye begins to lose its capacity for accommodation, but visual acuity remains much the same until the age of about forty when sharpness of vision quite suddenly declines. Many begin wearing glasses for reading and other fine work. While the majority of people never lose the ability to hear low-pitched tones, the progressive loss of hearing for high-pitched tones continues and is clearly noticeable after forty. For this reason the enjoyment of concerts drops slightly.

The human body is a finely adjusted complex of systems, organs, and servomechanisms which maintain physiological homeostasis. With age, this balance declines, and recovery from illness or a disturbed condition becomes more difficult. Due to a slowing of metabolism in the early forties, many people experience difficulty in maintaining their normal weight. Since in many cases physical exercise declines, the tendency to become overweight increases. Other undesirable metabolic tendencies begin to show up. Signs of diabetes may appear, uric acid percentage in the blood may rise above the average range; early lesions and tumors indicative of neoplasm and cancer may also show up. Gallbladder and kidney stones form more easily than before. These are some of the reasons that suggest a need for a thorough physical examination at this phase of life, even if one feels well. The question then is "How well physically am I?" Many systems of the body should be examined, including the gastrointestinal, genitourinary, gynecological (female genitalia), and cardiovascular systems. From about forty years of age it is very reasonable to consider periodic physical examination which from time to time will reveal the need for some X-ray and other thorough expansions of the basic medical checkup by the general practitioner. It is important for any person of this age to realize the detrimental effects of any strain, whether physical, emotional, or social.

Total physiological vigor and soundness of health are frequently manifested throughout the middle adult years, but gradually decline in later years. Both the rate of illness and the death rate persist at the minimal pace until the progressive acceleration occurs at about fifty. It is interesting to note that the causes of death are age-related. Accidents are the important factor until middle age; from that time on, degenerative conditions such as heart disease and cancer become increasingly prominent.

Activities in hobbies and in interests continue to decline from their high level before marriage. Near the end of the middle adult years, one finds his leisure time lengthening considerably. During the years that follow those who cultivated hobbies in their youth readily take them up again, often in a modified form to reduce physical exertion. Apparently there exists an urgent need for education in the use of leisure time, for while the need for activity and exercise of one's powers persists, a great many people neglect taking up sports and hobbies to gratify this need.

Interests, or activities one has a "liking for" rather than a wish to participate in, show definite age-related trends. Sedentary and noncompetitive diversions, such as listening to music and visiting historical places and museums, become increasingly popular, but active competitive activities show a continual decline.

Mass media of communication—radio, TV, newspapers, magazines—claim the largest portion of leisure time. The effect of mass media on the individual personality is great, but declining. There is much doubt, however, that the vicarious experience in the ready-made fantasy world which they provide is a wholesome replacement for personal efforts that gratify basic human needs and maintain physical vigor.

In a world of timesaving devices, automation, and shortening working hours, leisure-time activities gain prominence by supplying the satisfactions of acquired human interests and concerns. Time-killing pastimes should be omitted in favor of more creative, constructive, and noncompetitive activities. This constitutes one of the major developmental tasks of this stage, the stage of preparing for the late adult years and for old age.

PARENTAL ASPECTS

During the middle adult years most parents find that their offspring are no longer children but adolescents and young adults. Parental guidance and protection are vastly altered because teen-age children find less of their time and activities associated with home. As the children carry out higher educational responsibilities and join their friends in various group activities, they gain in motivational strength leading to greater self-reliance and increasing independence from their parents. Many parents get into difficulties with teen-agers by requesting their assistance with chores, such as caring for younger siblings, or by expecting them to return at a prescribed hour.

Despite the problems of parents with their adolescent children, the presence of children at home is challenging and reassuring. Many kinds of enjoyment increase at the time the adolescent is approaching adult status. Mutual growth in understanding and appreciating each other's interests and activities is the key to successful cooperative efforts in pastimes, projects, and the resolving of situations that previously provoked conflict. Parents often regret that this phase is rather short-lived. When they really begin to feel gratified by their offspring and desire this equilibrium to continue, their children, having completed their education and job training, are ready to move away, to marry, and to establish families of their own.

Late in the middle adult years and the years immediately following, the stage of "the emptying nest" begins with the marriage of adolescent or post-adolescent children, and moments of bleakness appear and multiply. Signs of the "dull residue of existence" may or may not show up, depending on the dominant attitudes and goals set earlier for self-fulfillment in this period of life. Changing one's attitude and outlook must begin while the children are still in their teens. For example, the mother who has the ingrained attitude that her children desperately need her assistance enters this stage with much anxiety as she realizes she is no longer needed. Again, the father who has forced his son to depend upon him for all his material needs is likely to enter this stage with regrets that his son fails to live up to his expectations.

Frequently the development of new or modified attitudes is not sufficient for the middle-aged adults who are trying to adjust to an empty home. By increasing their activity in organizations and clubs, and by greater participation in civic and religious responsibilities, each helps himself to gain added maturity and equanimity in the face of the problems arising at this stage.

Also, the discovery of new satisfactions in expanding the comforts and aesthetics of the home, in closer relationship to his spouse and other relatives, in enjoying freedom for social visits, hobbies, and travel, all these will contribute to adjustment and also to the enjoyment of this phase of life.

REEVALUATING THE SELF-CONCEPT

When a person begins to notice his difficulties in making progress at work or a hobby, or that his attempts to learn something new are less efficacious than in the past, and, especially, that some declines in these areas are quite obvious, he will, understandably, become concerned. In addition to these changes, he may experience less satisfaction in his usual recreational pursuits and recognize the law of diminishing returns in his energy expenditures. Such experiences readily lead a person to the conclusion that he is growing old.

The already anxious person magnifies incipient signs of old age and even invents some new ones. Time and again a disease or ailment of middle age and the following convalescence offer some free time for the purpose of self-reappraisal. Anxiety is intensified when the idea finds subjective support that he is losing some of his most appreciated qualities and abilities. Sexual capacity and appeal is one of them. Memory and the ability to learn are others. Emotional ambivalence and oscillation, reminiscent of the turmoils of early adolescence, often appear and lead to the second major crisis in the person's life. Deep philosophical and religious questions pertaining to the meaning of life and to the value of the goals pursued during adulthood appear and press for answers; failure to resolve these problems can boost anxiety to disturbing levels. If routine activities lose their motivational strength because they seem purposeless, the person may resort to neurotic self-defenses, such as withdrawal or depression, or attempt to engage in experiences that had much personal meaning earlier.

Throughout childhood, adolescence, and early adulthood, the individual feels he is in the process of becoming what he wants or what he ought to be. Usually through the thirties, he continues to advance his status or improve his self-concept in some respects at least. He labors, and expects "a break" to his advantage in realizing his personal aspirations. At about forty, however, many realize they are merely holding their own or actually losing ground, long before their aspired ambitions have materialized.

The reevaluative step at this age often favors self-justification and placing the blame on closely related persons and circumstances. A husband blames his wife for unsatisfactory support in his strivings toward goals, while the wife spots many inadequacies in her husband in her attempts to safeguard her integrity. Statistics show that in the period 1950 to 1965 one in every ten marriages broke up after the twentieth year of marriage [9].

For the majority of adults, the early forties are the years of "retest and realignment" for at least a belated achievement of some selected life goals. New attempts at vocational promotion or improvement and at marital reintegration usually encounter obstacles. After two or three years of trial, the middle-aged person feels forced to make a final estimation pertaining to his present level of success. Not many come to positive statements and see meaning in their renewed effort. Many recognize that they continue to fall short of their still-optimistic aspirations. This is a phase when a person can profit considerably from further adult or college education. Because of the fast rate at which knowledge increases, many people, including professionals, need refresher courses and seminars.

Some people show inability to reconcile themselves to the lack of appreciable gains during this phase of life. The tendency to blame themselves or others often reaches neurotic or, in a minority of cases, psychotic dimensions. Some react by escaping into alcoholism, psychosomatic illness, or paranoic hostility. Attempts to destroy obstacles and enforce success at times lead to adult delinquency. Not many are fortunate enough to change goals in terms of their ability or to acknowledge failure in a stoic attitude. Frequently compensation is sought through association with the more fortunate ones or by means of pressing their children to raise the family status.

As the middle and late adult years merge, one has fewer and fewer opportunities for self-assertion. This is a key psychological factor, prompting feelings of inadequacy and anxiety. If one cannot prepare himself to meet this problem, he will react by demanding exceptional performance from others, including those under his supervision. New interpersonal conflicts arise which increase tension and often make the situation unbearable. One becomes more entangled if complications of previously ignored problems arise. As a result, symptomatic relief is unknowingly sought and a delayed neurotic pattern takes hold.

To many persons, the period of reevaluation of self is a temporary upheaval. The futility of such outbursts and turmoil is recognized, and renewed attempts to regain control over oneself and external situations lead to a stabilization and readjustment long before the stage expires.

RECAPTURING YOUTH

Some drives and urges that have been satisfactorily controlled during adulthood now reappear with new strength and high frequency. An analysis will show a relationship to pubertal and adolescent drives and impulses, many of them sexual in nature. The earlier sexual and aggressive tendencies, inhibited or repressed into subconsciousness, now reappear because they remained unsublimated. In addition, their vitality has accumulated through formation of complexes involving related urges.

For many adults, an Apollonian, or intellectually ordered and tempered, way of life gives way to Dionysian expressiveness and disregard of the moderate and conventional. Older men entertaining adolescent girls or dealing in sex magazines are examples of such behavior. With age creeping up on him, a man may feel urged to engage in sexual and related gratifications before it is too late. Oral gratifications are excessively sought after, and returns to masturbation also occur. This is more likely to happen to individuals whose maturity and personality integration were never completed processes. Adequate character formation and an explicit philosophy of life are powerful deterrents to such attempts to recapture youth by returning to immature or perverse modes of behavior.

Development of character enables a person to control such drives and urges, while a proper Weltanschauung assists him to direct his energies toward constructive and socially acceptable channels of activity and self-expression. Activities motivated by integrated character traits tend to bring greater ego satisfactions than mere behavioral discharges of drives and impulses. For this reason, gratifications gained by altruistic, religious, and related activities are deeply satisfying to human nature and contribute much to the preservation of general welfare and, particularly, to mental health.

Among the helpful sources for the understanding of the conflicts and adjustments at this middle phase of adult life are E. Bergler's *The revolt of the middle-aged man* [4], Roy A. Burkhart's *The freedom to become yourself* [5], and Bernice L. Neugarten's *Personality in middle and late life* [2]. This is a period of life that has received little attention from the social scientists.

COMPENSATING DECLINE

A program of objective self-examination will typically show many beginnings of decline, slow and barely noticeable in the early part of middle-adult years yet continually increasing as the stage advances. There is a moderate decrease of psychomotor speed and strength. The biochemical equilibrium is in some cases disturbed by diseases of middle age, such as kidney and bile stones and respiratory or circulatory difficulties. If menial, mine, or factory-line work has been engaged in throughout the adult years, old-age signs now begin to appear prematurely. Poorly used cognitive functions deteriorate at a fast rate. General organismic decline may become conspicuous toward the end of the phase. David Wechsler's evaluation [8, p. 206] points to gradual but significant declines of brain weight and to lower intelligence-test scores as age increases.

Cognitive decline is usually more gradual than physical decline, while personality deterioration is rather exceptional in this phase. Occasionally some gains are observed, especially among professional categories. Wherever vocational specialization and progress are possible, morale is easily maintained. A high level of self-realization is then made an actuality. Mental health and alertness may be preserved by the labor and lower class population by taking advantage of indirect forms of compensation. Through diversified interests and hobbies, the range of activities and achievements may be considerably expanded and other than vocational gratifications secured.

Decline in the social dimensions of the individual present a vivid contrast to the various other dimensions considered. In a survey of the community life of American adults, Robert J. Havighurst [6] found by interviewing 234 persons in greater Kansas City (Kansas and Missouri) with respect to their functions and competence in their communities that the period from forty to seventy is a plateau period with a slight decrease toward the later years. The structural aspects of social life decline sharply during this period, especially after sixty years of age. Figure 21–1 presents Havighurst's hypothetical curve of biological equipment and social functioning in two forms of society.

One of the most efficient ways of compensating for early decline is maintaining awareness of developmental tasks of this stage of life and engagement in age-related activities, supplementing and superseding the more energy-consuming activities of the earlier stages of life. The following section is a list of tasks related to the developmental level of middle-aged people.

Figure 21–1 Relation between function and structure through the human life cycle. (Robert J. Havighurst. The social function of middle-aged people. *Genet. Psychol. Monogr.*, 1957, **56**, 297–375, fig. on p. 345. By permission.) *Society A:* One giving high status to older people and opportunity to continue their social functioning under favorable circumstances. *Society B:* One marked as a "youth-oriented society," which devaluates middle and old age.

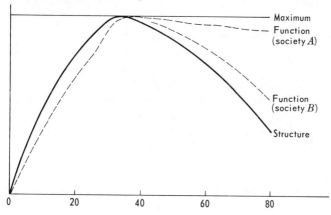

DEVELOPMENTAL TASKS AT MIDDLE ADULT AGE*

1. Helping growing and grown-up children to become responsible and socially integrated adults.

   Freeing their time for social and recreational opportunities by taking care of their little children. Such duties are frequently enjoyable.

   Encouraging grown children to participate in civic activities and supporting them with practical and moral aid when they need it.

2. Developing new satisfactions with one's spouse.

   Exploring new hobbies, club activities, and community projects.

   Expressing appreciation for one's spouse in his attempts and his successes.

   Sharing his feelings and thoughts, aspirations and disappointments.

3. Creating a pleasant, comfortable, and aesthetically ordered home and yard.

   Acquiring household facilities for comfort and ease of upkeep.

   Remodeling and decorating in terms of the family's interests and values.

   Assuming responsibilities related to the entertainment of members of the extended family and old and new friends.

4. Increasing social and civic activities.

   Keeping informed on civic affairs, and national and international events.

   Taking an active part in church and civic organizations.

5. Finding new occupational satisfactions.

   Coming to terms with one's degree of success, and working with lesser tension and increased experience.

   Contributing to the success of others by timely advice and assistance.

   Letting younger persons take over some areas of responsibility without threat to self-respect or status; planning for one's eventual retirement constructively.

6. Making satisfying and creative use of increased leisure time.

   Enjoying a chance to engage in activities for which time was unavailable before.

   Sharing leisure-time activities with one's spouse and friends.

   Balancing recreation in terms of activity and passivity, group participation and privacy, self-indulgence and service motivation.

7. Accepting and adjusting to the physical and mental changes of the middle years.

* In this section we have drawn heavily on an excellent presentation of developmental tasks for fathers and mothers by Evelyn M. Duvall in *Family development* [1, pp. 397–410].

Getting regular medical and dental examinations; using glasses, hearing and other aids when prescribed.

Maintaining a physical exercise program appropriate to age and endurance.

Observing adequacy of diet and appropriate appearance; restricting tobacco and alcohol consumption.

Increasing records and order to balance decreasing power of memory.

Maintaining a variety of interests, with emphasis on the intellectual, artistic, and religious phases of life.

Making use of modern counseling and psychotherapy before problems, worries, or depression produce severe detrimental effects on personality integration.

Reaffirming moral and religious values of life and engaging in related practices that have real and transcendent meaning.

GROWTH OF PERSONALITY AND CHARACTER

It is possible to gain additional roles in middle adulthood and in some fields an individual can continue to specialize and even to rise in status, but for most people, personality and character are the only vital growth components at this stage of life.   Because of the great influx of societal and cultural changes in the modern world, everyone is pressed to refashion his personality at each phase of adult life.

Some changes in attitude result from self-reappraisal when an individual admits the impossibility of regaining youthfulness with its intense gratifications.   If the developmental tasks of early adulthood are sincerely undertaken, a person may make fruitful advances in orienting himself toward the constructive channels that remain open to him.   Increased perspective, a capacity for detached appraisal, and calm evaluation of each step contribute to success in many social and business enterprises.

While indifference and apathy erode the personality structure, a certain degree of emotional detachment is helpful because it affords a more objective approach to life, with less ego-involvement and fewer deep conflicts and worries, than an emotional attitude can command.   With detachment, past experience and new information serve as guides toward success in various undertakings.   Routine activities also retain significance if they are attuned to the hierarchy of lasting values.   Gaining internal peace and character stability are probably the most appreciated achievements of a lifetime.   Significant steps can be made in this direction since boundaries for character growth are usually set by the individual.

People expect all persons in their late adulthood if not before to gain in moderation and balance, for an assertion of a scale of values. The natural tendency toward lowered emotionality as years increase assists in development of a preponderant reliance on rational judgment. Therefore, a higher consistency of character traits in middle adulthood is a frequent outcome of earlier oscillations and search for lasting values.

The mature person in his forties should conclude that life will not continue to be a supercharged carrousel; he will not be able to recover so effectively from mistakes caused by spontaneity and impetuosity. He ought to examine more carefully his motives and behavior, becoming more steadfast in his cherished principles and ideals. Before a person enters the late adult years, a certain degree of inflexibility is often attained. As a result, a general reliance on the habitual begins to expand into various behavior areas. This tends to promote the order and consistency of behavior and conduct by which late adult years are frequently marked.

QUESTIONS FOR REVIEW

1. At what age does middle adulthood begin? Describe the leading characteristics of this period.
2. Explain which factors contribute the most toward the socioeconomic standing of persons in middle adulthood.
3. How do vision and audition change in the early forties? Why?
4. Why do weight problems often start during middle adult years?
5. How do fathers and mothers react to the leaving of home of their adolescent and postadolescent children?
6. Describe reevaluation of the self-concept by middle-aged persons. What has this reevaluation to do with their aspirations?
7. What factors deter from attempts at recapturing youth in late middle adult years?
8. What are the means applicable for the reduction of physical and cognitive decline during middle age?
9. List several developmental tasks for middle-aged people.
10. Describe changes in several personality and character traits during middle adult years.

REFERENCES

I. Selected Reading

1. Duvall, Evelyn M. *Family development.* (2nd ed.) Philadelphia: Lippincott, 1962. A comprehensive and well-written work on the expanding and contracting families of the present; stresses dynamic interactions among family members and family tasks.

2. Neugarten, Bernice L., et al. *Personality in middle and late life: Empirical studies.* New York: Atherton Press, 1964.

3. Thomas, John L. *The family clinic.* Westminster, Md.: Newman, 1958. A collection of practical questions and answers on husband-wife-child relationships, authority, child education, and related topics.

II. Specific References

4. Bergler, E. *The revolt of the middle-aged man.* New York: Wyn, 1954.

5. Burkhart, Roy A. *The freedom to become yourself.* Englewood Cliffs, N. J.: Prentice-Hall, 1956.

6. Havighurst, Robert J. Social function of middle-aged people. *Genet. Psychol. Monogr.,* 1957, **56**, 297–375.

7. Lehman, H. C. *Age and achievement.* Princeton, N. J.: Princeton, 1953.

8. Wechsler, David. *The measurement and appraisal of adult intelligence.* (4th ed.) Baltimore: Williams & Wilkins, 1958.

9. *Vital statistics of the United States: 1964.* Vol. III. 1968.

LATE ADULT YEARS

The individual enters the phase of late adulthood when declines in health and performance are not sufficiently recovered and when large losses are compensated by lesser gains. The chief task of this period is the maintenance of the achieved level of performance and participation. Because of accumulated experience, most men are able to function at their highest vocational level. This often involves considerable responsibility and extensive self-application. The progress at this stage chiefly consists of economic gains, expanded civic participation, and character stabilization. Some progress in personality development also occurs as many traits become more salient and effectively expressed.

The intense responsibilities related to child guidance and education usually terminate at the onset of late maturity, if not before. Following the departure of the last grown-up children, women ordinarily gain additional leisure time. Menopause usually occurs when women enter this phase of life. Men move into a less noticeable climacteric at the age of about fifty-five when their sexual capacity declines and prostate enlargements become more frequent. The physical and cognitive deteriorations accelerate to a moderate rate. These changes are irreversible and the individual slowly moves into old age from about sixty to seventy, if not earlier. Late adulthood is practically a *terra incognita* for behavioral sciences. There is a dearth of psychological studies and any conclusions made about this age are very tentative.

MOTIVATIONAL CHANGES

A general decrease in drive is a major factor in changing the total motivational structure at this level of life. The variety of interests of adulthood tends to decrease moderately as some interests and concerns wane, while additional interests are not easily acquired. The functional decline varies with the function measured. Speed begins to fall off slightly at the age of thirty to thirty-five, while coordination remains fairly stable until about sixty-five. Health often declines in the early forties, and strength at about forty-five. The individual variation in general biological aging and in nodal points must always be taken into consideration. Because of genetic factors as well as diseases and accidents, metabolic changes and various declines may start much earlier, but also much later for some individuals [3, p. 14]. Frequently, moderate deterioration in sight and hearing presses for adjustment of many activities at this time.

Sexual decline

For males, the slight decline in sexual capacity during late adult years accelerates at about fifty-five and produces the climacteric. Changes in the male's gonads show little effect upon the body's functioning or the individual's personality. Men simply find their desires for sexual outlets decreasing, as sexual activity becomes less gratifying.

In females, the menopause lasts for a period of about two years, when natural cessation of the menstrual cycle takes place. Women traverse their change of life in the mid and late forties with little or no diminution of erotic excitability. For many of them, however, the menopause is quite upsetting. When the ovarian productivity declines and ceases, many of the body's biochemical controls are somewhat disordered. The accompanying powerful emotional reactions are often disturbing to the individual. During their menopause, some women are subject to marked excitability, hot flashes, sweating, dizziness, sensitivity to heat and cold, and other symptoms of a confusing nature. Usually they become more irritable, restless, or depressed than before. There is a noticeable decrease in self-control and feeling of adequacy. Adolescent maladjustments to self and others are often reactivated. These trying days may continue for several months or last for a few years. When menopause changes are gradual, there is time for a woman to get used to a new picture of herself. In addition to hormonal medication, forbearance and understanding from the woman's husband and older children are most helpful in assisting her through this phase of life.

Preceding the menopause a considerable number of women strongly desire to have another child or experience increased sexual preoccupation. Some enter into sex-related activities in order to "make up for lost time." Erotic excitability and decreased self-control permit vivid symptomatic behavior. Following the menopause, some women lose allergies that had bothered them for many years. Women's behavioral stability and self-reliance also rise and are maintained for about a decade. Excepting the phases of stress, neither sexual desire nor orgasm are lost. Affectional and sexual desires last for life, but there is a moderate decline in old age.

Occupational concerns

Motivational changes are also greatly affected by family changes when the last children leave home and become fully independent of their parents. This is especially true for the mother. It is difficult for most parents to accept the fact that their children do not need them, and that they like moving away. The parental home is now too large, yet the couple often hesitate to sell it and buy a house appropriate for their personal needs. Memories are cherished, and the large home, they maintain, will serve well for the visits of their grandchildren.

This "empty nest" situation presents a new opportunity for self-evaluation. The parent can no longer use chilren to excuse his failure to develop his intellect and personality through reading and adult education. Too many adults are out of touch with their former friends, relatives, and civic affairs. If they have not followed the developments of science they know less than the present day adolescents know. Vocationally, some are embarrassed in finding themselves in competition with young people whose life experiences are often less than half of their own but who are efficient contributors in their specialized fields. Expertness at late adulthood is a typical expectation, and one must measure up to it, if only to maintain his ego adequacy. Even at this late phase of life the decision to grow or to vegetate is a very real one. It is not easy to write off one's high aspirations for occupational superiority. A dearth of pertinent knowledge at this age is a frequent product of early neglect of additional growth and specialization. Late adulthood is not the proper time to turn completely to the utilization of past experience, though it is difficult to retain future orientation throughout this phase of life.

The vocational situation is often much worse for women who now become free and desire employment. If a woman completed her academic or professional studies over two decades ago, she usually cannot show vocational efficiency with the skills acquired so long ago. Too many subjects, methods, and techniques which are used now were unknown when she went to school. The current skills and techniques must be acquired for today's vocational practice. For a professional re-establishment she often needs refresher courses to pass state board examinations. Additional course work and training are indispensable for most professions and many trades. Throughout adulthood the desire to learn new subjects declines and an ever increasing number of persons reject additional training opportunities.

A former high school teacher may feel forced to take up another activity requiring no examination or additional course work. Yet such inappropriate changes are disturbing. While it is not good for women to stay at home without a sufficient amount of work, full-time employment often proves too much for many of them. Then too, at this level, the financial needs do not require such employment. The best answer lies in part-time or seasonal employment that leaves time for personal interests and concerns.

Financial disadvantages of full- or part-time female employment are probably nearing the point of no return. Statistics compiled by the President's Commission [11] showed that one in three of 1,900 companies has dual pay scales for equivalent office jobs in favor of men. In the U. S. one in ten families is headed by a woman, and "at least half of them are carrying responsibility for both earning the family's living and making the family's home." The Civil Rights Act, however, ends the legality of dual pay scales for men and women.

At this stage it is good for men and women to further mutually supportive relationships with their grown children's families and with aging parents. In cooperation with other individuals and organized groups, they can help promote civic, religious, and cultural activities. Religious values and practices often gain much meaning and carry reassurance of personal salvation as the certitude of an afterlife rises with advancing age.

DEVELOPMENTAL TASKS AND CONCERNS

Adjusting to family changes and preparing oneself for old age necessities are the tasks of this phase of life. Health, family, and one's role in life are probably the chief concerns marking this level of adulthood. The developmental tasks consist of (1) helping grown-up children, (2) gaining in leadership, and (3) adapting oneself to the accelerating process of aging. One can help grown-up children perfom their responsibilities by developing mutually supportive relationships with them, as well as with their close friends and relatives. It is possible and desirable to gain new friends through services and occasional entertainment of relatives and friends. Since gains in leadership are feasible at this age, by exercising cooperativeness with neighbors and by joining several organized groups, an older person may do much in promoting worthy civic objectives, and political and cultural values as well.

Keeping up with scientific, political, and cultural changes provide multidimensional interests for people of this age. They may investigate the arts, sciences, philosophy, religion, law, and politics. Consider scientific developments alone. As Robert Oppenheimer stresses, knowledge which used to double in millenia, then, in centuries, now doubles in a decade.   One either reads many articles disseminating scientific achievements or loses his touch with modern science.   With the current rate of discoveries and technological advances, not wisdom but ignorance accumulates, unless one keeps in step with the scientific developments of each year by reading daily papers and weekly magazines.   With regard to the world and man's relationship to it, while geography became much more complex with the rise of new independent nations, the world became much smaller through greatly improved transportation facilities.   A young person experiences little difficulty in accepting scientific achievements and the fast pace of the technological age, but an older person whose world image was formed during his teens and twenties, is baffled by the developments that confront him through television or direct experience.   To avoid this confused state an adult must keep pace with the changes in society.

Only by applying oneself to intellectual and cultural concerns, is one able to maintain a comparatively high level of cognitive functioning.   W. A. Owens' follow-up study [10] points to insignificant decline of mental powers during the fifth decade of life.   He tested a sample of 127 college freshmen in 1919. From this sample 96 subjects were retested in 1950 and tested again in 1961 with the Army Alpha in all three testings.   The findings show that the decade from age 50 through age 60 was one of relative constancy in mental ability, since the apparent downward trend was statistically insignificant.   The author makes one important implication: cognitive decline, like cognitive development, is conditioned to some extent by the nature and intensity or environmental stimulation.

SELF-CONCEPT AND CHARACTER

During the years of late adulthood, most persons consider themselves middle-aged and try to convince others that they are not old, still capable of doing the same things they did when they were young.   Gradually, however, they begin to feel differently as physical speed, vigor, concentration, and alertness decline.   Staying young and keeping as active as they were earlier is a difficult course to pursue.   Hence many persons after some unsuccessful trials reverse their attitude and deliberately slow down and search for additional comforts.   Very often this mode of living is the follow-up to an illness and the doctor's advice.   They begin studying what is good for them and what is not, and try conforming to the former and avoiding the latter.   Aging occurs against the desire or consent of the individual, and it is irreversible.   The direction of the total development cannot be changed significantly.

Despite accumulation of experience and dexterity, many older persons begin showing some difficulty in applying themselves.   This difficulty in part springs from the accelerated rate of the technological changes requiring acquisition of new abilities and skills. As we have mentioned, the readiness for learning new subjects subsides in later years. Then, too, significant declines in observational accuracy and speed add their share to the problems of the older person. At this age "to learn the new they often have to unlearn the old and that is twice as hard as learning without unlearning" [8]. Generally there is less transfer and more interference as age advances. While learning is always desirable, it is much easier to learn at fifteen or thirty than at fifty-five or sixty. Pressures to learn are dreaded by many middle-aged persons. They prefer to rely on experience.

Creativity and inventiveness subside greatly. Notable and very superior contributions to most fields of human creative endeavor are usually made by young adults. It has been found that as a rule the very superior contributions to the field of chemistry were made by scientists who were not more than twenty-six to thirty years of age. For practical inventions, physics, botany, and electronics the ages were thirty to thirty-four; for surgical techniques, genetics, and psychology thirty to thirty-nine; for medical discoveries, bacteriology, physiology, and pathology thirty-five to thirty-nine [8, p. 342].

The tendency of asserting oneself through consistency and rigidity is frequent but not very helpful in a culture of rapid successions and changes. General reliance on the past and specific inclination for applying the habitual earn fewer and fewer dividends. For ambitious persons, decreasing amount of success stirs up emotional currents which breed intensified problems of adjustment. Without some success tranquility cannot be preserved for any long period of time. Inability to gain additional competence is always difficult to accept. A significant number of poorly adjusted persons start using projection as a means of self-defense. It is easier to blame somebody else or to claim a "degeneration" of society than to accept one's inability to learn and profit from the new changes, so eagerly embraced by the young.

The exposure to the many influences and vicissitudes of life have produced deeply engraved traits and attitudes in the older person. Many traits carry a personal significance; there is ego involvement. The oscillations of adolescence and of the early forties produced some revisions to the early personality structure. Now in late adulthood the final stabilization and encrustation is taking place. Resistance to change is more often felt. Step by step the movement toward the rigidity of age gains in power and spectrum. The person is less willing to change his ways of acting and believing. His reliance on the past and the habitual is now more frequent and only rarely does he compromise with new fads, fashions, and renewals. He often rejects opportunities to acquire s'ills related to modern technological advancement. "Personality patterns are firmly established long before middle age and they tend to continue throughout adult life" [9].

The general future orientation of adolescence and early adulthood declines in intensity during this stage. Now, recollections from the past begin to play an increasing role and take more time. Hopes for future success succumb to the disappointments of the recent past. The need for continuous expansions deteriorates. Attitudes toward one's exceptionality, giftedness, and superior worth become toned-down as slides of realism are imposed upon one's thoughts and fantasies. Except in the cases of the most gifted and successful people, disruptions and uncertainties press toward maintenance rather than rise of one's occupation, status, or reputation.

The social-class differences in adjustment have been attested to by investigators of this field. Lower-class people often have poorly developed and unresourceful personalities which interfere with their adaptability from middle age through senescence. A majority of the middle-class people have fairly differentiated and adaptable motivational systems—an asset for the progressive modern society. Upper-class people have additional advantages springing from accumulated knowledge, civic leadership, and financial resources. Yet for people of all classes, there is a slowly rising difficulty in adjustment with the advancing age as ego integration slowly or moderately declines. David L. Gutmann's projective (TAT) study [7] of 287 white urban men and women aged forty and seventy shows that with advancing age there is increased difficulty in the management of inner life for both men and women. The active mastery style decreases with age, and the passive and magical mastery increases. Older men and women are more frequently prone to illogical thought and to motivated misperception of stimuli. Reduced self-confidence and satisfaction with life was also observed.

A recent stress and health study [6] of two elderly samples ($N=301$ and 258) disclosed that persons in their fifties and sixties who had experienced "stressful situations during the previous ten years tended to have poorer physical health than did comparable persons who had experienced less stress during this period." This was true for both a sample of severely disabled persons and a sample of non-disabled older persons living in the community. Apparently, a person cannot manage much stress effectively without detrimental effects to his health. This is consistent with the assumption of "wear and tear."

The late years of adulthood are marked by a lessening capacity for *self-repair*. This applies to bodily functioning and health, as well as to social relationships and cognitive processes. Any person can lose and lose much, but any gains are rare and do not come as easily as in early adulthood. One is pressed for conservation of his health, material goods, and of his personality gains. Attempts at self-improvement bring barely observable increments. At this age a person must prepare for even bigger slides downhill. This will be shown in the next two chapters on senescence.

QUESTIONS FOR REVIEW

1. Explain the basic motivational changes during the years of late adulthood.
2. Describe the effects of menopause and compare them to the "climacteric."
3. What are the effects on parents when all their children have left the home?
4. Describe the vocational problems for men and women in late adulthood.
5. List the developmental tasks of late adulthood and explain one of them.
6. Give reasons for the difficulty in keeping up with the scientific and cultural changes at this age.
7. Explain why learning of new subjects is difficult at this level of life.
8. Give some reasons for character stabilization and for the tendency toward conservation.
9. Explain the role of the past on personal adjustment during late adulthood.

REFERENCES

I. Selected Reading

1. Birren, James E. *The psychology of aging.* Englewood Cliffs, N. J.: Prentice-Hall, 1964. Biological, cognitive, and social changes; learning, personality, and pathology—all are subjects of this fairly comprehensive presentation.

2. Neugarten, Bernice L., et al. *Personality in middle and late life: Empirical studies.* New York: Atherton Press, 1964. Personality patterns of adulthood and later phases, including ego functions and sex roles.

II. Specific References

3. Anderson, John E. Psychological research on changes and transformations during development and aging. In J. E. Birren (Ed.), *Relations of development and aging.* Springfield, Ill.: Charles C Thomas, 1964. Chap. 2, pp. 11–28.

4. Bayley, Nancy, and M. H. Olden. The maintenance of intellectual ability in gifted adults. *J. Gerontol.,* 1955, **10**, 91–107.

5. Bossard, James H. S., and Eleanor S. Boll. Marital unhappiness in the life cycle. *Marriage Fam. Living,* 1955, **17**, 10–14.

6. Gray, Robert M., J. M. Baker, J. P. Kesler, and W. R. E. Newman. Stress and health in later maturity. *J. Gerontol.,* 1965, **20**, 65–68.

7. Gutmann, David L. An exploration of ego configurations in middle and late life. In Bernice L. Neugarten et al., *Personality in middle and late life: Empirical studies* (see **2** above). Chap. 6, pp. 114–148.

8. Lehman, Harvey C. *Age and achievement.* Princeton, N. J.: Princeton, 1953.

9. Peck, Robert E., and Howard Berkowitz. Personality and adjustment in middle age. In Bernice L. Neugarten et al., *Personality in middle and late life: Empirical studies* (see **2** above). Chap. 2, pp. 15–43.

10. Owens, W. A. Age and mental abilities: A second adult follow-up. *J. educ. Psychol.,* 1966, **57**, 311–325.

11. President's Commission on the Status of Women. *American women.* 1963.

Part 9
Late Phases of Life

This period is characterized more by declines than by developments. However, the present trend toward increased life expectancy permits a large number of individuals to reach late adult years and to grow old. As a result, the percentage of older people in the population is steadily increasing. The following two chapters will consider the deterioration of various abilities and the contingent limitation of activities which mark senescence.

The theory of *disengagement* [8, 13] holds that aging is accompanied by a mutual withdrawal on the part of both the senescent and others in the social system to which he belongs. This "disengagement," initiated either by the individual himself or by others, results in social distance. For many individuals beyond fifty, disengagement adequately characterizes the modal tendency in the developmental process [16]. The commonsense theory of *activity* stresses the need to maintain vocational and recreational interests in order to make the individual's later years pleasant and productive. As the problems of adjustment multiply for the aging person and his particular needs intensify, his ingenuity, humor, and wisdom will often be called into play to make the final stage of life balanced and gratifying.

BIOLOGICAL
AND COGNITIVE CHANGES

As the later years of life approach, there is a marked decline in the physical qualities of the individual. The onset and rate of deterioration varies, however, from one organic system to another and from one person to another. The sequence depends upon many factors, including hereditary endowment and specific past experiences, such as diet and exercise, illnesses and injuries. The kind of life that has been lived determines the pattern of aging. The process of aging is also related to personal and social adjustment during the years of adulthood. Satisfactory adjustment in adulthood promotes the integration of feelings of self-fulfillment that aid in maintaining higher activity and achievement levels during middle age.

The exact time of the onset of old age is difficult to specify. Some people reveal noticeable changes in traits as early as forty; others still appear "young" at seventy. Just as no single criterion can be employed to delineate adolescence and adulthood, no decisive criterion can be given for the onset of old age. Individual variation is very great within each community and nation. Generally the mentally deficient, those with borderline deficiency, and physically handicapped individuals deteriorate early, and often at a fast rate. At the age of thirty or even earlier, defectives begin to exhibit signs of old age.

Their life expectancy is very short.   On the other hand, many well-endowed persons seem to be capable of resisting accelerated decline until seventy and eighty.   Although the spry senior may be in much better physical condition than persons who are several years younger, he is not as strong or vigorous as he was earlier, though he still manages to maintain a youthful attitude. The average person takes the middle ground.   He begins to deteriorate earlier than the well-endowed person, yet his rate of decline is moderate.   Ultimately each individual has his own rate and pattern of aging, similar to many others yet always distinct in some traits and features [6].   Empirical studies [14, 15] suggest that approximately half of the individuals between sixty and seventy identify themselves as middle-aged rather than old.   Identity crisis is apparently a part of growing old.

DISTINGUISHING SENESCENCE AND SENILITY

A distinction between senescence and senility may be clarified at this point. Senescence is a period of life somewhat arbitrarily identified by the chronological age of a person.   The age of sixty-five or seventy is now held as the point introducing this last stage of life.   The accelerated rate of deterioration is a more definite criterion.   Retirement also points to the beginning of this phase of life.   Marked deterioration of organic systems, cognitive powers, or of acquired skills is not yet implied.   Preservation of many adult qualities and traits is frequent.   Lessened activity and poorer application are usually implied.

Senility, on the other hand, although closely allied to senescence, implies a substantial loss.   The retention of earlier adult powers and characteristics is slight.   Senility is closely associated with a considerable loss of physical and cognitive functioning, whether in old age or prematurely.   Impairments of brain tissues and motor coordination, high irritability, considerable loss of memory, orientation, and self-control are typical signs of senility rather than old age.   A regression to mere biological and emotional need satisfaction is frequent.   Senility is fairly common in old age.   Severe cerebral arteriosclerosis will result in senility symptoms, but frequently senility appears because of psychological rather than organic factors.

Generally the period of old age is one of widespread and sometimes drastic change.   Possibly only the years of early adolescence offer a comparable challenge to the individual.   As in adolescence, the late years of life are characterized by physical, social, and emotional upheavals.   But, as in the early years, proper preparation for such changes can prevent them from being too stressful and too disruptive.   Indeed, the late years can be ones of considerable equanimity and happiness.

As a person notices creaking joints, increasing weakness of sense organs, a decrease in usual energy and speed, fast change in quantity and color of hair and teeth, and distinct decline in sexual potency, all combined in varying degrees, he becomes very aware of his own aging. He begins to think about the role of an elder and makes some adjustments to it. Social expectation and cultural pressure act together, often forcing a new mode of life upon him before the personal need exists or the declining powers demand.

The theory of *disengagement*, originated by Elaine Cumming and her associates [7], is apparently the first fairly well elaborated psychosocial interpretation of the elements of aging. Originally this theory was based on the following three hypothetical steps: (1) rate of interaction and variety of interaction lessen with age, (2) changes in amount, and variety, of interaction are accompanied by concomitant changes in perception of the size of the life space, and (3) a change in the quality of interaction accompanies decrease in the social life space, from absorption in others to absorption in self, and from evaluative to carefree. The empirical data of the interviews, based on 211 fifty- to ninety-year-old subjects, suggest that disengagement starts during the sixth decade with a shift in self-perception accompanied by a constriction in the variety of interactions with others [7, pp. 25–34]. An elaborate statement of the disengagement theory may be found in Elaine Cumming and W. E. Henry's *Growing old* [8, pp. 210–218].

BIOLOGICAL AGING

Fundamentally, biological aging is marked by a lower metabolic rate, which slows down energy exchange within the organism. Hence, its resources for behavioral self-expression are gradually curtailed. Energy, when overused, is not fully recovered. The person impairs powers by overactive exertion or prolonged activity. Genetic damage results from lessened ability for cell division. For example, brain and heart muscle cells show an increased amount of insoluble pigments. The rise of insoluble compounds interferes with vital cell functioning. Neurons are very highly differentiated, and there is no further mitotic division after the early years of life [12]. There is a moderately accelerating decrease of brain weight. The general health situation becomes precarious, and chronic diseases are more frequent and severe in the older age group. Heart, kidney, bile, genitourinary disturbances and other ailments are more frequent than in earlier years. Injuries and wounds heal at a much slower rate, and sense receptivity becomes much less efficient. Difficulties with vision and hearing are frequent and severe.

The decline in cellular functioning depends on the extent of damage to the nucleic acids of the chromosomes. With injuries to the deoxyribonucleic acids (DNA) defective messenger molecules (ribonucleic acids, RNA) are produced that are unable to synthetize the enzymes for maintaining certain basic cell functions, especially at the time of mitosis [2, p. 52]. In many cases the chemical *oncogens* (initiators) form simplified or neoplastic cells, including neoplasms (benign and malignant tumors) [20]. Any accumulation of deleterious mutations accelerates aging [9]. Other causes of aging include somatic mutation and chromosomal aberration [22].

During the late adult years, biological aging is a gradual debilitating process. It is also a process that cannot be stopped or reversed. Practically all bodily systems deteriorate in both their structural and functional efficiency. Functional abilities chiefly depend upon the circulatory system, which supplies the total organism with oxygen, fluids, and nutrition. The walls of blood vessels—arteries, veins, and capillaries alike—harden and narrow as adult age advances. This, in turn, interferes with the optimal circulation of the blood. The hardening of the capillaries disturbs the supply of nutrients to various bodily systems and organs, including the central nervous system. Consequently, this starts gradual muscle and tissue atrophy, which, in turn, produces a loss in weight, immunity, and strength among some very vital organs, such as the brain, lungs, and heart. When the heart loses weight, the blood pressure mounts. At a certain phase of this process a physiological insufficiency of the heart results.

Physical work or exercise easily strains the circulatory system. Climbing stairs increases the heartbeat and oxygen demand considerably. Any continuation of such action will disturb the heart and general organic equilibrium. While the amount of oxygen used is an indication of bodily strength, a person in late adulthood soon demands more frequent periods of rest that decreases oxygen exchange. There is a lessened overall utilization of oxygen with advancing years. The lung capacity is only about one-half of what it originally was from about twenty-five to thirty.

A smaller calorie intake is another sign of organismic aging and points to a loss in work capacity. Clinical experience indicates that biological aging can be slowed down by well-controlled athletic activities. Continuing moderate and regular physical exercise throughout the years of adulthood slows down the degenerative processes and helps to preserve organic structures and physical welfare for several years longer than is normal and also raises life expectancy appreciably. Leisurely cycling or walking, if practiced during late adult years, may be continued into old age.

Sensorimotor coordination gradually becomes less balanced. Reaction time increases, some movements become awkward; speed and gracefulness, when necessary, are difficult to attempt, if possible at all. Therefore, accident proneness increases. Especially among women, the loss of previous poise and attractiveness is evident.

Every physical impairment or limitation produces notable changes in the personality of the individual. Some of these modifications are a direct result of physiological functioning, for example, the memory losses following certain arterial disturbances.   Other psychological alterations, however, represent somewhat remote aftereffects of physical malfunctioning.

It is noteworthy that a person functions, not in terms of the strongest systems of his organism, but in terms of the weakest links in his bodily structure.   Usually one vital organ or system "wears out" early in comparison to other physiological systems.   Consequently, illness or even death results from such an impairment.   Forces maintaining life are only as strong as their weakest vital component.   Whenever a vital link "breaks," the resulting stress leads to death.   When an old person engages in strenuous exercise of any kind, he has to take this principle into consideration [21, pp. 274–276 and 299–301].

One major change resulting from physical impairment is the gradual restriction of the individual's environment.   In infancy and childhood, a major contribution to psychological development was the increasing ability to go beyond the immediate home surroundings.   Late in life, the trend is typically reversed.   Decline in vision reduces the degree to which a person can depend upon the written word for knowledge of the outside world.   Auditory loss likewise reduces the effectiveness of verbal communication, especially in a group situation.   Losses of motor strength and coordination similarly reduce the individual's ability to travel from place to place.   Even with an automobile, which so greatly facilitates contact with distant persons and places, a gradual restriction is present.   Visual and orientation deficiencies, increased reaction time, reduced coordination, and liability to intense fatigue, all contribute to a loss of mobility and its serious consequences for personal adjustment.

With old age many physiological deteriorations occur.   Loss of hair and change of its color to white, folding of the facial skin, "old-age spread," and the "dowager's hump" are some of the easily observed senescent features. Accumulation of fat, especially in the abdominal region, and a lowered position of the head are also related to aging.   Affliction by disease speeds up, changing appearance beyond the biological schedule.   This also depends on the earlier patterns of living and adjustment to stressful situations and events during adolescence and adulthood [12].

DECLINE OF COGNITIVE ABILITIES

When memory declines at a noticeable rate, it is often replaced at least in part by imagination, a condition that leads to many confabulations (the joining of separate events as one), especially in attempts to report recent happenings.   Memory for events in early life is retained fairly well.   This makes a person refer frequently to remote rather than immediate experiences.   Failing memory and a decrease in perspective are two key factors influencing his general orientation and perception of time and space. Time appears to pass at a much faster rate than before, and the old person has difficulties in adjusting to consequent inevitable changes. As he forgets the names of streets, buildings, and their appearance, and loses track of his whereabouts, he sometimes experiences estrangement even in familiar surroundings.

Despite his accumulation of experience, an old person gets lower scores on intelligence tests than before, indicating a decline of his higher functions and performance. In order to preserve IQ constancy, computation is usually statistically adjusted to the normal rate of decline of mental abilities in the later years of life. With his narrowing alertness it is rare for an old person to accept readily any new ideas or ventures. Making choices becomes difficult. Creativity, if it has developed and been utilized, also declines, probably at about the same rate as cognitive abilities.

In vocational activity, an old person usually experiences a loss in efficiency. By the early sixties, many individuals begin to show some inadequacies in performing their accustomed work, and they become tired more quickly than before. Retirement, set arbitrarily at a particular age, for example, at sixty-five, is usually unfair to individuals who are still capable of performing their job well. Besides a feeling that he is not needed, a lack of proper recreational facilities for the retired also elicits feelings of inadequacy and depression. If the retiree has no outlet for exercising his powers and abilities, the resulting feeling of uselessness is detrimental to his security and status. The psychological effects of "empty time" are damaging to many but especially to those who lack a variety of interests and hobbies to substitute for employment.

Although the amplitude of emotional experience and the control over feelings and emotions decrease to a great extent, emotional sensitivity does not. As a result, affective irritability rises somewhat and emotionally toned discontentment is frequent. Tendencies to rationalize and to blame others by projection are two frequent means of self-defense.

Decreased engagement in social activities is often due to less satisfaction from such interaction. Difficulty in attending to a conversation and lack of information concerning current events are two factors contributing to the decline in interpersonal communication.

When a wholesome pattern of living and adjustment has been established and practiced, the aging process proceeds smoothly with little distress and anxiety. A person is often ready to accept aging and to make the best possible adjustments to it. If, on the other hand, emotional upsets have been frequent and defense mechanisms, such as projection and rationalization have been used intensely, difficulties usually become magnified in the later years of senescence. Earlier disguised attitudes of selfishness and superiority tend to become more marked, and are frequently exhibited by old people. A desire to be honored by others is a form of self-aggrandizement that now appears with considerable vividness. A tendency to boast over past accomplishments is common.

Persons who do not develop healthy control and sublimation within the earlier years of adulthood are likely to crave for oral gratifications with aging. Since affectional needs are less often satisfied at this age, compensation by excessive eating and drinking is frequent. Constant complaining about younger relatives or their health and finding faults in others are frequent means of compensating. These problems make this stage of life appear as another period of crisis, comparable to puberty. In a significant number of cases, this turning point in life is accompanied by psychosomatic disturbances and, to a lesser extent, by senile psychotic outbreaks.

The frequent tendency to emphasize minor injuries and symptoms seems to serve several purposes: it provides an excuse to avoid unpleasant obligations, it justifies egocentric demands, and it obtains the concern and attention of others. The tendency to hold on to life somewhat corrects this despairing situation. Reactionary and conservative attitudes come into prominence as psychological flexibility and a readiness to experiment disappear. Unfavorable experiences of the past make many older persons tenaciously thoughtful and cautious. Anxiety, worry, and sensitivity to dangers greatly inhibit an old person and promote withdrawal from challenging activities [19, pp. 62–64].

With old age there is also a substantial increase in leisure time. When children marry and leave parents and, especially, when retirement comes, the remaining energy has to be directed toward previously neglected hobbies and new activities. Neglected potentials may now be used. Old age is an appropriate time for developing artistic and intellectual interests. Writing, drawing, painting, and a variety of crafts are good ways to engage energy and obtain enjoyment. Church activities, charity drives, and civic projects are usually gratifying engagements at this age. Active participation in some individual and group activities is of crucial psychological importance for maintaining self-esteem and a sense of belonging. It is advantageous for the old person to have opportunities for serving or assisting others [4].

Lifelong emotional reaction patterns, attitudes, and sentiments related to values and various spheres of living influence the kind of emotional disturbance to which one is prone during this phase of life. Adjustment difficulties at the adult level tend to intensify significantly late in life [14].

Most fundamental needs are felt more intensely now than earlier. Recognition and respect, affection and achievement, security and self-esteem are all strongly sought by an old person. Most of them experience difficulties in gaining gratification of these needs. Unduly high demands on the part of old people not infrequently cause friction in social relations.

Evelyn M. Duvall [10, p. 441] attributes the following developmental tasks to aging families: (1) finding a satisfactory home for the late adult years, (2) adjusting to retirement income, (3) establishing comfortable household routines, (4) nurturing each other as husband and wife, (5) facing bereavement and widowhood, (6) maintaining contact with children and grandchildren, (7) caring for elderly relatives, (8) keeping an interest in people outside the family, and (9) finding meaning in life.

PERSONALITY CHANGES

Changes in personality structure and organization encompass practically all their dimensions in senescence. The usual decrease in motivational strength is linked with a narrowing range of interests and activities. Lesser gratifications result from poorer performance in most fields of endeavor. As powers decline, some interests, habits, and attitudes disintegrate. The general decrease in flexibility and ability to learn is directly proportional to an increase in rigidity and constriction. Many self-expressive activities, including speech and conversational skills, begin to decline. Ruminating over earlier and more satisfactory experiences preoccupies the old person and influences his conversation with others. Repetitiousness and habituation to routine activities increase at a considerable rate.

Success in preserving integration of personality and its operative traits shows widespread individual differences related to former personality development. Individuals who acquired an attitude marked by a desire to learn whenever opportunities existed now earn high dividends. Likewise, those who faced reality in all its dimensions throughout the stages of development, and in adulthood acquired the needed reservoir of abilities, interests, and skills, are able to cope with emerging problems and novel situations. Their functional level of self-expression is consistent with their endowments and, as a result, many gratifying experiences of self-actualization result. Such experiences enhance the ego and facilitate readjustment to the old-age status. Lacking conflicts and disillusionments, such individuals preserve personality integration during their advancing years.

Many others, because of unfavorable parental and social influences or a lack of personal effort, acquired little knowledge of the complex art of modern living. They failed to develop their endowments and, internally, remained in either an acute or a dormant conflict situation. In such cases, personality disintegration takes hold early and often leads to pervasive results. Early senility is a frequent result, appearing in later years of adulthood or early in old age. Many such individuals finish their lives in mental and similar institutions.

Mental health cannot be substantially improved during the late stages of life. Experts in psychotherapy find a poor response to counseling and psychotherapy after approximately forty-five years of age.   Emotional disorders, hypochondriasis, and a general senile dementia are frequent.   Apparently many individuals failed to deal successfully with moderate and severe deprivations, conflicts, and problems during their twenties and thirties and became predisposed to psychosomatic and mental disorders.

Many sixty-year-olds, for example, see their environment as complex and dangerous, and there follows a movement from outer-world to inner-world orientation and preoccupation with self.   A shrinking of the life space and avoidance responses develop [18].   Turning of all cathexes inward is taking place, and the person moves away from both old and new engagements [8, pp. 222–226].

QUESTIONS FOR REVIEW

1. Explain the differences between senescence and senility.
2. Give some reasons for biological aging and indicate the more conspicuous signs of it.
3. Explain the need for regulation of physical exercise as one grows old.
4. Present Selye's theory of causes of stress and death.
5. Give some reasons for decline of cognitive functions.
6. Why does the increase in leisure time occur suddenly?   Suggest proper activities for utilizing this time.
7. Why is there much redundancy in speech and habitual activity during old age?
8. On what factors does adjustment during old age depend?   Analyze the significance of one of these factors in the light of a particular experiential background.
9. How do elderly persons tend to interpret their environment?

REFERENCES

I. Selected Reading

1. Anderson, John E.   (Ed.).   Psychological aspects of aging.   Washington: American Psychological Association, 1956.   Research possibilities analyzed under the auspices of the Committee on Research, Division of Maturity and Old Age, American Psychological Association, in Bethesda, Md., April 24–27, 1955.

2. Birren, James E.   The psychology of aging.   Englewood Cliffs, N. J.: Prentice-Hall, 1964.   A study of biological, social, and cognitive changes, including the senses, learning, pathology, and personality.

3. Burgess, Ernest W.   Aging in Western societies.   Chicago: University of Chicago Press, 1960.   Consists of three parts: various aspects of aging in several countries (income and retirement, housing and family, health and research); case histories; and selected statistical tables.

4. Donahue, Wilma, et al. (Eds.). *Free time: Challenge to later maturity.* Ann Arbor, Mich.: University of Michigan Press, 1958. A collection of papers by twelve authors, dealing chiefly with old-age adjustment and uses of free time.

5. Drake, J. T. *The aged in American society.* New York: Ronald, 1958. A comprehensive study of the status and implications of old age.

6. Welford, A. T. *Aging and human skill.* New York: Oxford, 1958. The final report of the Nuffield Unit for Research into Problems of Aging, which was active in Cambridge, 1946–1956. An appraisal of various achievements from early adulthood to the seventies.

II. Specific References

7. Cumming, Elaine, L. R. Dean, and D. S. Newell. Disengagement, a tentative theory of aging. *Sociometry,* 1960, **23,** 23–35.

8. Cumming, Elaine, and William E. Henry. *Growing old: The process of disengagement.* New York: Basic Books, 1961.

9. Curtis, H. J. Biological mechanisms underlying the aging process. *Science,* 1963, **141,** 686–694.

10. Duvall, Evelyn M. *Family development.* (2nd ed.) Philadelphia: Lippincott, 1962.

11. Frank, Lawrence K. Gerontology. *J. Gerontol.,* 1946, **1,** 1–12.

12. Gilbert, Jeanne G. *Understanding old age.* New York: Ronald, 1952.

13. Henry, William E. Engagement and disengagement: Toward a theory of adult development. In R. Kastenbaum (Ed.), *The psychobiology of aging.* New York: Springer Publishing, 1965. Pp. 19–35.

14. Kastenbaum, Robert, and Nancy Burkee. Elderly people view old age. In R. Kastenbaum (Ed.), *New thoughts on old age.* New York: Springer Publishing, 1964. Pp. 250–262.

15. Kutner, B., et al. *Five hundred over sixty.* New York: Russell Sage Foundation, 1956.

16. Maddox, George L., Jr. Disengagement theory: A critical evaluation. *Gerontologist,* 1964, **4,** 80–82.

17. Montague, M. F. A. *Direction of human development.* New York: Harper & Row, 1955.

18. Neugarten, Bernice L. Personality changes in the aged. *Cath. Psychol. Rec.,* 1965, **3,** 9–17.

19. Pollak, Otto, and Glen Heathers. *Social adjustment in old age.* Social Science Research Council, Bulletin No. 59, New York, 1948.

20. Rous, Peyton. The challenge to man of the neoplastic cell. *Science,* 1967, **157,** 24–28.

21. Selye, Hans. *The stress of life.* New York: McGraw-Hill, 1956.

22. Sinex, F. Marott. Genetic mechanisms of aging. *J. Gerontol.,* 1966, **21,** 340–346.

THE SENESCENT'S
SELF-CONCEPT,
NEEDS, AND PROBLEMS

With the increasing physical and cognitive decline characteristic of the late years of life, certain personality modifications seem to be inevitable. The aging person's self-concept usually undergoes some change. Personal needs and suitable means for satisfying them are modified. In addition, the individual's role in society is altered. With all this, new and varied adjustments and problems are bound to occur. This is a period when the individual is called upon to utilize resources he has developed during the preceding decades. Moreover, it is a period during which the assistance and understanding of society is greatly needed.

HEALTH AND ILLNESS

As indicated in the previous chapter, the later years of life are characterized by a general decline of the biological systems of the organism. Despite the fact that wide individual differences in the rate and amount of deterioration exist, some physical impairment is inevitable. Visual, auditory, and other sensory defects become increasingly prevalent and incapacitating. Reaction time, strength, and endurance are all affected. Arthritis in its various forms afflicts many persons. The cardiac reserve is lowered. This can be seen in the number of illnesses and accidents, together with a lowered recuperative power, as the organism is approaching illness and death. These symptoms of aging are psychologically significant not only in themselves but also in the effect they have upon the personality and behavior of the individual. If health is defined as "a state of complete physical, mental, and social well-being and not merely the absence of disease or infirmity" [15], senescents are un-healthy, even though many have no symptomatic evidence of illness over varying periods of time.

The dependence of the cognitive and emotional functions upon the integrity of the neurological and chemical systems of the body is well established. Any gross change in these systems as a result of disease or injury is usually re-flected in the behavior deterioration of the individual. Equally important, however, are the personality changes that reflect the individual's reaction to his physical condition. Such somatopsychological changes, as Barker and his collaborators [4] have termed them, are often just as significant as those biologically induced. Moreover, such changes sometimes occur even in the absence of serious or disabling physical changes.

With the rise of physical and psychosomatic symptoms the individual's con-cept of himself undergoes some restructuring. Just as the bodily changes occurring with the onset of puberty forced the adolescent to revise his view of himself, so too the old person alters the picture he has of himself to a certain extent. While his self-image may remain relatively intact, his abilities do not. Sooner or later he must accept the fact that he is no longer the robust, healthy individual he was in earlier years. No longer is he capable of the many activities that were previously part of his daily living. Increasingly he must protect his general well-being. Even if he is still in relatively good health, a reassessment of declining abilities and rising limitations, as well as the awareness of potential dangers, seems unavoidable as he sees his friends and peers beset by physical ailments, which in many cases result in death. He must adjust his exercise, diet, reading, and general participation as his physical and cognitive powers decline.

Some reorganization of the self-concept is both normal and desirable. Since man's behavior is largely a reflection of how he perceives himself in relation to his surroundings and other people, it is imperative that he have a realistic view of himself. The individual who refuses to accept the fact that he has new limitations is obviously rejecting reality. To the extent that his concept of himself fails to correspond to his own condition, he will be inade-quate. Similar problems arise, of course, in the case of the individual who exaggerates the physical changes he perceives in himself—the person who regards himself as completely limited, inadequate, and dependent upon others.

In addition to the rather direct impact that physiological changes have on the personality of the individual, be he young or old, other effects also are observed. One subtle effect is the gradual restriction of exciting and pleasant experiences and intellectual stimulation. In childhood, the acquisition of motility, spoken language, and reading skills meant the enlargement of the child's psychological world. More and more he was able to reach beyond his immediate environment and experience many new events. As new restrictions are imposed upon the individual by physical limitations, the world of personal experiences shrinks. Visual difficulties frequently limit the time a person can spend in acquiring new ideas through the written word. Such deficiencies also tend to reduce the individual's freedom to leave his immediate environment. Hearing defects, especially if severe or uncorrected, cut the person off from many personal contacts and the information and stimulation they ordinarily provide. Motor disabilities, even if only the lack of sustained endurance, reduce the opportunities for experiences and social interaction outside the immediate home environment.

MAINTAINING A VARIETY OF INTERESTS

With the gradual restriction of activities and the consequent limitation of intellectual, emotional, and social stimulation, it becomes increasingly essential that the individual maintain a wide variety of wholesome interests. There is, of course, no specific approach or pattern that may be considered as the best approach, but the need for some genuine sources of activity and amusement is a necessity. The present adjustment of the individual is dependent upon past attitudes and habits, as is revealed in the breadth of interests of the older person. Activities that have long held his attention typically tend to be continued. This is particularly true when such interests do not conflict with specific physical or social limitations. Because of the increasing limitation of activities in the later years and the consequent conflict between interests and abilities, it is imperative that interests be extensive in range. In line with the theory that activity is beneficial, Erich Fromm [6] urged the older person to become more responsive to the world around him. He should learn to re-create through his genuine interest in the world. Fromm also predicted that perhaps fifty years from now, old age will be any age above forty because nobody will have to work after that age.

Although many elderly persons acquire new and rewarding interests, the task of doing so becomes increasingly difficult with the passage of time. For one thing, the opportunity for adequately testing new areas gradually is restricted. Entirely new, truly satisfying interests characteristically require a considerable time for development. Consequently, occasional or sporadic contact with areas of potential interest is generally of little value. Moreover, because of increasing difficulty in coping with totally new and novel situations, untried areas of interest are not so likely to be sampled.   One again, therefore, is faced with the conclusion that the years prior to old age are the time during which genuine interests and areas of satisfaction should be developed. Even more essential is the formation of healthy attitudes regarding these interests.   All is not lost if a certain activity is restricted; related or new areas can provide sources of personal satisfaction.   With such a background, the individual is prepared for whatever the future may bring.   Even should certain sources of personal reward later be denied the person, he has the needed ability to face the loss and turn to other areas.   He thereby is prepared to enrich and enjoy life rather than lapse into a state of self-pity or continuous reminiscence, either of which is unrewarding and leads to stagnation and deterioration of the entire adjustment.

INTELLECTUAL AND RELIGIOUS CONCERNS

The pattern of decline prevalent during senescence occurs with the intellectual activities as well.   Without the intellectual stimulation provided by extensive and varied communication with the outside world, the individual is forced more and more to rely upon what he has learned previously.   This limiting of experience and the decreasing sharpness in memory for new and novel concepts readily account for much of the constriction and rigidity of intellectual activities so frequently associated with old age.   Tendencies to reminisce and relive the past likewise become understandable.   The decline of cognitive capacity reported in the later years may well reflect in part the absence of stimulation.   It is clear that the lack of exercise of any capacity or system, bodily or mental, ultimately leads to its deterioration.

Because of the lack of varied intellectual stimulation, the excessive amount of leisure time, and the awareness of bodily changes heralding the eventual approach of death, the individual typically is impelled toward further self-examination.   Was it all really worthwhile?   Why were there so many mistakes?   By such questions the individual is guided toward a reappraisal of his philosophy of life.   Many get interested in personal memoirs; some attempt writing them.

In keeping with his concern for a philosophy of life and a workable hierarchy of values is the individual's concern with religion.   In seeking a permanent system of values and resolutions of the fears and vicissitudes of life, it is only natural that he should examine his ideological and religious commitment.   This growing interest in religion is vividly illustrated by the finding of Ruth Cavan and her colleagues [5].   Whereas only 71 percent of the men questioned in their sixties reported a certainty of afterlife, 81 percent of those in their late eighties reported this conviction.   Interestingly, 83 percent of the younger women revealed a certainty of afterlife; 90 percent of the older group did so. Moreover, 100 percent of both men and women who were ninety years and older held to an afterlife. C. T. O'Reilly [12] studied a Chicago working-class community's population of persons over sixty-five. His sample included 6.5 percent of the 4,511. His results showed an increase in religious activity among older people. However, those who were lonely or unhappy did not turn to religion more than other people. A major survey [9] of religious studies concluded that interest in and concern about religion increases even into extreme old age, and that religious attitudes and feelings intensify during senescence, yet ritualistic behavior outside the home tends to diminish.

SOCIAL NEEDS

Throughout his entire life span, the individual lives in a social environment. He depends upon his fellowmen not so much for physical support, as for psychological support, affection, and stimulation. This dependence fails to diminish during the later years of life. In fact, in many respects it frequently tends to increase. With old age, however, the total interaction of the senescent with the kin and community to which he belongs tends to decrease significantly. The person is less able to maintain achieved roles and positions. There are practically no significant roles at this age that the senescent can fill. He usually lives apart and away from his children and grandchildren. He is often removed from companions of younger days. As a rule, his social isolation is greater than at any other period of life.

Yet, by means of social intercourse, the individual may be provided with a wealth of experience and manifold stimulation. Just as the child's boundaries of experience were vastly extended by meeting many youngsters in the school situation, so the elderly person's boundaries are partially determined by the scope of his personal contacts. New ideas, interests, and attitudes are needed, and these stimuli can be compensated for by less personal substitutes, such as reading, radio, and television only to a limited extent. The opportunity, however, for the individual to express and test his own ideas, beliefs, and attitudes is not provided by such media. Nothing less than direct personal contact will suffice. It is essential that the individual communicate his ideas and attitudes, that he test them in the light of others' reactions. Personal contact also is necessary for the stimulation of feelings and emotions. With the absence of normal social interaction, either a gradual impoverishment of affectivity or inappropriateness of reactions may be expected.

The safeguarding of cognitive and affective processes is by no means the only function of social communication. The fundamental needs of recognition, love, belonging, and status depend upon interaction with others for their satisfaction. Frustration of these basic needs quite naturally leads to unhappiness, and is accompanied by use of a defense mechanism whenever achievement of goals is thwarted, for example, aggression, withdrawal, or regression.   Just as the adolescent, upon viewing the gross changes of his own bodily and cognitive structure, needed the reassurance of his peers and a feeling of dialogue with them, so does the senescent who witnesses in himself the widespread losses of advancing age.   Contact with others his own age also helps the aging person accept gracefully his decline in physical and mental powers.

SOCIETY AND THE SENESCENT

In addition to the adjustments required of the senescent as a more or less direct result of the aging process, certain problems arise from his changing role in society.   Some of these are related to his family and immediate friends, some to the community and society in general.   Whereas earlier in life the individual was the head of the household, helping to shape the lives of his children and others younger than himself, in his declining years this role is lost.   Instead, frequently the roles of parents and children are reversed to such a point that the parents are dependent upon the children to a considerable extent.   Such reversal cannot help but alter the individual's concept of himself and present new problems of adjustment.   Should he regard himself as a nuisance or a burden?   How much personal freedom should he relinquish?   A multitude of questions naturally arise for the old person.   His happiness and that of those about him depend upon the answers he receives to these questions.

Intimately related to this entire problem area is the attitude of the younger members of the family.   Is the senescent to be regarded as a liability, for example, or, at best, an ever-available baby-sitter?   Or is he someone who needs constant care and protection even to the point of being treated much like a child?   Should he be sent to a home for the aged or perhaps even to a mental institution?   Any behavior that depreciates the dignity and self-assurance of the individual naturally produces serious adjustment problems for him.   Old people want to be close to their families and yet maintain their independence from them.

The general attitude of American society toward the senescent is improving. The growing concern over the older population has brought about charitable and legislative action for their welfare.   This is marked by provisions for proper housing of the elderly in many communities, by rising social security benefits, by the pension plans of many companies, and by improvements in general medical care provisions.   By furnishing the sheer necessities for him, the senescent can be independent of his offspring.   There is still a need to utilize the services and contributions of senior citizens for the benefit of society at large. Sidney L. Pressey and Alice D. Pressey's "inside" study [13] of four modes of life in old age suggests many improvements to the present situation, especially through the increased participation in senescent groups and service to other old people of the competent senescents capable of such activity. Despite rising rigidity, old people are aware of their social environment and remain willing to contribute even as age advances.

CONTRIBUTING TO THE COMMUNITY

During preceding decades the elderly person was a full participant in the civic and economic life of the community. He bore full responsibility for his own welfare as well as that of others and along with such responsibility enjoyed corresponding privileges and status. With retirement and increasing physical limitations, however, this role changes, even to the point where the individual is financially dependent upon those about him. Such a reversal of role lowers his status and self-confidence. At the same time, the scope of personal privileges becomes somewhat restricted, creating additional adjustment problems. The transition crisis of retirement is serious for all men who have not been prepared for it.

During the years of adulthood, the individual was physically, emotionally, and intellectually capable of helping chart the course of his community economically, politically, and culturally. Because of his age and experience, he has had a greater voice than young adults. With advancing age, however, this position has changed. Evidence of this is the fact that no one younger than forty-two years of age or older than sixty-eight years has, as yet, been elected President of the United States of America [11]. For a variety of reasons, including increasing physical limitations, the maturity of the children who formerly looked to him for help and guidance, his partial or complete retirement from gainful employment, or perhaps his inability to modify long held views to meet changing circumstances, the old person typically forfeits most of the control and direction he previously exerted.

By gradually relinquishing his role in and contribution to the community, the individual is faced with still another break with society. Without such participation, he tends to lose contact with the wide circle of peers and younger persons so necessary for intellectual and emotional stimulation. The result is naturally unfavorable for the personal well-being of the individual. Loss of such contact leaves the individual less prepared to deal with the problems of society and to contribute to the welfare of the community.

RELATING TO THE INCREASING LIFE SPAN

The social and personal problems related to old age continue to increase. Because of the rapid advances in the medical sciences and the improved

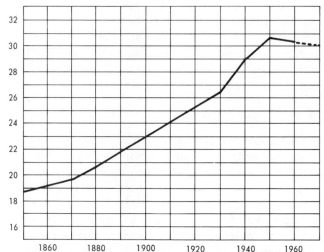

Figure 24–1 Median age of American population: 1850–
1970. (U. S. Bureau of the Census. *Statistical abstract of
the United States: 1967.* (88th ed.) 1967.)

general conditions in which we live, man's life span has been steadily growing.   Figure 24–1 reveals that the median age of the American population
has risen from less than twenty years in 1860 to more than thirty years in
1960.

As the older age groups continue to show remarkable growth, the median
age of the population also has consistently increased.   While the total number of persons in the United States approximately doubled between 1900 and
1950, the number of individuals sixty-five years old and over was four times
as large.   In 1950, the older group constituted only 4.1 percent of the total
population, in 1965 almost 10 percent.   Moreover, government census pro-
jections show that this age group will steadily increase from the 16,159,000
persons found in it in 1960 to 21,171,000 persons in 1975, and to 25,006,000
in 1985 [14, p. 6].   Figure 24–2 illustrates the past and the future changes
of the senior population.

With the increasing number of individuals living to old age and with the
ever-growing number of years that individuals tend to live beyond retirement,
new problems beset society.   Greater time, effort, and resources are required
for researching the medical, psychological, and social problems of the aged.
Additional facilities are needed for the treatment and care of the elderly population.   In addition, the general well-being of the elderly depends upon opportunities for leisure-time activities and for productive endeavors: opportunities
to do, to achieve, to feel success, and to make a real contribution to society.

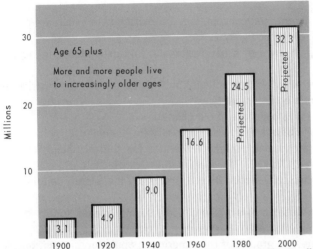

Figure 24–2 Increase in American older population. (U. S. Bureau of the Census. *Current population reports: estimates,* series P-25, No. 251; for population 2000, Division of the Actuary, Social Security Administration.)

Such opportunities demand the cooperation of society as a whole, not merely the aged society. The distinguished historian Toynbee declared: "A society's quality and disability can best be measured by the respect and care given to its elderly citizens." After quoting Toynbee, President John F. Kennedy in his message before the House of Representatives in 1963 noted:

> Our senior citizens present this nation with increasing opportunity to draw upon their skill and sagacity and the opportunity to provide the respect and recognition they have earned. It is not enough for a great nation merely to have added new years to life—our objective must also be to add new life to those years [8].

The problems of increasing age are, of course, not merely social. Each adult must prepare for a greater life span. Each must look forward to a greater number of years spent in retirement. There will be more time for finishing lifework, for autobiographical retrospect, and for contemplation. Hence, every person must anticipate more and longer-termed adjustments to old age than were common in past generations. However, with the sympathetic cooperation of society and the acquisition of wholesome attitudes, interests, and activities, the individual need not look ahead in despair but rather with hope for continued constructive work and accomplishment.

QUESTIONS FOR REVIEW

1. Describe the physical condition of old people and enumerate illnesses frequent at this age.
2. What changes in the self-concept may be expected to result from the gradual decline of the bodily systems?
3. What is the significance of a psychosomatic interdependence in regard to behavior?
4. What important effects on personality and behavior does the restriction of the senescent's environment have?
5. Explain the religious concerns of old people.
6. Why is a diversity of interest areas necessary for the elderly?
7. In what ways are social contacts essential for the well-being of the elderly individual?
8. What changes typically occur in the status of the elderly within the community?
9. What are some basic provisions American society makes for its older citizens?
10. Indicate how the age groups of the American population are shifting in proportion.

REFERENCES

I. Selected Reading

1. Birren, James E., et al. (Eds.). *Human aging: A biological and behavioral study.* Bethesda, Md.: National Institute of Mental Health, 1963. This Public Health Service publication, No. 986, includes articles by twenty-two contributors, among them several medical studies.

2. Kastenbaum, Robert (Ed.). *New thoughts on old age.* New York: Springer Publishing, 1964. A presentation of the theoretical perspectives, clinical explorations, and assessment of characteristics of older people.

3. Wolff, Kurt. *The biological, sociological, and psychological aspects of aging.* Springfield, Ill.: Charles C Thomas, 1959. A study of the various aspects of aging in terms of their effects, as well as suggestions for the welfare of the old-age population.

II. Specific References

4. Barker, Roger G., et al. *Adjustment of physical handicap and illness: A survey of the social psychology of physique and disability.* (Rev. ed.) New York: Social Science Research Council, 1953.

5. Cavan, Ruth, et al. *Personal adjustment in old age.* Chicago: Science Research Associates, 1949.

6. Fromm, Erich. Psychological problems of aging. *Child Fam.,* 1967, **6,** 78–88.

7. Havighurst, Robert J. Successful aging. *Gerontologist,* 1961, **1,** 8–13. See also Ewald W. Busse, Geriatrics today—An overview. *Amer. J. Psychiat.,* 1967, **123,** 1226–1233.

8. Miles, Walter R. Human personality and perpetuity. *Gerontologist,* 1965, No. 1, Part 2, 33–39.

9. Moberg, David D. Religiosity in old age. *Gerontologist,* 1965, **5,** 78–87, 111–112.

10. Moss, Bertram B., with Fraser Kent. *Caring for the aged.* New York: Doubleday, 1966. A practically oriented book for those who cope with problems of the elderly.

11. Murray, Alan. *U. S. A. at a glance.* Boston: Houghton Mifflin, 1956.

12. O'Reilly, C. T. Religious practice and personal adjustment of older people. *Sociol. soc. Res.,* 1957, **42,** 119–121.

13. Pressey, Sidney L., and Alice D. Pressey. Two insiders' searchings for best life in old age. *Gerontologist,* 1966, **6,** 14–17.

14. U. S. Bureau of the Census, *Statistical abstract of the United States: 1964.* (85th ed.) 1964.

15. World Health Organization. Constitution of the WHO. *Public Health Reports,* 1946, **61,** 1268–1277.

Part 10
Recapitulation and Conclusions

This section is self-explanatory. It is helpful to reexamine the entire life span and to note crucial developmental factors and processes of various phases of life in relation to our American technology and culture. As has been pointed out, each stage of human development has needs, tasks, and problems of its own.

By parental influence and personal endeavor one learns the societal and cultural norms and adjusts oneself to them, and by personally motivated pursuit of goals one greatly influences one's conscious and unconscious search for one's own identity, for status in the community, and for meaning. The intricacies of our present society and culture with their space-age ramifications and opportunities, as well as dangers, intensify challenges and responsibilities for the present and future generations.

25

SYNOPSIS OF HUMAN DEVEL-
OPMENTS THROUGHOUT LIFE

The process of human development as a whole is a differential growth and cyclic structuring producing a personality and identity which are greatly determined by individual equipment and environmental opportunities. Like a spiral, it presses upward for more than two decades, then maintains the level which has been achieved for about two decades; then there follows a long period of decline until a point is reached when a major organ or system fails and death occurs.

As the human individual grows and matures, he displays many qualities far removed from his animal origins and has enormous plasticity in adapting himself to his environment and culture. For the purpose of self-protection he usually becomes a master of defense mechanisms and in maneuvering others to suit himself. He is a creature both "made" by others and making others to the image of himself [1, pp. 663–666].

KEY FACTORS IN HUMAN DEVELOPMENT

Parents play the major role at the outset and during the early periods of development. The "psychic birth" [9] of most individuals occurs within the setting and atmosphere of the family.   Peers and acquaintances are potent modifiers during the later stages of life.   Early patterns of feeling and emotion toward various dimensions of reality largely determine one's later attempts at self-direction and search for status in life.

In this child-conscious century one would suppose that most people receive a satisfactory start in life.   Some facts, however, seem to contradict this assumption.   A large number of children are reared without one or both of their parents.   In fact, over 9 percent of children live with a stepmother or a stepfather.   Figure 25–1 illustrates familial conditions as they existed in 1960.   An undetermined percentage of families also, although still physically functioning as a family unit, are separated by frequent dissension and psychological isolation from a meaningful sharing of attitudes, interests, and activities.   A beginning and continuation of life without both parents results in serious deprivation of proper sources for self-identification.   Its undesirable impact on later life is difficult to overestimate.   After reviewing nearly a thousand studies on trait and personality development from birth to adulthood, Benjamin S. Bloom [5] concludes that the most important period for personality formation is between birth and the onset of schooling.   Individual tendencies in motivation become more and more striking with increasing age. The individual unfolds his early dispositions in accordance with environmental opportunities that stimulate their development.

Psychological bisexuality and other human qualities are developed within the confines of the total environment.   The child must be highly influenced both by his father and by his mother so that the desirable qualities and traits pertinent to both sexes may be adequately developed.   He must learn to iden-

Figure 25–1   Living with and without parents.   (U. S. Bureau of the Census. *U. S. census of population: 1960.*   Vol. 1.   *Characteristics of the population, 1964.*)

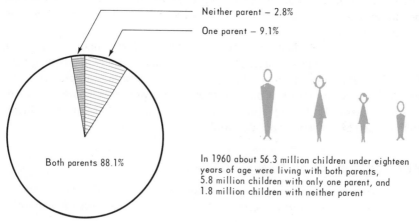

Neither parent — 2.8%

One parent — 9.1%

Both parents 88.1%

In 1960 about 56.3 million children under eighteen years of age were living with both parents, 5.8 million children with only one parent, and 1.8 million children with neither parent

tify himself with both male and female figures. As compared to the family, no other environmental contributor exerts even a comparable influence upon the formation of a child's personality. The deepest needs of the child (affection, acceptance, and security) are gratified through a dynamic interaction with his parents.

As was indicated earlier, the present trend toward lengthened education in some ways prepares the individual for the complexity of modern life. Children and youth need a longer and better educational preparation for efficient adult living. Indeed, education is becoming a lifelong process. At the high school level it should include courses in family life as well as dependable citizenship.

FOUNDATIONS FOR LIFE

Prenatal, infant, childhood, and adolescent periods form the foundation for an adult pattern of life. Each makes significant contributions to adult traits and characteristics by the influence it exerts on the subsequent periods of life. Thus, prenatal development lays a foundation for developments during infancy. What happens in infancy affects life and adjustment during childhood. Subsequent developments during adolescence can also be traced to childhood and, to a degree, to infancy. There is considerable support for the psychoanalytic theory that the basic personality pattern is established during the first five years of life; yet many extensions and modifications occur later. Let us retrace the most influential developments contributing to a person's total personality formation.

The prenatal period. The prenatal period is a stage of extreme dependence upon another during which physiological structures, individual motility, and sensitivity to stimuli have their beginning, and it continues until the individual is ready to function outside the mother's uterus. Although the developments occurring during the prenatal stage represent physiological growth primarily, this stage is also of psychological significance. The profound relationship between the physiological integrity of the organism and its behavioral functioning is a key reason for this. Physical development provides the foundation for most future behavioral and personality patterns and characteristics of the individual.

Birth and infancy. Birth brings the ejection and exposure of the fetus to a personal and increasingly autonomous existence. At this traumatic point, the newcomer's needs have to be met by others who may or may not have satisfactory attitudes and information to safeguard his welfare. The newborn may be welcomed by his parents, or he may enter into a discordant group of persons barely managing to live under the same roof.

Infancy is a preparational phase of life because all the major developments that mark human life appear before this stage gives way to childhood. Scientists interested in human development and adjustment do not fail to acknowledge the crucial role of the first two to three years of life. Certain universal essentials must be supplied if unhampered development is to occur. Florence L. Goodenough and Leona E. Tyler [4, pp. 523–527] term these essentials "raw materials," some tangible, for example, food, and some intangible, for example, love. Both are indispensable in promoting feelings of acceptance, security, and individuality. Many infants are deprived of the intangible essentials for their psychosocial development. When the general sensitivity to stimuli begins to rise from about the age of three or four months, the infant needs a large amount of sensory stimulation, including touching, patting, cuddling, and moving. The infant needs a variety of stimuli long before he can discover them on his own initiative.

During infancy the pattern of living and adjusting gradually becomes structured. If the parental personality traits and the atmosphere of the home do not produce any distortions of this structural organization, the physical and mental well-being of this individual is ensured by a sound foundation and a certain strength to meet situations during the later periods of development. Opportunities for experiencing sufficient stimulation with humans and objects, as well as exercise in initiative and exploration are of major assistance for the psychological development of the individual.

Childhood.   Childhood depends upon the development and experiences of infancy. The timing of progress in developmental tasks serves as a basis for predicting further developments and overall adjustment. Figure 25–2 illustrates the average time for the beginning and completion of several developmental tasks. It may be noted that some tasks are comparatively simple, while others are complex. An infant, for example, readily takes solid foods and chews them. To learn to eat solid foods he merely needs opportunities at the right time. The task of self-control begins early but extends well into the twenties. A great deal of help and encouragement is needed to master one's impulses successfully.

An outstanding quality of the child is his self-awareness and the beginning of his self-regulation. While organismic regulation is established long before birth and becomes strengthened during the early weeks of postnatal life, desirable forms of behavior regulation take years of effort. Although the child is exposed to many environmental influences, his selectivity increases and, more important, his self-concept appears as a third major directing force of his activities and adjustment, heredity and environment being the others. The self-concept the child has acquired becomes an important influence upon further trait and attitude formation. "From childhood on, a person's own *choices* determine to a considerable extent which possible courses of development are to be followed, which to be closed out" [11, p. 506].

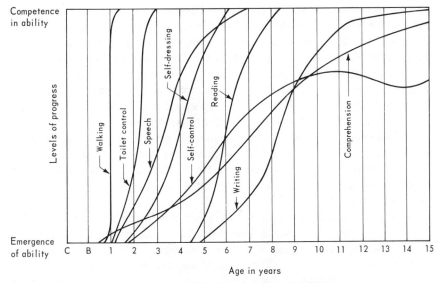

Figure 25–2   Hypothetical curves of sundry developmental tasks.

Many events have a great importance for the child—such, for example, as when he recognizes the importance of speech as a means of communication, when he leaves the confines of home for the first vacation trip, and when he begins to attend a kindergarten or school.   In middle childhood, the consequential event is when the child finds a companion in whom he can confide. Each event of this order reorganizes the child's *eigene Welt* (own world) significantly, and carries repercussions for his self-concept.

Neighborhood and school begin to play important roles as the years of childhood advance.   The child's milieu expands to include many variables in his environment and culture.   His curiosity impels him to explore most of the observed, imagined, and intellectually apprehended phenomena.   His suggestibility adds its share to his socialization.   Thus, a child moves continuously into the world of others (*Mitwelt*) and into the objective world (*Umwelt*), as well as into a world of his own (eigene Welt).   It is beneficial for the child if these three worlds largely fuse into each other rather than differ and distort each other.   In some cases, a child lives too much the life of others, or he withdraws too deeply into the world of his own creation.   Most disturbances and disorders have their origins in the years of childhood if not before.   Excessive parental demands, for example, may strain the child's ego to the point of disintegration.   Lack of mothering and affection may stunt his absorption of desirable emotions and attitudes.

Children move into peer society before the span of childhood expires, and establish a basic pattern for later identifications with contemporaries. Success with peers is crucial for later adjustment. Acceptance of one's duties and responsibilities is an important lesson that must be learned within the years of childhood. Personal competence in working toward perceived goals and ideals increases during the preadolescent years. An affective pattern of living and adjusting to situations that he encounters makes the child eager and ready to enter higher levels of maturity during the years of adolescence.

Adolescence. This period includes pubertal growth and later developments leading up to an adult pattern of life with its final traits and features. Intense self-observation, heightened emotional experiences, and moral-religious stirrings usually occur within the period of adolescence. It is a period of conflict and ambivalence.

Self-consciousness and emotionality reach new heights because of turbulent rates of physical growth, sexual maturation, and the resulting difficulties in behavior regulation. Heterosexual associations contribute to the further rise of self-consciousness. The voice of conscience becomes vivid at this stage of life. Feelings of uncertainty, guilt, and remorse run high as the adolescent ventures into experiences conflicting with his own standards and values.

Maturation of intellectual power is followed by much doubt and rumination, with attempts to discover answers to puzzling questions. A critical attitude toward parents and authority is often a marked feature of the adolescent. Tendencies toward perfectionism and social discrimination are also heightened. The search for identity for the male is marked by strivings for achievement and independence from parents; the female seeks to establish a network of intimate interpersonal affiliations and loves [7, pp. 343–347]. Both sexes look for and usually find adults on whom to model their personalities. Young male and female adolescents wonder what kind of person they would like to be and what goals and purposes in life they should rely upon.

The need to encourage capable adolescents to remain in school and develop their potentialities as fully as possible has been recognized in many quarters. For many young persons school opens their eyes to various cultural opportunities and chances for employment and self-improvement [8, p. 9].

Sexual maturation and interest in members of the opposite sex is frequently accompanied by ups and downs, with both encouraging and discouraging feelings about personal adequacy in heterosexual relationships. For many adolescents emotional ambivalence and irregularities in sexual function confuse the overall picture of maturation. Frequent attempts to conform fully to the standards and actions of their peers contribute to clique and crowd formation, which, in turn, provides opportunities for deep interpersonal identifications.

Rapid developments of personality, while producing a temporary loss of organismic equilibrium and self-control, also indicate the approach of adulthood. Increasing adequacy in self-appraisal improves efficiency of performance and stability of behavior.

Toward the end of adolescence, the adolescent's self-concept is clearer and more complete. The person is then capable of visualizing his present roles and of projecting himself into future needs and goals. Now he realizes what he wants to become. Many life-determining decisions are made before the individual enters adulthood. The direction of development is often significantly changed by a confidant, a life mate, or just the decision to disregard bothersome aspects of experience. Apparently the adolescent chooses one of many possible selves as he accepts his adult identity.

ADULT PHASES OF LIFE

Experience and adjustment on an adult level depend greatly on the solutions to the conflicts and frustrations of adolescence. Finding satisfactory outlets for emotional and sexual drives is essential for a healthy adult pattern of living. Constructive self-regulation of energies and drives usually involves a considerable use of compensation and sublimation. Adjustment in adulthood is largely determined by strengths and weakness in earlier life.

During adult life, marital dissension and vocational disappointments are two frequent sources of maladjustment. Personal insecurity and lack of orientation based upon one's capacities and assets represent the principal etiological conditions that produce and intensify neurotic patterns of adjustment. With the achievement of vocational and marital stability, on the other hand, adaptation to one's total environment is greatly facilitated.

Since at the adult stage of life most abilities peculiar to the individual constellation of endowments are developed to a high level, their integration and application in terms of vocational opportunities represent major developmental tasks. One has to find his niche in life and settle down before his abilities begin to decline noticeably during the middle phase of adult life. During the years of early adulthood, the individual has good possibilities for correcting his personality weaknesses by his own efforts or with the assistance of professional counselors.

If a person makes efforts to apply his abilities and skills, if he develops civic and cultural interests, cognitive decline is often retarded. Adherence to physical and mental hygiene is a necessary adjunct to proficient living during the adult years of life. Moreover, a religiously oriented philosophy of life is generally helpful in promoting meaning in life activities and an adaptation to reality in all its aspects. Old age, for example, frequently starts before a person is ready to accept it, although decline in abilities increases.

THE DECLINING PHASES

Aging is a lifelong process, but its disadvantages are concentrated in old age. During the years of later adulthood a gradual decline begins. It accelerates as late adult years merge into senescence. Decline or deterioration affects all structural and functional powers. Structural deterioration usually precedes functional decline. Some organs and systems deteriorate at a faster rate than others. For example, the kidneys may fail and lead to death with an otherwise high level of vitality. A heart attack may also occur at an early stage of decline. Amplitude of memory narrows extensively, while the powers of reasoning may show no significant decline until the late seventies. Any deteriorated organs or powers, however, have significant repercussions on the total organism and personality.

Many elderly persons tend to cling to the image of themselves as it was in early or middle adulthood. Therefore, they continue to set long-range goals and to propose additional self-realization for the future. The difficulty in approaching these goals is often due to the decline of ability and to the occurrence of illness. The person forced to deal with his actual self often faces an identity crisis, especially when age is considered a misfortune.

Difficulties in maintaining former social status and in making adjustments multiply. Withdrawal from physical and social activities should not create an abrupt change in the pattern of living. In order to avoid major financial setbacks, many older persons continue to work as long as employment is available to them. Both unmodified continuation and sudden dropping of work tend to be unhealthy. Not fully realizing the extent of their declining abilities, some people strain their hearts by engaging in strenuous physical work, such as shoveling snow or working in the garden. Observation of elderly people confirms the fact that they exhibit tendencies toward activity as well as disengagement.

TERMINAL DECLINE AND DEATH

To the young adult death is a strange phenomenon, difficult to comprehend. His thoughts about it are accidental and short in duration. His attendance at funerals is often an external necessity rather than a moving event. The situation changes in later years. On such an occasion a senescent easily gets ego-involved, and his ideas of identification or self-reference become disquieting if not disturbing.

During the senescent years of life, ideas of death begin to enter consciousness more often. For many persons it has a strong depressing power, something they avoid facing and suppress. When the *terminal* decline begins, usually about one year prior to death, there is a noticeable departure from earlier stability. Psychomotor skills, cognitive functions, and self-control, all fail greatly, and incoherence and gloominess usually set in. Even untrained observers notice the difference.

The idea of being near death produces anxiety and stimulates preparation for it. To many people the depressing idea of bodily extermination gives way to a resigned or an anticipative outlook toward death and the hereafter. When Socrates was sentenced to death and given a glass of poison to drink, his philosophical attitude moved him to utter a still immortal message: "Only my body will die; my soul will eternally exist and be judged by a Supreme Being in accordance with the good and bad deeds of my life." This insight of a pre-Christian philosopher reveals much about the human belief concerning this aspect of transcendence.

Reveries that survey life are often vivid in old age, especially at times when discomforts and pain subside. Reviewing past events is beneficial if they have been in keeping with his philosophy of life and its key values. Evelyn M. Duvall [8, p. 430] puts the matter in these words: "Nothing can bring greater satisfaction than finding that life all adds up, and that together the two (husband and wife) know who they are and where they are headed in the business of living." Christians see death as the entrance into a life with God for those whose life accomplishments measure up to His justice and mercy.

Charlotte Buhler [6] is preparing a book on the course of human life in its goal aspects. Biographical, clinical, and questionnaire (Goals of life) data will be integrated in this study of goal-finding, goal-developing, and goal changes throughout life. The factorial analysis of the goal questionnaire "established" seventeen factors, such as having the necessities of life, accepting limitations and denials, developing best potentials, and having success and status. Among other factors that emerged were being highly regarded, a value dominant in male preferences, and being attractive and glamorous, a value dominant in female preferences.

Figures 25–3 and 25–4 identify the leading causes of death in the United States in the 1960s. It can be noted that heart diseases account for about one-third of all deaths. The death rate for kidney infections increased by about 93 percent from 1954 to 1964. During the 1960s most of the yearly variations in death rate were slight rises or decreases. Tuberculosis mortality continued to decline, while the death rate from malignant neoplasms (cancer) increased fairly steadily. In 1965, the provisional figures for cardiovascular (heart) diseases reached 503.8 and malignant neoplasms 152.9 per 100,000 population.

In 1961, for the first time, life expectancy for the U. S. population exceeded seventy years. In 1965, the life expectancy for newborns was 73.7 years for females and 66.9 for males. For the later 1960s it continued rising at a moderate rate.

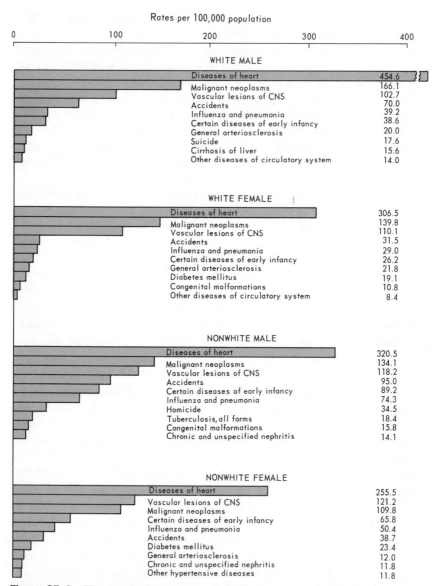

Figure 25–3 The ten leading causes of death in groups classified by color and sex: United States, 1960. (*Vital statistics of the United States: 1960.* Vol. II. *Mortality.* Part A, Fig. 1–2, 1963.)

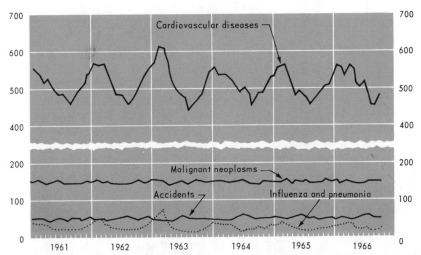

Figure 25–4 Major causes of death: U. S., 1960–1967. (U. S. Dept. of Health, Education, and Welfare. *Health, education, and welfare indicators.* 1967.)

Table 25–1 recounts some occurrences essential to each stage of life, including developmental tasks, hazards, and important considerations in regard to motivation, personality, and the self. This schematic presentation permits an overall view of the subject matter and concludes this study of human growth and decline.

QUESTIONS FOR REVIEW

1. In what areas do parents greatly influence their children?
2. What basic differences are there between children with both parents and those with one?
3. What are the fundamental essentials for unhampered development?
4. What are the qualities that distinguish the child from the infant, and the adolescent from the child?
5. When and how does the child begin to control his behavior?
6. List the major characteristics of an adolescent and compare them to adult traits.
7. How does vocational development contribute to adulthood?
8. Identify some significant changes which occur during middle adulthood and relate them to the developmental tasks of that age.
9. Identify and discuss several leading causes of death.

Table 25-1 Review of key human developments

Level of development and approximate age	Physiological growth and psychomotility	Dynamics and motivation	Developmental tasks	Major hazards	Personality and the self-concept
Prenatal: zygote, 0 to 2 weeks embryo, 2 weeks to 2 months fetus, 2 to 9 months	Conception Implantation Differentiation of tissues and bodily systems; emergence of motility and of sensitivity; approaches postnatal functioning power	Maintenance of organismic equilibrium; reflex movement	Proper physiological foundations for postnatal developments; biochemical controls; rise of viability	Defective heredity; endocrine and circulatory malfunctions; certain maternal diseases	Transition from tranquility to motility
Neonatal (early infancy)	Increase of sensitivity and beginnings of sensorimotor coordination; integration of gross and refined central nervous system functions	Satisfaction of bodily needs; affective excitement	Preservation of life: adjustments to new external and internal conditions, eg, temperature, food, etc.	Birth complications; disequilibrium and infections	Adjustability vs excitability
Middle infancy, 2 to 15 months	Rapid growth in size and weight; refinements in neuromuscular coordination; further integration of lower and higher central nervous system mechanisms	Greater interest in environment; recognition of mother and familiar objects; intense need for mothering; rapid emotional differentiation; strong drive for activity	Gain in control over neuromuscular and vocal systems; acquisition of new attention-getting techniques; establishment of emotional security	Lack of physiological stability; perceptual deprivation; lack of mothering	Adaptability to parents; awareness of one's individuality

Table 25–1 Review of key human developments (continued)

Level of development and approximate age	Physiological growth and psychomotility	Dynamics and motivation	Developmental tasks	Major hazards	Personality and the self-concept
Late infancy (toddling stage), 15 to 30 months	Advance and completion of phylogenetic motor patterns; control over fine muscles	Greater initiative in exploration of surroundings; emergence of childhood motivation; increasing resistance to parental demands and suggestions	Progress in initiative; acquisition of speech facility; establishment of toilet controls	Difficulties in relating oneself emotionally to parents and siblings; distrust and fears; maternal deprivation	Narcissism; rising awareness of self; strong attitudes toward self and others; acquisition of strong likes and dislikes
Early childhood, 2½ to 6 years	Acquisition of ontogenetic motor patterns; increase in gracefulness; decline in the rate of physiological growth	Interest in distant environmental and social relationships; fantasy preoccupation; make-believe; emergence of sentiments	Increased use of verbal communications and social play activities; distinguishing right from wrong	Insecurity and childhood diseases; withdrawal from social stimulation	Great increase in social response; growth in self-consciousness and attitudes toward oneself; rising identification with parents
Middle childhood, 6 to 9 or 10 years	Greater control over fine muscle groups, eg, dressing oneself and ball games; decrease of physical growth	Growth of realism in attitude and adaptability; recognition of role relationships; interest in friendships	Control of negative emotions; development of a scale of values; cooperative attitude; a sense of sex identity	Lack of achievement and self-acceptance; attitudes of inferiority and defeatism	Extroverted and enthusiastic; appearance of character traits; growth in personal responsibility
Late childhood (preadolescence), 9 or 10 to 11½ or 12½ years	Rate of physiological growth ebbs, then increases; ready acquisition of various motor skills	Sex identity; established adventure and novelty sought; scientific questioning arises	Adaptation to peer society; experience of group security	Poor peer relationships; lack of industriousness	Greater preoccupation with self; loosening of emotional identification with parents; wondering about the years ahead

401

Table 25-1 Review of key human developments (continued)

Level of development and approximate age	Physiological growth and psychomotility	Dynamics and motivation	Developmental tasks	Major hazards	Personality and the self-concept
Puberty (early adolescence): girls, 11½ to 14; boys, 12½ to 15½ years	Turbulent growth of many organs and systems; approach to adult size and proportion; biochemical balances disturbed; external awkwardness increased	Strivings for independence; negativism; emotional vascillation and moods; ambivalence, emergence of powerful sexual drives; erotic fantasy; strivings for interpersonal intimacy with peers	Self-reorganization; gains toward independence by emancipating self from family; control over sexual impulses	Isolation and excessive daydreaming; lack of self-assertiveness; extreme rebellion; peer rejection	Increase of introversion; indecision; search for human models and oneself
Mid-adolescence: girls, 14 to 16; boys, 15½ to 18 years	Reduced rate of physiological growth; large gains in fine motor control and strength	Powerful drive for social companionship, including members of opposite sex; expansion of intellectual quests and reasoning	Acceptance of a masculine or feminine role; identification with peers	Peer rejection; perfectionistic aspirations; moodiness	Lack of integration; ambivalence and antagonistic strivings; magnified social awareness; search for standards
Late adolescence: girls, 16 to 20; boys, 18½ to 22 years	Appearance of adult characteristics; adult level of performance; biochemical equilibrium	Approach of heterosexual adjustment; striving for maturity and popularity	Selection of an occupation; improved self-control; formation of Weltanschauung	Rejection of self and neurotic or delinquent solutions of conflicts	Crystallization of character in terms of social and moral norms; concern over the future
Early adulthood: women, 20 to 30; men, 22 to 35 years	Optimum level of physiological development and psychomotor controls	Establishment of a relatively persistent hierarchy of motives; active social and civic participation	Establishing economic independence; selecting a mate and starting a family; performing	Fixation of pubertal and adolescent attitudes and modes of adjustment	Integration of behavior-organizing factors into a personally acceptable pattern; increase in ex-

Table 25–1 Review of key human developments (continued)

Level of development and approximate age	Physiological growth and psychomotility	Dynamics and motivation	Developmental tasks	Major hazards	Personality and the self-concept
			a paternal or maternal role		troversion; maintenance of flexibility;
Middle adulthood: women, 30 to 45; men, 35 to 50 years	Moderate decrease in speed and strength; increasing appearance of physical limitations	Interest in children, comforts, and stability; concern about vocational status	Management of a home and care of children; sense of responsibility in the community; preservation of adult personality traits and abilities; gains in leadership	Lack of a philosophy of life; inability to maintain economic or social standards of living; lack of readiness to release children; family dissension	Decrease in flexibility; reliance on the habitual and ideological
Late adulthood: women, 45 to 60; men, 50 to 65 years	Problems in health preservation; decline in physical strength and endurance; sight and hearing difficulties	Decrease of interest and drive; moods and worrying more frequent; leisure time activities sought; decrease in desire to learn new subjects	Adjustments to family changes as children leave home; preparation for retirement; desire to help others	Presenile diseases; excessive demand for reverence; acceleration of aging and lessened capacity for self-repair	Increased rigidity and decrease of resourcefulness; reliance on past
Senescence: women, 60 to death; men, 65 to death	Further deterioration of sensory activity and motor skills; lessened ability for even daily routine	Desire to be of use; withdrawal from social functions; loss of interests; restriction of activities	Maintaining frequent contact with children and grandchildren; maintenance of health; integration through maintenance of self-esteem	Physical strain; isolation from relatives; skepticism and depression; excessive preoccupation with self; loss of meaningfulness of life	Difficulties in relying on past and habitual; self-fulfillment or apathy and rapid disengagement

403

10. What is the life expectancy for boys and girls born between 1965 and 1970?

REFERENCES

I. Selected Reading

1. Berelson, Bernard, and Gary A. Steiner. *Human behavior: An inventory of scientific findings.* New York: Harcourt, Brace & World, 1964. A fairly systematic presentation of 1,045 findings in the field of behavioral science.

2. Coleman, James C. *Personality dynamics and effective behavior.* Chicago: Scott, Foresman, 1960. A study of human resources and abilities, personality and behavior theories, and means of assisting human development and adjustment.

3. Fulton, Robert (Ed.). *Death and identity.* New York: Wiley, 1965. Discussions by various contributors on theories of death, and attitudes and reactions toward them, as well as the management of grief and mourning.

4. Goodenough, Florence L., and Leona E. Tyler. *Developmental psychology.* (3rd ed.) New York: Appleton-Century-Crofts, 1959. Chap. 26. A presentation of conditions necessary for optimal human development.

II. Specific References

5. Bloom, Benjamin S. *Stability and change in human characteristics.* New York: Wiley, 1964.

6. Buhler, Charlotte. The human course of life in its goal aspects. *J. hum. Psychol.,* 1964, **4**, No. 1.

7. Douvan, Elizabeth, and J. Adelson. *The adolescent experience.* New York: Wiley, 1966.

8. Duvall, Evelyn M. *Family development.* (2nd ed.) Philadelphia: Lippincott, 1962.

9. Jung, Carl G. *The development of personality* (translated by R. F. C. Hull). New York: Bollingen Foundation, 1954.

10. Moore, Bernice M., and Wayne H. Holtzman. *Tomorrow's parents: A study of youth and their families.* Austin: University of Texas Press, 1965.

11. Tyler, Leona E. *The psychology of human differences.* (3rd ed.) New York: Appleton-Century-Crofts, 1965.

Glossary

Achievement quotient (AQ) The ratio between the individual's scores in scholastic performance and the standard.

ACTH Adrenocorticotrophic hormone produced by the pituitary gland to stimulate corticoid production in stress situations.

Adjustment Process and behavior that a person uses to satisfy his internal needs and cope effectively with environmental, social, and cultural demands.

Adjustment, emotional A state of emotional maturity proper to the age of the person and marked by a relatively stable and moderate emotional reactivity to affect- and mood-eliciting stimuli.

Adjustment, social Reaction patterns toward others conducive to harmonious relationships within family and other reference groups.

Adolescence The developmental period beginning with the onset of major pubertal changes up until adult maturity.

Adrenals A pair of ductless or internal-secretion glands attached to the kidneys and secreting adrenalin and cortin, important in emergency and stress situations.

Adult A person who is mature in all major areas and capable of a satisfactory adjustment to himself and to his environment.

Affect A vital feeling, mood, or emotion characterized by specific physiological (psychophysical) changes and states.

Age, mental (MA)   The level of intellectual efficiency as determined by a test of intelligence; the age at which a computed score on an intelligence test occurs.

Age norm   The average for a given age as revealed by sample group performances at this age.

Aging   The continuous developmental process beginning with conception and ending with death during which organic structures and functions of an immature organism first grow and mature, then deteriorate.

Alienation   A process or a state wherein familiar persons and relationships appear strange or unacceptable and the individual reacts with criticism and withdrawal.

Altruism   Deep unselfish concern for others often expressed in charitable activities.

Ambivalence   Internal tendency to be pulled (physically or psychologically) in opposite directions, e.g., acceptance-rejection, love-hate, participation-withdrawal.

Amnesia   Defensive forgetting caused by a strong mental conflict and repression.

Anesthesia   Lack of psychophysical response to sensory stimuli. No awareness of pain.

Anoxia   Deficiency in the supply of oxygen to the tissues, especially the brain, causing damage to their structural integrity.

Anxiety, neurotic   The experience of distress and helplessness due to ego damage or weakness, accompanied by an expectation of danger or misfortune.

Apperception   A mental process for interpreting and assimilating new experience or behavior in the experiential background (apperceptive schema).

Aptitude   A recognizable context of capacity or potentiality for specific achievements, if the person is given proper training.

Aspiration, level of   The intensity of striving for achievement, or the standard by which a person judges his own activity in reference to expected end results.

Atrophy   Progressive decline of a part, or its decrease in size, or degeneration.

Attitude   An acquired persistent tendency to feel, think, or act in a fixed manner toward a given class of stimuli.

Autistic   Self-centered; with perception, feeling, and thinking unduly controlled by personal needs, desires, and preferences at the expense of sensitivity to others or to situational demands.

Autogenous   Self-originated, as distinguished from what is initiated by outside stimuli and learning.

Behavior   A kind of reaction, including complex patterns of feeling, perceiving, thinking, and willing, in response to internal or external, tangible or intangible stimuli.

Birth injury   Temporary or in some ways permanent injury to the infant which occurs during the birth process.   Many disabilities are attributed to brain damage occurring as a result of birth injury.

Cathexis   Attachment of affects and drives to their goal objects; direction of psychic energy into a particular outlet.

Cephalocaudal   The direction of growth from head to extremities (tail).

Character   The acquired ability to act and conduct oneself in accordance with a personal code of principles based on a scale of values, and facility in doing so.

Child   An individual between infancy and puberty.

Childhood   The period of development between infancy and puberty (or adolescence).

Chromosome   The minute threadlike body that carries many DNAs, RNAs, proteins, and small amounts of other substances.

Compeer   An age-mate. Cf. Peer.

Conception   The merging of the spermatozoon and ovum in human fertilization.

Conditioning   As used in the present work, a mode of training whereby reinforcement (reward or punishment) is used to elicit desired (rewarded) responses.

Conduct   That part of a person's behavior, including insufficiencies and reverses, which is guided by ethical, moral, or ideological standards.

Confabulation   An attempt to fill in the gaps of memory without awareness of the falsification involved.

Conflict   An intrapsychic state of tension or indecision due to contrary desires, ungratified needs, or incompatible plans of action; also between conscious and unconscious choices.

Congenital   Referring to characteristics and defects acquired during the period of gestation and persisting after birth.

Constitution   The organization of organic, functional, and psychosocial elements within the developing person which largely determines his condition.

Conversion   As used in the present work, transformation of anxiety and energies elicited by a conflict into somatic symptoms.

Culture   A country's manner of living, characterized chiefly by intellectual and societal aspects of a given civilization; its methods of child rearing and education, customs and mores, traditional civic and religious practices.

Daydreaming   A form of withdrawal from unpleasant or frustrating reality into the realm of fantasy and reverie, frequently of a pleasant, wish-gratifying type.

Defense dynamism or mechanism   Any habitual response pattern that is spontaneously used to protect oneself from threats, conflicts, anxiety, and other conditions that a person cannot tolerate or cope with directly.

Development, level of   A period in a person's life marked by specific clusters of traits, interests, and attitudes and by a similarity in interests and concerns among individuals of that period of life.

Developmental-level approach   In psychology, that approach in which the total personality of the individual is considered at each phase of life.

Developmental psychology   A division of psychology which investigates the growth, maturation, and aging processes of the human organism and personality, as well as cognitive, social, and other functions, throughout the span of life.

Developmental task   An increase in the ability to produce more complex behavior patterns in any dimension of growth specific to one of the successive levels of human development, adequate performance and application of which promote adaptation to reality and an attitude of personal adequacy.

Differentiation   The process by means of which structure or function becomes more complex or specialized; the change from homogeneity to heterogeneity.

Dimension   A coherent group of processes having a particular denominator; e.g., intelligence, emotion, language may be seen as dimensions of personality.

Dimensional approach   In psychology, the approach in which a specific aspect or area of personality is considered throughout various phases of life.

DNA   Deoxyribonucleic acid molecule, containing the genetic code—"the molecule of life."

Drive   The tension and arousal produced by an ungratified need and directed toward a chosen object or end.

Dyadic   As used in the present work, it refers to active relationships between two persons, e.g., mother and child; father and son.

Dynamic   Refers to forces and potent influences that are capable of producing changes within the organism or personality.

Dysfunction   Disturbance or impairment of the functional capacity of an organ or system, including mental abilities.

Ectoderm   The outermost cell layer in the embryo from which structures of the nervous system and skin are developed.

Ego   The core of personality, which exercises control and directs drives and impulses in accordance with the demands of reality.

Embryo   As used in the present work, a human organism in the early phases of prenatal development, from about two weeks to two months after conception.

Emotion   A conscious state of experience, characterized by feeling or excitement, which is accompanied (and frequently preceded) by specific physiological changes and frequently by excitation of the organism to action.

Endocrine glands   The ductless glands of internal secretion, such as the pituitary, thyroid, and adrenals.

Endoderm   The innermost of the three cell layers of the embryo, from which most of the visceral organs and the digestive tract are developed.

Endowment   Capacity for development, physical or mental, conditioned by heredity and constitution.

Envy   A distressful feeling aroused by the observation that another person possesses what one now desires to have.

Etiology   The investigation of origins, causes, and factors contributing to a trait, attitude, or disease.

Euphoria   An intense, subjective sensation of vigor, well-being, and happiness, which may exist despite some problem or disability.

Extrovert   A type of personality whose thoughts, feelings, and interests are directed chiefly toward persons, social affairs, and other external phenomena.

Fantasy   A function of imagination marked by engagement in vicarious experiences and hallucinatory actions; reveries, daydreaming.

Fetus   As used in the present work, the human organism in advanced stages of prenatal development, from two months after conception to birth.

Fixation   The persistence of infantile, childish, pubertal, or adolescent response patterns, habits, and modes of adjustment throughout successive phases of development.

Frustration   The experience of distress and morbidity induced by failures and by thwarting of attempts to gratify one's needs or ambitions.

Gene   A complex protein molecule consisting of cistrons, mutons, and recons in the chromosomes of reproductive cells carrying (or contributing to) a specific hereditary trait.

Genetic psychology   The branch of psychology that studies the human organism and its functions in terms of their origin and early course of development.

Group, reference   The group a person belongs to or is interested in belonging to, e.g., peer groups, usually with a molding influence upon the individual.

Growth   Increment to an organism or its structures, change structurally or functionally toward a more differentiated state.

Guidance   Refers to a variety of methods, such as advising, counseling, testing, use of special instruction and corrective teaching, by means of which a person may be helped to find and engage in activities that will yield satisfaction and further adjustment.

Habit   An acquired or learned pattern of behavior, relatively simple and regularly used with facility, which leads to a tendency to use such acts rather than other behavior.

Hedonism   As used in the present work, a psychological system of motivation explaining all behavior and conduct in terms of seeking pleasure and avoiding pain.

Heredity   The totality of physiological influences biologically transmitted from parents (and ancestors) to the offspring at conception.

Heterogeneous   A term used to describe any group of individuals or items that show marked differences in reference to some significant criterion or standard.

Homeostasis   Cannon's term for the relative constancy the body must maintain to function properly, e.g., temperature, blood pressure, heart-beat rate.

Homogeneous   A term used to describe any group of individuals or items that show marked similarity or low variability in the qualities or traits considered.

Homosexual   Centered on the same sex; marked by a tendency to find sexual and erotic gratification with a person of the same sex.

Hormone   A specific chemical substance, produced by an endocrine gland, which effects certain somatic and functional changes within the organism.

Hypothesis   A tentative interpretation of a complex set of phenomena or data on the basis of supportive facts or findings.

Id   A psychoanalytic term which denotes the instinctive and impulsive drives that seek immediate gratification according to the pleasure principle by which they operate.

Ideal   A standard approaching some level of perfection, usually unattainable in practice.

Identification   An unconscious effort to gratify certain deep-seated needs through affiliation with and imitation of another person, group, or ideal.

Imprinting   In many animals, a species specific innate disposition accompanied by a strong drive to follow (imitate) the parent or its surrogate in a very early phase of life.   In humans, basic emotional and social patterns are followed but to a lesser degree and with less precision.

Incubation   A period in assimilation and the problem-solving process during which certain presented ideas gain in motivational strength and begin to condition a part of behavior, especially during childhood.

Individuation   Differentiation of behavior into more distinct and less dependent parts or features.

Infancy   The first two to three years of human life, during which all major human abilities originate, marked by almost total dependence on others.

Infantile   Pertaining to the lowest level of postnatal maturity; mode of behavior or adjustment resembling the infant level.

Inferiority attitude or complex   An emotionally conditioned and frequently unconscious attitude with reference to one's own organism, self, or personality, characterized by serious lack of self-reliance and notions of inadequacy in many situations.

Inhibition   Prevention of the starting of a process or behavior by inner control, although the eliciting stimulus is present.

Innate   Existing before birth and accounting for a particular trait or characteristic.

Intelligence   As used in the present work, the practical application of sensorimotor and cognitive functions, shown by standardized performances that are measurable.

Intelligence quotient (IQ)   The index of mental capacity obtained by testing, originally a numerical ratio between mental age and chronological age. Now it more commonly refers to the statistical concept based on standard scores and on normal distribution and deviation from the mean.

Introjection   A basal (crude) form of identification in which the individual assimilates simple behavior patterns of other persons.

IQ   See Intelligence quotient.

Juvenile   Pertaining to an older child or adolescent.

Kinship   Blood relationship between two or more persons; usually includes marriage and adoption ties.

Latency period   A psychoanalytic term referring to the period, from approximately four to eleven or twelve years of age, during which interest in sex is not apparent.

Libido   A psychoanalytic term which designates the total undifferentiated life energy (C. G. Jung), sexual in nature (S. Freud).

Life cycle   The total time from birth to death, divided into a number of stages and phases and emphasizing recurrence of certain important events.

Malfunction   See Dysfunction.

Matrix   A framework or enclosure that gives form or meaning or perspective to what lies within it.

Maturation   Developmental changes manifested in organismic functioning primarily due to heredity and constitution; organismic developments leading to further behavioral differentiation.

Maturity   The state of maximal function and integration of a single factor or a total person; also applied to age-related adequacy of development and performance.

Median   The measure of central tendency which has half of the cases above it and half below it; the fiftieth percentile.

Mental conflict   See Conflict.

Mental hygiene   The art and science of mental health; application of the principles and measures necessary for its preservation and promotion.

Mesoderm   The middle of the three fundamental layers of the embryo, which forms a basis for the development of bone and muscle structure.

Metabolism   The physicochemical changes within the body for supplying, repairing, and building up (anabolism) and for breaking down and removing (catabolism).

Method   A logical and systematic way of studying a subject.

Mother fixation   Deep identification with the mother to the practical exclusion of other females as models or idols.

Motive   Any factor that stimulates or contributes to a conscious effort toward a goal.

Need   Any physicochemical imbalance within the organism, due to a lack of particular nutrients, which arouses tension and drives.   By analogy, psychological and personality needs are recognized.   Primary or genetically determined needs and derived needs (generated by the operation of primary needs) are usually distinguished.

Negativism   A primary mode of expressing one's own will by persistent refusal to respond to suggestions from parental and authority figures.

Neonate   A newborn infant.

Neuromuscular   Pertaining to both nerve and muscle, their structure and functions.

Neurotic   Mentally and emotionally disturbed; characterized by recurrent symptoms often caused by unconscious conflicts.

Normative   Based on averages, standards, or values.

Ontogenesis   As used in the present work, origin and development of an individual organism and its functions from conception to death.   Cf.   Phylogenesis.

Organismic age   The average of all basic measures of a person's development at a particular time, such as carpal development, dental development, height, and weight.   Often it includes achievement and educational, mental, and social age.

Orthogenesis   A theory assuming that the germ plasm is gradually modified by its own internal conditions and that an organism (and personality) has a specific, species-related course of development, unless blocked.

Ovum   The female germ cell.

Parallel play   The side-by-side play of two or more children with some independence of action yet heightened interest because of each other's presence.

Peer   Any individual of about one's same level of development and therefore equal for play or any other mode of association.

Percept   A unit of the perceiving response or reaction; immediate knowledge of what one perceives.

Perfectionism   The tendency to demand frequently of oneself or others a maximal quality of achievement, without a proper consideration of limiting factors.

Personality   Generally, personality refers to acquired consistencies of behavior.   More specifically, it consists in the multilevel functioning of those qualities, traits, and characteristics which distinguish a human being and determine his interaction with social and cultural factors.

Phyletic   Pertaining to a line of descent according to species.

Phylogenesis   Evolution of traits and features common to a species or race; rehearsal of the prehistory of man.

Projection   A self-defense dynamism, by which an individual attributes to others his own qualities and traits, usually undesirable ones, such as hostility or dishonesty.

Proximodistal   Pertaining to movements near the body axis that differentiate and specialize earlier than the more distant ones.

Psychosomatic   Pertaining to the effects of psychological and emotional stress upon health and pathology; indicating that a phenomenon is both psychic and bodily.

Psychotherapy   The various techniques for the systematic application of psychological principles in the treatment of mental or emotional disturbance or disorder.

Pubertal   Pertaining to anything related to the developmental period of puberty.

Puberty   The period of physical (especially sexual) and cognitive maturation, characterized by rapid somatic growth and the assumption of adult traits or features.

Pubescent   Pertaining to an individual in the early part of puberty or to anyone who exhibits significant characteristics of that period of maturation.

Rationalization   A dynamism of self-defense whereby a person justifies his activities or conduct by giving rational and acceptable, but usually untrue, reasons.

Readiness, principle of   Refers to the neurological and psychological disposition to attend to and assimilate a category of stimuli to which sensitivity and learning responses were previously lacking.

Regression   Returning to an earlier and less mature level of behavior and personality functioning.

Reinforcement   Any facilitating influence or condition for strengthening selected behavior patterns.   Cf. Conditioning.

Resistance   As used in the present work, opposition offered by a child or adolescent to the suggestions, orders, or regulations of his parents.

RNA   Ribonucleic acid molecule playing the role of a messenger for vital DNA functions.

Role conflict   The situation in which a person is expected to play two or more roles which he cannot integrate into his self-system.

Self-concept   The individual's awareness of and identification with his organism, cognitive powers, and modes of conduct and performance, accompanied by specific attitudes toward them.

Self-direction   Independent selection of goals and of the proper means and actions to attain them.

Self-realization   The lifelong process of unhampered development marked by self-direction and responses in terms of one's capabilities or potentialities.

Senescence   The period of old age.

Senile   Refers to appearance and behavior in old age.

Senility   Marked loss of physical and cognitive functions in old age or preceding it.

Sentiment   An affective and cognitive structure of related attitudes toward a particular value or object.

Sibling   An offspring having the same parents as another or others.

Socialization   A progressive development in relating and integrating oneself with others, especially parents, peers, and groups.

Somatic   Pertaining to the body or organism.

Sperm   The male germ cell, or spermatozoon, containing chromosomes, DNA, RNA, protein, and other substances.

Strain   The condition within a system or organ when it is exposed to stress, e.g., overactivity.

Sublimation   A dynamism of self-defense whereby the energies of a basic drive are redirected into a higher and socially more acceptable plane of expression; a mark of normal development.

Superego   A psychoanalytic term which refers to that part of the personality structure that is built up by early parent-child relationships and that helps ego to enforce the control of primitive instinctual urges and later functions as a moral force; analogous to an early form of conscience.

Temperament   The affective disposition and expression of emotional energies in terms of reaction speed, depth and length of emotional experiences, and relevant behavior.

Tension   A state of acute need, deprivation, fear, apprehension, etc., which keeps an organism or certain organs in a state of intensified activity, e.g., adrenal glands.

Trait   A distinctive and enduring characteristic of a person or his behavior.

Trauma   Any somatic or psychological damage to the individual, including stressful and terrifying experiences.

Unconscious   The area of motivational structure and thought process of which the person is not directly aware.

Valence   A Gestalt psychology term (K. Lewin) referring to an individual's subjective appraisal of an object or situation in his life space, by virtue of which the object is sought (positive valence) or avoided (negative valence).
Value   The worth or excellence found in a qualitative appraisal of an object by reliance on emotional and rational standards of the individual or of selected reference groups.
Viability   Refers to the organism's, e.g., the prematurely born's, capacity for surviving outside the uterus.
Vital capacity age (VA)   A relationship between lung capacity and age.

Weltanschauung   A configuration of attitudes and views toward all dimensions of reality, the material and the metaphysical; key tenets of a philosophy of life.

Zygote   As used in the present work, a new individual formed by the union of male and female gametes, and the resultant globule of cells during the first phase of prenatal development following conception and lasting approximately two weeks.

Selective List of Journals

Below are the titles of selected journals, with their Library of Congress (LC) catalog numbers and formal abbreviations, which publish theoretical and research studies in human development.

Title	LC number	Abbreviation
Adolescence	HQ796.A35	Adolescence
Aging	HQ1060.A27	Aging
American Academy of Arts and Sciences. Proceedings	Q11.B7	Proc. Amer. Acad. Arts Sci.
American Academy of Political and Social Science. Annals	H1.A4	Ann. Amer. Acad. Pol. soc. Sci.
American Association for Advancement of Science. Summarized Proceedings	Q11.A51PR	Sum. Proc. Amer. Asso. Advancem. Sci.
American behavioral scientist	H1.A472	Amer. beh. Scientist
American educational research journal	L11.A66	Amer. educ. Res. J.

Title	LC number	Abbreviation
American journal of human genetics	QH.A31.A1A5	Amer. J. hum. Genet.
American journal of orthopsychiatry	RA790.A1A5	Amer. J. Orthopsychiat.
American journal of psychology	BF1.A512	Amer. J. Psychol.
American journal of science	Q1.A52	Amer. J. Sci.
American psychologist	BF1.A518	Amer. Psychologist
American scientist	LJ115.A57A5	Amer. Scientist
American sociological review	HM1.A52	Amer. soc. Rev.
Annals of human genetics	HQ750.A1A5	Ann. hum. Genet.
British journal of psychology	BF1.B7	Brit. J. Psychol.
Canadian journal of psychology	BF1.C3	Can. J. Psychol.
Catholic psychological record	BF11.C3	Cath. psychol. Rec.
Catholic University of America, Studies in psychology and psychiatry	BF173.A257	Cath. Univ. Amer. Stud. Psychol.
Character and personality	BF1.J66	Char. Pers.
Child and family	HQ769.C4	Child Fam.
Child development	HQ750.A1C45	Child Developm.
Child development abstracts and bibliography	Ref. HQ750.A1C47	Child. Developm. Abstr. Bibl.
Child study, the bulletin of the Institute of Child Study, University of Toronto	LB1101.C4	Child Study Univ. Toronto
Children	HV741.C536	Children
Developmental psychology	BF723.J	Developm. Psychol.
Exceptional children	LC3951.J6	Except. Children
Family	HV1.J56	Family
Genetic psychology monographs	LB1101.G4	Genet. Psychol. Monogr.
Genetical research	HQ431.A1G395	Genet. Res.
Genetics	QH431.G43	Genetics
Gerontologist	HQ1060.G4	Gerontologist
Hereditas	QH431.A2	Hereditas
Human biology	GN1.H8	Hum. Biol.
Journal of abnormal and social psychology	BF1.J79	J. abnorm. soc. Psychol.

Title	LC number	Abbreviation
Journal of applied behavioral science	H1.J53	J. appl. beh. Sci.
Journal of applied psychology	BF1.J55	J. appl. Psychol.
Journal of educational psychology	L1051.A2J6	J. educ. Psychol.
Journal of educational research	L11.J75	J. educ. Res.
Journal of experimental child psychology	BF721.J64	J. exp. child Psychol.
Journal of genetic psychology	L11.P4	J. genet. Psychol.
Journal of genetics	QH431.J621	J. Genet.
Journal of gerontology	HQ1060.J6	J. Gerontol.
Journal of heredity	S494.A2J7	J. Hered.
Journal of personality	BF1.J66	J. Pers.
Journal of personality and social psychology	HM251.J56	J. Pers. soc. Psychol.
Journal of projective techniques and personality assessment	BF698.J65	J. proj. Tech. Pers. Assessm.
Journal of social psychology	HM251.A1J6	J. soc. Psychol.
Marriage	HQ1.M35	Marriage
Marriage and family living	HQ1.J6	Marriage Fam. Living
Merrill-Palmer quarterly of human growth	HQ1.M4	Merrill-Palmer Quart.
Psychological abstracts	BF1.P65	Psychol. Abstr.
Psychological bulletin	BF1.P75	Psychol. Bull.
Psychological monographs	BF1.P8	Psychol. Monogr.
Psychological record	BF1.P68	Psychol. Rec.
Psychological review	BF1.P7	Psychol. Rev.
Review of educational research	L11.R35	Rev. educ. Res.
School and society	L11.S36	Sch. Soc.
Science	Q1.S35	Science
Society for Research in Child Development. Monographs	LB1103.S6	Monogr. Soc. Res. Child Developm.

Name Index

Subject Index